The Robert Hall Diaries
1947–53

Lord Roberthall

The Robert Hall Diaries 1947–53

Edited by
ALEC CAIRNCROSS

London
UNWIN HYMAN
Boston   Sydney   Wellington

Published by the Academic Division of
Unwin Hyman Ltd
15/17 Broadwick Street, London W1V 1FP, UK

Unwin Hyman Inc.,
8 Winchester Place, Winchester, Mass. 01890, USA

Allen & Unwin (Australia) Ltd,
8 Napier Street, North Sydney, NSW 2060, Australia

Allen & Unwin (New Zealand) Ltd in association with
the Port Nicholson Press Ltd,
Compusales Building, 75 Ghuznee Street, Wellington 1, New Zealand

First published in 1989

Cover from a painting by Perilla Hall.

British Library Cataloguing in Publication Data

Roberthall, Robert Lowe, *Baron*, *1901–*
    The Robert Hall diaries 1947–1953.
1. Great Britain. Civil service. Roberthall,
Robert Lowe, Baron, 1901
I. Title   II. Cairncross, Alec, *1911–*
354.41006′092′4
ISBN 0–04–445273–X

Library of Congress Cataloging in Publication Data

Hall, R. L. (Robert Lowe), 1901–1988
    The Robert Hall diaries, 1947–1953/ edited by Alec Cairncross.
        p.   cm.
Bibliography: p.
Includes index.
ISBN 0–04–445273–X (alk. paper)
1. Hall, R. L. (Robert Lowe), 1901–1988—Diaries.   2. Economists—
Great Britain—Diaries.   3. Great Britain—Economic policy—1945–
I. Cairncross, Alec, Sir, 1911–   II. Title.
HB103.H25A3   1989
338.941′0092′4—dc 19   88–39007
[B]   CIP

Typeset in 10 on 11 point Times by Nene Phototypesetters Ltd
and printed in Great Britain by Cambridge University Press

Contents

Preface

Robert Hall (as he then was) came to Oxford as a Rhodes Scholar in 1923 after taking a degree in civil engineering at the University of Queensland (his father was a mining engineer). He read for the newly established PPE degree, specializing in philosophy but taking three optional papers in economics, and was awarded first class honours. This led to his appointment in 1927 to a Fellowship in economics at Trinity College where he continued to teach until the outbreak of war in 1939. There were at that time many young economics dons in the new PPE school at Oxford and they were encouraged by their seniors to join in an 'Economists' Research Group' of which Hall became a prominent member. The Group undertook empirical research on business behaviour in order to test how far it conformed to what was assumed in economic theory and reached rather negative conclusions that attracted much attention. Particular interest attached to pricing behaviour, which was the subject of an important article in 1939 by Hall in collaboration with the American economist C. J. Hitch.[1] Hall also published before the war a book on *The Economics of a Socialist State*.

During the Second World War he was recruited to the Raw Materials Department of the Ministry of Supply and was assigned shortly after America's entry into the war to service in Washington, where he spent two years in the Combined Raw Materials Board. There was in fact very little combined planning as distinct from exchange of information; but the experience allowed Hall to familiarize himself with the ways of a large government machine, get to know America and American institutions and make many American friends.

At the end of the war the Raw Materials Division of the Ministry of Supply was absorbed by the Board of Trade. Hall returned to Oxford but continued to engage in work for his old department on a part-time basis, helping in the preparation of a buffer stocks scheme for staple commodities. In April 1945 James Meade had tried to induce him to join the Economic Section, in effect as his Deputy, but Hall declined. When approached two years later to take over the direction of the Economic Section, he agreed. He was released to join the Section on a part-time basis in June 1947 before taking up his duties full-time from 1 September.

From 1947 to 1961 Hall was adviser to a succession of governments.

---

[1] R. L. Hall and C. J. Hitch, 'Price Theory and Business Behaviour', reprinted in *Oxford Studies in the Price Mechanism* (ed. Wilson and Andrews), Oxford, 1951.

He served under eight Chancellors and exercised more influence on economic policy than perhaps any other official. Fortunately – although it was contrary to Civil Service rules – he kept a diary and in it he recorded events as they occurred from day to day and his reflections on them. The diary is an absorbing account of what went on inside government in the postwar years and provides a valuable insight into the shaping of high policy in those years.

More than any other source it reveals the thinking and argument that lay behind the advice on economic policy offered to ministers. It does so in a lively and readable way and allows us to trace, week by week, the current preoccupations of the Chancellor's advisers – something very difficult to do from the vast mass of official papers in the Public Record Office. It also contributes to a judgement of the grounds on which policy was based and the capabilities of those who shaped it, whether as ministers or officials.

The post which Hall held throughout was that of Director of the Economic Section, a body which originated in the Cabinet Office in 1939–40 and moved to the Treasury in 1953 when Hall was given the title of Economic Adviser to HMG and knighted. The Economic Section was the first group of professional economists to serve as economic advisers at the centre of government in Britain (or perhaps in any country). A history of the Section from 1939 to 1961, which has just appeared, provides a useful amplification of some of the material in the diary. Other recent or forthcoming accounts of the period covered by the diary are listed in the Bibliography.

This diary is not the first to appear by a former Director of the Economic Section. Robert Hall's immediate predecessor, James Meade, has recently published his diary for the period between November 1944 and September 1946. For about half of that period, however, Meade's diary is almost entirely blank and the entries are limited to three short periods at the end of 1944, the end of 1945 and the middle of 1946. Hall's diary, on the other hand, extends over the whole of his fourteen years in the Economic Section with only minor breaks in 1948 and 1953.

There is another difference between the two. Meade made long entries at weekends, giving a systematic account of the work in hand. His diary dwells more on what was going on within the Section, and deals with it in a more considered way, than Hall's diary which looks outward from the Section and usually records his immediate reactions, although there are lengthier entries when he is abroad or on board an aeroplane and free from office duties.

It was not originally Lord Roberthall's intention that his diary should be published during his lifetime. Its very existence remained a secret (except from Lord Trend, Cabinet Secretary in the 1960s). Under the thirty year rule none of it could have been released for publication before 1977 and what appears in this volume would have had to wait until 1984 at the earliest. Soon after he had begun to consider publication, Lord Roberthall had a stroke that ruled out any prospect of his editing the manuscript himself. With his agreement I undertook the task but he died on 17 September 1988 just as the editing was completed.

I have been anxious to let the diary speak for itself wherever possible and have therefore confined my intrusions to a few passages intended to provide a background for readers unfamiliar with the period. Once the narrative gathers pace and the same names recur, any initial difficulties in following the course of events soon disappear. Where someone is first referred to I have inserted in square brackets (provided I thought it necessary) some indication of the post they held or the department to which they were attached. I have also inserted in square brackets, for the convenience of the specialist reader, the reference number (and sometimes the PRO call number) of documents mentioned in the text where I have been able to trace them. All other explanatory Notes are put at the end of the text (pages 283 ff.) and so also are four Appendices describing the main committees mentioned, with their functions and PRO call numbers, providing fuller details of the main official characters in the story, listing the members of the Economic Section in the years covered by this volume and spelling out the various abbreviations scattered through the diary.

The present volume covers only the years 1947–53 but it is the intention to issue a second volume covering the years 1954–61 as soon as authority to publish can be obtained.

My task as editor has been made materially easier through the assistance I have had from Neil Rollings, especially in tracking down papers in the Public Record Office and in preparing the note on committees in Appendix I, and from Mrs Anne Robinson who typed the not always very legible diaries with unfailing accuracy. This assistance was possible thanks to grants from the Nuffield Foundation and the Leverhulme Trust to both of which I gladly acknowledge my indebtedness. Others to whom I am indebted are Mrs K. Jones of the National Institute of Economic and Social Research, J. D. Bailey of St Antony's College Oxford, Rodney Lowe of Bristol University and Charles Slansky of *The Economist*.

A.K.C.

To my wife
Perilla
without whose love and support
my life would be the poorer,
and these diaries could not
have reached publication.

Introduction

When Robert Hall took over the direction of the Economic Section they were a small group in the Cabinet Office numbering about a dozen. Most of the older and more experienced members had left or were on the point of leaving; by the end of the year nearly half the staff he inherited from Meade had gone. There was no full-time Director between April and September and the staff were also without ministerial direction since Morrison, the Lord President, to whom they reported, had also fallen ill early in the year and was now fully occupied in other directions. In contrast to the apparent decline of the Economic Section, a new Central Economic Planning Staff, announced in March 1947, was being manned up over the summer months. This staff, under Sir Edwin Plowden, the government's Chief Planning Officer, was at first located in the Cabinet Office and attached, like the Economic Section, to the Lord President, Herbert Morrison. By the end of September, however, Morrison had given up his duties as co-ordinator of economic policy, and from then on, both the Economic Section and the Planning Staff served under Stafford Cripps in one capacity or another.

Nineteen forty-seven was a year of crisis. First there had been a fuel crisis in February when a large part of British industry had been forced either to close down for lack of electricity or to curtail output for lack of coal. This had meant a serious loss of production and exports and set back the process of conversion from war to peace. A foreign exchange crisis followed. There was throughout the year a dangerous imbalance between exports and imports and an even larger one between exports and imports paid for in dollars. This produced a drain of gold and dollars from the reserves which gathered force with the introduction of convertibility of the pound in July 1947 in fulfilment of an obligation under the Loan Agreement with the United States. Within six weeks, on 20 August, convertibility had to be suspended and what was left of the US dollar loan was frozen. It was still uncertain whether the Marshall Plan for European recovery would win the approval of Congress. It was necessary, therefore, to review urgently how much could be imported in 1948 without trenching too deeply on the limited reserves still available.

It was with these problems that Robert Hall had to grapple as he took up his duties. Not only was the import programme under revision but it had been decided to introduce an autumn budget in order to reduce the inflationary pressure that had become increasingly obvious. On his very first day as Director he circulated to the Budget Committee an assessment of the economic situation with proposals for higher taxes and lower food subsidies.* Dalton was still Chancellor until November, but at the end of September a new ministry was created under Sir Stafford Cripps to manage economic policy, Harold Wilson taking over from Cripps at the Board of Trade. Six weeks later Dalton resigned and Cripps was appointed Chancellor, merging his new Ministry of Economic Affairs and its staff with the Treasury. Within three months from the commencement of the diary there had been two major political upheavals. First Morrison and then Dalton had gone and Cripps was left the undisputed overlord of both economic and financial policy.

Three separate staffs were now advising Cripps: the official Treasury under its Permanent Secretary, Sir Edward Bridges; the Central Economic Planning Staff (CEPS) under Plowden, now part of the Treasury; and the Economic Section, still in the Cabinet Office, but virtually an independent part of Cripps's staff. It had been agreed earlier that Plowden would rely for technical economic advice on the Economic Section and he and Hall soon entered into a powerful partnership which continued throughout the period covered by this volume. For his first year, 1947–8, Plowden also had the benefit of advice from Austin Robinson, who brought with him from Cambridge three young economists, Kenneth Berrill, Robin Marris and Patricia Brown. This did not make for an altogether happy relationship with the staff of the Economic Section, but as time went on, the two staffs worked increasingly closely together.

One of the principal activities of the Economic Section from 1945 to 1947 had been the preparation of an *Economic Survey* which was the nearest thing the government had to a plan and which dealt with the prospects and problems of the coming year. The early Surveys were intended only for ministerial consideration but in February 1947, for the first time, an *Economic Survey for 1947* had been published after being completely rewritten by Stafford Cripps and R. W. B. Clarke, a Treasury official. The Economic Section had also been engaged in 1945–7 in preparing, in collaboration with the CSO, a *Long-Term Economic Survey* looking five years ahead. Work had proceeded in a rather desultory way in consultation with the government departments concerned but had never been completed. Much of Hall's time in the summer months was taken up with this task. On his return from America early in June 1947 one of his first duties had been to take the chair at a meeting to consider a draft *Economic Survey for 1948–51*. The draft was subsequently revised and a new text was circulated in mid-October.

Cripps had asked for the completion of the *Survey* by mid-November with a view to publication in December. As was pointed out by the Treasury, however, this was out of the question. How could any published document base itself firmly on the assumption that there would be no Marshall Aid (as in the draft) or alternatively that there was some specified amount of Marshall Aid (when Congress had still to

* 'The inflationary pressure', note by the Head of the Economic Section, 1 September 1947, in PRO T 171/392, '1947 Supplementary budget'.

vote on the subject)? The Planning Staff were also laying claim to responsibility for the *Long-Term Survey* and arguing that the Economic Section should confine itself to an annual *Survey* of the usual kind for 1948. What was finally agreed in October was that effort should be concentrated on an annual *Survey*, looking ahead where necessary and indicating perhaps that a long-term plan would appear at an early date. A draft for ministers was circulated in January 1948 and the published version appeared in March.

The *Economic Survey for 1948–51* was never submitted to ministers. Instead, Austin Robinson embarked in 1948 on an *Economic Survey for 1948–52* which was completed in July (EPB(48)25) and formed the basis for a *Long-Term Programme* submitted to the OEEC in Paris on 1 October and published in December (Cmd 7572) after a leak in New York (see the diary entry for November 23rd).

The really pressing problem was that of the balance of payments in the wake of the suspension of convertibility. Advice on this was mainly the responsibility of OF (the Overseas Finance Division of the Treasury), which came under Sir Wilfrid Eady, a second secretary, but in which R.W.B. ('Otto') Clarke, although only an assistant secretary, was the man who mattered. As a staff advising on economic policy as a whole and engaged in the drafting of an *Economic Survey for 1948*, the Economic Section could not avoid pursuing the subject. The Treasury, as Meade had found earlier, was not very forthcoming and this led to a good deal of friction.

As the diary opens, the problems uppermost in Hall's mind were staff shortages, relations with the Planning Staff and the Treasury, the drafting of the *Long-Term Economic Survey* and the outlook for the balance of payments. He made almost daily entries until mid-November and then broke off for four months before resuming, more intermittently, towards the end of March 1948. From then until the middle of 1953 the diary continues without any similar break.

I

From the convertibility crisis to devaluation,

1 September 1947 to 15 September 1949

Monday, September 1st 1947

Today I began as full-time Director of the Economic Section of the Cabinet Office, in succession to James Meade who had to resign because the strenuous life gave him stomach ulcers. I think he took everything too seriously. I was asked to take the post in April and was transferred on a part-time basis from the Board of Trade from June 1st. This was mainly to work on the draft Economic Survey, 1948–51. But as the balance of payments position became worse I had to spend more and more time on it, including a good deal of August when I was supposed to be on leave.

Nothing much today but I was sent for by the Lord President [Herbert Morrison], mainly to be told that I must get more staff. This is a worrying problem as four of Meade's senior people have left or will be gone by Christmas. It is not at all easy to get people back from the Universities as there are so many undergraduates there now and no one who is starting again after the war wants to interrupt his career once more so soon.

Tuesday, September 2nd

Saw Plowden [Chief Planning Officer] today. He wants us to make a study of the current position as he is convinced that it is more serious than Ministers suggest. I said we couldn't do it until we got new Treasury estimates [of the balance of payments] as no one knew what exactly the reserves and liabilities would be after the heavy losses of August. But we would ask the Treasury.

Wednesday, September 3rd

Saw Norman Brook (Secretary to the Cabinet) today and discussed various things including staff. Told him that the Lord President's idea, that because there was a crisis everyone would rally round, was wrong – many economists felt that the present Government was hopeless. In any case all universities had raised their salaries and the Economic Section was not as attractive as it used to be. We also talked about the events leading to suspension of convertibility and he said he would see Marcus Fleming (Deputy Director, Economic Section) who had all along been nervous about Treasury freedom with the sterling balances but had been assured by Eady [Treasury Second Secretary] that the Treasury had this well under control.[1] Marcus and his assistant Nita Watts feel very bitter about this but it is partly their fault as they never succeeded in getting the Lord President to see the point, so that they made him feel that all was well when even on their own analysis it wasn't. But to lose all the American loan so quickly shortens our remaining time.

I suggested to Brook that we try to get [Donald] MacDougall, now at Wadham [Oxford], and he welcomed the idea but doubted if it would come off.

Thursday, September 4th

[Economic] Planning Board. The TUC members were away at the annual conference and we had quite a pleasant time discussing methods of cutting investment – the FBI members want industry to do their own but it is hard to see how this would work. However even an exhortation might help.

Monday, September 8th

The Treasury refused to make any balance of payments estimates as they were getting new programmes in to ERC [Exchange Requirements Committee] and couldn't say. We will have to do our own. Austin Robinson [Planning Staff] began to draft the survey, which Plowden wants to put to the Planning Board.[2]

Wednesday, September 10th

Robinson and Marcus Fleming working all the time on the current survey. Fleming doesn't make it look very bad, but we think he believes that exports can be forced into dollar countries if we refuse to let the other countries draw their sterling balances. Tress [Economic Section] thinks that this involves an easier diversion of exports than is practicable.[3]

Friday, September 12th

Plowden showed Bridges [Permanent Secretary of the Treasury] the draft tonight. The Treasury are furious that we have dared to make our own estimates and Bridges has given them till 10.30 tomorrow to reply. They wouldn't let Austin Robinson and me go to Bridges with Plowden unless B. had all *his* staff along. After dinner P., Austin Robinson and I went to see Stafford Cripps [President of the Board of Trade], who had just made a very good broadcast on his new export programme. He is acting for the Lord President and we wanted his permission to circulate the survey to the Board. As it is very critical of the adequacy of the present measures, we felt he should see it. He is very nice and extremely able and I enjoyed the evening – he only wanted a few changes in tone to suggest the determination of the Government instead of the difficulties of the task. I got the 12.05 to Oxford and arrived very tired.

Monday, September 15th

An exhausting weekend as Paul Butler [a retired diplomat] was there all the time and several other people were in and out. Today Otto Clarke

[OF Division, Treasury], who was just back from Paris, made a violent attack on our survey because it was too optimistic. He objected mainly to Fleming's assumption that if we limited drawings on the sterling balances, we could sell increased exports to dollar countries. He wanted to do it mainly in terms of the dollar difficulty and we agreed. Otto and I lunched together at St Stephen's Tavern and he attacked the Economic Section for consistently overlooking the hard currency problem. He thinks that we ought to think mainly in terms of bilateral bargains and altogether believes in Henderson and Balogh as against Keynes, Robbins and Meade. Events have supported this and it is clear that everyone on both sides of the Atlantic was absurdly optimistic in 1945 about the prospects of recovery. Now all Roosevelt's advisers are gone and nearly all the UK side – Liesching is [Permanent Secretary] at Ministry of Food, Keynes dead, Robbins and Meade retired. Only Will Clayton [US Assistant Secretary of State for Economic Affairs] is left to plague us. I think Otto is too extreme and he minimizes the faults of the Treasury, who so arranged things that we lost about $600 mn for unblocked sterling in 6 weeks.[4] But our general attitudes are similar and we both hope we will get no more American help until we mend our ways.

Tuesday, September 16th

[Trevor] Swan, who has been lent to Economic Section by Coombs [Australian Prime Minister's Department], arrived today. He is said to be the best of the young Australian economists and to have been carrying a heavy load in Canberra. I lunched with [Duncan] Burn today. He is now Industrial Adviser to *The Times* and seemed to hold sensible views. We talked over our mistakes and both decided that our worst was to under-estimate the post-war level of activity in the USA, which has led to the present enormous demand for food and raw materials and altered all the prices. We could not have foreseen the troubles with Russia or the coal crisis or the bad harvests, but we ought to have done so on USA.

Wednesday, September 17th

The review was finished and looks very gloomy. Mrs Wyndham Goldie [of the BBC] lunched with me at Boulestin – she is in charge of economic talks on the Third Programme but finds is hard to get suitable economists. I said I would try to help but could not broadcast myself as it would get civil servants into politics, however careful I was. I said I would advise her unofficially about the various points of view that might be held. In the afternoon I went to the Investment Programmes Committee to support Bensusan-Butt [Economic Section], over machinery diversions. Depts were very obstructive but after a few rows we got them into a better frame of mind. If we can't divert machinery into exports we might as well give up.

Thursday, September 18th

Planning Board took the current review.[5] A useless discussion but they broadly accepted the conclusions and Plowden persuaded them to ask for draft recommendations to the Government on the additional measures needed. Afterwards I saw Plowden and said that I thought that we ought not to be discussing the failings of the Government with outsiders unless we had *first* told Ministers. The Planning Board was really a new constitutional development and quite contrary to all Civil Service practice: however it seemed that Ministers had intended this. We agreed to send a Minute to Cripps [President of the Board of Trade] telling him that we thought that more severe measures were needed and that we expected the Board to recommend this. I lunched with Howard Sykes [formerly secretary of the wartime Combined Production and Resources Board] who is on a visit for some slightly mysterious purpose. The State Dept had wanted to help him but he had refused. He seemed however to be on good terms with Snyder (Secretary of the US Treasury). He thought UK would not get any more US help until we showed that we could get by ourselves: it was thought that we were being demoralized by loans which concealed the extent to which we were living beyond our income. The US also considered that our failure on coal showed that nationalization was a disturbing factor and that if we nationalized steel, output would fall and US help to Europe would need to increase. Why should they pay for our experiments, especially when they disliked the objective?

Friday, September 19th

The new Committees for dealing with balance of payments are getting under way. The principal one is the Overseas Negotiations Committee, presided over by [T. L.] Rowan [PPS to the Prime Minister] who has come from No. 10. First meeting today – Rowan obviously has instructions to take a tough line. I think it will be a very useful Committee; the old B. of P. Working Party [a subcommittee of the Steering Committee] hardly ever met but this is to meet almost daily and to approve all negotiations and the general principles to be followed. Eddie Playfair is the Treasury man: he called Humphrey Mynors (Bank of England) *Roger* all through the meeting: an easy confusion as they look much alike.[6]

The other Committees are ERC which is little changed, and a new Export Targets Committee under Harold Wilson [Secretary for Overseas Trade], very like the old Export Promotion Committee.

Wednesday, September 24th

Plowden, Clarke, Hugh Weeks [Plowden's deputy], Austin Robinson and I met Cripps and J. H. Woods [Permanent Secretary, Board of

Trade] today on the Review and our Minute. He (Cripps) is really a very able man; he sees all the points and remembers relevant things which he has met before. He seemed quite prepared to let the Planning Board go forward even if it were critical of Ministers.

The ON Committee is meeting every day and making some progress. Rowan is a very good chairman and the Treasury seem genuinely anxious to get the best advice available.

The Investment Working Party is hard at work and reaching the end of their report.[7] They hope to cut the total by something like the £200mn announced by Cripps in his speech [on 12 September]. This £200 mn was just a guess I made at a meeting with Plowden, Weeks and Robinson, as Cripps was insisting on putting down some firm figure. It seemed to me the most we could have any chance of implementing, but the Working Party feel very gloomy about the building labour as they think it will nearly all go into the black market or under £10 house repairs.[8]

Thursday, September 25th

Planning Board. Plowden did a wonderful job and railroaded all the recommendations through with hardly a change. It was like a College meeting where no one dared to speak because the issues were so serious. We recommended more cuts in imports, stopping dollar leaks through sterling releases, measures against inflation, proper measures to get labour and material for exports, and full publicity about the gravity of the situation. John Henry Woods entered a caveat about the position of civil servants who must not criticize Ministers, but everyone supported the recommendations. Now they ought to go to Ministers. It will be interesting to see if they dare to turn them down.

Saturday, September 27th

At Oxford for weekend. Oliver Franks [Provost of Queen's College, Oxford] came in for an hour or so. He looked tired but seemed in good form; he talked about what he had to do in Washington in presenting the 'Marshall Plan' scheme.[9] He is very gloomy about the prospects for the UK until we realize how bad everything is. I think that he is very anxious to get back into public life if he can (a) square Queen's, (b) time his reappearance so that he can pull us out of our troubles. He thought that the 40s should replace the 60s – at least the former had some ideas and some knowledge of how to carry these out. When I took my new job I did not agree with Oliver's gloom, but now I suspect that he is right. Ministers are (so far) incapable of taking painful decisions.

Tuesday, September 30th

This morning it was announced that Cripps is to become Minister of
Economic Affairs, and Harold Wilson President of the Board of Trade.
I went to a meeting of the Exports Target Committee and saw Harold.
The changes are very good in the sense that Cripps is a realist and able
to understand a problem extremely quickly. It ought to be good for the
Section, as I am very doubtful if Morrison could understand the long
briefs we gave him. My own impression is that the Section has overdone
its academic integrity and taken the line that it should tell the truth,
however difficult it is and however long it takes: and that this applied to
all its activities. It is a problem as I quite agree that the Section would be
useless if it thought of itself as an administrative unit: there is enough of
that already. To be any use we must be a technical unit. But the truth in
these cases depends on the impression you make. If Morrison goes away
thinking that the Economic Section is such and such, it doesn't help that
his brief didn't say that. It is a dangerous field as if you go too far you
begin to ask what you want done and what advice is most likely to lead
to that result. The only danger with Cripps is that he may set up a new
Ministry of Production which I am sure is not suited to Whitehall as it is
now.

I lunched with Maurice Green, one of the City page men of *The
Times*. He seemed a nice man – we talked about inflation but he
couldn't really say how bad the situation was. It is technically impossible
to measure an inflationary gap but I think we are fairly close to the
proper order of magnitude.

Wednesday, October 1st

I lunched with Heymann who does Commodity Policy for *The Times*
[and *The Economist*] and is correspondent of the *Neue Zurcher Zeitung*:
he brought his Swiss editor [Aschinger?] who seemed a charming man.
We talked about planning and how hard it was to *do* anything. Dined
with Howard Sykes who was full of ideas. The one that interested me
most was the suggestion that US capital should finance urgent Empire
development, such as Wankie Colliery [in Rhodesia] or the petroleum
companies: on a debenture basis with some share in the equity. He
thought that US business would feel that London houses understood
these things better than they (US) did, and that there would be no real
trouble if it were properly explored.

Thursday, October 2nd

Talked to Austin Robinson about the Survey.[10] It is very obscure as he
really wants to do it and I think it would be giving up too much of the

Section's work to agree. In any case, it is extremely difficult and he is very erratic – he would need to use my staff and why shouldn't they get the credit? I spoke to Butt who was very much opposed to the idea and later saw Plowden and warned him not to do anything precipitous.

Friday, October 3rd

Saw Plowden again. Cripps wants a memo on the inflationary position and what might be done on it, and also on the line he should take on wages.[11] The PM [Attlee] and Isaacs [Minister of Labour] had seen the TUC about the letter calling attention to the Government's desire that wages should stay put, and had run away from it: S.C. wanted to retrieve the position if possible.

Later in the day Marquand [Paymaster-General] sent for me – he had also been asked for his views and wanted us to write something. This sort of situation occurs quite often and one has to be very candid – I told him we were already at work but would give him a copy. He was rather annoyed and felt that he ought to have been told but said he would clear with S.C. He has had a bad time as almost immediately after he was made Paymaster-General with an eye to long-term plans, Plowden was appointed and since then he has been almost in the cold. Now he hopes to be drawn more into the picture.

We worked until midnight and I got the first train or rather the 9.45, on Saturday, having left a draft for Plowden.

Monday, October 6th

Discussed our draft with Plowden who said we were too weak on wages: but I pointed out that there *was* no remedy in an inflation except to deflate and meanwhile to make appeals. The Government would not use a wage-stop and there was the trouble that the least desirable occupations are those least easily controlled. No one could stop employers paying more than minimum rates and they would do so if profits were easy and they had to keep their labour.

Fennelly [Board of Trade] dined with me at the Reform and afterwards we talked to Maurice Hutton [British Food Mission in Washington] and A. Robinson. Maurice thinks that we shall have to get a US loan and that we are mad not to begin now – it will take a long time. We all argued that we ought not to get US help until we had showed that we could help ourselves, and that Ministers would not face the situation until they had to.[12] He has been so long in Washington that the usual trouble has set in – he can see *his* problems very clearly and thinks that it is only *our* incompetence that prevents us doing the things here which will ease *his* path. I have often felt the same myself when I was in Washington.

Tuesday, October 7th

We settled (I hope) that Economic Section could take the responsibility for the re-write of the [Long-Term] Survey with Austin Robinson's help – he would take it over perhaps at Planning Board stage. Plowden didn't seem to mind at all – I think the trouble is that Hugh Weeks committed himself to A.R. without discussion.

Party at night at the Gorell Barnes [Adviser to Prime Minister at No. 10], who have a very nice house in Hampstead and had provided an opulent supper. Plowden and Lady P. were there – she is keen on farming. I had a long talk with Peggy Jay [wife of Douglas Jay, then Adviser to Prime Minister at No. 10] who told me the names of the new Ministers. Everyone was delighted that Shinwell has gone from Fuel and Power and Hugh Gaitskell got the job [of Minister of Fuel and Power]. Shinwell consistently refused to believe that coal was going wrong last winter or that he needed more men: I think he is more responsible than any other man for our troubles now, as it is impossible to say where we might have been if the export drive had not been checked and especially if we had been able to bargain with a little coal. Cripps has now got three young men whom he seems to trust in the Board of Trade [Wilson], Supply [Strauss] and Fuel and Power [Gaitskell]. Marquand is to take the allocating committees so it won't be for lack of power if Cripps fails – he has all the key posts.

Wednesday, October 8th

Lunched with Plowden, mainly to discuss whether we needed any help from US. He agreed that we ought not to start until we were sure we would cope at this end, and I agreed to do a memo for S.C. Gorell Barnes agreed to brief the PM in the same sense.[12] In the afternoon we had a first Survey meeting with Campion [Director, CSO] and A. Robinson and got the lines cleared except for the question of 1948 or 1948/51.

At night I called for the Chancellor [Hugh Dalton] who drove me to our dinner with Mrs Cannan [widow of Professor Edwin Cannan of the LSE]. I was surprised that he had accepted – it was a gracious act towards the wife of an old teacher. Rita [Cannan] had ordered a table for 7.30 and we were late – the table was given away and we had to wait. The Chancellor didn't seem to mind and at dinner he boomed away about old mutual friends. Rita asked him how he would invest some money and he took it very well, advising Dalton 2½s – it would have been a good tip if she had taken it! She went early and he took me back to No. 11 and talked a while of the difficulties of a deflationary budget: but he seems to be going to introduce one. They are of course most worried about reducing the subsidies. I left early and worked late.

Thursday, October 9th [Friday 10th?]

Lunched with George McGhee [a former Rhodes Scholar] who is in charge of US aid to Greece and Turkey and is on his way back to US. He talked a good deal about the conditions US would certainly attach to any loan to UK, and whether we could accept. I told him that I thought conditions *could* be useful – the Harriman Mission was useful whereas the export White Paper had been disastrous.[13] We both felt that it would be extremely useful if we got a UK Mission going in Washington again – we are very short-handed there.

After lunch I discussed inflation with Cripps, Plowden and Rowan [Cripps's Permanent Secretary]. Stafford Cripps was full of ideas for possible taxes, and gave me a great deal to do including notes for a speech. The Section had a busy afternoon but we got through – the main trouble is that they *will* write briefs that are too long. No wonder Morrison could not understand them.

Dined (late) with Kennedy. Fennelly, Westerman and Bugbee (US Embassy) were there. A good dinner. Bugbee is leaving and his successor (?) was there too. Talk was very general. I got the 9.50 and had a lazy weekend as I was tired.

Friday, October 10th [Saturday, 11th?]

Spent most of the day in Trinity giving [Anthony] Crosland a lead; I dined there and everyone extremely nice to me.[14]

Monday, October 13th

Planning Board all the morning and Steering Committee [of Permanent Secretaries] most of the afternoon. All on the Investment Working Party report (EPB(47)17). No real criticism except on small points – no one could cope I suppose. Nearly everything is taken at such short notice that if you don't participate in writing the drafts you have to be very strong to have any effect. Bridges has an even better technique for steam-rollering than Plowden – he seems conciliatory but gives nothing away.

It's odd how £200 mn has stuck: it was a figure [for investment cuts] I thought of quickly one day at a meeting with Plowden, due to the fact that Stafford Cripps was determined to put *some* figure in his speech.[15] The main snags are (a) can building labour really be diverted, (b) will there be steel enough with these cuts, for the export drive. But Whitehall is being increasingly worried about the dollar problem which means that if we reach the export targets we will be sending a good deal of stuff to places that can't pay.

Tuesday, October 14th

Cripps at 10, the rest of the day mainly on the new balance of payments statement which the PM has demanded at once (before the House meets).

Cripps had Marquand there and was very nice though he let the talk wander too much. It was partly on the staff question, where he did not have any suggestions: partly that he wanted me to do various things and especially a review of the economic situation for the debate on the King's Speech. The staffing is almost impossible – we want a senior man and they aren't available.

At 10.30 Bridges took a special balance of payments meeting to consider the new proposals, for fairly heavy food cuts and more export direction. Ince [Permanent Secretary of the Ministry of Labour] was very anxious for a realistic statement, while he always takes the line on labour proposals that the Ministry of Labour is powerless. On the whole, everyone agreed – the paper is to go up from the Chancellor [Dalton] and Stafford Cripps and we met in Bridges' room at 6 to consider a new draft. Otto Clarke did all the work – he is obviously a very hard driver and when we dispersed at 7.15 he had to draft again and get copies to the Ministers and the printers before 8 a.m. It is to be taken at Chequers on Sunday.[16]

I lunched with Lionel Robbins at LSE and got some good advice about the Section and relations with A.R. He says that the latter was very temperamental when he was himself with the Section when Lionel was Director. The best thing was to get help from Norman Brook. Lionel as usual is very bitter about the Chancellor. He is closely identified with the Loan and regards its failure as due to the Chancellor's bad monetary policies. I think there is a little in this but that the chief internal villain is Shinwell. Outside, we all under-estimated the American boom, and the slowness of recovery, and most people (but not Churchill or I) the political deterioration with Eastern Europe.

One thing that horrified me today was Eady's attitude during the final drafting. He really did not seem to understand the problems of 'unrequited' and 'frustrated' exports which now bothers Whitehall so much.[17] Yet he is the chief negotiator for all the bilateral deals we are expecting. I do get the impression that we are going to make the worst of our new bilateralism – all the odium in US and all the downward spiral, and none of the cakes and ale.

Wednesday, October 15th

Mostly working on an outline for Stafford Cripps' speech. I lunched with Max Nicholson [Lord President's Office] at PEP [Political and Economic Planning] to see a possible candidate for the Section – Ogilvy Webb. Hard to decide – I am a bad chooser. Saw Plowden later and suggested Oliver Franks as the US Ambassador – he could be just the man to keep the conditions for the loan tolerable. Plowden very favourably impressed and will 'float it' as he says.

The Section hard at work – Butt, Nita Watts and I all worked till nearly midnight. Butt is doing very well with the Survey but he will need to as Stafford Cripps wants to *publish* in December. It all has to be re-written and the two crucial divisions – on imports and on investment – still to be taken.

Talked to Campion in the Club at dinner. He suggested that the Treasury were promoting Rowan to be Cripps' Permanent Secretary in order to fill up his time so that Clarke (Chairman of Exchange Requirements Committee) could get back for the Treasury the general authority on balance of payments questions now with Rowan as Chairman of Overseas Negotiations Committee. *If*, as I suspect, the PM put Rowan there, it is a very subtle move *if* Campion is right. I can believe it though don't think it would be altogether conscious. 'In tragic life God wot no villain need be'. The Treasury is the tragedy and there may well be no villains.

Thursday, October 16th

This afternoon Rowan, Plowden and I saw Stafford Cripps about his speech: he suggested a number of changes and in general wanted the full story on the events since the August debate on the State of the Nation. Rowan took me to dinner with his wife at the Carlton Grill: she seemed very nice. They first met on the QM [*Queen Mary*] when Rowan was Winston's PPS [Principal Private Secretary] and she was an ATS (or perhaps WREN) going with Winston to Quebec. After dinner we both went back and I worked on the speech till midnight and started again at 8 a.m., getting the first draft done by about 9.

Friday, October 17th

This was discussed with Rowan who wanted the order changed a bit. I had done it by problems – convertibility, exports, imports – he wanted it by time. This wasn't very hard and I went back to the June 30th announcement of the first programme cuts. There are two fundamental difficulties: (a) the failure to do anything serious about the dollar drain, though it was evident by August 5th that this would put us through the loan by October, (b) Cripps' Central Hall speech which, though it was generally agreed to be the most realistic of them all, yet suggested that the export targets would be enough and thus he concealed the magnitude of the dollar problem. After a bit of rewriting, I got the whole thing into shape by about 7 p.m. and managed to get the 7.35. The Inner Council of Ministers is meeting at Chequers on Sunday to take the paper on export [import?] cuts, before the Cabinet meets on Monday.

Monday, October 20th

The Cabinet took all the import cuts *and* the whole investment reductions today. I gather that it was a tight thing on the food cuts: Strachey [Minister of Food] had argued that there were other things to be done, especially more investment cuts.[18]

Dined with M. Hutton at the Reform Club; a big party, mainly to talk to Bob Brand [Treasury representative in Washington 1944–6] about how to present the UK case in Washington. Plowden, Tommy Brand [Lazard's], Lionel Robbins, Hugh Weeks, Austin Robinson, Otto Clarke and Feavearyear [Ministry of Food]. A good deal of discussion. The general view was that we ought to have a stronger team in Washington but also that we would have to show that we were going to do something by ourselves before we could expect any help. P. told me later that it had practically been decided that we should ask for US help and that John Henry Woods would probably lead the UK team.

Tuesday, October 21st

King's Speech announcing the proposed change in the Parliament Act, which Attlee later said would be to cut the veto to one year. Apparently Nye Bevan [Minister of Health] insisted on this as the price of deferring steel nationalization.[19] Ministers are mad to do this when they are asking for national unity in face of the balance of payments crisis. It is worse than they think. We had a meeting with the Board of Trade to discuss diversion of exports and the Board of Trade argued that it would do more harm than good and that no action should be taken on any account. They are responsible for the export drive and obviously don't feel the urgency of the problem at all.

Thursday, October 23rd

Stafford Cripps made his speech which was very well received and hailed on all sides as a realistic and non-party one.[20] But it was said to be ill-matched by the proposals on the Lords.

Friday, October 24th

We had to keep Pakenham [Parliamentary Under Secretary, War Office] informed so that he can put the Government's economic case in the Lords. I went to see him and found him on the point of going to Germany and on the hop meanwhile at the call of Bevin [Foreign Secretary]. I arranged for Jefferies [Economic Section] to work with his secretary, March, for the speech he is to make in the Lords on October 28th.

Thursday, October 30th

This has been a week mainly of working on bits of the Survey. Plowden's people have hardly been visible as they were trying to do a White Paper on the investment cuts. However we had a long session with Reeder of the Ministry of Labour about the labour distribution in 1948. The main problem is the number of unemployed, which in the end we put at 465,000 – largely by difference.[21] The only important figures are the coal and textile targets and the building ceilings.

Today there was a paper [CP(47)298] from the Ministry of Food asking for permission to buy more wheat, probably for dollars, to end bread rationing. Strachey is trying all sorts of devices to get out of the food cuts which have been imposed. But so far he has been turned down. The true problem is animal feeding stuffs – if we cannot get these the new agricultural programme cannot be carried through.

Monday, November 3rd

Took Butt to dine at the Reform where we saw Colin Clark [the well-known statistician], who is on a quick visit from Australia. Afterwards we worked late on the Survey. He [Butt] is rather an erratic draughtsman and sometimes tends to put in much too detailed recommendations on things he considers wrong. But he is able to do it, anyhow, and it is wonderful to have someone to take the place of Tress.

Tuesday, November 4th

A long day, mainly on Survey. In the morning there were two papers on an approach to the US to get some help to maintain our reserves: they had already been to Ministers so I had no chance of saying anything. Apparently Lew Douglas [US Ambassador] asked on Saturday for something in a rush.

In the afternoon had a long talk with Plowden. He was furious because Ministers had refused his White Paper on Investment and wanted something much more flattering.[22] He had refused to do this and Stafford Cripps had offered to do it himself which was deflating as Stafford Cripps is already far too busy and in any case the one man P. respects. Nye Bevan is trying to cut out all reductions in building labour, which will make nonsense of the Report as nearly half the investment cuts come there.

Afterwards I talked a bit about the Survey and about affairs generally. P. wonders if he has done any good – I am sure that he has as at least he has got these decisions on imports, exports and investment. I respect him more and more, since he does do things in the right order and on the whole gets them straight. But he thinks Ministers are in a panic both about the very bad situation, and about their own prospects.

They are all disturbed by the results of the municipal elections which seem to show a very big change in opinion.

Monday, November 10th

All the intermediate days have been mainly on the Survey: we had the first main meeting on Friday 7th and it went off fairly well: at any rate no one wanted any big changes. But it will be a desperate job to finish it in time. There is a good deal of trouble between Marcus Fleming and the Treasury over 'unrequited' exports and exports of capital. It is clear that the UK will almost certainly pay off its sterling debts by £200 or £300 mn over next year but the Treasury are very reluctant to admit this.[23]

Today we spent a long afternoon discussing the situation of coal with Fuel and Power. Francis Hemming [Under Secretary, Fuel and Power] was very anxious that we should be pessimistic, not only about the chances but about what could be done. We are committed to 6 mn tons of exports under the Marshall Plan and will be promising several million tons more as a result of the trade agreements we are now making.

Wednesday, November 12th

Went to Stafford Cripps' morning meeting to discuss the paper on the overall balance of payments, which is now ready for Ministers [CP(47)31.1]. The main problem, coming out more and more clearly, is that as we cannot earn enough dollars, we will be 'unrequited' in some sense or other for a good deal of exports [to non-dollar countries] if the targets are reached. And it will be difficult to decide when to start cutting down on the exports and how to explain it and what to do with goods which cannot be sold. Not much talk at the meeting. Marquand, Plowden, Rowan and me. Marquand not very happy, as usual, though I think he is a little more in the picture.

Afterwards I gave a lecture at the Imperial Defence College on New Economic Trends. An interesting discussion afterwards but *not* about my lecture. I was hotly cross-examined about inflation, and the relation between fiscal policy and planning. So the view that all is not well in the Treasury is spreading: I couldn't speak very freely.

A lot of rush jobs in the afternoon. UKCC [UK Commercial Corporation, a state trading body] paper, where the Ministry of Food and Cabinet Office want to do something and Board of Trade thinks all is well. I feel sure that we will have to improve on our traditional trading methods and so does everybody else except Board of Trade which is actually responsible. The Survey is now running a little late but in any case it has become very uncertain whether we can publish anything as the US seem to be moving much faster on Marshall than we had expected: and all our work has been on the assumption that we shall not get anything.

Thursday, November 13th

The Budget yesterday was quite unsatisfactory from our point of view as the surplus for which the Chancellor budgeted was too small for us to learn anything about the extent of inflation.[24] I worked late on Survey questions with Butt who is doing very well indeed.

Friday, November 14th

A bombshell this morning as the Chancellor has resigned because he told the *Evening Standard* lobby correspondent about the budget as he was going into the House. The man telephoned the Office and it caught the Stop Press and technically appeared before the announcement in the House. At first Winston condoned it but later decided that he must ask for an inquiry. Everyone (including I myself) feels sad about the way it happened even if we did not agree with Dalton's policy. But it is clear that there was no option but for him to resign. I felt so grieved that I wrote him a little note, which I rarely do on such occasions. Stafford Cripps is to be Chancellor but to retain responsibility for Economic Affairs. This will be a very good thing if he has time to think about it.

I saw Plowden late in the day about a suggestion Broadley [Deputy Secretary, Ministry of Food] made to me at lunch, that M. Hutton should be in charge of UK economic interests in Washington. Apparently Hutton is not altogether at one with Liesching, his Permanent Secretary. But I think that Hutton would do very well in the job suggested, which will in any case need doing badly if we are to get Marshall help, as now seems far more likely than it did even a few weeks ago.

Plowden said he gathered that Dalton was excited about his speech and having to wait in the lobby because the House wasn't ready, he told the reporter (whom he knew well) what he was going to say, without even thinking what he was doing. The reporter either didn't know he would catch the Stop Press, or didn't think either. It was all a complete muddle and reflects nothing but rashness. Everyone gives away secrets every day but they know the people concerned and no harm is done. Apart from personal regrets, it ought to be a good development as Stafford Cripps has been dying to get financial and economic planning together. P. wants us to write a paper on inflation. He says Stafford Cripps intends to go on as at present but fears he will be far too busy. The ideal arrangement would be if he got a rather junior man to run the technical side of the Treasury and himself did the overall things. But where is such a man?

At night we worked on the Fiscal Policy section of the Survey, which should be easier now Stafford Cripps is Chancellor. After a long argument, Swan convinced me that there are dangers in too much anti-inflation; he points out that in present condition of physical shortages, to cut down expenditure far enough to ease these would probably cause under-consumption of the things that can be supplied fairly easily. We decided to bring this point out in the Survey and in our paper on Inflation. It *may* be a turning point in British policy, though I doubt it.[25]

Monday, November 17th

Worked on Saturday and got the draft on National Income and on fiscal policy finished and off to Proctor [Treasury Under Secretary] for Treasury comments. I saw Peggy Jay in Oxford on Sunday – they are very much upset about Dalton as Douglas Jay had just become his Parl. PS and this has traditionally been the stepping point to Under Secretaryships. In any case they liked Dalton and fear the effect on the Party. I don't think the effect will be much as the tide has turned against it anyway.

Today a meeting of the Working Party on Marshall Aid – Clarke, Gorell Barnes, Makins [Assistant Under Secretary of State, Foreign Office], Weeks and I. It is going to be the most important single subject in economic policy. We all agreed on the general line and are going to meet frequently to work it out in detail. The essential thing is that it should help us along and that the conditions should not hinder us.

Over the winter of 1947–8 the economic situation improved markedly. The 'dollar drain' fell steadily and in the first quarter of 1948 there was actually an inflow into the reserves, thanks largely to a gold loan from South Africa and drawings on the IMF. Exports resumed their climb and over the year as a whole there was a rough balance on current account, the deficit in hard currencies being counterbalanced by the surplus in soft currencies. Shortages of food, materials and energy were less acute; and as Dalton's November Budget took effect, there was a perceptible diminution in inflationary pressure. Congress had not yet voted for the European Recovery Programme. But with rising tension between the United States and the USSR, first over the Communist coup in Prague and then over the Soviet blockade of Berlin, the chances of receiving Marshall Aid were much stronger.

The Economic Survey for 1948 *was published in March 1948 and work continued on the* Long-Term Economic Survey. *This came to assume added importance as the European Recovery Programme developed and a Continuing Organization of participating countries (OEEC, now OECD) was set up in Paris. Members agreed to aim at 'viability' (i.e. getting along without Marshall Aid) by 1952 and were asked to submit plans showing how this was to be done in co-operation with other members. On 1 October 1948 the United Kingdom submitted a* Long-Term Programme *derived from the* Long-Term Economic Survey *and other countries followed. The question then arose how far the various programmes submitted by member countries were compatible with one another, as well as the more fundamental question how far the various recovery programmes represented a joint effort and could be regarded as a move towards European integration. In Britain ERP was viewed as a*

joint attack on the dollar problem without further commitment. The
Americans, on the other hand, wanted Britain to take the lead in bringing
about European integration (i.e. creating some kind of Common Market)
and the French also wanted a more lasting association, possibly through a
Customs Union.

March 1948

I seem to have come to a dead stop there. The main events since have
been working with Cripps as Chancellor: the developments on ERP
(European Recovery Plan) and the publication of the Survey.

In the past 3 months there has been a revolution in Government
policy since Stafford Cripps has been the undisputed master in the field
and on the whole Plowden has been his prophet. All the old barriers are
coming down between Treasury and other policy and there is very little
of a rearguard action. In many ways it has been rather frightening since
E.P. and I get almost anything we want and we don't really know
enough to justify this faith in us, or more truly lack of faith they have in
themselves. The more I see of S.C. the more highly I think of him – he is
anxious to tell the truth, he is a man who is completely fair in his
outlook, and completely bold if he is convinced that a particular course
is right. The Treasury have given up the struggle altogether on the home
front – they still fight a bit on overseas matters, where they have
stronger people and we know less. But it is here that they are doing
worst. In spite of the repeated statements to the contrary, the gold drain
goes on and a fair bit of it is due to leaks of one kind or another. I am
beginning to wonder if we are not paying too high a price for the sterling
area: we are certainly paying too high a price for the luxury of not
blocking the sterling balances, and I doubt if we will really get credit
for it.

On ERP, the working party reported just after Christmas and the
report [EPC(47)33] was accepted. Then an Executive Committee of the
London [European Economic Co-operation] Committee was set up to
run the show. Clarke as Chairman, Weeks, F. G. Lee [Deputy
Secretary, Ministry of Supply], Makins, Lintott [Second Secretary,
Board of Trade] and I are the members with a Cabinet Office Secretariat. Gorell Barnes was there too at first but he was soon moved on
promotion from No. 10 to the Colonial Office, and gave up. We did a
great deal of desultory work but didn't get very far. I went to
Washington for a week at the beginning of March to see what was going
on. The main conclusion I reached was that nothing could be clear until
an Administration was appointed – and that the State Dept at present
felt that the Aid should be divided in Paris by the 16 [i.e. OEEC] – I
think this would split them up, at any rate in the first year – once the
supplies began to move it would be different.

The Survey [for 1948] got gloomier and gloomier. Austin wrote most
of it in the end but Ministers thought it too long and D. Jay did the final
version; mostly he cut out Austin's additions, which pleased Butt. I was

in Washington when it was published [Cmd 7344] but found on my return that it was called the 'Black Paper'. At any rate it tried to be realistic. Butt was so sad when it finally saw the light that he resigned, but I managed to persuade him to stay.

Wednesday, March 24th

On Monday Oliver Franks* telephoned and I took him to lunch at the Reform where he had a triumphal progress. Oliver was in very good form: we talked about the house and servants and some of the problems; also about the set-up for ERP. He said he wanted Frank Lee in Washington, which contradicted what he is alleged to have said in Paris, 'that it did not matter as he would do it himself'. I don't believe he would have said this seriously. He wants someone of Permanent Secretary rank to run the London end. We also talked of general matters including the mounting tension in US against Russia. He was very optimistic about the outcome of any war, largely on the grounds that ABs [atomic bombs] whatever else they might not do, could immobilize railway junctions.

In the afternoon I saw F. G. Lee and told him (at O.'s request) that he would be *persona gratissima* as head of the Supply Organization. He is obviously very anxious to go for a year but does not want anyone to think so – in fact everyone does think so.

Developments on ERP over the weekend have been so rapid that it now looks as if we shall get nearly all the money we want, at least this quarter. But the problem is whether we will be able to produce any evidence on which they will pay: all the private account stuff will be hard to bring in in a hurry. There have been meetings all the week about the programme for which we have just been asked: on Tuesday the Economic Policy Committee agreed to the figures we have been collecting [for submission to the US authorities, EPC(48)19] but also that there was to be an end to the dollar drain, i.e. that if ERP was not enough for our import programme we were to cut the programme. I don't believe that they will stick to this if it hurts – as long as there is a gold reserve they will use it. But Cripps means it – he at least has principles, and courage.

I have been arguing with Gilbert [Joint Second Secretary, Treasury] about the presentation of the Budget and on Tuesday afternoon S.C. had a meeting about whether we should publish figures showing the split between items on capital and income account. It was decided not to publish much this year but S.C. suggested that I write an article for the Royal Statistical Society making a tentative analysis. I don't want to do this but suggested that James Meade might do it. This was agreed.[26]

---

* See entry above for October 15th 1947, when I suggested Franks to Edwin Plowden as US Ambassador. After a good deal of difficulty this carried the day and after a good deal of hesitation, Franks accepted. His wife Barbara was in tears for two days as she thought now the war was over they were going to have a quiet life at Queens.

We have made astonishing progress in 12 months and are approaching a position where we can honestly say what we are doing – I can hardly believe that all these things which would have been so impossible when I came to the Section, are open now. To crown all, Edward Bridges sent for me this afternoon to ask what I thought about the policy of the Bank [of England] and whether we should give them directions about the control of credit. There are a lot of papers started by Douglas Jay who has been enlightened at least in this.[27]

I have seen a lot of M. Hutton this week. He is too positive in all he says and puts up people's backs, though he is often sensible. He is resigning in June and coming back to UK – he had hoped to fix up a job on this brief visit but has not been successful.

Hugh Weeks' appointment as Co-Director of the Colonial Development Corporation was announced on Saturday. E.P. doesn't seem to mind him going and I think he is right. He has no ideas about a successor and asked my advice but I could not think of anyone really good – I suggested Caine [Colonial Office], Binney, Bretherton [both Board of Trade], Fleming, Muir [Ministry of Works] and Gorell Barnes. I can't say I think any of them are ideal. It is extraordinary how thin we are on the ground now, or seem to be.

E.P. is very much up and down these days; on the whole I think he is gloomy but he must realize that he has made a big difference. Stafford has saved the country from a complete débâcle and Plowden has been his chief adviser in all this.

The Budget is on April 6th and I have been writing bits of the speech. I begin to feel some trepidation about whether we are not overdoing it, but all my calculations so far as I can make any suggest that if anything we are on the easy side. Yet we contemplate an astonishing surplus – if it turns the tide, we shall certainly have earned the right to do something handsome the other way in a slump. But we shall be blamed for the turn. We have a lot to learn about full employment yet.

Thursday, April 8th

The main event since I wrote last was the Budget. This was the day before yesterday and as it was the first time I had had anything to do with it it was very interesting. The speech was re-written three times with comments from the [Budget] Committee – I was mainly concerned with the references to inflation. The result of last year was to give a very big surplus and this year's seemed even bigger but we stuck to the argument that the situation had to be judged by comparison with the previous year and especially in connection with the big reduction in the foreign deficit. But I got a bit in to make it clear that we can change our policy if we go too far. It is the first time anyone has ever tried to make a Budget designed to affect the whole situation and it is all rather frightening, though I don't know why, since to do nothing or to take a conventional course is just as bad or worse than to take any other mistaken view. Anyway it is a great tribute to Plowden – he and I made it together as the Treasury were not prepared to take a line at all.

The proceedings were complicated by the appearance of the National Income White Paper on April 5th with a whole set of new calculations since the Survey, which reduced Austin to despair. He is very up and down and became convinced that we had overdone it, and conveyed this to Douglas Jay [Economic Secretary]. Everyone was very cross with Campion and quite right too – the figures were all different from the Survey and neither the Treasury nor the Economic Section had a chance to comment. However, I calmed Douglas.

The Chancellor spoke very clearly but with hardly a gesture and little change of tone. The House did not seem to appreciate the main points and only cheered the obvious ones. Afterwards Winston made a short speech; he seemed to enjoy it but I thought he was rather confused, especially in casting back to Gladstone's days when he said that in the old days people (apparently Labour) talked of letting savings 'fructify in the pockets of the people'. The Chancellor gave the Budget Committee a dinner afterwards and Plowden made a little speech of congratulation telling him this was the first 'planning' Budget.[28]

Tuesday, April 13th

I have read all the Debate and listened to some of it, though Austin Robinson took nearly all the shifts in the official box. This afternoon Plowden and I went to see Stafford at the House to discuss his winding-up speech. Austin, after his panic last week, was so impressed by the criticism that the Budget was not deflationary enough that he wanted to give a set of Nat. Income calculations. I managed to reduce these a bit though they still proved that we had gone too far. But all my fears, that it would be said to be too deflationary, have proved to be unfounded. It has had a very good reception on the whole, of course the whole Right has attacked the Special Levy but we expected that.[29] The Stock Exchange was actually upward after the Budget, so they can't say it destroyed confidence, but actually it turned down on Monday.

On that day, Bridges had a meeting about Price Control and I suggested that we needed to examine the whole field of Government action to help or hinder competition. To my surprise, Bridges and John Henry Woods accepted this and all the Permanent Secretaries present agreed, so J.H. was told to go away and produce a scheme.[30]

Thursday, April 15th

The Budget is now over though of course a good deal is still to come in the House. It has been widely welcomed and so far Cripps has had to make only one concession, on children's non-utility clothing. I had a meeting of the Economic Section this afternoon and we agreed to keep watch for deflationary tendencies, although I doubt if anyone would let himself take the same view as I did. It is a great comfort to me to find how few economists there are available who understand Nat. Income accounting and even less who would check (the figures of the Government).

Friday, April 16th

I think I must have fallen asleep at that point but I think I meant to write that I was comforted to find that so few economists can understand inflationary calculations and even fewer who can (or have) compared the various figures, especially those in the Survey and in the White Paper. Plowden and I have now written to Bridges suggesting that the Budget Committee should meet regularly, not under such pressure as it works under when preparing a Budget, and discuss the general issues of Public Finance.[31] If we get that and the Board of Trade investigation [into government and competition] it will be a beginning. But we are far from having a Plan yet.

The ERP [European Recovery Programme] Act has been law for ten days or more and Paul Hoffman has been made Administrator. Hall-Patch [Foreign Office] is to go to Paris to lead the UK team. We are told that most of the work will have to be done there by the Continuing Organization [OEEC] and I have been trying to persuade London that we must not only make programmes there but also get down to the organization of individual studies of commodities where independence of Western Hemisphere can be achieved.

This spasmodic diary-writing is very bad and leaves lots of loose ends. We solved the Downie problem by transferring him temporarily to CEPS [Planning Staff] where he will put some sense into the Investment Programme and at the same time learn a good deal more about it. My staff is still very mediocre. Peggy Hemming is away ill most of the time and [Bryan] Hopkin cannot get loose from the useless Population [Royal] Commission which seems to be going on for ever. Shackle cannot be made to do anything that is any use and Jefferies is something of a weak brother. Fleming has great abilities but is a little lazy and has fits of academic conscience in which he feels that the truth as he sees it is more important than anything else. This would be all right if he took the trouble to check his facts and his reasoning but like all economists he is an escapist and thinks he is being virtuous in taking a high line when he really hasn't done enough to justify *any* line.

Plowden has so far not found anyone to take Weeks' place and gets little help from the Treasury. He is in a mood of gloom at the moment, short of staff and nothing very obvious to do. But we shall get going soon, on the real business of planning. Now that we have ERP we can breathe for a year at least and in that time should make great strides. But of course it *may* demoralize us: though I fear that political developments will over-shadow economic – the split between East and West is complete and though the Russians can turn right round in a moment if they see fit, they show no present signs of wanting to do so.

Thursday, April 22nd

The BC met yesterday to discuss our paper on future plans of work. It was readily accepted and as a next step I am to write a paper on the burden of expenditure and the lack of incentive in the tax system.[32] No difficulty at all. Bridges speaks very well but is discouraged by the weaknesses of politicians and the ineptitude of his own staff who load him with far more work than he can do. He is too nice to get rid of his top men, and consequently he has no time himself and all our reserves drain away more or less fruitlessly.

Friday, April 23rd

Yesterday I dictated two memoranda to Plowden, one called 'Have We Got a Plan' in which I tried to set out all the things which I thought we were doing or ought to be doing, and one on the first quarter balance of payments. The Treasury Statistical Office [OF Stats.] had just done a very good statement on this, the sort of thing we ought to have had long ago.[33] The results were encouraging in some ways as we were doing more or less what we had intended. But we had lost much more gold to Belgium, and to Canada (on S. African account) than we had planned. Far worse than these was the continuing outflow of capital into the sterling area – if this goes on all our other efforts are hopeless of success.

Thursday, May 20th

At the beginning of May I went to New York to the 3rd meeting of the Economic and Employment Committee [of the United Nations]. This was even worse than the previous ones as there were the two reports of the Sub-Commissions to be taken and the Russians fought over almost every word. The main trouble was the Report on Development which condemned colonial powers for neglect to develop colonies. The CO [Colonial Office] were much upset and wanted us to make a show about it. But there was a lot of trouble on the other report and altogether I felt that it was a battle-ground rather than a meeting of people with a common problem.

New York was more opulent than I had ever seen it. No signs of depression: and the war fever is over for they have all made up their minds that there will be a war very soon and are now beginning to arm for it. The main interest was in the Republican candidate. Stassen was coming up fast but many people thought that the result would be a compromise on Vandenberg.

Since my return, I have been working on a paper which will try to find out the extent to which price control and material control preserves the existing pattern of industry, whether it is efficient or not. This was suggested first at the Prices Committee by me, and everyone took it up, so J. H. Woods was asked to write a paper on it and then we discussed that. I was asked to formulate questions. My first draft terrified Bridges as it was so detailed and he got Gilbert to see me; but poor Gilbert is not very forceful and it is still as I left it.[34]

Other things happened: I have got John Hicks [Nuffield College] to write a paper on the Budget accounts. Ministers want an inquiry into Government policy on the distributive trades and Douglas Jay is to be Chairman – he is anxious that I should be on it. Everyone is beginning to think the Budget *is* deflationary, and I am starting to watch for signs of this.

On the ERP front, we have got our first quarter allocation, $300 mn grant and $100 mn loan if we want it. So now we really have got a year to breathe in and I am anxious that we should now start on plans to advance our viability. It will be a fearful struggle to stop Ministers from increasing consumption standards and they have given way on cheese already. Tom Finletter, with whom I used to work in Washington, is to be the London representative of Hoffman and Harriman [the latter being the President's Special Representative in Europe]. We could not have had a more sympathetic appointment.

This week I dined with Hall-Patch, who told me that he had no staff at all: and lunched with several people including Otto Clarke who seems to be getting a bit more sensible. I plugged rather with both of them the importance of getting the Working Parties started on joint action in Europe, especially on the agricultural front where we may miss this year's ploughing if we do not start now. Hall-Patch had already been discussing these things in Paris especially with the Scandinavians who he thinks are very good.

The whole future is very obscure according to Clarke, who thinks (a) that on any view the terms of trade are going to stay against us so that we ought to shift the population away; (b) that we are likely to have a war with Russia soon and ought to be planning for this instead of neglecting it; (c) that we would do much better to join the USA if they would have us than the 16 European countries. He is a bit like T. Balogh (not that *he* would advocate such things, quite the reverse) in being so plausible however wild or advanced his views are – one feels they are almost certain to be right.

Oliver Franks is sailing the day after tomorrow, with at least 5 servants he collected in Oxford. He is full of ideas about what he will do and is of course much refreshed by his long rest.

The gold drain is very much less for the first 6 weeks of this quarter than it has been for more than a year. But April and March imports are both shockingly high.

Wednesday, June 2nd

There was a leading article in the *Financial Times* today about the progress of deflation, which was very sensible. It said that the tide was already turning, but that there would not be a slump and that we must welcome the easing of tension which would be brought. Plowden thinks that the Chancellor is getting worried about signs here and there, but Plowden and I have made an attack on the new issue of 12 [clothing] coupons for 4 months. It is very disappointing that H. Wilson has given way to the clamour of the wholesalers – no decision recently has been so much against our general objectives.

Dalton is back in the Cabinet as Chancellor of the Duchy, with a roving brief – it has not taken long: the papers say it is because he has been making such difficult speeches and I expect they are right. Everyone in Gt George Street is gloomy and afraid he will be making mischief.

We have been working on the terms of the bilateral agreement with US for ERP, which has been drawn very loosely but with all the discretion on the US side. It has very much the air of 'beggars can't be choosers' and we are going to try to modify it though I don't see how we can do this except by persuading the US that it isn't wise to put it this way – if the Agreement is published it will support all the Russian arguments about it being a weapon for economic domination, though of course the spirit is exactly opposite.

Wednesday, June 9th

Ministers were much upset by the terms of the Agreement and have taken a very uncompromising line: 'in no circumstances will they agree' to this or that [EPC(48)48–9, 55–7, 59].[35] I wonder what they would say if they were told that in that case there would be nothing for them, after they have staked employment and the rations on getting help. However I hope that it will not come to that – it would be gratifying if we showed so much spirit, and on the whole very good for us to have to stand on our own feet at once. But it would be very bad in the short period for Anglo-American relations and would probably wreck the ERP programme entirely, support the whole Russian thesis, and lead to the early establishment of Russian domination in a good deal of Europe. None of the other Paris countries likes the bilateral agreement and I suppose we will make some sort of common front.

S. C. Leslie (the Chief of the Economic Information Unit) told me today that the Chancellor is getting worried about possible unemployment. I suppose the City is full of rumours and there have been a number of approaches on the purchase tax, alleging severe unemployment already. We discussed it today with Wilson Smith [Additional Second Secretary, Treasury], whom I hardly knew but who seems very nice. Rowan, Leslie and Hitchman (who is taking Weeks' place [as Plowden's Deputy]) were there. We all agreed that the position on ERP was precarious but that otherwise we need not worry. Of course there will be some unemployment and that is exactly what we want. But there is no danger of it affecting the investment industries unless we cannot get enough timber for the houses, and so we can stop it whenever we like. The trouble will be that Ministers will get in a panic as soon as there is any difficulty about any particular place – what they need is strong stomachs. The more I think about it the more convinced I am that no one should be allowed to plan unless he can hold firmly to a line he has decided until he is quite sure it is wrong. In this case we actually wanted some unemployment. However there are no signs of anything yet though we are always a bit behind-hand with our figures.

We talked yesterday with the Chancellor, Jay, Glenvil Hall [Financial Secretary], Soskice [Solicitor-General] and Croft [Chairman, Board of Customs and Excise] about the purchase tax and decided to make a few remissions. The worst spot is alleged to be the wireless industry but I am sure that people won't buy many more sets if the price falls because everyone has one already – however this may speed up replacements. The House sat all last night over the Finance Bill and the Chancellor promised to look at all the things we had discussed in the morning.

Plowden is fishing in Scotland. Franks made his first speech this week, to the National Press Club – he seems to have done it well, with neither manuscript nor microphone according to *The Times*.

No sign of Dalton yet.

Thursday, June 10th

This morning I arranged with Sir David Milne [Permanent Secretary, Scottish Office] for the work, accommodation and so on for [Martin] Fearn who is going to be the Economic Adviser to the Scottish Home Department. He has been with us since February and done very well. I took Hitchman to lunch at the Reform: he is a very quiet and sensible man who shares my views about the need for getting a plan into the form of a phased action programme – I hope he will help me with Plowden – our idea is to have a high level Committee to parcel out the work.

In the afternoon to the Dollar Drain Committee where Otto Clarke told us that the Imperial Tobacco Company have decided that dollars will stay short for tobacco and that they must develop Rhodesian production in a big way. Otto asked whether we should encourage this as he feared the effect on the tobacco lobby in Congress. Rowan, P. S. Beale of the Bank and I all felt very indignant and said that this was the declared policy of Ministers and the way we had all agreed would be needed if we were to get into balance. Bridges on the whole agreed but thought we should play down the publicity.

The King's Birthday but the Trooping of the Colour was cancelled because a thunderstorm was feared and it would spoil the scarlet and busbies of the Guard! This is austerity. The main people I knew in the Honours List were Hinshelwood [Dr Lee's Professor of Chemistry, Oxford], Hutton and Helmore [Second Secretary, Board of Trade]. I am glad for Hinch. Helmore is still rising fast but I suppose his next step will be his last – the worst of the Civil Service, that once you are a Permanent Secretary there is so little else, unless you are in the Foreign Office or can become Head of the Treasury.

I cannot make much progress with all the things I really want to do, especially my paper on taxes.

Wednesday, June 16th

There is now a great deal of silly talk about the impending deflation. The Chancellor asked for a note on it and is now going to give a Press Conference for which I am doing the brief. He also got me to write a foreword to the Fortnightly Economic Report, saying that we must be calm and resolute.[36] There were very good leading articles in *The Economist* and *Financial Times* about this, and the unemployment figures show a decrease this week on the April ones. Nevertheless there is a feeling of panic or at least apprehension which I find both feeble and exasperating. Marquand has written a note to the Chancellor which was mentioned yesterday and I am to see Bridges this morning about it – fortunately we have been on the look-out for some time but no very plain signs yet.

Thursday, June 17th

I saw Bridges and did a note for him later on saying that there was still a long way to go but that we were watching the position – and he asked me to send them a note once a month telling him what we felt, which he would forward to the Chancellor.[37]

Fearn left yesterday for Edinburgh – he is a pleasant and competent man.

Helmore, to whom I had sent a copy of my paper against the 12 coupons, wrote to say that though he did not agree that the Board of Trade were wrong, he would see that we were consulted in future before any more decisions of this kind were made.

There seems to be very heavy weather in Washington about the bilateral agreement – the US will not accept our views on the rate of exchange [but] now agree that we should be free to give up the whole of our obligations if they do not give us enough help. It is very awkward since we cannot possibly see eye to eye on this, yet neither side can afford a break-down.

Meanwhile Harriman has told the 16 in Paris that they are expected to split up the aid among themselves which we had previously said would probably wreck OEEC. I still think that it will be very hard to do, especially as the US want to reserve the right to say what we will get in grant and what in loan. The programmes which they ask for are causing a great deal of work and Otto thinks that OEEC will break down on clerical shortages alone. But we are of course trying to go on. I sometimes wish that Ministers *would* refuse the aid – it would be very popular and do the country a great deal of good, and people might actually work if they had the prospect of independence in front of them.

Monday, June 21st

Everything is going on much the same. We had a meeting on Friday about the bilateral agreement – the US have been very conciliatory and most of the points are settled, especially the termination clause which was the most difficult for us but which has somehow been kept out of the papers. The Chancellor has said that we must try again to get the US to divide the aid at least in the first year, so there is to be another approach to Harriman. Nothing else seems to me insuperable although there has been a little difficulty about stockpiling, and this may get worse as the latest version of the Appropriation Bill sets aside 5% of the local currency fund to buy strategic materials. This means, of course, 5% less aid than before but it may be offset if the stockpiling keeps the prices of our raw materials higher than they would have been. My own feeling is that only a change in the terms of trade can help us much and I would prefer (on the narrow ground) no stockpiling anyway except as materials come into surplus. However strategy will not wait for that.

Today I was summoned to see Marquand and found Douglas Jay and Campion there – it was about watching for signs of a slump and Campion and I agreed to do it but I pointed out that economists were very bad at such predictions. We have, of course, been watching for some time but we shall do it more formally now. There will be a great outcry before long and probably the best thing to do is to anticipate it so that when there *is* any increase in unemployment we can say we planned it and there is no cause for alarm. Indeed I wrote a piece for the Chancellor's speech at the end of the Finance Bill along these lines.

Thursday, June 24th

Ministers have been very sticky about the bilateral and yesterday the paper done by Butt in March on 'Consequences of No ERP' was circulated to them to make their flesh creep.[38] It was a gloomy picture but we have not agreed yet and the gossip today suggests that all the other countries are ready to sign and that we may be isolated. Ministers of course will have to persuade Parliament and the country that the conditions are in our interests, and if they don't it will be useful propaganda for USSR. On the other hand, it is almost inconceivable that the negotiations should be allowed to break down and it is clearly in the interests of the US that they should not.

I lunched today with Neil Caplan (Board of Trade) who has just been promoted and is now A/S in charge of Export Programmes. I am very glad he has got this step which he well deserves – he is young but has had five arduous years as a Principal. Our futures have been linked at many times, first in RMIA for a few weeks in 1940 – then in Russian, or rather Allied, Supplies in 1941 – then for a while in RM(PW) in 1944, and in the Commodity Policy section of RMD and BOT from 1945 until last June when I began in the Economic Section. We agreed to keep in close touch. He told me that they are running rather quickly into consumer resistance in exports of boots and shoes, apparel and a few other lines and that we cannot hope in 1949 to maintain even the present level of exports unless we can get up the capital goods.

Butt had already made the same point in dealing with the IPC report, which will have to fix home investment in plant and machinery after looking at exports. It is an awkward decision however we look at it, and we ought to cut imports of food in order to keep up home investment. But I don't suppose we will. It was decided this week to end bread rationing soon because it is breaking down in practice, and they took the opportunity to increase issues of coarse grain for pig and poultry feeding, thus throwing away about £5 mn in hard currency; all we will get out of it is a little more eggs and bacon.

Plowden and Hitchman and I discussed this morning how best to direct and to progress import saving and diversion: we are all agreed that some one body should co-ordinate all the spasmodic work now being done and having added it up decide what more is needed. But we did not agree on whether Plowden himself should do it, or Eric Roll who is Vice-Chairman of the Programmes Committee in whose terms of reference the job now is.

Another small landmark today was the first meeting of the new Committee of Second Secretaries to investigate Controls and Efficiency.[39] In a small way I am the originator of this. Sir B. Gilbert is the Chairman and Dow [Economic Section] and Polly Hill [Board of Trade] the Secretaries. It was on the whole an encouraging meeting – James Helmore came back from leave and is anxious to make it go. We agreed to start by discussing the problems with a number of the people operating selected controls.

In the evening I saw Leslie about the Chancellor's Press Conference on Signs of Deflation. I doubt if there are any yet – it is less inflation rather than deflation. But the export trade is the worst spot if Caplan's story is correct.

Friday, June 25th

I spent an hour in the House today listening to the Debate on the final stages of the Finance Bill. The Chancellor said a good piece about the deflation having to go much further yet but nobody else said much. Unfortunately I went to sleep just as Glenvil Hall (FST) came to ask me about the floating debt. He only said 'O, I do envy you'. It is a long process, 2½ months since the Budget; on the whole it has stood up very well.

This evening had a long talk with Plowden about planning after E.A.G.R. [Austin Robinson] goes on July 15th. We have to produce some sort of 4-year plan for Ministers and Paris but I hope it won't be published. Then I saw Butt who is anxious to take over.

This morning we talked again about the long-term steel demand and we all thought our present figure (17.5 mn ingot tons for 1952) was probably too low. Of course it is all terrific guesswork but if the Board of Trade are right we must export steel or bust.

Dewey has been nominated [for the US Presidency] in Philadelphia, with Warren as VP. I suppose it is not the best choice for us but it might have been much worse. Franks has been doing well on the bilateral and the Prime Minister and Stafford have been making a great appeal to

Douglas on political grounds, so it looks as if we shall get more or less what we want. It is odd that the US have been so insensitive to Russian criticism which one would think they wanted to avoid – but of course nearly all the difficulties have been because of Congress who are usually quite unaware of what other people will think and who kept on putting in their pet bits. The last crisis is on MFN for Japan where we have stood so firm that they seem to be going to give in, though apparently [General] MacArthur got the Army to get State to promise it.[40]

The IPC [Investment Programmes Committee] is running into fearful troubles as there is not nearly enough steel to meet the programmes and there will have to be drastic cuts all round, besides the general cut on plant because of the export problems. I will probably have to work on this soon. There is still too much to do but our relations with CEPS are going to be very good now that Hitchman and Roll are replacing Weeks and Robinson.

Plowden has squared H. A. Marquand over the deflation by telling him that all this drive to stop it is a Tory device to split the Labour Party.

Tuesday, July 20th (Paris)

It is a great pity that I have not been keeping on with this as I have done some very interesting things. This will have to be topics now.

E.A.G.R. has produced his balance of payments picture for 1952 [EPB(48)21]; it is very much crystal gazing but shows that we will be lucky if we export 145% of 1938 in that year, and that in that [case] we will have about 1947 imports – proposed that food should take the cut. My people have objected because they think the incomes should be higher and hence the trade. It went to the Planning Board and the ED (Steering) Committee and Ministers, who took it on Friday last – they didn't like it much but said work could start on this basis. The important thing is that Plowden has got his Committee working under Hitchman to progress import saving etc. so at last we can get down to actual plans instead of these general exhortations. As for the 4-year plan, Plowden has agreed that we should give precedence to the 1949 Survey:[41] Butt must get on to that as soon as he comes back from Corsica where he is now on leave.

IPC. After months of work the first draft of the new (1949) IPC Report is out [IPC(48)8]. It shows that we invested much more in 1947 than we expected and are well over the target in 1948. Steel will be the trouble for some time and the main recommendations are 175,000 houses, which we won't get agreed and even if we did we would build more; exports of machinery same in 1949 as 1948: the main cuts to come on railways and fuel and power. I expect there will have been frightful howls this week. I went to the last few meetings but Butt did nearly all the work from Economic Section side, or rather Butt and Downie.

Controls and Efficiency. This Committee which I got going has met every week and seen a number of people from Supply, Board of Trade and Works about particular controls. Everyone seems very control-minded and even in cases where it could obviously be relaxed they make all sorts of trouble. I don't know what we shall do – one of the main snags is that steel is the bottleneck but there is a rumour that we shall be giving up steel allocation all the same – I almost hope that we shall, the present allocations do not work and if IPC can keep down the big Government-sponsored projects all may be well.

Inflation. The present stage is a very interesting one as there is a good deal of easing of the situation yet unemployment is less than ever. We have now laid on information from Ministry of Labour and Board of Trade and will probably get some from Supply so at least will have a story. It is clear that the worst horrors are being stopped, really bad products losing money and luxury goods getting easier, e.g. gin, rum, wines, tinned non-points goods, hardware, some furniture, some clothes. But there is still this high investment demand, and although it is said that people are spending less on holidays, entertainments etc. they are still spending plenty. The Chancellor has been very good and made a Press Conference a few days ago when he was very firm about our having a long way to go yet. I made the outlines and it has had a good Press. I don't think we have any ideas where we are going at present, and all the figures are poor anyhow. But we have certainly checked the tide and I think it is going down a little.

Hicks has been working at his paper on Budget accounts but hasn't finished his draft. After immense agony we at last finished our paper on Budgetary Prospects and the tax system and got it round to the Budget Committee on Saturday. Now we will see if we can do anything about it.[42] Unfortunately I am away this week.

I dined with Finletter at the Reform on July 9th and he was very forthcoming about his problem, mainly the level at which his staff will approach our people. He hates this kind of thing but Congress made a point of taking ERP away from State and willy nilly he must stand up for himself. I think we have not handled it very well considering that we knew this, but the Foreign Office agreed with the US Embassy so on paper we have acted properly. I don't know how it has come out. Finletter is very good and we are lucky to have him but I think the Mission may have much less to do than we expect because of the division of aid in Paris – if the OEEC have done it, it can't be much criticized though it will be no doubt all the same. Anyway we have started to get the 2nd quarter bills paid and probably the 3rd quarter appropriation is through. The reserves are still running down slightly but it is very slight and we have gained 6 months even if we don't get a cent more. However we will almost certainly go on till next June on any view. I cannot be sure how it will go – there will be a great deal of trouble and annoyance. In some ways this seems a bit unreal because of the Berlin situation.

On July 15th Geoffrey Crowther [editor of *The Economist*] gave a small dinner at Brown's: Douglas (Jay), Plowden and me. Douglas came very late and was tired out but he gradually revived and talked a good deal, first about Berlin and the Russians, and later about the UK position.[43] He was very firm about Russia and felt, as I do strongly, that it is no good making concessions unless you think for some private reason that it is a useful move, i.e. that you don't expect them to change the Communists' fundamental views. He spoke about running a convoy through by force, as of course his own view. Plowden and Crowther were both rather aghast but in the end agreed that a retreat would ruin all we had been working for in Europe. I sometimes think however that in these matters Geoffrey allows his detestation of war to make him sentimental. Afterwards we all talked about the lack of incentive in the British system and how difficult it would be to recover properly when there was so little to stimulate either employers or workers to do more.

It was a pleasant evening and we promised ourselves more of it.

On July 17th I was suddenly asked by Leslie Rowan to go to Paris where I am now, having just come. The object is to arrange the 4-year questionnaire which is to lead to the answers to be made into the recovery plan. I left the office at 9.45, Northolt about 11.15, Paris about 12.45. Am now at the Bristol.

Monday, July 26th

I did not succeed in finishing and am now in London again. It was an interesting week. The Ex. Committee charged Hall-Patch with getting the questionnaire out and he handed it over to the Swede, Dåg Hammarskjöld, who set up a Working Party of independents, intended to be H. himself, Marjolin [Secretary-General of OEEC] and I. But the French insisted on being on it and in the end three of them came to most of the meetings. We did not have many disagreements however and in the end adopted a questionnaire more or less on the lines the UK had suggested, though with more stress on the description of the plans and intentions of each country. Hammarskjöld wrote an introduction on the problem, taken straight out of the ECE report. We kept the statistical material down as much as possible. At first the French wanted to collect a great deal of information to enable a central plan to be made at once, but in the end they accepted the view that detailed questions and detailed planning would have to be done by the Vertical Committees.

On Tuesday came from London Otto Clarke with a telegram from Franks to say that Hoffman had decided that after all aid had better be divided in Washington and that OEEC was to concentrate on planning for viability. He also said that the main thing the UK needed was to increase productivity and that Congress did not care about any country but the UK which always aroused deep emotion one way or the other. Eric Roll was furious at this as he had been sitting with Guindey [French Ministry of Finance], Malagodi [Italian Delegation] and a Dutchman [Spierenberg] to hear all the countries' cases and to make recommendations, and it was all going better than anyone had supposed. We stayed up nearly all night arguing about it – as I have consistently said that I did not think OEEC should do it, I suppose I ought to be pleased, but it is irritating to be told to do something you don't believe in and when you try hard and make it work, to be told it is to be done another way after all.

On Thursday a man called Lowe, a reporter on the *New York Herald Tribune* European edition, took Roll, Clarke and me to 'dine'. He had industriously gone to Shannon the night before in order to fly back with Hoffman who was coming to Paris. Hoffman had told him 'off the record' both that the aid would probably be split in Washington and that there was going to be a row about the lack of Ministers and the status of the ECA representatives in Europe. So these things leaked out quickly enough.

On Friday night Hall-Patch gave a dinner at the Crillon for 3 of the 4 'wise men' who were dividing the Aid; but as Malagodi is for some reason not bien vu by the Italians he asked Cattani [Head of Italian Delegation] instead. Also Alphand [Director-General, French Foreign Office], and the head of the Dutch ERP delegation [Spierenberg], Clarke and me and Ellis-Rees and Coulson [Treasury and Foreign Office members of UK Delegation]. After dinner they talked mostly about the division and whether, in view of the unexpected ease of the proceedings so far, it would not be possible to get the 4 to discuss their proposed recommendations with the countries concerned and try to make amicable adjustments and so perhaps cut out the wrangles which would otherwise take place on the Council.

I left rather early: at dinner talked mainly to Guindey who is in the Ministry of Finance and seemed very nice – we both had begun as philosophers but were caught by other things.

The Working Party on Long Term Planning got on extremely quickly and we were able to discuss the first draft with Hall-Patch and Alphand, and later with Bissell [Assistant Deputy Administrator, ECA], on Friday. It consists of a general statement to the Ex. Committee, a short analysis of European problems written by Hammarskjöld from the ECE Report, and a request for a general statement and illustrative tables very much on the lines of the draft the UK had submitted. Bissell was very nice indeed and seemed thoroughly sensible and helpful. In particular he said that the US had learnt that too much statistical forecasting was pointless and that they were now more interested in plans of action and so forth – this was exactly in line with our report. He wanted us to ask more explicit questions on internal finance than we had done while realizing that this was very delicate. Fortunately the UK is all right on this since at any rate the Cripps Budget.

I had a great deal of help from Figgures [Director of Trade and Payments, OEEC], in particular in establishing the proposal that the Vertical Committees should be the bodies who would ask the detailed questions needed for planning, e.g. agriculture or steel.[44] In general there seemed very little enthusiasm in Paris for *doing* anything concrete – everyone was willing to talk about general schemes particularly designed to make the façade of economic integration – customs unions, balance of payments committees and even general plans for the whole economy, but we were the only ones who wanted to get on with particular things which were obviously worth doing. I am quite sure that we shall not have any complete or even partial integration in any but the project sense in the time of the plan.

Friday, July 30th

A very busy week. On Tuesday and Wednesday I spent most of the day at a CS [Civil Service] Board seeing candidates for the Economic Section. There had been 57 applications for the two jobs but most of these completely useless and of the 12 whom we saw in the end only about 4 were possible. However one of these called Jukes seemed very good indeed and we will take him. He is a scientist who did operational research in the war and is now doing similar work for the ex-LMS railway; it is really applied economics. He got so interested in economics that he has been working at LSE in his spare time and has just got a good First. We also took Keane, whom I had taken as a temporary in December and who has been a success. Finally we also liked though with some doubts a man called Wiggs, now with the Control Commission in Austria (only it isn't called that) who has been writing what are in effect their Surveys and doing it well. So if I get Jukes and Wiggs I shall be much better off, especially if Hopkin really comes next month as promised. Both Plowden and Brook have been speaking to me about the staff of the Section but I have slowly been reaching the conclusions (a) that I inherited a very poor lot from James Meade, (b) that I cannot expect any help from anybody in getting people together.

Friday, August 27th

Jukes is coming and I saw him today to discuss what he might do. He confirmed my first favourable impression. Wiggs has decided to go to JIB [Joint Intelligence Branch] – I am rather sorry but as we were not prepared at that stage to offer him a job on a permanent basis, we cannot complain. I was on leave for the first two weeks of August and most of the third week, and had a letter from Edward Bridges about staff while away. He repeated Plowden's arguments and said that I ought to have a good Deputy and asked if I thought I could get one at say £2,000 a year: he feared Plowden would take on another economist if I did not find someone. I have not answered yet and feel very uncertain about what to say. It is very unlikely that he could get Austin again, especially as he has been asked for to go to Paris for three months in the last part of the year to help in writing the 4-year plan for USA.

There is a crisis in Paris on the combined problems of allocation of aid and intra-European payments. The 'four wise men' (of whom Eric Roll was our man) after weeks of work reached an allocation and most countries accepted it though the Belgians were at first difficult – the real recalcitrants were Turkey and Greece and they could have put in a minority report and left it to ECA. But at the same time the payments scheme was coming forward with the idea that some of the aid given to creditors (in fact UK and Belgium) should be offset by these countries making sterling (or B. franc) gifts ['drawing rights'] to European debtors.[45] Now all the debtors want firm guarantees of their deficiencies as a condition of accepting the ECA allocations. And today I gather that we are very near a split. I don't think this will happen: and even if it does I don't think US would cut off the present Appropriation. Our own position is now beginning to improve and if we can get enough aid between now and (say) next June to keep up our reserves, I think we could then stand on our feet if we must.

On Thursday we met Dewey, the Agent-General for the Congress 'watch-dog' Committee (*not* Tom). His job is to keep an eye, direct and through emissaries, on how the money is going and the whole thing working. He was very nice, large and elderly and apparently not very smart though he made a few sensible remarks. But I felt that he was someone we could deal with.

That night I had a drink with Abbot Low Moffat, now in charge of Trade and Finance with Tom Finletter. He was mainly concerned about strategic materials but did not say anything much. Then I dined with Rowan at the Union, to meet Guy Thorold who is an old friend from Washington and who has been borrowed from his insurance broking firm to go to Paris for three months and try to get the 'projects' started. This has always been the UK idea of how to get economic co-operation and apart from the payments scheme it is the only starter – but it is clear that the moment we do not press it on, it comes to an end. So he is going to stay there and press it: if it is not done there will be nothing to show in the Paris 4-year programme, on which we are now working. The questionnaire emerged from Paris on the lines on which I had left it, and Butt and Strath [CEPS] have been trying to get the answers (in the form of a report) due by Sept. 7th.

Thursday, September 2nd

The report [*The Long-Term Programme*, EPC(48)79] was sent to the printer today and Plowden is having a meeting on the 4th.[46] Planning Board on the 7th, ED on the 6th, EPC on the 14th. It has been rather a desperate job and annoyed Butt because so much was changed and softened. He hates the idea of tempering the truth as he sees it, and will not admit that there is a limit to what Ministers can take or will do. Fundamentally, it is clear that decisions will be taken one at a time and as they can be arranged and that an Economic Survey cannot be (as Butt would like) an opportunity to decide all the problems of the year at once.

Wednesday, September 22nd

The report went through fairly easily though Strachey made a fuss about the small increases in food consumption shown [EPC(48)82].

Butt is now making a few small changes in consultation with Douglas Jay. At the same time, reports written by the Programmes Committee and dealing with plans for 1948/49 and 1949/50 have been approved and are all going to Paris.[47] There was not much time to consider these and Otto Clarke is really triumphant for the time being in his struggle with Plowden. Otto is unpopular with many people because he wants to be the economic dictator of Whitehall, but he is so able and so tireless that no one can make much headway against him. I think there is a bad slip in the programmes as they under-estimate our exports for both years and since our situation and our need for help depend on what we achieve in exports, we shall not look too good in the end.[48]

The Chancellor has gone to Canada to try to get our trade prospects straight. It is very awkward since they have planned for some years to produce for our market and there is little sign of our being able to pay – they would like us to devalue our currency but we don't feel it necessary just now. Plowden is away for a short holiday this week. Before they went, we had a meeting of the BC to look at Eady's summary of our paper on taxation etc. The Chancellor agreed to look at the depreciation question:[49] various points were made on income tax simplification. Otherwise we left it over and are now making some advance estimates. Dow has just done some but they look very odd. Investment is up, the foreign deficit down, and the surplus a bit down – altogether the effect seems very small and yet it seems to me that in fact the pressure is a good deal less.

Hall was critical of the Bank of England's conduct of monetary policy. Discussions had been proceeding since early in 1948 (see entry for March 24th) on the basis of an initiative by Douglas Jay, who argued that it should be possible to use the budget surplus to reduce the money supply. The Budget of 1948, however, yielded only a small surplus 'above the line' in the first six months of the financial year while government borrowing for capital expenditure continued and bank advances continued to grow fast. The resulting increase in the money supply brought scathing press attacks in October and the Chancellor then called on Jay to chair periodic meetings on credit policy between Bank and Treasury officials. Jay and Hall, who was a member of the working party, contemplated a ceiling on bank advances, which Cobbold, the Deputy Governor, thought 'most unwise', while the Governor, Lord Catto, viewed the proposal 'with the utmost alarm' (Cairncross, 'Prelude to Radcliffe', Rivista di Storia Economiche, December 1987). Since the Bank was unable to make use of ratio control in order to limit the growth of the money supply and was denied freedom to raise interest rates, it had little choice but to let the money supply respond to the public's asset preferences and the rate at which the government could pay off debt out of budget surpluses.

Budget surpluses halted the growth in the money supply in 1948–9 while short-term interest rates remained unaltered until the change of government in 1951. Hall continued to press without much success for a more restrictive policy with a view to checking inflation. The Treasury, however, hesitated to accept the higher interest burden that would have been involved and after issuing nine reports without much action being taken, the working party was wound up. It was not until 1956 that any similar group discussed the fundamentals of credit policy.

Thursday, September 23rd

Talked a while to D. Jay yesterday about the Budget. He wants to make some concession to both employees and workers and I agree with him, though it is hard to know how much we can afford. The increase in exports and the extra investment have made the outlook for reduction poor, and now there is re-armament. I have started to do some calculations and we shall only be able to make trivial concessions.

There is quite a hunt going on against the Bank over the increase in deposits, and enormous calculations are being made by Compton [Treasury Under Secretary] and Eady. They are somewhat pointless I think, as the bankers can operate rather independently if they want. The fundamental things are that there is no *need* for increased deposits as far as Government finance is concerned, since we are paying off the floating debt a little: and that it must be against public policy to let the stock of money increase when we are trying to deflate. The Bank tends to the early 19th century heresy that *because* prices are rising therefore more money is needed. It is astonishing to find this view held in 1948. But the whole relationship is astonishing, especially after the nationalization of the Bank by Dalton. If ever there were anything done for show, not for effect, this is it.

Wednesday, October 13th

On Wednesday, Sept. 29th I flew to Paris by the late 'plane to spend a few days talking about the method of dealing with the Long Term Programmes, the questionnaire for which I had settled on the last visit (see July 26th above). Eric Roll crossed on the same 'plane and he was very helpful in the talks. We spent almost the whole of Thursday and Friday with Hammarskjöld, Marjolin, Figgures and Baraduc, the latter three from the Secretariat. We got on very well and worked out a skeleton for the report and a time-table. It is clearly an almost impossible task. The OEEC have just got MacDougall to leave Wadham for a year – Wadham had refused to let him come to me but on this occasion Bowra [the Warden] was just going himself on a long trip to USA. Austin Robinson is borrowed for three months to help the UK Delegation and my Swan is going to help. Guy Thorold is there already and seems to me to be doing well.

The UK programme was in on time (Oct. 1st) and Iceland came a day later: then Denmark on about October 5th. But today these are all that have arrived and it certainly looks as if they will find it impossible to digest them all, reconcile the main differences, and write the report by

Dec. 1st. At any rate the US cannot say we are not giving a lead on this – we have done all the work on the questionnaire, a great deal on the outline, and are the only major country to have a programme.

At home there has been much discussion about what we mean by 'European Co-operation' on which we had done little work. Caine, [Ivone] Kirkpatrick, Makins, Syers and I have written a note, arguing that full economic union is not a starter just yet and that we must stick to the 'projects' approach.[50] Unfortunately in Paris the projects have not made much headway and there will be very little to show by way of active co-operation when the long-term programme is drafted.

The weather in Paris was delightful and the food and drink very good. I had an easy time at the weekend and actually walked about a good deal and saw some pictures, Notre Dame, and a number of the places in the Quarter where I had passed so much time between 1923 and 1929. The appearance has not changed much but the morale of the people is apparently very bad. The FO think de Gaulle will get in soon and this seems to me almost certain since the Centre parties cannot agree sufficiently to carry on a Government for more than a few months at best. The CGT has started a wave of strikes just now, most people think at Moscow's orders. Nothing can delay the French recovery more. They are working hard and production figures are good but the inflation is wrecking their chances on the foreign balance.

Home Affairs. Before I went to Paris it was settled that we should do a 1949 Survey, to come out in January, and Butt has started on this. It ought to be fairly easy this time though he will want to bring as many problems to light as he can. We are going back to the old Survey Working Party technique which Austin could not work. Otto is being quite friendly – he does not seem to bear any malice and probably is not conscious that he offends people.

The Chancellor is back and taking an interest in money and inflation. A draft Speech for the Mansion House dinner on the 19th was made while he was away but he did not like it and yesterday I had to do one at very short notice. He seems in very good form and we had a full dress meeting at 5.30 when he made jokes about my draft, which however he accepted on the whole. The Speech is all about the progress of the Budget and disinflation.

Our economic affairs look better and better and we shall soon be in overall balance and struggling with problems of unrequited exports, the sterling balances, and the effect of success on US aid. But no one has really started to get down to this yet. We talked about it a great deal a year ago and are getting the old papers out of their files now.

There was a Budget Committee today to look over more of the preliminary problems – we all felt that we could not do much this year but that in time purchase tax should be low and the range extended. I have given up the idea of using it as an economic weapon because it is so hard to get it increased and everyone hates changing it: so that in practice it is more likely to do harm than good. We didn't get very far today but will have a field day next week on Depreciation Allowances etc.

The Committee on Controls and Efficiency has started again but makes very little headway. Departments will not run any risks.

Thursday, October 21st

The Mansion House speech had quite a good press, but there really isn't much more to say on economic affairs. Parliament meets on Monday and the Steel Bill will be introduced within a week: all the final touches have been given. It is drafted so that the transfer can be made before the election, by Ministerial order not subject to confirmation. I don't think this is a good idea: if the Labour Party wins the election they won't need it, and if they don't they will only cause confusion. It is very hard to know how opinion in the country is going.

We had another Budget Committee on Wednesday to talk about depreciation, when Inland Revenue took a very difficult line and we made no progress; they have gone off to set out their arguments in full. Plowden and I are feeling determined to go on.

Tuesday, November 2nd

Last Thursday I dined with Plowden and Crowther to meet the American members of the Anglo-American Council on Productivity. Phil Reed [Chairman, General Electric Co.] and all the others were there, also [George] Wansborough of the Bank, Sir Claude Gibb and several British business men. We dined at Brown's and afterwards all said what we thought. Geoffrey (Crowther) and I both felt it was a long process of deterioration, but most of the business men talked of their own experiences. In nearly all cases they concentrated on labour relations.

Yesterday I went to the House to hear the Chancellor on the Debate on the Address as I had written the bit about internal conditions. Afterwards [Sir Arthur] Salter spoke and picked up the main weak points – I found it all rather dull.

At Oxford during the weekend I met Paul Samuelson of Harvard, at the Baloghs. He is one of the best of the younger economists and made a great impression on me. He had read extremely widely, remembered it all almost verbally, and had I thought very sensible views. Isaiah Berlin was there and we had a pleasant evening.

Thursday, November 4th

All day yesterday was full of excitement about the Presidential election, which was a complete surprise to all. By 4 p.m. it was clear that Truman was in – if he is the man for it (which I doubt) he will have all before him for if ever a man was the architect of his party's victory it is he. The best thing for all is that the Congress will be Democratic and inclined to give the President his way, so at least there will be a fairly clear line.

Swan has done a paper which shows that the UK has planned to take all the surpluses outside the Western Hemisphere so that if our plan succeeds no one else will be able to recover through diversion. I have circulated it.[51] He himself has just gone to Paris to help Austin.

There is quite a lot to write about Economic Section staff, following a meeting with Brook and Plowden last week.

Friday, November 5th

Lunch with Plowden yesterday at the Travellers Club; there was a Planning Board in the morning. Rowan talked about OEEC but nothing new. Plowden has been very depressed since he went to Paris last weekend to be questioned about our 4-year programme. The French and Italians did the questions and he felt that they were quite unrealistic and were expecting to be carried, by US and UK, throughout the period. He said that Hoffman, who came impatient with the UK, went away thinking we were doing much better than we really were. At lunch he [Plowden] talked mainly of his own plans – he thinks of retiring next June but is not sure if he will find anything interesting to do – he would like to try steel really I think. Anyway he doesn't want to run any risk of being asked to leave by a Conservative Government, nor to leave of his own accord when an election is near. We talked about election prospects – I thought the Government might do well to go to the country fairly soon but he said he thought they would take their full term.

The October bank statements show that advances have increased a great deal in spite of all the assurances we have had.

Tuesday, November 9th

Plowden and I sent an angry minute to Bridges about the Bank statements and yesterday I was called by Eady in some agitation to discuss with him, Compton and Mynors of the Bank. They produced a lot of figures but on the whole seemed to think we had a case and indeed I had the impression that they were very uncomfortable. It is hard not to get the impression that the Bank, and the banks generally, do not think at all about credit control as economists do, and indeed that they don't quite understand what it is all about.

Thursday, November 11th

Eady has produced a rather disquieting memorandum on Bank Advances, largely showing that the increases in deposits were due to Government deficit, including borrowing for housing and Public Corporations. He told me incidentally that next year's expenditure will be enormously up on this year's, defence, the Argentine fund payments and especially the new health services which are turning out to be far dearer than was expected.[52] Dentists and doctors are working much harder and getting much better incomes.

We are now deep in the Survey for 1949 and Butt is beginning to get in a state again, though I think he is doing a very good job.

Thursday, November 18th

This has been an interesting week. The Steel Bill was given its Second Reading and the battle now fully joined. I did not go to the House but Leslie told me that Stafford made a wonderful speech on compensation and a very political and Cassandra-like one on the main issue. I should think the Government were shaken by the enormous fall in their majority at Edmonton but apparently not.

On Monday we saw the Chancellor and Strauss [Minister of Supply] on steel subsidies and I am glad to say S.C. held out firmly for no subsidies at all. We have also been attacking the ones on feeding stuffs, and are having some success, no doubt largely because of the tight position on the Budget. The Survey date has been postponed till late February or early March because of the probable large increase in the Estimates; by then they will be out, whatever they show, and we may have a policy to meet them.

On Tuesday at the 2nd Secretaries meeting I raised the balance of payments question and we agreed that it should be looked at – at that stage by the Economic Survey Working Party but later I saw Wilson Smith who had (quite rightly) decided that he would do it himself. Incidentally I had an argument with Otto Clarke about what had been sent to Paris – there is no doubt we *have* sent overall balance estimates for '48/49 and '49/50: and these show a much worse position than is likely. I have been urging strongly that we ought not to be borrowing or really begging money from the US on an exaggerated picture of our poverty. It is true that our dollar deficit may be as bad as we have said and that the favourable soft currency balance is no help there – but it must make us suspect to conceal it. Anyway we will have to decide quite soon what to do, if anything – P. and I on the whole want to import more to reduce the pressure of inflation here. It is a great thing, however you look at it, to be in overall balance once more. And to me at least it means that we could live if we had to, with no more US help.

The Economic Survey Working Party met this morning to look at the first draft for the Survey – we had a pleasant and friendly meeting only marred by the absence of Fuel and Power. Hemming told us later that his Minister had refused to let him attend – we must make a row about this. Gaitskell is a queer fish – a day or two before he sent a message to the London Committee that they were not to talk about coal exports and Rowan told the emissary that it was not in Gaitskell's power to do this sort of thing.

The other main development has been on Banking Policy, where we are at least making some headway. Following our meeting last week,

Mynors wrote a long letter – he then went to Rhodesia to help set up their Central Bank but Lucius Thompson-McCausland [Bank of England] is acting for him and came to see me today. We made quite a lot of progress and very nearly agreed: we both feel that there has been a great deal wrong with Government as well as banking policy, and that there must be much more borrowing from the market rather than from the banks for capital purposes. We both felt that Keynes had left behind a set of doctrines quite unfitted for the times in which we live as for the last 20 years of his life he was pre-occupied by questions of deflation instead of inflation – in a way he had been too successful. The only doubt really between us was on whether banks would work to a ceiling for total deposits without harm to the system, and whether credit deflation was too blunt a weapon. That is how the Bank talks – I think it is absurd and that all we are asking is that they should be neutral and not act against us in our struggle, as they must have been doing.

Douglas Jay told me this morning that he is going to take a working party of himself, Eady, Compton, Mynors and me to keep a steady eye on all this – it is certainly a great stride forward. A year ago Dalton was just falling – I was not even on the Budget Committee and the Economic Section was not allowed to talk to the Bank at all. Now at least we have got all this into the open. *Non nobis Domine sed Crippsei* (or whatever the Dative is).

The staff of the Economic Section is being changed quite a lot (see Nov. 5th). Jefferies is going to a Department – we haven't settled it yet. Jennifer Forsyth is leaving because she is marrying C. Dow and neither he nor I think that a wife should work in the same Section as her husband. I hope Peggy Joseph – Hemming – will get a job somewhere else. And I am trying to screw up courage to tell poor Shackle that we won't want him after his contract runs out – it is painful but he is really no use at all. Of these four, J., F. and S. are obviously the weakest of the Section and Peggy, though a first class economist, is never here. So we must be stronger without them. Meanwhile I am taking on a new man called Licence from the LSE and hope to get two or three good new boys at Christmas from a competition we are having. Butt is probably leaving for a while, or for ever, though I hope it will only be to go to Canberra. I don't quite know yet who will do the Survey but am almost inclined to think that it should be Keane, who is continuing to develop very nicely indeed. I am still over-worked and short-handed but we are much better off than we were a year ago, when we reached the depths.

Tuesday, November 23rd

We had another meeting of the Economic Survey Working Party yesterday, mostly about coal. The Minister of Fuel and Power wants to put in some smooth passage about next year, setting a target and explaining how it will be reached, with no indication of the uncertainties. Everyone else opposed this. On the whole the meetings have been good ones, though I have not felt that I was doing my best at them –

sometimes I wonder if this is not taking away my powers of thought and work.

Today however I had a top pressure job – the 4-year programme [for 1948–52] having got out in New York is being published in bits here and we decided at Plowden's Morning Meeting to try to get the Chancellor to see the Press this afternoon. I had to write a brief as there was no one else available and after leaving the London Committee at 12 worked on it till 1.30. It was typed by 2 and I handed it over and it was used with little change at 4 and Leslie told me that it was a successful Conference. The brief stressed the experimental nature of such programmes – when we publish about Dec. 7th, there will be a covering note to the same effect.

At Bridges' meeting yesterday I was asked to do a new appreciation for the Budget Committee – Dow has already done it, a fairly good job, and we can send it round shortly. The present conclusion is that we should make no tax changes.[53]

Wilson Smith had his meeting on balance of payments this afternoon – Plowden, Rickett, Otto Clarke and Cohen (Board of Trade) were there. We agreed on the whole that more diversion of exports to dollar markets was the first essential. Otherwise we were against reducing exports, or doing this to increase home investment (which is what Finletter wants): we were rather divided on more imports but Clarke is going to look on the Programmes Committee at the prospects, re-membering that less controls are a good thing and less pressure or inflation certainly good. Otto is nervous about letting in more inessentials, largely for temperamental reasons though he can rationalize very well.[54]

I saw Plowden later and he told me that Bretherton is under consideration [as Joint Deputy Director of the Economic Section] and that I may get a rise soon on the grounds that all the Chief Scientific Advisers are going to get them. I wish I knew if I really wanted him; but I can't refuse. E. Roll is probably being transferred to Paris and if so P. will probably get a man called Willis, whom I don't know but who was runner-up to [Laurence] Helsby for No. 10 [as PPS to the PM].

Last night I dined with the Tuesday Club[55] and sat between Crowther and N. F. Hall who told me all about his administrative or business staff college at Henley. He said it was a great success and that the entrants for the 3-month courses are of very high quality. Afterwards, Paul Bareau of *The Economist* spoke about foreign exchanges and said some very queer things: but we had a good discussion afterwards and that is the main test of a speaker. There was a good deal of difference about whether dollars will be permanently scarce, a remnant of mysticism I thought. Salter was there and very bitter against the Government because (I think) of his lost seat (they abolished the Oxford University seats): he says he won't try to find another constituency. Most people felt that things were improving, as of course they seem to be: they all deplored the recent optimism of the Chancellor as they felt this would bring about too much pressure from his colleagues to make him give up austerities all over the place.

Not much to write about – in some ways we seem to be in doldrums but I think there are plenty of problems if we could really work on them.

Tuesday, November 30th

We had the first meeting today of a Committee on Banking Policy under D. Jay. The others were Eady, Compton, Thompson-McCausland of the Bank and I. Eady had written a paper which we took. He was rather offensive to Jay but very polite to me. We made a certain amount of progress and the Bank put forward the interesting view that advances were being increased to cushion the shock of the policy of deflation. It would have been more convincing if they had not said previously that all this was due to the needs of Government finance; since we have proved that on balance the Government had been paying off floating debt, they had to find some other explanation. I had spent some of the weekend reading Keynes and Sayers [*Modern Banking*] so felt rather fortified. It is hard to know how much the Bank understand all this. I think Compton is beginning to get it and Eady hardly at all. But Lucius Thompson-McCausland has put forward some very ingenious arguments: I wish I could make up my mind whether they were genuine or a rationalization of what they want. D. Jay knows a little about it and was a good Chairman – he kept his temper very well under provocation. I think we are at least making some progress and it is a great thing to be able to talk about it at all.

The Chancellor has been on edge to go to Paris ever since Friday but hasn't been asked yet. All the Treasury officials concerned, and P. and I, have been trying to dissuade him. He wants to talk about fiscal reform but they would soon get him on to joint programming.

Wednesday, December 1st

Still a good deal of va-et-vient about S.C. and Paris. When I got to P.'s weekly meeting, there was great indignation about a BBC item in the 9 o'clock news, saying that all the delay on the 'master plan' was due to differences between the UK and France about our imports – later it was agreed at the London [European Economic Co-operation] Committee that there should be an explanation to the lobby correspondents that the delay was nothing to do with this.

The Economic Section's appreciation of the long-term programmes as a whole is nearly done[56] but Otto Clarke weighed in today with a long diatribe on the theme that we had better not collaborate with Europe at all except perhaps in the recovery period. He called in ITO to prove that we would be unable to discriminate against USA which is rather funny both because of his historic opposition to ITO and because our whole recovery assumes discrimination.

Tonight I saw Norman Brook for a while about staff questions. He suggested that if Bretherton came he could be an additional Deputy

Director which was just what I wanted as only in that way can I hope to keep Fleming in fair shape. Fleming has been doing some very good work lately. Brook also agreed to speak to Peggy Hemming (to whom I have at last written) if she doesn't get another job fairly soon. We had a bit of a talk about the place of the Section and agreed that it would be better where it is than in the Treasury, which has certainly not succeeded yet in integrating Plowden or Rowan. He said that the Section's present good relations with the Treasury were a new feature largely because of me – I wish I could think so, I fear it is due to Cripps. Anyhow there is no doubt that our relations at present are very good except for Otto who has established a sort of reign of terror which is a great tribute to the force of his personality: as he does not seem to mind at all contradicting himself and is in general either very unscrupulous or very much a man of the mood of the moment.

We also had a word about the (Lynskey) Tribunal[57] – he said he thought that it was doing the government a great deal of harm not only because of how Ministers had acted but because they had been hobnobbing with the scum of the Capitalist system while reviling the best elements in it. (I had said I thought that it was harming the Government for the first reason.) The Steel Bill seems to have fallen flat but I cannot help thinking that this will not.

I wrote a Minute to Plowden, Rowan and Wilson Smith about the estimates of our balance of payments in 1948/49 and 1949/50 which we are going to publish next week with the 1949/50 programme [see entry for September 22nd]. They seem to me to be far too pessimistic and I am afraid that we shall be accused of concealing facts in order to get money. I have been trying to get this faced for some time but not very successfully.

Thursday, December 23rd

The last three weeks have been extremely full, between trying to finish the draft of the Survey and working on the Paris document and on our paper for the Budget Committee.[58] There is a lot to say.

Bretherton has finally decided to come and will appear in the middle of February. I have not told Marcus [Fleming] yet but hope he will be able to bear it. Jefferies goes to Ministry of Supply in a few days and Jennifer Forsyth leaves about the same time. There are 70 applicants for the new economic assistantships and I hope that we get some good ones. Butt has at last decided not to go to the CO and I hope to send him to Australia to pay back our debt on Swan (who leaves in a few days). Butt shall go in March, when the Survey is published.

He has done a very good job on it, on the theme that 1948 saw the end of spectacular change and 1949 will be a year of progress if we can solve our real tasks. Everyone has been complimentary about it and it is going to the Planning Board almost as it left us. We have done it in three parts, a review of 1948, a forecast for 1949, and some notes on problems.

Wilson Smith has at last told Finletter about the overall balance of payments and I gather that Finletter was not surprised. We had a meeting of the Wilson Smith [Balance of Payments] Working Party today, to hear about progress. Board of Trade are looking at import licences on non-essentials and the Programmes Committee at the import programme generally. Plowden and I made a fuss about the slow growth of exports to dollar markets. Board of Trade are always looking at this and deciding there is nothing they can do: we think that they should regard it as having a good deal of priority.

From the London end, Paris has seemed like a mad-house and we have been meeting at odd times and at very short notice, to consider successive drafts. We take too much trouble with our suggested amendments, Cohen of the Board of Trade being especially captious: but while these are being telegraphed the draft itself has been torn up and a completely new text is on the way to us. Under this technique very little notice is paid to our amendments. It is all a great rush and the Executive Committee are meeting tomorrow and Rowan has called a meeting of his inner group on Monday – I shall *not* be there but am leaving it to Fleming. I think the Paris people must be very unstable – Austin certainly is. It would have been better to stick to a main text.

Tuesday, January 11th 1949

A good deal has happened. Bretherton began work yesterday: Marcus was very upset and I was disappointed that he took it so badly, considering how hard driven I have been and how many things we do not do at all. I am putting B. on the Investment Programmes Committee instead of me, and generally on to home affairs. The first draft of the Survey has been to the Planning Board and is to go to the Steering (ED) Committee on Thursday. It is a very good one and has had a favourable reception so far – no doubt partly because it is a success story.

Thursday, January 13th

We are having a lot of trouble over the next Budget owing to the large increases in social services. The Section did a long paper a few weeks ago and I have been trying to produce a simplified version which I succeeded in doing last night. As last year, the figures keep on changing. But one can do it in a fairly simple way which will stand up to criticism if one gets the right line.[59]

I've had a number of talks to Plowden lately, who seems to be worrying about whether to resign or not. He thinks that if the Government is changed he might be asked to go, which would be unpleasant. He does not want to become a permanent Civil Servant which is one alternative. But I think he does not really want to go either. Although he is so strong when it comes to taking a line and sticking to it, he is very much inclined to worry about things where he need not act now (as this) or at all (e.g. whether we are ruined or not).

Bretherton has made a good start and met everybody now but Marcus. He hasn't worried me much. Plowden seems quite to like him.

Today Plowden and I saw John Henry Woods in the morning about depreciation – it is doubtful if anything can be done this year as profits are running so high. We also talked a little about clothes rationing, which can probably be abolished fairly soon, though cotton will stay scarce. This afternoon the ED Committee took the Survey and we got through fairly well, except for Otto Clarke who had put Wilson Smith up to say that most of the balance of payments material must be re-written. As time is so short, this lets Otto re-write it without criticism. It is very unfair to everyone else and we had taken very strong objection to the Ministry of Fuel and Power when they tried to write their bit at the last minute. We are hoping to get a printed version to Ministers next week indicating the parts that we think might form the basis of a published version and those that are only for their information.

Afterwards Plowden had a long talk with the Chancellor and agreed the shape of the next Budget though the details are not quite what we suggested, especially on financing the extra health cost. Apparently S.C. is now all agog to spend a long stretch in Paris planning for Europe, and wants Plowden to give up here and become the chief planning officer for OEEC in order to write a European plan and see that it is carried out. It seems to me a poor idea and to show little comprehension that what is mainly wanted is a different attitude in Whitehall. But Stafford may be right and of course if there were a really high-powered man in Paris it would impose a good deal of co-operation on Whitehall from there.

Tuesday, January 18th

The last few days have been very unpleasant ones for me owing to the attitude of the Treasury to the Survey. At the ED Committee Wilson Smith, prompted by Otto Clarke, asked to redraft the Balance of Payments section: they sent in something late on Friday night, which was the deadline. It was a complete re-draft and it was clearly almost impossible to argue it with them and after some reflection I became very much annoyed over the weekend and protested strongly to Otto, then Plowden and finally Wilson Smith. Everyone did their best to soothe me and to promise that it would not happen again. There were special difficulties of course but it made me feel that the Economic Section was treated as a compiler or secretary, and that OF were getting out of all the hoops of the Survey WP, Planning Board and ED Committee that everyone else had to go through. All this has led me to feel that the Survey is gradually becoming an emasculated document which represents nothing but the minimum that will get by Permanent Secretaries and that if Ministers have any idea that it is an expert work they are quite wrong. I am writing to Norman Brook about it, but there is no easy solution as I do not think that the Economic Section is competent to write a Survey on its own and if it did the result would be more or less a collection of prejudices.

Butt is on the whole much better pleased than last year in spite of his troubles and I think has found he resented Austin altering his prose more than the Treasury altering his economics. He is almost certainly going to Australia in March to repay them for Swan, who is now in Washington for a few months in the Bureau of the Budget before returning. Coombs has become head of the Commonwealth Bank which is a quick rise and I don't know exactly what the new arrangements are.

There has been so much heat on the Survey that there has not been time for much else. The Treasury are looking at food subsidies, but will no doubt pass them by. S.C. has issued a ukase that there are to be no supplementaries next year! As P. says, it is like Canute and the tide – but I think it may do some good nevertheless. At the 2nd Secretaries this morning we spent most of the time looking at a speech which the Chancellor is going to make shortly on the 4-year programme. Meanwhile the country is very agitated about Palestine and I gather that the Cabinet is also.

We are keeping going in the general attack on the Bank but have not made much progress yet and on the whole I think we have got back to interest rates, which the Bank say would have to be raised until advances were checked. However I suspect that they have told the offending Banks all the same to go easy on their advances, and there are rumours that the new issue market is more difficult than it was.

Wednesday, January 26th

Roffey* next weekend (Feb. 5th). The general pattern is settled on the lines of our paper. I saw Bridges and told him it seemed very rash to commit so deeply on one man's advice but he said very sensibly that the Committee felt that the advice was conformable to what they thought the situation needed, even though they hadn't absorbed the calculations. It has not been decided at all where the extra money is coming from.

The Survey is going to the Production Committee today. After the agitations with OF Division it has gone fairly smoothly and so far no sign of Ministerial interest.

A paper has been written about our attitude to OEEC.[60] We still have no policy and this seems to me to continue on the same lines. We must make sacrifices but do no irretrievable damage to our economy.

---

* Roffey Park [a country house in Gloucestershire] where the Budget Committee finished the Budget off.

Tuesday, February 1st

A very heavy day today. Banking policy, Budget Committee, Food Subsidies, and to see the LP this evening about the Survey. I have resolved to write it down, as they are all important subjects.

The PC was very polite about the Survey, said it was very objective (which I wish it were) and only made minor criticisms. Butt has now begun to work on the version for publication. Meanwhile Leslie has shown me a scheme for the popular version which I find a bit pretentious as it talks of 6 Aims and 3 Choices like a work on Chinese religion. He is going to drop that part.

We are having an argument with the Board of Trade about export targets for 1952. After a long struggle have persuaded them that there are a large number of ranges.

Wednesday, February 2nd

Nothing much at the 2nd Secs. at 10 yesterday – the Government is going to set up a small body to look at the question of agents to help against Controls, raised by the Lynskey Report. At 11 we had the banking meeting, with figures for the whole of 1948. These showed that in the first 6 months both Government and the public were borrowing heavily but that it had almost stopped in second six months. The most interesting thing was the rate at which money is coming in now: the Government reduced its debt by £350 million in Jan. Also the very small effect this was having on the total of Bank deposits. However we were promised much more in February. On the whole I think this is coming to hand, and that the Bank is putting on some pressure although it declares that it cannot do so.

At 12.15 we talked to the Chancellor about Production Subsidies and I think may have made the first impact on what will be a very long job. He was much more ready to consider changes than I had expected. As a start we are to talk to the Ministry of Food about getting the estimates for next year below £500 mn with perhaps a change in some other indirect tax to make some cost of living offset.[61] But though this may come to nothing, it looked as if it would be worth going on in general to see if we could not make big changes, e.g. in the children's allowances which would be much cheaper than the present system.

In the afternoon we talked mainly about Hicks and decided to make no change on last year but to wait for the Crick Committee [on the form of government accounts, Cmd 7969] before deciding finally whether to put some or all of the accounts on a receivable-payable instead of a cash basis. We are to keep the alternative classification but look at the items again.

At 5 P. and I saw the LP about the Survey but as it turned out that he had not read it we spent a somewhat fruitless hour in gossip. P. said a bit about his fear for OEEC – I must write soon about the situation there – Morrison agreed that we should have a coal target and told us that there would be some trouble in having a combined Budget–[Economic] Survey Debate again as the Opposition might insist on dividing the time so that there were in fact two debates. He said that Winston was now so erratic that his own followers hardly dared to make any arrangements, e.g. about Parliamentary time, as he was quite capable of disregarding them entirely if the humour seized him.

Monday, February 7th

All last week Whitehall has been working on a document for Ministers assessing the outlook for West Europe, and for the UK long-term programme, in the light of the report to ECA which has been attempting to summarize the 16 long-term programmes. The London Committee set up 3 groups to work on this but in the end Otto wrote a report summarizing the work each group had done.[62] As usual, it was a brilliant piece of work, but as usual he took the opportunity to insert his own prejudices, in this case anti-European. The first draft implied that the only threat to the UK was the danger that we might be forced, by our own ill-considered benevolence or by US pressure, into getting mixed up with Europe. It quite ignored both our obligations to the whole plan, our dangers if we went our own way, and our political and perhaps economic interests in collaboration. This spirit led to rather doubtful treatment of a number of questions on which there had been arguments at the Groups, such as the levels at which trade might be balanced and whether the UK could really get away with pre-empting the non-dollar supplies of food and materials.

There was a long session of a working party last Wednesday and of the London Committee today at which I proposed some amendments but though many of these will be accepted, it is hard to change the tone of a document from that of the original draft. The next step is to be a great round of negotiation in Paris – S.C. intends to go, with P. and a team, to put forward our own views about how Europe ought to proceed. There is no doubt that we shall be heavily criticized, mainly because of our continued refusal to admit products which Europe used to sell us. It would be more to the point if they concentrated on our plans to grab so much of the cream of the non-dollar trade.

Frank Lee came to see me today; he is now getting settled into the Ministry of Food [as Permanent Secretary] and wanted my views of Peggy Hemming who is the leading candidate for the post of Ministry of Food economist. I told him I thought her erratic attendances were the worst feature but that she would need someone to keep an eye on her if she were to do her best work. He was most worried about whether she would antagonize all his people – she used to be a very fiery character – but here I thought that her marriage was being so successful that she no longer felt the frustrations about her work which were driving her from job to job. I hope she goes but felt nervous that I might be giving too favourable a picture. If she does, I will only need to get rid of Shackle and then all my first round problems will be over. This week we are trying to select some assistants to fill up our places.

The weekend at Roffey is just over and was very satisfactory on the whole. Just before I went we did the calculations again and they came out worse than before, mainly because of the foreign balance still improving. So there was no margin at all and indeed we wanted more rather than less. D. Jay got very nervous and tried to argue that all the calculations were phoney but G. Hall was much more strong-minded. In the end it came down to a desperate search for money and we decided on a few more attempts though whether any of them are adopted will depend on whether S.C. can persuade his colleagues. He is a most admirable character in every way, very quick and extremely fair and not afraid of anything, yet sensible about menaces and not prepared to fight just for the fun of it. Edward Bridges was very good at the critical moment. I was greatly helped because they took Compton this time and he knew something about our calculations which no one else did and indeed I am not always sure that I do myself. However they are conformable to common sense which is the great thing.

Thursday, February 10th

The document on OEEC ['The UK long-term programme and European viability' (EPB(49)6)] is nearly through and I think we have made most of our points. Marcus had a special session on the meaning of 'inessential' and seems satisfied. It went to Bridges yesterday afternoon but I could not go: nor can I tomorrow for EPB. On both occasions I am at a CS Board for economic assistants. We did not see anyone we really liked yesterday – one very nice man but he had a bad stammer and I doubt if we could keep him enough in a back room.

Plowden is off on the idea of a long-term review of budget prospects: when he gets an idea he sticks to it till it is carried through.

Friday, February 11th

A quiet day yesterday. I had a long talk to Plowden on familiar lines. He is now concerned about our long-term contracts lest they prevent us from getting any good from the possible fall in commodity prices. The break in US wheat has come happily for us as far as the Wheat Agreement goes but may lead to fearful troubles with Canada.

Tuesday, February 15th

Plowden and Cripps are going to Paris this morning. I saw Plowden yesterday and he said that Stafford Cripps was looking extremely ill. After Roffey he collapsed and stayed a week there but instead of getting better he is worse and talks of retiring.

We only got one assistant from the Board, a woman from LSE called Kelley. There was a very good one from Christ Church, but he did not appear, to my disappointment.

I have started Economic Section meetings again and we had quite an interesting one yesterday. Bretherton, who is being a great help, asked about our 1950 investment policy and everyone spoke freely. We all agreed: (a) that 1950 should not be increased over 1949; (b) that if possible it should be decreased; and (c) that it was becoming very hard to control it at all. Interest rates and credit policy seem to be out, and on the whole we all felt that the only thing to do was to get the agreement of the socialized or state-controlled sector to a rate which with the private would give what was wanted. Unfortunately the present trend of the socialized industries is all towards independence – it makes nonsense of the reasons for socializing.

Wednesday, February 16th

There was quite a good meeting of the London Committee yesterday. The French want to pass a pious resolution but we liked Hoffman's 6 points better and are trying to make them the basis of the resolution – to be passed at the present meeting of the Executive Committee [of the OEEC], where Stafford Cripps is. There are suggestions from Washington for another great programming and division of aid operation, which would effectively prevent any combined work on the real problems.

I am continually plagued by people who want to learn all about how we plan. They will not believe how vague it all is.

Tuesday, February 22nd

ED and EPB took the Survey yesterday in the version to be published. Fergusson [Perm. Sec.] of Fuel and Power was very captious. Gaitskell is obviously a very poor Minister. It is disappointing.

Friday, March 11th

The main events recently have been getting the National Income estimates into the Survey, making a quick study of the general situation for the final Budget Committee discussions, and the Chancellor's visit to Paris.

The National Income estimates proved to be as late as we had feared as Jackson (CSO) kept on changing them up to the last possible moment. We had both to keep the prose consistent and to ensure that any Budget decisions would not seem inconsistent. Jackson and Dow did very well and cooked where they had to but I do not like it at all.

Wednesday, March 16th

The Chancellor's weekend went off all right and I have been doing the first draft of the speech. The Survey came out yesterday and the first press conferences seemed all right.

Friday, March 18th

The only really nasty criticism of the Survey was *The Guardian*. The interest died away in one day and it will all be forgotten as soon as the weeklies are out. The most doubtful part is thought to be the neglect of what would happen if exports to soft currency countries fell off sharply. All conclude that it will be a severe Budget.

I have done very little on this Diary and ought to write about:

> Staff – Nita Watts and Butt.
> Paris – Plowden's scheme for a talk with Monnet.
>   – Costs Study.
>   – Stability Study.
> Depreciation of the £.
> Outlook in US and UK for slump.
> 1952 Review [*Long-Term Economic Survey 1948–52*].
> Home Agriculture.

Of the topics listed in the entry for March 18th what occupied Hall most over the rest of the year was 'depreciation of the £'. Although this did not occur for another six months, Hall had already concluded that de-valuation was necessary in order to improve the competitive position of British exports in North American and other dollar markets and as a precautionary measure in case of a deepening of the mild depression then in progress in the United States – a depression which was reducing the dollar earnings of the sterling area and threatening the limited reserves of gold and dollars.

When Hall approached Cripps towards the end of March to suggest an examination of the proposal, he received no support. Over the next few months, however, he gradually won round most of the senior Treasury officials, starting with Henry Wilson Smith when they visited the United States together in June. This meant that by the time Cripps had to go off for treatment in a clinic in Switzerland after a meeting of Commonwealth Finance Ministers in July, there was a fairly solid front at the official level in the Treasury in favour of devaluation. Economic policy was left in the hands of a triumvirate – Harold Wilson (President of the Board of Trade), Hugh Gaitskell (Minister of Fuel and Power) and Douglas Jay (Economic Secretary to the Treasury) – who were converted in mid-July and persuaded the Prime Minister of the need to devalue. By the end of the month the Cabinet was also of this view and Cripps on his return very reluctantly agreed.

In the meantime it had been arranged during a visit to London early in July by Snyder (Secretary of the US Treasury) that talks on what could be

done should take place in Washington in September between UK, US and
Canadian representatives, first at official and then at Ministerial level. The
decision to devalue was communicated 'to those of Ministerial rank'
during the talks but was not publicly announced until 18 September in a
broadcast by Cripps on his return to London. No other measures were
taken in September except to raise the price of a loaf of bread by a penny.

Wednesday, April 6th

It has been difficult to settle down with the Budget hanging over me.
The figures keep on changing and the feeling that we may be in for a
slump is getting stronger, so that although there are no statistics to
support this everyone has been in a state of nerves, especially Plowden
who has varied from being ready to resign because the Budget was not
deflationary enough, to being almost panicky because it was going too
far. We have made a few concessions on the Roffey position, and as the
figures have developed they have made the comparison between the
years look worse, but we had to take a view and stick to it.

However, today, Budget Day, came at last: and the speech just as last
year, which began by looking so odd, got better and better. And at the
last minute figures suggested that we were not near a slump yet. We all
got down to the House about 3.25 and the box was crowded, as was the
House itself. Stafford spoke for about 2¼ hours and in the end was
almost an orator. It is of course too long to be followed at all closely and
it was hard to know how much was taken in. But clearly the Government benches disliked the very plain statements that we had to pay for
our social services, while the Opposition applauded. No one seemed to
register anything but some gloom about the increase in food prices, the
least expected thing in the whole affair in spite of the published
Estimates, which had allowed for them. The 1d off beer and the extra
Death Duties both passed in silence but for some reason there was a
violent reaction against the increase in telephone charges, though I was
told later that he made a slip and said they were going up *from* 14/8 (or
whatever it is) to £5, instead of *by* that amount. Eden made a short
complimentary speech and we all went.

I saw Aidan Crawley on the way out, who spoke well of the Budget,
and Ungoed-Thomas who was at Magdalen with me and who was very
angry and said this would compromise Stafford Cripps' position. I don't
know what he thought could have been done. I also saw one of the
Australia House people who was rather shattered, and Ritchie of
Canada House who thought it was very fine and brave.

We all dined with the Chancellor at No. 2 Park St afterwards and
Douglas Jay said, what I expected, that the Labour people had not liked
it at all. I felt that Stafford Cripps would have to be conciliatory at the
Party meeting tomorrow and that by the weekend and next week public
opinion would have come round to Stafford's side. Both Bridges and
E.P. agreed and we hope he will do that. However I felt deeply enough
to do what I hardly ever do, and I called at *The Economist* and found
Roland Bird and Wilfred King writing their pieces. Fortunately they felt

as I did, that it was a very fine Budget so there was no need to go in for any argument. Edwin spoke later to Geoffrey on the same lines.

So now we must await the reactions. It will be a crucial test for the Labour Party and the British people. If they are unwilling to pay for their social services then we cannot get out, for we will neither meet our dollar gap until we have to because the gold is gone, nor check inflation.

Lots of other things have been happening and especially we are making studies of what to do if there is a slump – the problem is mainly that to keep up purchasing power at home will go against getting dollar exports – and I have launched an inquiry into the exchange question. I saw the Chancellor about this on Monday (this was really the first move towards devaluation – R. 1982), and as always came away feeling what a fine brain and what an integrated personality he has – one can say what one likes and get a good hearing and an intelligent reply. He is against it now but it is the first step: of course we shall not know even if there is a prima facie case until we have looked, though I myself believe that there is one.

We are just beginning to rewrite the Long Term Survey. Butt is going to Australia to replace Swan or rather to pay for him – his boat keeps on being put off and is already a month overdue. Downie has just been promoted and will act as Secretary. I have lent Nita Watts to Paris for a spell – she was getting stale and is glad to go. I have asked for some civil servants but I don't suppose I will get them.

Why must everybody make such a fuss? They scurry round and stir things up that would do much better if left alone. Why do they spend time creating crises? If only they would go away for a while things would solve themselves.

As the entry for May 26th explains, arrangements were made for talks with Monnet at his country house from 21 to 24 April. France at that time was seeking to come to terms with the reconstruction of Germany with American help and looked first to Britain for joint action before turning instead in 1950 to a reconciliation with Germany in the Schuman plan. Monnet wanted a dramatic gesture to catch the imagination of ECA and Europe. What emerged from the talks was something different. Hall and Plowden took away a sense of the need to resume normal trading relationships between the members of OEEC. Freer entry of goods from the Continent would expose British industry to much-needed competition and by absorbing purchasing power would counter inflationary pressure. Thus began the movement towards liberalization of trade in which the rest of OEEC joined from 1949 onwards (see also entries for November 23rd and December 23rd 1948).

Thursday, May 26th

It seems impossible to keep pace with this. The Budget went off all right in the end, but the Labour Party did much worse in the local elections immediately following it than they had been doing before, and this must have been partly due to the reaction. As far as the home front is concerned, there have been no signs yet that it was too severe. Unemployment fell more than seasonally every month since January and the mid-May figures are little more than those of a year before. We have been writing a paper for the EPB and the EPC on measures against a recession but it is quite clear to me that the recession will come from a fall in exports, and that internal measures to deal with this will be in contradiction to what we want to balance our external trade. This issue becomes increasingly the major one and no decision at all has been reached on how to deal with it.

Plowden, Hitchman and I spent 4 days in Paris from April 21st to 24th having the talks with Monnet which had been arranged between Cripps and Bevin and Queuille and Schuman [their French opposite numbers]. We talked at Monnet's country house and went over most of the economic problems of each country. Monnet felt that we must do something to catch the imagination of ECA and our own people, by way of economic co-operation. He had various suggestions, notably that we might deliberately plan for a big coal–meat swap, they changing their agricultural plan from grain to meat. I think there was a good deal in his feeling about what was wanted but that there is no one on either side with the energy and the position to carry through anything like this.

The French thought that they were almost on top of their inflation but that this was based on large Marshall and sterling credits and their only hope (with more chances than seemed likely before I went) was for an increase in production big enough to cover the foreign balance and offset the disinflationary effects.

I did not feel that we got very far somehow – the talk was too much in general terms and I doubt if much of it will get as far as discussion in detail. This might happen if Plowden and Monnet were Ministers. But Plowden certainly has other more pressing interests. We all agreed however that the pattern of trade was developing almost irrespective of costs and that more competition must be got into the system somehow. And as a result of this Plowden has fought a hard fight and got agreement to go in for many more OGLs (Open General Licences) for soft currency imports, the first step I think towards a little more liberal trade. Meanwhile we are making some attack on the home agricultural programme in an attempt to reduce its worst excesses, and have stood out against the Hops scheme and the proposal for a Tomato Marketing Board.

The 1949–50 programme for Paris has been completed and the main effect is to show a bigger dollar deficit than we expected, almost entirely due to larger losses to third countries. This is an inevitable result of an over-valued pound and brings the bankruptcy of our policy in this field into the open. Prices are falling in the US now and our exports also, especially cars where we are losing what bit of a market we had been building. The pressure to devalue is growing and has built up to something like an international attack on sterling. It was at first inspired by the US Treasury and ECA but once launched it runs along very largely on the facts themselves.

I went to New York between May 5th and 22nd, for the Ec and Emp. Commission Session. It was only interesting for the attack made at last by the members themselves on the uselessness of the Sub-Commission, which we voted to abolish, and the doubts held about the Commission itself. There is no doubt that the deepest evil is the complete split with the Slav bloc, who don't want to do anything the other countries regard as constructive and who poison the whole atmosphere by unremitting efforts to make anti-US–UK propaganda, mainly on the Colonies but also on alleged US Imperialism through the ECA and now Truman's 'point four' [i.e. technical aid to developing countries].

The most interesting thing to me was to study the US economy at first-hand. I concluded that the slump was going further than I had thought, partly because saving is appearing again and partly because the appearance of a down-turn has brought out a much larger body of old-school 'sound finance' thought than I had expected. This may be partly due to a genuine belief that some unemployed resources are necessary for progress. But meantime the mass of the people are more social security minded than they have ever been and I think that if the world isn't thrown into chaos the US is slowly but surely headed for the Welfare State.

I stayed with Oliver Franks at the Embassy for a weekend – he was in good form, his great labours on the Pact, Palestine and all the daily jobs London ask him to handle *personally* having been slacked off for a while. He is strongly in favour of re-opening direct UK–US talks on general topics again – they have been practically dropped for a year with the insistence that everything will go through Paris, a forum that leads on the whole to caution and slowness.

I saw a good deal of John Deutsch [Canadian Department of Finance] whom I like more each time I see him – I would like to go to Ottawa if I could arrange it. As a result of the PMs' Conference it was agreed that senior officials should visit within the Empire for economic talks, and Plowden has been given the job to arrange it. Whether he will get the staff is another matter. But I may come in on it.

Sunday, June 5th

I am writing this in the Shoreham in Washington, where Wilson Smith and I have come to begin again direct talks. When I got back to London I found that Oliver had cabled about these and Stafford had accepted the idea much more freely than anyone expected, and gave instructions that they should start as soon as may be. This was too soon for Washington but after some frantic cabling it was cleared, on condition that no one was committed and that publicity should be avoided; we have almost succeeded on the latter though something leaked here and came out in a *Daily Telegraph* article in London the day after we left.

We got here Thursday night and had a preliminary meeting in the US Treasury on Friday – Wilson Smith, Sidney Caine, George Bolton [UK Exec. Director, IMF] and I (Allan Christelow and Edgar Jones [both

UK Treasury and Supply Delegation] came along too). On the US side, William McChesney Martin of the Treasury, Willard Thorp of State [Assistant Sec. for Economic Affairs] and Bissell of ECA, each with one subordinate, and Hebbard of the US Embassy in London. Martin began by saying that the Treasury were anxious to discuss the future of the IMF and that they were all disturbed by the lack of progress which was being made towards convertibility and non-discrimination, which it had been jointly agreed should be UK–US objectives after the war. Ought we not perhaps to ask if these were still our objectives? There was a good deal of discussion about the unbalanced state of our payments, surpluses with soft and deficits with hard currencies. Was this the best we could do? Devaluation was touched on lightly.

On Friday afternoon and Saturday morning we had sessions with ECA, mainly Bissell who is inclined to give lectures though he is beautifully lucid and almost too fair-minded. He first suggested that rules might be adopted limiting the price (above the dollar price) which could be paid: this was part of the general scheme to narrow the gap between prices in the dollar and non-dollar world. He agreed under pressure that this could result in no trade and that deflation could not be pushed too far (though he thought more than at present would be healthy). This brought him to devaluation and we pointed out all our doubts about this, both of diagnosis and of the dangers that we would run of setting up forces which might counteract any good it could do. But I felt rather strongly that the balance of argument was on his side.

This (Sunday) afternoon we saw the Ambassador who urged us (quite rightly – on my preliminary prompting) to move in small rather than large parties, to entertain as much as possible, and generally to try to establish a meeting of minds and not to discuss any current negotiations unless for illustration. This was our instruction: but I think he was very useful as we had previously moved in a party of six and had made no arrangements for private talks.

Tuesday, June 7th

I have spent a good deal of my time these two days with the staff of the Council of Economic Advisers, mainly Walter Salant and Gerhard Colm, trying to assess the current situation. They feel that the re-emergence of saving is the really serious factor (as I do) and that there will probably be a steady decline, and not the revival in early 1950 which the more optimistic predict. Investment is declining slowly as is the foreign surplus; Colm however thinks that public expenditure will be much higher this year than last, though he agrees that it has shown little effect so far (it may of course be concealing an even bigger shift to savings). We discussed the size of the problem a good deal but ended with the view that no one knew what was needed to sustain a GNP of $250 billion. My guess is that it will be a great deal. Salant has been reading articles on the propensity to consume and thinks that it is possible that in the long run people save the same proportion of their incomes but this seems very unlikely to me, no less so than Pareto's Law. Anyway we all felt that until the US Government began to spend on a large scale things would slide down, and we all felt uncertain when this would be, especially as Congress is not expecting an autumn session this year (both Chambers are being mended!).

The general assumption is that the UK will devalue before long and that if it does not it certainly ought to. It is also expected that Congress will become increasingly protectionist-minded as things get worse here, and Walter thinks that if we *are* going to devalue we ought to do so soon because otherwise there will be objections and at any rate talk of exchange dumping.

On Monday afternoon we had a long session at the Treasury, with Martin and Southard, who used to be their principal civil servant and is now the US Executive Director of the IMF. Southard for the US had proposed that in future no Fund advances should be made to countries with exchange restrictions and various other signs of 'fundamental disequilibrium'. Bolton had objected strongly and we spent the afternoon on this. It was soon apparent that they thought (and I think rightly) that any automatic advances at present would soon use up all the Fund's dollars and would be so much more European or world relief. Bolton however was arguing that if the rules proposed were adopted permanently, it would never become possible, e.g. for the dollar to become a scarce currency. The trouble is that all the institutions set up after the war were set up in the expectation that an international equilibrium would soon be reached, and that it has not been. Thus we are trying to start from a position which no one expected we would dream of starting from.

We got on to devaluation and Wilson Smith said how much objection was taken in the UK to the action of introducing this subject at a Fund Meeting. Southard said (again rightly) that if it couldn't be discussed by IMF, what was IMF for? However it was made clear that a good deal of damage could be done to a currency like sterling by this sort of thing, whereas the Fund could and did discuss the parities of minor countries regularly. This was left open.

Today we had another talk with Bissell, mainly on the conditions which would make a world of continuing discrimination against the dollar less objectionable. He was in very good form and in effect staked out rules like those of the sterling area as the ones that should be applied. He made a great point of the need to keep the prices between the two systems not too much out of line with one another, as, if they were, the administrative measures would have to be more severe than the countries concerned could tolerate. The conditions necessary were:

(1)   common monetary policy, balanced budgets, etc.;
(2)   willingness to make a success of it;
(3)   some dollar ration for those in special circumstances;
(4)   level of costs and prices not so far out of line with dollar prices as to make the temptation to cheat too great.

The whole talk went very well and I thought we were much more on a common level than before.

I lunched with Walter Lippmann [US commentator] and went in the evening to a meeting of Government economists who discussed the possible effects of a US recession on the position of other countries.

Walter Lippmann impressed me very much, both as a person and for the breadth of his mind. He very quickly makes me feel that he can follow any train of thought however speculative and whatever the background required: the sort of thing one gets with a few good academic people, e.g. Oliver Franks. We talked mainly about the dollar problem – he is convinced that we shall have it for a long time, that US capital exports will be too small for many years; and his solution is that the US should be willing to buy a few key foreign currencies and especially sterling, on condition that there was no inflation, and to hold them indefinitely. (This would give much the same effect as if the UK suddenly discovered a large gold mine with just the annual output needed to balance an overseas account based on free imports.) I haven't worked out the detail yet: his main point is that *once Congress accepted the plan* it would be automatic. And he thinks that in the end it would be easier with Congress than annual grants. It is certainly more a plan for 'tomorrow' than 'today'. We also talked at some length on Germany where he is very much concerned though I doubt if he has cleared his mind of what I regard as the fundamental loose thinking of all our policy – that we cannot make a success of a policy of keeping Germany not a menace to peace *and* making her a willing and active partner. My solution is stolen from Monnet – that we ought to invent things Germany and other OEEC countries, mainly UK and France, have to do jointly.

The meeting with the economists was more interesting than enlightening. A man called [Albert] Hirschman spoke from a paper and made a number of theoretical points which I did not think valid. He assumed that a recession was coming in Europe as well as in US, instancing Belgium and Italy. The fall in prices would diminish the dollar gap and the home deflation would make the countries concerned more competitive, so that some might not 'be able' to spend their US aid and all this would not help the US position. I said this seemed very unlike the picture as we saw it in the UK and that we were afraid that it would make things worse for us. Everyone in later discussion assumed that we would probably devalue: their analyses were more realistic than the speakers. They asked me a good many questions especially on the impact of devaluation on UK wages and costs.

Saturday, June 11th

We are now at La Guardia waiting to leave after a 24-hour delay. The BOAC service is really intolerable. In 16 crossings I have been on time only twice. It is said to be due to there not being enough 'planes for the service so that they can never keep them properly repaired. However the time has been useful in private ways and I feel much more relaxed than I did. The Washington talks were more exhausting than I had expected.

On Wednesday morning we had a rather barren morning with the US Treasury, mainly on convertibility (and on Article 9 of the Loan Agreement),[63], where they seemed to me very doctrinaire and completely oblivious to all the difficulties of their own position and to have quite overlooked, in their belief in convertibility and non-discrimination, the objects towards which these were going to contribute. In the afternoon we talked a while to State Department people under Wynn-Brown about the oil and the Argentine troubles. We seem to have infuriated their oil people by a 5-year agreement which will exclude US oil, at a time when they are running into a surplus. And to have added fuel to the flames by not telling them about it until it was too late to do anything. This is a clear case where we ought to be allowed to discriminate because dollars are scarce: we have right on our side but they the law (in Article 9) on theirs.

After dinner, which Caine had with us, we talked about where we were and what we should do. We agreed a line to be followed at the final meeting – and to get Oliver to approve it before.

(a) We had gained a great deal and hoped the talks would continue; (b) without attempting either to negotiate or to arrange a UK–US policy to be put over, e.g. in Paris or at the Fund; (c) we were going more impressed by the difficulties of the situation than we had come. While we still wanted convertibility and non-discrimination, we had to recover and to do so with political stability. Our own recovery had slowed up and the dollar drain was growing again now there was a slump in US; (d) on devaluation we had said that UK policy was quite against it and would re-affirm this. But as officials we had thought, were thinking, and would report; (e) on the Fund, while we could not accept the criteria in Southard's memo, we sympathized with their fear that all the money would be used up before the world had got anywhere near a position in which currencies could be stabilized.

We put all these points to Oliver next morning and he agreed with our general diagnosis, that US thinking was back in 1945 and that it had forgotten all about the objectives of 1947 and 1948. He made a few suggestions, mainly that we should labour the difficulties of our position and the impossibility of any sharp internal deflation. I saw him for a few minutes afterwards and also at his garden party that evening – he seemed quite pleased about it all. My own feeling is that the outlook is very grim but that Wilson Smith has learned a lot and established good relations with Martin which is a great step forward.

Afterwards we went to a final meeting in the Treasury and Wilson Smith went through the points, quite well. Martin replied, saying chiefly that they were very glad to find that our ultimate objectives were the same as theirs – they had been feeling increasingly that this was not so. Willard Thorp spoke briefly and said how hard we were making it for them especially with things like the Argentine agreement. Afterwards we lunched at the Metropolitan with Hoffman, Bissell, [David] Bruce

[ECA Mission Chief, later Ambassador, in France] and an ECA man
whose name I did not get. On our side Franks, Wilson Smith, Caine and
I. I liked Hoffman but as he was in the middle of a stormy session with
the Senate Appropriations Committee he had to go after 20 minutes,
and his team soon after. Bissell is I think the ablest of them all and can
think in very broad terms but he is so busy that he takes the ideas of his
staff too easily and there is no doubt that they are pressing towards
non-discrimination and convertibility.

On Friday morning we flew to NY and lunched at J. P. Morgan's with
Russell Leffingwell, the senior partner, and Whitney, a fairly senior
one. It was an interesting lunch quite apart from the surroundings which
I felt rather awesome. Leffingwell was against devaluation and against
public works for the US. He said that the recession had really begun in
September 1948 and that the Federal Reserve's credit restrictions since
then had been the main cause of the movement. This was an interesting
view of a weapon now considered out of date, though the Bank of
England seems to think that it is too severe for use. Leffingwell wanted
lower taxes and easier credit policy. His main idea was that the US
should support sterling freely, as long as we balanced the Budget and
pursued a proper monetary policy. This was the same idea as W.
Lippmann's, who no doubt got it from Leffingwell.

We had a 24-hour delay in New York and had to wait 6 hours at
Gander because Prestwick was closed – then we went into Heathrow
after all. The prestige of BOAC is very low indeed – mainly because
they have not enough machines but they always give me the impression
that time is no object, and their stories to the passengers are always
unconvincing. I have made 16 crossings in Constellations and been late
14 times, from 6 hours to 30.

Wednesday, June 22nd

Since we got back I have talked about very little except devaluation –
the dollar drain is so high since April that a new policy has to be found
and this brings devaluation right into the picture. I feel very frustrated at
the moment as I seem to be surrounded by invincible ignorance and
prejudice.

Friday, July 8th

After a long and violent series of arguments, Plowden and I managed to
convince the other Treasury officials and those of the Bank what was
needed. However Ministers would not take our prescription. They
agreed reluctantly to announce import cuts, though not really to make
them. And to have talks with the US. But nothing on expenditure,
money or exchange rate – no fundamentals in fact. It is a tragedy that
S.C. should be so ill at this time, it is almost impossible to get anywhere
with him and he told P. that he felt suspicious of all his advisers and had

to read all their stuff to see that they did not slip anything over on him that was flatly against his party beliefs. I feel very bitter against the Bank on all this. They have been against doing anything on exchange or interest rates and have been as negative as possible while all the time keeping a hedge out. 'These measures won't help'. 'We may be forced to devalue'. 'We must consider interest rates' and so on. It is absolutely intolerable that there should not be a clear line on these things from the people who have the primary responsibility.

Monday, July 11th

Today was rather amusing. Ministers had seen Snyder [Secretary of the US Treasury] on Friday and Saturday and had discussed it all after lunch at Chequers on Sunday. I gather that Snyder said nothing positive and a certain amount negative but that he had been authorized to agree to official talks in Washington at the end of August, to be followed at once by Ministerial ones. The next question is to prepare the UK brief; EPC had given a general blessing to the paper we had concocted after the dinner at 2 Park St (on June 29th) but it was very sketchy.

Anyway at 12.45 I saw Plowden who said that Bridges wanted Wilson Smith to lead both in preparing the brief and on the official talks and that Wilson Smith had asked for *me* to help him. P. had said that I would no doubt be very glad to do what I could. But on later thought he had decided that as the issue was so crucial to our whole future, he (P.) ought to come very closely into it. Did I agree? I said I thought that at least all the papers should be taken by P.'s Working Group of the ED [Steering] Committee.[64] P. said he would see Bridges in the afternoon.

At 3 p.m. I was sent for by Douglas Jay who swore me to secrecy and told me about the weekend talks at Chequers. These had apparently been directed largely against reactionary (laissez-faire or liberal) officials and economists and it had been thought that Ministers must supervise the preparation of policy more closely, and that they ought to get in an economist especially to help. Thus he (Jay) had been charged to lead in the preparation of the brief. (a) What economist could he get? (b) Would I give as much help as I could? It seemed apparent from this that I was not the target of the attacks, though I did not know why I was excluded from the brief making. We discussed Balogh (rejected as bad collaborator), Kaldor (alpha if available), Worswick (good), Austin Robinson (I did not like), Tony Crosland (to my surprise – too young), and Cairncross. It was left that I should talk to Jay and Wilson Smith tomorrow. But obviously Jay wanted me to come in as much as I could.

When I got back to my room at 4, I found a message from Oliver and he came a few minutes later. He said that a plan had to be found which *he* could put to Dean Acheson [US Secretary of State] and that there was nothing as yet and that he and I would have to think one out. He suggested that the US should be persuaded to take over the sterling balances in return for our dropping the sterling area and going back to convertibility. This would please the US but really cost us nothing as with full convertibility the sterling area became meaningless anyway. (I found later that he had just got this idea from P. whom he had seen at 3 – P. presumably got it from George Schwartz in yesterday's *Sunday Times*.) Oliver talked as if at the least he would take a large part in the Washington talks.

At 5.15 we had a 2nd Secretaries Meeting and decided that the draft, which the Chancellor had prepared during the weekend for his speech in the House on Thursday, was no good. It said very little about what we would do, apart from the cuts in imports. And it was wrong in many places. Incidentally P. told me that Stafford Cripps was in such bad shape that he was going off on Monday for six weeks' holiday – alas! the horsemen of Israel and the chariots thereof. It was agreed that E.B., E.P., and W.S. should see Cripps tomorrow at 10 to tell him his speech was lousy.

Afterwards Wilson Smith asked me along and told me the story again. His version was that Ministers wanted the brief to be prepared by people who were not over-loaded already, and had wanted Oliver and a new economist to be found. However Oliver did not want to lead here, because he was on holiday, nor in Washington where he wants to keep out of the arena. So E.B. was going to propose Wilson Smith for the job. They hated the idea of a new economist, and would I be prepared to give up most of my time? I agreed against a new high level economist though I thought Worswick would be useful. A problem was to fit Douglas Jay in but they would cope somehow. Wilson Smith was obviously pleased at the idea of getting in on top of all this and wanted my help. So we shall see what happens. As far as I can see (a) Ministers want O. with Douglas Jay to keep it straight re home politics, (b) Douglas Jay wants to lead all through but has all the officials against him, (c) E.P. wants to get in himself and keep Wilson Smith as much out as he can, (d) O. wants some part in it all but is not sure what. The whole lot seem to want *me* to be the chief economist and brain, so it ought to be flattering.

Tuesday, July 12th

No progress on the above today. I saw E.P. in the morning and found him more disgruntled and at his request saw E.B. at 4.30. He was obviously so bothered about stopping Douglas Jay from taking charge that he hadn't considered the Wilson Smith/E.P. relationship at all. Saw E.P. again – he is very temperamental and had been told by his brother at lunch that he ought to resign so he was thinking of it – although in the morning he had been full of fight.

P. had a meeting in the afternoon of the ED Working Party to talk about the differences between UK cost of materials and finished goods, and those in other places. Partly the 'two worlds' problem and partly the consequences of bulk buying.[65] We had very stupidly sold materials at cost on the rise, to help the White Paper policy, and now were reluctant to lose on the fall. It was not a bad meeting and (a great score) we appointed Frank Lee to take a group to report on facts and policies. He was dying to get into this again and Helmore, who really ought to do it, has no time and neglects a lot of things he should do.

Wednesday, July 13th

Found E.P. in a rage this morning. He was due to see S.C. at 2.30 and proposed to offer his resignation because he and S.C. were out of sympathy. If this were refused, he would then say that it was idiotic to bring in new people to deal with a situation for which CEPS had been created – and that unless this were changed he *would* resign. I told him I agreed but that S.C. had clearly not thought out what he meant by new people. He came in later in the afternoon to tell me of the interview which had gone quite smoothly with no threats. S.C. had been keen on some outsiders still (because the machine was overworked) but obviously wanted P. kept in. Incidentally P. denigrated the Bank and Cobbold [recently appointed Governor], and apparently S.C. agreed that Cobbold was no good and said (a) he had only appointed him because he could not get anyone else, (b) he had turned out far worse than had been expected.

E.B. had a meeting at 3.15 to lay on the first work for the US talks. Frank Lee had invited himself on the strength of yesterday's job. Otherwise it was mostly a 2nd Secretaries meeting. But neither D.J., nor O.S.F., nor H.W.S. were there – three of the original quadrumvirate settled at Chequers for this job. The Economic Section drew inflation and US obligations against deflation. I think we shall have to do a good deal.

The unemployed figures today showed a drop of over 40,000 since mid-May; this is very sad and shows that inflation has come on again.

The Commonwealth Talks began but I did not hear anything about them.[66]

We talked to P. this morning about the 1952 Survey and practically agreed to drop it. The facts are quite uncertain, and Departments have so much else to do that they are reluctant to work hard at an exercise they consider useless.

Tuesday, July 19th

Last night P. and I had Coombs to dinner at the Travellers Club. It was the first time I had seen him since he became Governor of the Commonwealth Bank. We had a long general talk on the situation and how to handle the US talks. He suggested that we ought to persuade them that Central Banks should be authorized to invest in the International Bank – this would have the advantages of the Leffingwell–Lippmann solution that it would only need *one* legislative change and then be administrative discretion. But he thought that investment would *seem* more sound than currency support. We encouraged him to put it forward and I think he will. The more solutions of this kind are on the table, the more likely that one will be accepted.

We also discussed devaluation where I think we shook him a good deal – at least he said it would be a useful weapon – and the IMF, where we asked him to press the Australian application for a drawing, in order to keep the scarce currency question alive. He is really a very nice man indeed now and his successes have mellowed him so much that one would not recognize the character that I first met at Hot Springs at the 1943 FAO Conference. At times I even thought I saw the emergence of the Central Banker in its most conservative form – Central Banks against the world – but of course this is not real and if it were he would not share it. It is our own Central Bank which I find so difficult.

Wednesday, July 20th

The main features of yesterday were a meeting of 2nd Secretaries to discuss arrangements while the Chancellor is away, and a conversation with D.J. Apparently the P.M. is to take general charge with H. Wilson, and later Gaitskell, to act on high policy matters with him. Ordinary affairs to go as usual to Finance Secretary or Economic Secretary with E.B. having a veto. There was some talk about Washington but we are to meet again today. The team is not chosen yet, mainly because E.P. wants to go. He told me O.F. wants *me* to go, as I think does Wilson Smith who is to lead.

D.J. has changed his mind on devaluation and told me so – he is now working on Gaitskell. I think some of this is due to Nicki (Kaldor) whom I persuaded to try to work on them. It is a great relief to me. I feel that just as the officials began to come round, so now Ministers are – there will soon be a party and then a band-wagon. The main reason Jay gave was the very good one that HMG are losing grip and ought to do something. The LP is putting in a paper to the same effect and I have got Norman Brook to persuade the PM to do the same.

At this afternoon's meeting, Bolton said that the reserves would be down to £350 mn by the end of this week. However, when I got the statement today, it showed a loss of only £7.5 mn on the week and the total at £391 mn so he must have been exaggerating.

Very little else is happening, or at least gives me time to think about it. The [Long-Term] Economic Survey has been put off, partly because Departments won't work on it and partly because the bases are so uncertain.

Marcus is writing two notes, one on the rate to which we should go (by the way, Nicki said that Triffin [Professor of Economics, Yale University] told him we should float the rate and that IMF would not mind): the other on the US obligations to maintain employment etc. Bretherton has taken on a good deal of miscellaneous stuff. But the Section is very weak for a number of reasons – Butt and Nita away, many on leave, Hopkin still not quite clear of the Population Commission although it has reported.

Thursday, July 21st

Today P. and I had a long talk with O.S.F., ostensibly to take a line for the first talk with Jay about the briefs for Washington. He spent about 1 hour telling us what *he* thought was wrong and ought to be done. The only really new feature was his belief that the sterling area has been draining off all our dollars: he says that the figures prove it. I can hardly believe this but it may be so. Otherwise he wants to admit that it is our own inflation that has been the trouble; and he would like to cut expenditure by 10% or so, mainly from health, housing and the swollen Civil Service. At times he was very impressive and I began to wonder if he were our new Keynes. P. seemed a bit jealous at times.

This afternoon I went to the Garden Party – a very hot and clear day. I talked a bit to Bob Brand who is to speak in the Lords on Monday – he felt much as I do. As I was leaving I met Harold Wilson who took me aside and told me very cordially that he was arranging a talk between himself, Gaitskell, Jay, Bridges, Wilson Smith, Cairncross and me. This was because Jay and Gaitskell had now come round (v. July 20th) to a view *he* had long held. This was most encouraging – he had hardly spoken to me for a year and now was obviously anxious to get on the right side. I feel sure that he has known for a long time what was needed but would not take a line until he felt fairly sure he would not be alone. No doubt Cairncross has helped a lot. Anyway I feel that we have won now and may even have something in hand for the Washington talks – earlier I was in despair about this. It is all going a good deal better than I expected.

Wednesday, July 27th

There were more meetings on Friday and I had to come up early on Monday to a meeting with Harold Wilson, Gaitskell, D.J., E.B., W.S. and me. There we were asked mainly on the timing, it being assumed that the course itself was desirable. G. indeed said that if the Government decided to do this *and nothing else*, would it not be all the more important to push on with this? They practically prevented any discussion of the disinflationary measures which we had said should be included.

That evening E.B. gave a dinner at the Athenaeum, at which there were O.S.F., Plowden, W.S., Eady, Frank Lee, Helmore, Otto Clarke, Leslie Rowan and Roger Makins, whom I sat next to at dinner – he was at the House [Christ Church] when I was at Magdalen and must have known all the characters of *Brideshead Revisited*. It was a pleasant evening. After dinner we talked the whole crisis over. Oliver began (I had seen him at 6 p.m. to suggest this) by making it clear that he thought there was no point in trying to bargain and that we should go to Washington with action already taken if possible. This was accepted without question. For the rest we seemed more or less agreed except for timing on devaluation. At 2nd Secretaries on Tuesday this was taken a little further and I was told off to write a note to the PM setting out the common view of all officials, so that it should be clear what this was.[67] Stafford had not told the Cabinet that all his advisers thought the drain would not be stopped by what was announced in the Debate.

Since then there has not been much that came my way. I think that a good deal of intrigue is going on among Ministers because of this complete change of attitude by the three young economist ones. I have done a bit on several papers for Washington. There has been a great flap in Paris because of our revised deficit (1,500 instead of 1,100 mn dollars): this is thought to be a bid to get a bit more than our share of the appropriation, now reduced by Congress.[68]

Friday, July 29th

A meeting yesterday afternoon in the President's rooms at the Board of Trade. The same people as on Monday morning but Oliver, Plowden, Makins and Helmore joined it – far too many. I feel a bit inhibited as Wilson, whom I used to regard as a junior colleague, seems to expect me to say nothing. He has got very conceited and I feel he has also become a great temporizer, but this may be only my own feeling that he almost goes out of his way to be rude to me.

Anyhow we did not get very far. It has quickly been accepted that we are not to use devaluation as a bargaining weapon.

This afternoon, however, I went to see P. and Max Nicholson was there and told us that at a secret meeting late last night, the economic Ministers, PM and LP only, it was decided to do it fairly soon – no time to be fixed, as H.W. has to break it to S.C. which he will do during his European motor holiday, which gives a pretext for a call. At first I thought, especially in view of the meeting of yesterday evening, that the LP had got it wrong: but P. got it confirmed by Jay. A curious thing was that the PM sent for E.B. to discuss things and *did not tell him* of the meeting. He was very cross.

At this morning's Cabinet, which Oliver attended, the PM said he would do whatever was needed during the holidays as it would look bad to summon Ministers. So he got carte blanche – this is the best thing he has done yet that I have seen.

Apparently all this was decided without a word about the new rate. I set Jukes on hastily to finish the paper he was doing, which comes out at 25% or more. Calculations are not much good anyhow and it will have to be a hunch but it is as well to be able to produce the best economic essay possible.

Monday, August 1st

The House sat on Saturday, the first time for 10 years, and did its business and now it and Ministers are all on holiday. But the crisis will not take a holiday and I think the PM will have something on which to exercise his discretion. I begin to think also that there may be an autumn election, though there is no possible evidence for this.

Tuesday, August 9th

I was on leave most of last week. This week has had one very interesting development. Bridges asked Rowan and me to outline a brief for Ministers on the Washington negotiations – it followed a good deal the paper I had written on the main issues. But in our discussion we ended on the view that the future could only be handled by some sort of continuous machinery for discussion, like that being done for the Joint Defence arrangements. Then we found that Lucius Thompson-McCausland had made a similar suggestion in a paper he had done for the Washington talks: and R. Makins said today that the Embassy had suggested the same thing six months ago. However it began, it really is a new idea. E.B. had a meeting today to consider the outline and after a good deal of discussion it was practically accepted, including this idea. I spoke a good deal about it, illustrating from our experience with Combined Boards. So it will at any rate go to Ministers.

On Monday I went to a meeting with Jay and Gaitskell about the brief for the Washington talks. Gaitskell impressed me a great deal – he seems to get all the right points and to have a very good mind indeed. During the meeting, Harold Wilson's Secretary, Max Brown, arrived to report the talks H.W. had had with S.C. in Switzerland. But I have not yet heard what the conclusion is – it is of fundamental importance.

This dominates everything else and I have seen hardly anything of the Section on other matters for weeks.

Friday, August 26th

I later gathered that S.C. had not been at all well and had reacted somewhat unfavourably to the proposals, thus at least making it quite certain that nothing would be done in August and little before the talks. He was not flatly against devaluation but also very doubtful if it would do any good. The week ending on August 13th was entirely given up to writing and re-writing the paper for the Cabinet on the line to be taken in Washington. Rowan and I did most of the work and he most of the drafting. The Bank as usual were impossible to pin down on the question of bank rate and my feeling of dissatisfaction grew even more. In a meeting they seem to agree and when it comes to the final draft they water it down so much that it is worthless.

I went off on leave on August 14th and was at Bredannay near Annecy until the 24th. Plowden was staying near and I took him a letter from D.J. suggesting that he should return early to try to convince the Chancellor of the urgency of action. However he very sensibly decided that he might as well finish his holiday. S.C. was due back on the 19th and the Cabinet fixed for August 25th.

Towards the end of my stay I found to my annoyance that I had to go to Washington on the 25th and I had several messages asking me to call in Paris and leave time for London. Actually I got to Paris on the night of the 24th and found that Roll and Hall-Patch had gone to London that day to discuss the situation on the division of aid. The UK created such hostility by putting up our deficit from 11 to 15 hundred mn dollars that we have been under fire ever since. However it seems to me to be coming out all right or rather as well as we could have hoped.

I flew to London on the 25th and saw Brittain [Third Secretary, HM Treasury] who told me that there had been a preliminary meeting at Chequers which was rather inconclusive, that S.C. had returned in very bad shape, and that the Cabinet itself was fixed for 29th and S.C. and Bevin to leave for Washington on 31st. This made the whole time-table almost impossible. One cannot exaggerate the seriousness which S.C.'s illness has been to all our affairs in this period. The one man who had them in hand to go off and actually to become the chief obstruction – it ought to be a general lesson that if the leader gets unfit he should step right out until he is better or resigns. The dollar drain has been less in the last two weeks.

Norman Brook saw me in London and told me that my salary had at last been raised to £2,750 p.a. This is *instead* of any changes that might have come from the Chorley Report which he feels is not likely to be implemented for some time. It is personal to me in recognition of the particularly heavy load of responsibility I have had to take. It is the most I have ever got: before I went to the Economic Section I got £1,120 from Trinity plus £800 from the Board of Trade plus £150–200 in fees and it was on that basis that I felt I lost money on the change – of course the work is enormously more exacting than it was then, though one cannot deny that it is absorbingly interesting and that there is quite a lot of standing also.

The salary is now more suited to the prestige and if Government and especially university salaries do not rise much further it ought to be about right. Nevertheless the whole thing is absurd in the context of the decisions actually left to me and those which ought to be in the sense that no one else in the present set-up is competent to take them. It is absurd that a Government of professed planners should not only have no one who understands planning, but also no one who understands monetary policy and the theory of international trade. I do not say that it is essential that these should be left to theorists, but at least there ought to be more than one person who is capable of appreciating the theoretical considerations. The Bank seems to me to be quite unaware of all the work that was done about its own behaviour in the 19th century.

To cut this short, I left London at 5.30 on the BOAC 'plane. We had to wait at Gander as one engine cut out over the Atlantic and were finally transferred to a Pan Am 'plane and got to Washington, where I now am at the Shoreham, at 8 p.m. this evening. Goldman [Treasury Chief Statistician] flew with me and Wilson Smith, Holmes [Second Sec., Board of Trade] and Bolton were here already having arrived by sea yesterday. We have our first talk with the State Department tomorrow.

Wednesday, August 31st

I don't feel as if these talks are being at all successful. On Sat. and again on Monday we met twice in full force at the State Department, about 50 altogether. It was clear that we could not make much progress in that atmosphere and in fact the whole feeling was one of shadow-boxing. The US side clearly were not going either to offer anything or to make any criticism.

On Monday night Webb [Under Secretary of State] gave a dinner at the Mayflower. He brought Willard Thorp, Nitze, Kennan [State Dept.], Martin [Treasury] and Bissell [ECA]. The Canadians were [Norman] Robertson [Cabinet Secretary], Towers [Governor of the Bank of Canada], Deutsch. We were Hoyer Millar [Foreign Office], Wilson Smith, Holmes and myself. We got on much better and agreed to keep the future meetings much smaller, and yesterday (Tuesday) we consisted only of 5 US, two Canadians and five of us. But though we talked more amicably it was in a very sketchy way, running through the proposed Agenda and stopping to argue about certain points on the way. Webb said plainly on exchange rates that it was a matter of UK domestic policy on which they did not propose to intervene, but that they would like to hear our views if we had any. It is quite clear that both they and the Canadians are desperately anxious that we should somehow make a rapid improvement in our comparative cost position and that this is the only way they can see. But they are not going to be placed in the position where we could say that we did it at their behest. The same on internal finance. I gave a talk about our position and they were plainly interested but were reluctant to press us, and as we can say nothing of our intentions the talk soon comes to an end.

Sunday, September 4th

I now feel much more cheerful, partly perhaps because Oliver came back on Thursday and has taken hold, but mainly for two reasons: (1) the President's speech [see below, page 73] and the consistent friendliness of the Americans, (2) the indications both that our Ministers have become aware of the problem and that they have something in their hands to deal with it.

After the rather bad meetings on Tuesday, the official talks went much better. On Wednesday morning Harry (Wilson Smith), Caine and Bolton went and talked about the sterling balances on lines we had previously agreed – that they were a great burden but chiefly because of India, and that this had been a political necessity and was the cost of what had been the biggest UK achievement since the war and the only solid thing about US–UK politics in Asia. We did not draw the contrast with China but it was obvious, and the State Dept people fully agreed. This rather drew the US fire though there was something on S. Africa and a few general questions.

The other meetings, which went on up to Friday morning, went fairly well. They were on specific points, mainly about things we thought they might do such as the US practices on shipping and rubber, stockpiling, the tin agreement. A good deal of time was spent on the draft Agenda for the Ministers. We had set up a number of working parties which reported: the main one was on UK costs and prices, where both the US and Canada produced a good deal of evidence to show that we were not competitive. Holmes gave a very lame account of what the UK was doing to improve its competitive position, but they took more interest in the report than in what he said.

On Tuesday night came a cable reporting the Cabinet meeting on Monday [29 August]. This had approved the final draft of the paper Rowan and I had begun in the second week of August [CP(49)185, the brief for Washington] – it had changed in many ways since then. But it had firmly toned down the parts about internal policy and given instructions that our representatives were not to mention our internal measures unless pressed, and were then to say only that we were pruning inessential expenditure and would continue to keep inflation in check. All references to Caliban [the code-word for devaluation] had been removed from the paper and there were no references, of course, in the cable. The total effect of all this was to make me feel very doubtful about the attitude our Ministers would take and the account they would give, as all that was left was the import cuts and I feared that these might be regarded as impeding recovery.

On Monday afternoon President Truman made a speech to the American Legion Convention at Philadelphia which was plainly meant to create a favourable atmosphere for the talks: among other things it said that the US must not interfere with other countries' domestic affairs, and that the US was not in this or in other matters 'engaged in a charitable enterprise'. I noticed it at the time but as the week went on we became clearer and clearer that it was of major importance. Meanwhile the atmosphere of all our talks got noticeably better, perhaps because of the speech, perhaps because we had got away from the awkward subjects. Webb also got better and better and in the end we were much impressed by his friendliness, firmness as a chairman, and we began to think ability too. Wilson Smith had dinner with him and found out that his background at the Bureau of the Budget is an enormous help to him now because he knows so much about how to handle the Washington Departments.

We ended with a meeting of the full group on Friday afternoon and I felt that it was something to have got through the week at all in so friendly an atmosphere. At the last small meeting on Friday morning, Wilson Smith was fairly frank about our position and said that the US and Canadians were not to be gloomy, because it had been inevitable that we could not say what *we* were going to do. But they need not suppose from this that our Ministers would do the same. Webb replied in the same spirit and said frankly how important it would be to them to know what we intended to contribute.

Meanwhile two cables had come from the *Mauretania* which made a great alteration in my views and spirits. These made it clear that Ministers *did* have some major contribution to make, which from the tone could (I think) only be Caliban. (So S.C. must have been converted in the end and the long struggle which began for me in March when I first asked Bridges to have it looked at, and saw the Chancellor, has ended. I suppose that it was the logic of events and not of R.L.H. that has brought this about but at any rate Plowden and I had to convert first officials and then Ministers, in the face of opposition at every turn from the Bank of England, who have been as obstructive as possible and who will doubtless take the credit if it is successful. Incidentally they have also fought violently against doing anything in the monetary field, and their only contribution was to say that neither of these would do any good unless we made cuts in public expenditure which were so large that it was clear that the Government could not take them. In fact they behaved as if they wanted to drive the Government into deflation or the country into collapse.)

A second cable suggested that Ministers were getting worried about the whole outlook for the talks and were thinking much harder about the proper tactics, which was at least a sign of grace.

Oliver had Harry Wilson Smith and me to dine on Friday and afterwards Hume Wrong, the Canadian Ambassador, and Norman Robertson came in and we talked until nearly 12. But did not get very far. The Canadians have done their best all the week but have been disappointed that we were unable to say more. We had some discussion about the time-table for Wednesday when the talks begin. Our people want a very small and very secret huddle at noon and the US seem to want a fairly big meeting to start the proceedings in the afternoon. A great deal of care is required to keep Snyder in the picture in the way which we want.

Last night (Sat.) Oliver dined alone with Dean Acheson and this morning as I was writing briefs for the Agenda he telephoned and asked me to lunch. We lunched with only Aubrey Morgan who is a sort of public relations/confidential aide: and spent the whole afternoon discussing the situation. Dean Acheson said that if we wanted to hold the position till after the elections it was o.k.: or if we wanted 'to talk business' it would be. But if the latter, what they would try to do would depend on our action. We would be judged (a) by our short-term stand – would we carry out the import cuts, would we do Caliban, would we take the dollar export drive more seriously? (b) by our long-term intentions, would we really work with them on productivity, would we try to settle the sterling balances (they would be able to help because of their Far Eastern interests), would we state now (and work for) our belief in one world? On the latter they did not really trust Stafford. There were also points about Snyder – keep him in the picture – and about Wednesday, etc.

This was all most encouraging as we actually do want to do all the things listed and can give assurance at once on A1 and A2 and I would hope a sincere promise on A3 as it is our often-stated policy. During the afternoon another telegram came from the *Mauretania* making it quite clear that our people wanted to give a good lead on UK intentions. So we felt much better and went on to work out the whole strategy for Tuesday (the boat meeting till the sleepers at the Penn. station) and Wednesday. At 6 there was a meeting at the Embassy of the top 9 people when we agreed the tactics just decided. We all stayed to dinner, then the others were sent off and Wilson Smith and I stayed and drafted telegrams to the boat (also agreed in the afternoon) until nearly midnight. I came back to the Shoreham feeling very much better.

George Bolton said at 6 p.m. that he had been told that Snyder was *really* our best friend but needed care. We ought not even to mention a higher price for gold.

Clutterbuck was at that meeting and at dinner. I used to know him well in 1941 when he was the Dominions Office man at the inter-departmental meetings on general economic questions, which we used to think were so important – the inner ring so to speak. As we were all Assistant Secretaries I have since wondered if we were, but in a way it was a sort of open conspiracy, and everyone in it has gone ahead very fast since then, including Bill Hasler until he was drowned. Clutters seemed to me then to be by far the least able of the group but he is now Canadian High Commissioner and is well liked there. He had a very good manner last night and seemed on the whole a proper High Commissioner; he talked well. But I still doubt if he has much of a mind.

Tuesday, September 6th

Yesterday was Labor Day and a public holiday, and we spent the whole day in preparing briefs for Wilson Smith to take with him when he leaves at 9 a.m. this morning with Oliver. They are being taken in a fast cutter to the *Ambrose Light*, where they join the *Mauretania*. All the rest of us will be able to do little or nothing today which is a blessing as we have been at it ever since we came and I have been out to dinner almost every night. The briefs are very mixed in quality, having been done each by the man with the main Departmental responsibility, and very little time to discuss them, especially the line and the tone. Wilson Smith seems to me to be improving rapidly in his powers of dealing with the Americans and he has been on the whole good at leading his very varied and rather weak team in the last week. But he has not yet got the art of determining the line to be taken and rehearsing his performers in advance – in this there is an enormous difference between his technique and powers and those of Oliver.

Holmes is a very upright and on the whole lovable character but not at all good at dealing with the Americans, nor to my mind at getting anything done. One of the great weaknesses in our whole position for 18 months has been the lack of energy we have put into the dollar drive. Holmes in this is characteristic of the Board of Trade and undoubtedly gives the US the impression that in our minds an excuse is as good as an achievement. On negotiations, his Civil Service conscience (weak, I fear, in me) leads him almost to overstate his own case especially if there are features in it which will be unpalatable to the other side: then when he comes back he is loud in his condemnation of his own side. Somehow, it seems to me, he ought to have made more impact on his own side before he went to negotiate, and in the negotiations he should seem at least to see the others' point of view.

Bolton is essentially an operator and one who takes snap decisions by instinct and finds any reasons that come into his head to justify them. This makes him a baffling opponent as he will reverse his view, and apparently his reading of history and his logic, in a very short period and seem, and I think be, quite unaware that he has done so. Something of what used to baffle me with Lord Beaverbrook who either was unaware that he had changed his mind or was quite uncommoded by this. In academic circles, where arguments of any importance are recorded on paper and usually in print, this would be impossible and an academic person is at a great disadvantage in dealing with the situation in practice, and particularly in appreciating that if the decisions are on short-term matters it is probably right to make the changes, e.g. Bolton would make more money and Beaverbrook more 'planes by going on in this way than would anyone who was concerned by 'foolish consistency'. It makes him a very bad man, however, on a Mission like this as he does not know what it is all about. And I gather that he is not at all popular at the Fund and that the UK stock there is low.

Incidentally, there has been a curious contradiction all the week – Truman announced at Philadelphia and Webb said in plain terms to us that our internal policy (especially, said Webb, Caliban) was entirely for us. The USA would not press us on such a matter. But Southard on the Fund has been pressing violently all this time that the Fund Report should contain a strong passage practically calling on the UK to devalue: and clearly doing it on Treasury instructions, though no doubt he was strongly in favour of them. On Saturday Southard, who has the great US block of votes and enough client countries in his pocket to get a majority, refused any further drafting amendments and called for a vote. Tansley, our deputy who has been acting, then asked for an adjournment in order to consult his Government, the matter being so important. Southard asked for a recess of an hour to consider this and in the interval clearly consulted *his* Government about what he should do – at the end he agreed. But a great deal would be made of a situation in which, the Fund being in Washington, the US representative can get an adjournment to ask his Government if another representative can have an adjournment to consult his. It also shows that at bottom the US Government *are* pressing us on Caliban, whatever they say. Not that I mind, but it may be useful later on.

Sidney Caine has a very good mind and a good feeling for what is going on in Washington and what the US point of view is. In negotiation, however, he is given to thinking aloud and his thoughts are often unrelated to the case he is urging or to the political realities of the whole

situation. In fact he gives the impression that he has no personal interest
in the problem at all. This makes him, in my experience, an awkward
colleague. Lionel Robbins used to say that he and Frank Lee were the
best men in Whitehall and ought to run the Treasury. I agree about
Frank but I think Lionel was a little prejudiced on Sidney by the sweep
of his mind. On the whole, I think that this is by far the weakest team
and the one most badly organized for any major negotiation I have
known. Acheson told Oliver that it was the Conference for which the
preparation was the worst *he* had known and that it must not be allowed
to happen again. They have been, like us, so busy preparing a great
mass of documentation that no one has had time to consider or use it.

Tuesday, September 6th (evening)

We had a quiet day today and I did very little except to begin to write a
note about how we might organize for 'continued consultation'. There is
already a good deal of difference of view among the UK people here,
partly due to personal prestige, I think: e.g. I suspect that Wilson Smith
does not want anyone else to go on with the talks he began in June and
has continued. The Ambassador on Sunday had talked to me very
eloquently – he wants something like a Combined Board and I think
Dean Acheson, who had a lot to do with the wartime Boards, wants the
same. George Bolton asked me to lunch at the Mayflower to talk about
it but when I arrived he had brought Rasminsky, the Canadian
economic expert [later, Governor of the Bank of Canada], and Tansley
the UK Deputy on the Fund. So we all talked about it, but in a much
more tentative way. We all agreed that ECOSOC was a complete failure
and that Governments were turning away from it. But when George
suggested that the UK and/or the US might want to wind up the IMF,
Rasminsky said he thought that this would be politically impossible at
this time, at any rate for the US which had done such a big job in selling
it to their own people.

I said that I thought that the UK had not got far enough to have any
constructive ideas yet but that we were very much impressed by the
failure to get anywhere at all in the existing bodies, and by the great
strain that these were imposing on our manpower. It was clear that
nothing much could be done round a table unless those who were there
wanted more or less the same things. This ruled out the Russian bloc
and many other countries who were unable to take any but a very
narrow view. Secondly, the UK and the US were quite unwilling to
discuss their real problems in public with a lot of other countries
present. Consequently there was a tendency to keep on setting up new
bodies, e.g. OEEC, to do things which constitutionally speaking
belonged to others already in existence. The Atlantic Pact was an
instance in the political field (but nothing had come like it in the
economic) of a completely new departure. London was very dissatisfied
with the old framework but had no clear idea of the new. The main
point I stressed was that it was not so much the fact that IMF, ITO etc.

were set up on faulty analyses that mattered, as that there seemed to be no way of agreeing a UK/US analysis to replace the original, which had been agreed. Rasminsky did not dissent from all this but he had no suggestions – he may, however, come up with some.

It is interesting to note how many people feel the same climate at the same time. I have begun to feel in the last week that a US/UK economic union is probably much nearer to being practicable than most people supposed – US opinion has moved a great deal, and since UK opinion approves of Western union why should it not go further? This afternoon Pitblado [Treasury Under Secretary] said much of this to me – he had been stimulated by the Strasbourg vote for European Union and said that we must now begin to study the alternatives. Redvers Opie [ex-Oxford economist] spoke very much on these lines when I dined with him on Saturday.

The President made a speech yesterday on the achievements of the present (81st) Congress in which he went at length into his plans for public control and welfare, and attacked the special interests opposing these things. There was nothing he said that one of our Ministers could not have said.

Thursday, September 8th

The Ministerial party arrived about 7.30 and I had breakfast with Wilson Smith. They had had a good trip in the cutter to the *Mauretania* but found the party on board a little tired and ragged. Stafford Cripps not much recovered and Bevin in very poor shape. A great deal of the time had been spent in argument and not in expounding what had (as we thought) to be done. Edwin P. told me later that much of this was about Caliban where S.C. had come most unwillingly to the view that we were going to do it at all; wanted as little as possible; and wanted to ask the US and Canada what rate they suggested. He was talked out of the last in the morning, not long before he went off to the 12 noon meeting.

While this was going on Oliver had a meeting to decide the outline of the speech he was due to make at 4 p.m., on which no work at all had been done. Sidney Caine and I wrote this out and S.C. approved it about 10.45. Then I went off to the Bradford and dictated it, finishing about 12.30. Then we had an argument about the rate and finally agreed (W. S., Bolton, E.P. and I) that $2.80 or $2.90 was the right one. After lunch we took the draft speech to Stafford and went through it with him, a painful process with time so short and 8 people in the room. By the time this was done it was time to go: but I did not attend, going back to the Bradford to dictate the arguments in favour of the rate we had agreed on. Then at 5.30 we went back to the Embassy to consider the Agenda for today and finally I had to go and left E.P. to have my memo re-done and to include a bit on the free markets from G. Bolton.

I dined with the Lacys, but was rather weary after so rushed and unsatisfactory a day. I do not like to write speeches at all and particularly not in a hurry. The whole thing was a good example of the folly of leaving it all until the last minute but I suppose S.C.'s health made it essential. We were all wrong also about the speech – we should have made a draft or made sure, instead of assuming, that they were going to do it.

Stafford said that the noon meeting went very well indeed so I assume that our contribution was welcome. Oliver was there but I have not seen him yet. I gather that the afternoon meeting was all right and that the general atmosphere is enormously better than during the Snyder talks in London.

Now I have to write a broadcast, a thing I determined to do long ago, when the idea of Caliban first entered my head. Unfortunately I did not do it. S.C. is going to fly back in time to deliver it. For the next ten days the timing is very tricky.

Friday, September 9th

Not a great deal yesterday. An early meeting at the Embassy where (at Oliver's insistence) a paper was produced giving all the subjects that might be discussed and suggesting which should be referred to Committees and which discussed by the Ministers. This was for their meeting at 11. If Oliver were not here I wonder very much how the thing would have got itself organized at all.

The senior UK officials met in the Bradford at 11 to discuss the form of continuing organization. It went much better than I had expected because W. S. had become convinced that Ministers were set on it and so withdrew his opposition to the whole idea (he wanted continued but not continuous discussion by the 'responsible officials' and did not relish having a high level man in Washington as well as Rowan and Plowden at home).

After lunch the Committees were started but the one I had to do, raw materials and stockpiling, did not meet until 9 a.m. today. We sat about waiting to be told this until nearly 6. I wrote a few ideas for the broadcast. At night Oliver gave a dinner for about 30 senior people of the three Governments and on the whole I enjoyed it. I sat next to Abbott [Canadian Minister of Finance] and across the table from Lew Douglas who wore no eye patch and seemed in fairly good shape though much older.[69] He was full of plans for more fishing.

We talked a fair bit on the subject of Keynes and how irresponsible and wrong-headed he had been in the later stages and especially the loan agreement. Lew said that he had begged him to leave out convertibility and non-discrimination and urged that no loan would be better than that. We all agreed that Keynes had come to Washington intending to get something quite different and had problably never intended the UK to carry out the commitments. But as he died so soon afterwards all the minor characters left behind had to do the best they could. I myself have seen his policy on cheap money which the Treasury and the Bank acted on until I started to argue them out of it late last year – it assumed that slumps would be the problem though paying lip service to the view that all the sterling about would make the transitional problem perhaps inflationary. He changed his mind very freely but had such predominance in the Treasury that the views he happened to hold when he died became crystallized into the right doctrine.

Today I went to two meetings about tin, rubber etc., the National Press Club lunch where Stafford spoke, a reception by Snyder and dined here with the Chancellor and a few officials. The first was at Commerce at 9 and was taken by the Secretary [of Commerce] Sawyer who is said to be a very difficult man. However he was nice enough – we were asked to repeat our case and he asked a few stock questions. C. D. Howe [Minister of Trade and Commerce] came to my surprise to lead the Canadians – he was obviously being helpful as he volunteered almost at once that Canada would double her tin and rubber stockpiles. The US made no offers – at 5 p.m. we were called again to agree a report for Ministers at 11 a.m. tomorrow, but it also was just a statement of what we asked and what the US said. But Tom Blaisdell who presided then indicated that Ministers would probably be told something.

The Chancellor was in very good form at lunch at the National Press Club, which was crowded and turned away as many as came. The lunch itself was almost too modest but I don't see why not. The speech seemed to me to be very successful and afterwards he dealt with the deliberately awkward questions with great dexterity. So we all felt pleased. At Snyder's party I saw Arthur Smithies [Harvard professor, then in ECA] looking very well – we had a little talk about US business conditions but he was not very sure and inclined to wait for the automobile figures.

Afterwards we had a little dinner at the Shoreham as the Chancellor did not want to dine with Oliver who had 12 visiting English bishops. I gathered that S.C. did not want to meet Wand, the Bishop of London, whom I used to know when he was Chaplain of Oriel. Stafford was in quite good shape and he went off at 9.30 and I hope had a long night.

At dinner he gave authority for a cable to Playfair in London to start Caliban which is now called Rose: so they have cut the 14 days that were said to be the best time to 8. It felt a little like one supposed a mobilization order would. I wish I knew exactly what the steps were. So far no leak, perhaps because it has been freely predicted for so long.

Sunday, September 11th

Sam Goldman told me yesterday however that a run has begun on the reserves, and that they are now going very fast. I spent most of the day doing a draft for the broadcast and going through it with Edwin. At 9.15 we went through it with the Chancellor who made a lot of suggestions. Afterwards he went off, and O.S.F., W. S., Roger Makins, Edwin, Bolton and I had a long and slow discussion about the rate and how we could persuade Ministers to what we wanted. All the arguments had been written out by me some time before. It is now touch and go but I suppose it will be all right. The button has been pressed. George Bolton says that we *must* decide tomorrow and ought to do so today in order to let the right people know. The Canadians of course know the fact but not the rate.

Ministers had two meetings yesterday and ours seem quite pleased though I do not think that they have got anything tangible yet. Wilson Smith spent a lot of the afternoon in drafting the communiqué. I feel a bit vague about all the other items, having been so concentrated on my own.

I had lunch with Walter Salant who obviously felt as I did before we arrived but who has not been at all in the picture this week. He said that he wanted to make some suggestions about what *we* could do and what they could do if we did the right things, to put forward after we leave. He wants to try them out on someone here.

Monday, September 12th

Yesterday I spent the whole day at the Embassy, mostly with Plowden on telegrams about bread and guidance, and on re-drafting.[70] E.P. is a very slow drafter and fusses a good deal – it took him ages to get it as he wanted, though he was right to be worried about the bread cable since they couldn't do the sums except on some hypothesis. In the end we suggested a series of them.

S.C. had got up early and done a draft for the first three pages, not very good we thought especially on exchange rates which he had not understood, and I still doubt if he does. He wanted to say 'Of course there is no reason why the rate should be at one level rather than another' which implies, though he did not of course mean, that the markets are extremely imperfect and like the price in the kinked demand curve. Anyhow we did a re-draft to include the main points made on Saturday night, and left it there.

At 3.30 we interrupted our labours for a meeting about the draft communiqué which Harry had been working on. It seemed to me to go a good deal further than I had hoped, though Bolton and Holmes were very captious. Partly their temperaments. B. kept on saying that it would not cheer up anyone in London and Holmes that it took too meekly the US attitude on tariffs. I must say that I felt rather impatient. We have gone a lot further than we had hoped and I do not think we ever thought we would collect much cash. On tariffs, we can't make our friends in Congress go any further than their enemies will let them, and a communiqué that provoked a struggle would do us no good at all. Incidentally, I saw this (Monday) morning the re-draft, largely done by the US, which seemed to me to go further than the one we saw last night.

Today the Finance Ministers are going to talk from 9 to 11, then the whole party on the communiqué, and most of the afternoon on finishing it and handing it out. At 9.45 this evening we (the small group of UK officials) are meeting with our own Ministers to settle finally the actual figure. But Roger M. had a crack at E.B. yesterday and he seemed quite o.k. – and I think we will be all right. It seems wonderful to have got such a solid front in the end.

Last night I dined with Lippmann and his wife, and Dean Suter of the Washington Cathedral who wore a lovely red dinner jacket, like the Trinity Claret Club but much more beautiful. Walter seemed to me to be very gloomy because he felt that nothing was going to be done and that we were going to pretend that there *was* no crisis because we could not solve it. We talked a bit about the sterling balances and I tried to cheer him up but I do not think I had much success and indeed I felt that he thought I was very superficial. Ferdinand Kuhn of the *Washington Post* and his wife, who had crossed with the *Mauretania* party, came in later and we talked mainly about Communism and not very well at that.

Roger Makins told me this morning that he had dined with Bissell and the Alsops last night and that there had been equal gloom there. It is all very awkward for us as we cannot give them the missing piece and until we do we seem fools to suppose that there can be either new hope or new spirit to meet the situation. And they can't really assess the cuts either, or the run element. However I do not feel at all depressed.

Thursday, September 15th

I am writing in the air, having left La Guardia about 4.15 p.m. I flew from Washington by the 10.45 'plane, lunched in New York. I feel pleased to be so far only ½ hour late but the Captain has been told to get me on at all costs if he is held up, e.g. at Gander. I have the second last draft of the broadcast, which the Cabinet is to see tomorrow or Saturday. The Chancellor is flying tomorrow and the gun goes off at 9.15 p.m. on Sunday. However we all have nerves now and each day this week has seemed to me to be one day to the good. As time passes and more people are told it gets more and more likely to leak. In any case, as soon as the Fund Meeting is called (after lunch Sat. – for that evening) the reason will be obvious and of course as soon as the story is given to the Board it seems certain that one will give it away.

The whole thing is extremely romantic. It is clear that the US and Canada have been completely silent – we expected no less but it is gratifying. Enough Canadians have been told to allow them to settle what they will do and it seems almost certain that they will go one-third of the way. At the beginning of the week the other 'white' Dominions were told. The Indians are to be told tonight but they have got so near to guessing that they flew Rama Rao, the Governor of their Central Bank, back yesterday as he is the only man who knows enough about it to cope. Gutt [Managing Director of the IMF] is to be told tonight and Bolton thinks he is very likely to let it out. The papers have a number of rumours including one said to have been released by a Minister in Canberra. Anyway I don't suppose we can lose the whole reserve on Friday.

On Monday night Wilson Smith and I dined with Bissell and Joe Alsop – they pressed me a bit on how we could implement our promise to push dollar exports. I went through the old stuff. We had to leave at 9 for a meeting at the Embassy. S.C., the Foreign Secretary, O.S.F., E.P., G.F.B., R.M., W. S., W. Armstrong (the Chancellor's PS) and I. Here the final decision (as to the rate) was made – I do not dare to write it down but it was about right. R.M. had been working on E.B. and after a little talk he agreed, so did S.C. – they were impressed most by the argument that we ought to be safe – easy to go up. For once W. S. and G.B. agreed with the rest of us. The rest of the time E.P. and I worked on the speech and the Chancellor rewrote it and finally last night we had a meeting at which E.B. was rather critical. But we accepted his main points and Armstrong and I agreed our drafts. I had been sent for from London to clear up a few points but as I had already booked today it made no difference.

Apart from this, there has been a terrific coming and going of cables on all sorts of related matters, especially guidance, the time-table and bread. I do not know the final decision on the last but S.C. and E.B. want to put up the price, not only to cover the increased cost, but to make the loaf whiter and to increase children's allowances by 1/- a week. I do not know all the drill about who has to be told, who has to get guidance, and when. But S.C. very rightly has taken the line firmly that the broadcast *is* the guidance and that no one else will get anything until he has spoken.

A bit of work has been done on the continuing organization and on bodies for same. It has been decided to take Leslie Rowan for Washington, to work just below HE (His Excellency] and above S. Caine. Only a very small staff, most of the work to be done by the existing chaps or others brought *ad hoc*. In order to keep OF [Overseas Finance] in their place, it is to report to the London Committee, which E.P. wants Hitch to chair. And all the real policy points to go to the Steering Committee Working Party under Bridges or E.P. as his Deputy.

O.S.F., R.M., E.P. and I had some chat yesterday about bodies generally, and whether to move Hall-Patch from Paris. I should be sorry if this had to be done but it is very bad that he does not get on with Harriman and I gather that S.C. and E.B. have both got sour about him (my own view is that this is because US Ministers have told them what Harriman says). Anyway this was left. I suggested bringing Frank Lee back but the others were against it – I don't think they trust him.

We have decided that the next steps at home are to cut expenditure and to wake up the people in the Board of Trade doing the dollar export drive. *Everyone* on the UK talks in Washington agreed that Holmes was a disaster and I assume that he will be shifted. It is also agreed by everyone but the Ministers that H. Wilson is no good, ought if possible to be shifted from the Board of Trade, and certainly ought not to succeed S.C. If any young one is to do it, it is to be Gaitskell.

Well the talks are over and so is this book. We have done all that we could and now we must let the machine run out and see what happens. In two years I have helped to make very large changes in the two great weapons of the economy. We got a Budget Surplus of £600–700 mn and now we are making a big change in the rate. The third thing we ought to have done was to tighten up Bank Credit but here we have been defeated by the direct cowardice or else disingenuousness of Cobbold, whose people have on several occasions agreed to do something and then gone back on it.

Anyway it has been a most interesting period for an economist.

Incidentally, if anyone who writes so glibly about devaluation had to do it, he would think twice before he advocated it for a world-wide currency. We shall set the trading world ablaze and have no idea of all sorts of complications that may set in. And the operation itself is enormous and requires secrecy which will make it very unpopular if kept: and a failure if not. It is probably much easier for a small country. But it is a fearful thing for us.

(5.30 p.m. DST in flight from NYC to Gander.)

II

From devaluation to the change of government,

26 September 1949 to 15 October 1951

On his return to London Hall emphasized the danger of inflation which would undo the effects of devaluation on the trade balance. The home market was booming and unemployment falling quite sharply in spite of the loss of exports and a worsening of the trade balance by over £20 million per month. A stiff dose of disinflation was called for if the opportunities opened up by devaluation were not to be lost; and the fact that the Budget surplus looked like being £160 million less than was expected in April while small savers were drawing down their deposits by about £40 million per annum pointed to £200 million as a measure of the cuts required to restore the pressure of demand to the level originally planned. A further cut of £100 million would free resources for additional exports and for necessary changes in the pattern of production.

Ministers, however, were hard to convince that public expenditure and investment should be cut. They had resisted any suggestion of this kind in July when it was put forward as an alternative to devaluation. They could only be persuaded to take the necessary accompanying measures in October after a long battle and threats of resignation (on widely different grounds) from no less than four Ministers including the Chancellor. The cuts were supposed to add up to £140 million on government current expenditure and £140 million on investment. But many of them never came into effect or were not genuine cuts or were revoked later. Investment, for example, increased in 1950 by £100 million, the amount originally expected.

Meanwhile financial markets at first responded unfavourably to devaluation and there were expectations of another and worse crisis. But by the end of the year the reserves were recovering strongly and the gold and dollar deficit had for the time being almost disappeared.

Monday, September 26th 1949

The first book closed with me on the way from New York on Thursday, Sept. 15th. I got to London about 6.30 p.m. on the 16th and the draft speech was at once sent to be duplicated. Then I saw Bridges and later Jay, and gave them an outline of Washington and of the Chancellor's mind on the broadcast. On Saturday we went through the draft and sat about till he came, very late, about 6.30 p.m.

There was a Cabinet at once, very secret with the Ministers coming in at the old Treasury door in Whitehall and going to No. 10 through the tunnel. The main changes were bread to be 5½d instead of 6d and the family allowance scheme dropped. Frank Lee drove me to Paddington and I got the 9.50 to Oxford. The news did not seem to get out much next day [Sunday 18 September] and at 9.15 p.m. I heard the broadcast. Abbot Moffat of ECA London was there and seemed much upset. He had been against devaluation and was shocked by the low rate. ECA had written a paper estimating that we would earn less dollars than before.

On Sunday I wrote a speech about Washington for the Chancellor to give to a Press Conference on Monday. He used it more or less as it stood but to our horror, in answering questions he said that there were to be no cuts in defence or social services.

The week was painfully crowded and there were a number of 2nd Secretaries' meetings to consider all the things to be done next. On Wednesday it seemed likely that Parliament would meet and we began to write a speech which was given to Cripps on Friday. He took Sat. in bed. I had so much to do all the week that I cannot think much about it. Otto Clarke is writing a great many papers about future problems; he wants us to step right out of OEEC. He is still very bitter about liberalizing trade and thinks (or says he thinks) that we have lost control over our balance of payments.

Thursday, September 29th

The Chancellor wants to put a paper to his colleagues about the inflationary situation and I have been writing it.[1] The most interesting thing is that Government expenditure is almost certainly rising rapidly and we are likely to have supplementaries of £140 mn or so. This explains where the exports we did not make after March have gone. Mostly health and defence. The cuts in expenditure for which the PM called [in CP(49)170, 4 August] add up to only £26 mn against the £150 mn expected. I make it that we want at least £200 mn to put us back to April, plus at least £100 mn as a start to create the extra exports we shall need now we are back in the sellers' market. I have suggested £150 mn off Government expenditure and £150mn off investment, but I don't suppose they will take it.

I wish we could have the election soon, so that we could put some guts into something. There is no sign at all that Ministers are willing to cut anything. Harold Wilson, who must know better, put in a paper on timber saying that we ought to keep on the housing programme and be ready to spend dollars if we ran short. Plowden says that the BEA have got power stations all over the country full of turbines but no boilers.

The debate has not produced much except to rub in the increased cost of imports that are likely. Ministers are rightly more worried about holding the wages line than anything else, hence the [increase in] profits tax. We had several meetings with Stafford last week on this.

Yesterday Bridges called me in to say how worried he was about banking policy. He fears a clash between the Government and the Bank and says it is our duty to prevent it. He has got Cobbold to agree to a working party of Trend [Treasury Under Secretary], Eady, Mynors and Peppiatt to educate one another and wanted me to join. But if so would I behave like a permanent civil servant, i.e. not write or talk about what I had learnt when I left the Service? I was doubtful as this seemed to be an attempt to muzzle me but finally agreed. E.P. and I had seen H.G. earlier in the week to ask his advice about where to go next on this, as we were defeated by the Bank. He wanted me to write a paper and if necessary to have a clash with Cobbold and accept his resignation if he offered it. I am not sure but that this is probably the right thing but I suppose I must work on the party. It is very unfortunate that Eady is in charge of all this. But Trend should be a great advance on Compton (he has been most helpful on Government expenditure). And I feel better that Peppiatt is coming as I think he really understands all this.

Otto Clarke came in for a chat. He is predicting frightful things about the balance of payments on the ground that the new OGL [Open General Licences] for soft currencies will cost us the most frightful sums. I find it hard to believe this unless we cannot do anything to check inflation. However it may be that Ministers will refuse it.

Wednesday, October 5th

I have had a great deal to do on the paper on Inflation, which was finally agreed yesterday and will be circulated today. It contains only diagnosis, no remedy. We ask for £200 mn to get back to April plus £100 mn to prepare for the export drive.

I dined last night with Plowden and Crowther.

E.P. is very worried because he says we have done the Chancellor great harm by allowing him to be so optimistic in his broadcast. The public expected him to apologize for changing his mind on devaluation, and those who understand these things think that he minimized the harmful effects and especially misled the country about the effect on the cost of living.

I saw Leslie about this and he said it was true but that it would not matter if it were not that the Tories think that he is afraid to do anything about deflation. Consequently they are trying very hard to exploit the loss of confidence in Cripps, as he was the great asset of the Labour Party as far as the middle vote was concerned.

Thursday, October 6th

Planning Board, to take a note giving the main calculations on inflation. The members were rather gloomy: Tewson [General Secretary, TUC] said that the people kept on being asked for further efforts and when they made them they were told there was another crisis. This is the vicious consequence of going on increasing Government expenditure. Graham Cunningham [Chairman, Triplex Safety Glass Co.] was very angry because, as he rightly pointed out, the Government takes no notice of what the Board says. I said that it was not the planning but the refusal to carry out plans which was at fault.

Plowden took Clegg [Chairman, Cotton Spinners' and Manufacturers' Association] and me to lunch. We talked mainly about the possible cuts in cotton, and about the Anglo-American Productivity Council of which he is a member.

In the afternoon talked to Rowan about Washington – he is going on

Monday for first talks about the Continuing Organization. Also to D. Jay who is very angry about the £300 mn deflation, said it was an amateurish calculation and that all the figures were wrong. In particular, he attacked the £100 mn for exports on the ground that we would make the switch.

Wednesday, October 12th

The EPC took the main paper [EPC(49)102] on Monday and nearly all the Ministers made a strenuous attempt to whittle down the £300 mn in various ways. The Chancellor put in a second paper on Tuesday [EPC(49)110], getting it down to £285 mn to make allowances for the profit on wool which the Board of Trade have made. We took the opportunity to look at the 3rd quarter import and export figures which are just as bad as those for the 2nd quarter and fully support the view that there must have been a good deal of renewed inflation to have had all these extra goods and no unemployment. The Ministry of Supply found some supplementaries they had not expected and this partly offset the Board of Trade gains. The papers were taken again and after a lot of argument it was agreed that something substantial would need to be done. But it was also clear that they would shrink very much from anything really unpleasant by way of remedy. And at 5.30 this afternoon Bridges, Plowden and I saw the Chancellor to discuss the very hard question of the figure at which he should resign rather than accept [the absence of] further cuts. He told us that Bevan had already said that *he* would resign rather than cut housing or make a charge for the health service, both of which were in the proposals we are circulating.

It was very hard, since if the Chancellor resigned he would split his party, lose Labour the election, and start again the lack of confidence in the country. On the other hand, if he did nothing or [accepted] what we all thought inadequate, he would be deceiving everyone and opening the way for a new crisis. We all thought that £200 mn was the absolute minimum and that it would be cutting things much too fine even at that. He felt, however, that he might in the end get them to accept £280 mn and then make cuts off this rather than cut down the figure and feel that they were meeting the situation.

Monday, October 17th

All last week was taken up by the cuts and it is still going on. I was very much embarrassed on Friday as Hugh Gaitskell pointed out that there was an inconsistency in the balance of payments figures in the supplementary Memorandum [EPC(49)110]. I had used c.i.f. figures for imports in one table and f.o.b. in another without pointing out that the basis had changed. I felt very much upset – it is also rather scandalous that no one else should be competent to pick up such things.

Tuesday, October 18th

Parliament met today but they have had to put off the statement as there is an impasse – they have about £220 mn and want £30 mn more, off defence or health, and neither Minister will budge. The Foreign Secretary says defence will cause our foreign policy to collapse, and Bevan that he will resign if he does more (he has taken £35 mn off housing and £12 mn from a prescription charge). S.C. was full of gloom today and E.P. the same. P. had lunch with me and I told him that the Chancellor's alternatives, to accept too small a figure or to resign, were both wrong: he must win. So P., who was seeing him at 4.15 on this, took that line and called me later to say that he had had a successful interview.

An ED Committee yesterday on the import cuts brought out clearly that in a few lines production would fall when they were made. It is a dilemma – S.C. swore in Washington that we would make them, yet Ministers want him in his speech on the cuts to talk about more productivity most of the time. It is a silly idea anyway as he has said it twice already since devaluation. Today there was an ED WP on liberalization of trade [ED(W)(49)13] and that also brought out a dilemma. We are now afraid that we shall import too much, because of the inflation here: and thus have overall balance of payments difficulties. We *could* then plead these to go back on the liberalization. But it would be clear that if we did this we should have to say it was because we could not control inflation. And we are committed to that by Point 1 of the OEEC Plan of Action, in which S.C. took a leading part.[2]

S. C. Leslie had a long talk to P. and me today. He said that the Labour Party was breaking up and that this was because they had not grasped the seriousness of the situation. He wanted me to write and P. to process, a paper for S.C. to circulate giving the plain story. It was, he felt, our plain duty. But we felt that we had done all we could and that it would only make things worse if we tried again. Ministers had accepted £290 mn as a target and were only stalling on political grounds – this was their constitutional weakness, to choose the half measure and to put off but not anticipate or avoid the evil day.

Leslie Rowan is back from Washington, where he got a house. He leaves again on Nov. 2nd and wants to take an economist. I have suggested Jukes of the Economic Section or [Dudley] Seers of the Oxford Institute of Statistics. I don't know if either would go or if he would like them but they both seem to me very good.[3]

Friday, October 21st

Rowan is now thinking of taking van Loo [a Treasury official] from Paris: I think he would do very well. Yesterday at 3 p.m. E.B., E.P., B. Gilbert and I went to see the Chancellor to hear the final decision, which is about £260 to £270 mn. E.P. is in a very bad temper as it includes £30 mn a year off defence although it is thought that defence next year will be *up* £80 mn on last year – this calculation is £30 mn off £790 mn. So the whole sum will be wrong if he is right. But when I put this to S.C., he said he agreed and would insist on a cut either here or elsewhere.

Tuesday, October 25th

When I got back to Oxford there was a message to ask me for a draft of the speech by 10 a.m. Saturday, when a despatch rider came for it. On Monday Stafford had done a first draft and we have all been messing about with it. The PM's statement had a bad reception, largely because of the way he made it and the gossip there had been before. Cobbold said to E.P. yesterday that if all this had been announced on September 18th it would have seemed wonderful to everyone.

E.P., Crowther and I had dinner at Brown's on Monday with Nye Bevan. It was very interesting and I got an impression of great ability and of a philosophical basis for his thought which I imagine few other Ministers have. C. and P. flattered him a great deal which I thought silly but perhaps they know what he likes. He talked a lot about the 'polarization' of the parties and that he must express the extreme view or someone else would do it worse or else the discontent would grow because not vocal.

Everything seems in rather a mess now, mainly because S.C. is tired and bewildered and most officials are too. My own feeling is that things will go better now.

Friday, October 28th

The Debate is over at last, thank goodness: I did not go to any of it but spent about an hour with H. Morrison yesterday on his speech, and have to see Pakenham this morning about his. The Opposition criticized the cuts heavily on the ground that they were too small. I think they will be plenty if carried out.

Tuesday, November 1st

Everything seems much easier now the debate is over and S.C. and E.N.P. gone to Paris. *The Economist* on Saturday was very bitter about the cuts being a 'flea-bite'. I think they made a mistake in their calculations as they said we ought to allow for the change in the terms of trade, which is self-compensating. I wrote Crowther a note on this and have also suggested to Burchardt [Director, Oxford Institute] that he get someone from the Institute to write. I lunched yesterday with Austin Albu MP whom I had not met before – he was quite nice and able. Trying to get a line for his broadcast debate with Quintin Hogg [the future Lord Chancellor Hailsham].

Saw Bridges in the afternoon about OEEC economist – they are in despair. E. Roll rang me earlier in the evening and we agreed a list of Americans but that we would have a last try for Cairncross. E.B. asked Helmore and we should know today. Then we had a chat about the cuts and I told him I felt sure they were enough if carried out and that it was our business to see that they were. He has got a Committee of Treasury 3rd Secretaries to police and extend the Government expenditure. Bretherton said they were having great trouble with investment. No one would play and neither the Board of Trade nor the Ministry of Supply would divert any exports. I feel sure that we must put the utmost pressure behind all this.

Wednesday, November 2nd

Things are much quieter than they were and I was able to read the first draft Downie has done for the Survey. The theme is devaluation and the balance of payments. He did not agree that inflation had increased but his criticism of my paper did not shake me.[4]

Meade had lunch with me at the Reform and I saw W. King who had seen my note to Crowther. I tried to get Meade to write to *The Economist* on the same point.

Thursday, November 3rd

Saw Jukes. Gave Leslie a note on the cuts. Question of export price policy. Cairncross probably going to Paris.

Friday, November 4th

Cairncross came in and said that in the end he had decided not to go to Paris. He is changing houses and jobs, and has three small children, and he feels rather tired. I told E.B. who wanted me to hold up until he had told S.C. Cairncross stayed on and talked for about an hour about the need to get Ministers to take some more steps – he might almost have been *The Economist*. I told him I did not think it was as bad as all that and that I doubted if we could get a clearer picture of where we were going than we had now, until we had had several months' experience.

Tuesday, November 8th

I went to a Conference in Sidney Sussex over the weekend to discuss the next five years' work for the National Institute of Economic and Social Research. Austin Robinson presided, also present were Robbins, [Sir Dennis] Robertson, [John] Jewkes, [Michael] Postan, R. G. and G. C. Allen, H. Mynors, Habbakuk, Cairncross, Geoffrey Crowther. Cairncross told me he had seen the Chancellor who had persuaded him to go to Paris for three or four months. We talked mainly about a memo Crowther had written, asking for a study of the reasons why capital is put into industry. I thought it was not very inspiring as we had so many different points of view and bickered so much about minor matters. However they are all very nice. There was a letter in *The Economist* from Burchardt against their calculations of the gap – I had suggested this to Burchardt. G.C. did not apologize in the paper or to me but he was very affable to me and I felt that he wanted to be on good terms. Plowden told him last week that he thought the leading article on 'Salvation by Fleabite' was very irresponsible.

I am going to Paris tomorrow for a few days to talk to Roll and Hall-Patch and to do a few jobs. I saw Hitchman today to pass on the views of Abbot Moffat on purchase tax on soldiers, tourists etc. and also on the Colonial Office failure to ask for any ERP Development Appropriation.

Wednesday, November 16th

Most of the time in Paris was spent on discussing the content and form of the new [OEEC] Report, which was very much under discussion.[5] McDougall [Economic Adviser, OEEC] had produced an outline but it was much too diffuse. I talked it over first with Roll and Hall-Patch and then at lunch with McDougall and Marjolin. We all seemed to see very much eye to eye, and especially that the report should concentrate on viability, that it should be as frank as possible, that it should discuss the meaning of 'integration', and that it should deal with a few major questions, of which I thought devaluation should be one. There was a meeting of the Working Group on Monday and the Executive Committee on Tuesday and a new outline was agreed almost exactly as we had thought. Hall-Patch then arranged with Harriman that [Milton] Katz and [Lincoln] Gordon should come to London this week to discuss the form etc. of the report and outline with some people here. Then it would be for us and ECA to persuade the French, and in the end the job might just be done on time. There is an immensely difficult time-table point, in that the reports of the OEEC countries on 1950/51, 1951/52 and from then on are not even *expected* until December 15th. No one knows exactly or even roughly what they will show, yet the outlook will colour the whole report.

Hall-Patch took me to see Monnet on Saturday and we had a long talk. He was very gloomy and thought that UK–French relations were the key to European stability and that neither of us had an idea of where we were going or what to do with Germany. He returned once more to the idea of a deal on coal and meat (or wheat) mainly to show the world that we believed in one another. If they cut their coal investment and we promised to find them coal even if we were short ourselves; and if we cut our agricultural programme and they promised to keep up to their commitments even if they had to ration, it would be a great act of confidence. He expatiated at length on the harm done to our relations by the manner of devaluation. Hall-Patch told him that S.C. had warned Petsche [the French Minister of Finance] two months before that *if* we had to do it, we could only give two days' notice. And these two days were given. But Monnet said that whatever the truth was (he did not dissent or agree on this) there had been a deplorable lack of imagination on both sides. Surely the last two days could have been used for 'a cloak of consultation'. As it was no one in France would believe that we cared a damn for consultation. I felt very much as Monnet did about the need for good Anglo-French understanding, though I do not know if coal and meat would do it. But I don't think anyone in the Foreign Office cares about all this, or cares that there is no German policy. Incidentally, Bevin spoke in the House today about the improvement in Anglo-French relations *and* the new German policy, so perhaps Monnet is out of date.

I had two long talks with Robert Triffin, who is with the IMF and is their Paris representative, and whom I had not met before though I had seen several articles and his book on Imperfect Competition since the war and knew he was rising. He is a nice man though a bit concentrated in his ideas – he talked for hours about a possible Payments Scheme where his ideas are not unlike Fleming's.[6] I thought a good deal about this during the week and have a few ideas at last instead of the vacancy I had had before. I now think that all the schemes are too timid and that we ought to go for full inter-convertibility, with increasing penalties as limits are approached – and the idea that the very soft and very hard should be excluded as soon as possible leaving everyone in the middle to carry on.

I got back late on Monday night. Not much changed. P. is very worried (and has been for some time) about his own position. He is afraid that the Tories may get in and fire him and he wants to be first. But he obviously hates the idea of going at all. He says that the Government has decided on an election early rather than late and he is trying to find out what the Tories would do about *him* if they got in. He seems to think they *will* get in which is more than I do – I think it is very doubtful indeed in the sense of very open, and that much depends on what happens between now and then.

My own view of the economic situation is on the whole optimistic, though I agree that it is a close thing. The good points are (a) the reserves have risen *every* week since devaluation, (b) October exports about £156 mn, (c) the feel of the investment and labour markets is much less inflationary, (d) the Government has had an astonishing success with the Trade Unions in wages so far: much more than I had thought likely. The only point at all dark is the lethargy of exporters to dollar markets – there is a good bit of evidence that they are not taking advantage of their chances.

This morning we had the talk with Gordon and Tasca (the balance of payments man – Katz did not come) which Hall-Patch had arranged with Harriman about the ERP Report. It was very helpful. They obviously wanted us to make some commitments about integration, and payments. We seemed to be very close on most things, including the need to play up devaluation. Gordon came to see me in the afternoon and we had a pleasant talk. He was [a Rhodes Scholar] at Balliol 1933–36.

P. had a bad time at the Planning Board this morning, on the investment cuts. I don't know why: I wasn't there. He said that even Verdon-Smith [a director of the Bristol Aeroplane Co.] attacked him. He was a bit gloomy about wages and thought we ought to have a *very* deflationary Budget, including abolishing all food subsidies, ready for such a contingency. I agree that we have to get one ready but there isn't much we can do for a month or so as we shall have no more information for a while yet. If my hunch is right, we may be able to have an easier one than I had feared, as if wages are held down we can afford to give some tax concession or other.

There is a good paper on the Sterling Balances before Ministers [ED(W)(49)11], to be a brief for Leslie Rowan. But I expect we shall go on being too generous.

The Investment Cuts paper [EPB(49)20] is also before them.

Downie is now at work on the draft for the Survey [for 1950].

Marjolin told me he was delighted to be getting Cairncross. I have arranged to get Nita Watts back at the end of March.

Leslie's counter-depression campaign seems to me to be meeting with some success. At any rate the papers have stopped criticizing the Government: and after the gloom of last week the Stock Exchange is rising again and gilt-edged have recovered 5 points or so from their low. The Stock Exchange is mad anyway and I don't think we should take any notice of them.

Monday, November 21st

Ministers have approved the Sterling Balances paper. Rowan has had a success already as the US have agreed to a fairly substantial diversion of dollars to sterling oil. Tomorrow the Investment Cuts are coming up. Meanwhile the Defence Committee are meeting regularly to try to reach some agreement about next year's estimates but so far there is a clash between Bevin and Cripps – Foreign Policy or Social Services or Inflation. I saw E.P. tonight and he wanted to know if we could compromise on say £780 mn now and the final decision after the Election. My own feeling, that we are probably over the turn of the boom, is a little stronger than it was and I thought we could manage all right. P. wants us to get a paper, on Economic Policy for the next 5 years, ready for whichever Government is returned.

On Saturday night I spoke to the Pol. Ec. Club at Oxford about devaluation. A long discussion but I did not feel much impressed by it and on the whole felt that I knew more about the current situation than they did; I certainly ought to, and it is some comfort to feel that. Hubert Henderson made the best point, that the Government was nearly always too optimistic and when they felt that things were going well, we ought to brace ourselves for a shock.

Thursday, November 24th

Lord Linlithgow, for the Clearing Banks, sent the Chancellor through Cobbold a memo objecting to the idea either of credit restriction or of a ceiling for advances. As Marcus pointed out, it showed that they had learnt nothing in 100 years and I pointed this out to D.J. who sent the note to S.C. Yesterday we three and W. Eady had a little meeting and to my great delight S.C. not only agreed with me but undertook to write to Cobbold saying that he could not accept the view that the volume of money was at the discretion of the Clearing Banks. I made a draft last night. Eady is much alarmed and fears that there may be trouble. But if there is, so much the better – *I* fear that Cobbold will only temporize. Catto [former Governor, Bank of England] told S.C. last week that Cobbold was very weak. Marcus says that their people on his Committee on IEPS, ERP etc. are deplorable.

Wednesday, November 30th

I have been extremely busy but on a great variety of things. E.P. now says that the election may be postponed after all, mainly because the winter is said to be such a bad time to get out the vote. He changes his mind every day and now thinks that the Tories are certain to be returned, largely because there has been a *News Chronicle* Gallup Poll which shows a big shift away from Labour. He keeps on nagging me to do something on Economic Policy for the future but I haven't had time. The Survey is slowly taking shape but meanwhile the Programmes Committee has done a sketch to send to Paris on 1950/51 and so on which is very like a Survey.

Marcus has written a paper called 'One World?' which was discussed at a Section Meeting yesterday [EC(S)(49)30]. Peggy also did one [EC(S)(49)34]. Both called for discrimination in import restrictions as a necessary regulatory instrument. They feel that Whitehall is moving too fast towards the view that deflation should be the main weapon for dealing with balance of payments problems. It was a useful discussion.

I forget if I have recorded that the Section now has working for it [Fred] Atkinson, who used to be at Jesus and shared the lectureship with Trinity – he has gone on to IPC and Hopkin is to replace Jukes on balance of payments: also we have a new man called Grieve-Smith who is working with Dow. There seems to be a feeling in the Section that I am too much of a deflationist but I do not know what level of employment they want, so I have asked for a paper on it.

Marcus told me yesterday that he wanted to go to the LSE as a Reader – it seems very small beer. Undoubtedly one of the factors is that he is still deeply disappointed about Bretherton. I had a talk with Norman Brook about it today. He thinks that on the whole it will be a blessing: and I think I do too; he is a good though not brilliant economist but a difficult character and not up to anything like the load that has to be carried either by me or by a Deputy. Indeed if he had been more industrious he would have got away without Bretherton.

My days are full but as I have said there is no special thing. Today (Wednesday) I went to Plowden's morning meeting which he has every week at 10 on Wednesday for his senior staff, Nicholson, Leslie and I. I spoke about a paper which declared that with low raw material imports the cotton industry would need no more labour. Strath was asked to cope. Max [Nicholson] talked at length about Tizard [Rector, Imperial College, 1929–42] and the DSIR, mainly seeming to say that the scientists were often doubtful about proposed new investments, on technical grounds. He seemed to want the ESWP to deal: it was left that Strath and I should talk to him.

Then I dictated a note to the Board of Trade about a proposal to drop export volume targets in the Survey, about which Downie and Hopkin had been indignant. I read some papers and dictated a bit more and lunched with Eugene de Scrowtisch[?] who said the French were very corrupt but that everyone in London seemed far better than 18 months ago. After lunch I saw the reserves statement – the reserves are still rising and may well recover all last quarter's loss this quarter – and did a note on it for the PM. Then I agreed a line with Trend about the proposed Working Party on Internal Financial Stability: dictated a bit, saw Plowden about a B/E plan for a European Payments Scheme, which neither of us could understand – then saw Norman Brook, had a word with Marcus, read a few more papers and left about 6.20 as I had promised to have a drink with the Moffats. Most nights I am there till 7.15 or so.

I also wrote a note for the Chancellor on 'Trends since Devaluation', in conjunction with Otto: he wants to talk about it to NPACI on Friday: and I checked a note by Hitchman's people on Dual Pricing, after a meeting yesterday of Plowden's ED Working Group on the same subject [ED(W)(49)14]. The trends since devaluation still look good to me.

Tuesday, December 6th

There still seems little definite to write about. Yesterday there was an ED Committee to discuss the 1950 Balance of Payments for Ministers [ED(49)22 and EPC(49)157], and the submission to the OEEC for the 2nd Interim Report [EPC(50)158]. The latter showed that if we got $720 mn in 1950/51 and $360 mn in 1951/52 we would at least get the reserves back to $2,000 mn by the end of ERP. And on the whole it was rather cautious except that it assumed a high level of US activity and continuance of present policies here. But the Permanent Secretaries felt that it would create a very bad impression if we showed a build-up of reserves from ERP, and they scaled the figures down. It may be right – but it seems to me that if we had a run-down at the beginning and between April and September 1949, we ought to be allowed a compensating run-up.

The first draft of the Survey is nearly done, and we shall start our troubles next week.

Tuesday, December 13th

There has been the usual disturbance with Otto about the Balance of Payments part of the Survey. It is very annoying and I always tend to lose my temper. This time he said that the draft was all right but that as Ministers had just had it in the Programmes Committee material, he thought that they ought to get only what was intended for publication. We had a meeting with Plowden and Wilson Smith about it and agreed that the Ministerial version [of the *Survey*] ought nevertheless to contain a summary, but Otto and W.S. then roundly declared that Ministers had never had forecasts for the dollar position for the 2nd half of 1950. I was rather taken aback and later discovered that this was practically a lie, as the great bulk of the figures were in the ED Committee Report which had gone to Ministers as an Appendix to the paper. It is always troublesome. Otherwise it is going fairly smoothly: but I have had a great deal to do and feel a bit weary at the end of the day.

The first BC is on Friday.

Friday, December 17th [16th]

BC today. So far as we can see at present, there won't be much change next year, and politically this will probably be right. We looked at various taxes – D.J. has brought up petrol which was turned down the last two years. Also purchase tax, another old friend, where much could be done if there were some money to spare. And we looked at the possibility of allowing 'self-employed', e.g. lawyers and accountants, to have some of the benefits of a man under FSSU.

The Survey Working party has met all this week and we seem to have reached a compromise with O. Clarke. The National Income part has led to a great many arguments both theological and statistical, but it all looks like no change. However [Christopher] Saunders of CSO has raised an awkward problem on investment, where it seems that the IPC under-estimated the probable output in the engineering industry. At the moment it looks as if the £140 mn cuts will be off a larger total than we had expected. It is awkward because of what Ministers have been saying about the cuts. However we haven't discussed with IPC yet.

There are great misgivings about cheap sterling.[7] S.C. feels that there is a campaign by *The Times* to discredit the £ and that this is leading to the distrust behind the sales in New York, which are taking place mainly on French a/c. At the back of it all is the feeling that until the sterling balances are tied up we must remain vulnerable: I wrote a memo on it but have only showed it to Plowden so far – this advocates a loan, from Morgan's or the Federal Reserve, to support the rate. Cobbold who is just back also wants to support the rate but doubtless with our own money and for the wrong reasons. The reserves are still rising and will probably be well above $1,600 mn – they look like $1,670 mn or so at present.[8]

Tuesday, December 20th

Plowden and I had Walter Lippmann to lunch yesterday at the Travellers Club and afterwards he sat down and wrote out an outline of a plan for stopping ERP to the UK straight away and giving it instead to India, to be free dollars so that we could earn some of them, and to be accompanied by a reduction in the sterling debt of the UK to India of the same amount. Of course if India got the $720 mn for which we are hoping, and we could earn a good deal of it, and at the same time write the balances down by £260 mn or so, it would be wonderful. He asked how the counterpart fund worked and also for my views on Robbins' recent *Lloyds Bank Review* article.[9]

The first draft of the Survey is almost through the ES WP – we had a meeting on Friday afternoon to finish investment and on Saturday morning on 1950 balance of payments and yesterday afternoon on long-term balance of payments. There is a good deal of difference of view about the prospects for the latter.

S.C. has gone to Paris. P. says he will certainly resign unless the Labour Party has so small a majority that all hands are needed. Otherwise, he thinks Nye Bevan will be the next Chancellor.

Thursday, December 22nd

Saw P. this morning. He told me that they had now decided on the time. And all about his talk with Nye. He pressed me very hard to write the promised 5-year economic policy for the UK, so I wrote most of it this afternoon.

Friday, December 23rd

I finished the memo and sent it to P. who sent a copy to E.B. It was a review of the last 5 years and a policy (*not* a plan) for the future.

(a)   Keep down Government expenditure.
(b)   Keep down investment.
(c)   Keep down sterling releases and capital transfers.

The only fundamental controls needed are (1) IPC, (2) Programme Committee, (3) Exchange Control.

Monday, January 2nd 1950

I got a CB today and had some very kind messages, mainly from Civil Servants implying that this was the cachet for Civil Servants. I was much more pleased than I had expected to be.

In the afternoon, meetings with E.B. on cheap sterling, and on the statement on the last quarter's movement in reserves. We actually gained nearly $260 mn to bring them up to about $1,688. The statement attempts to distinguish 'continuing' from 'temporary and abnormal' factors but I fear this is an easier concept to formulate than to apply. I cannot help thinking that the publication will have a very good effect, and even to some extent on the cheap sterling NY quotations which upset the Chancellor so much. The *Financial News* said today that it was expected that the loss of reserves this quarter would be negligible or even a small gain. So there cannot have been much leak.

Wednesday, January 4th

It seems almost agreed now that the election will be next month, as indeed has seemed almost certain for a long time. But Senior Civil Servants now discuss it openly. I have had a great many letters and it is much pleasanter than I had expected. A really handsome one from the Chancellor, who, I thought, would not have bothered: and to my great surprise, letters from the Governor of the Bank of England and from 'Hoppy' [Sir Richard Hopkins, formerly Permanent Secretary, Treasury], who cannot know me well. Very nice notes from Lionel Robbins and Dennis Robertson. And a letter from E.P. saying that all his successes were due to me.

Had a long talk with him and one with Strath. The main feature developing is very bad relations with the US. But I think for once they cannot afford to let us down. For we could very nearly get by with no more ERP after June but I doubt if they could afford to give us none and let Stalin say 'I told you so'.

Thursday, January 5th

Gaitskell and Jay have written a memo to S.C. saying that we are giving up planning and that the Socialist Government will lose its character if we do so.[10] The occasion, and the main objection, is the 'liberalization' of trade by the new OGLs for soft currency trade. Jay has been at it for a long time. The interesting part was the first explicit recognition that high profits and inflation may be inevitable with full employment. The rest was based on a rather mystical view of the distinction between essentials and inessentials.

Tuesday, January 24th

Things are a lot quieter now as the election approaches but a good deal has happened in between. On Jan. 6th I spoke to the AUTE at Liverpool on the current situation, and introduced the problems of full employment and wages policy, about which I think a great deal. Not much reaction.

The Survey was taken by EPB and ED Committee, and got through fairly easily. We have had the first BC of 1950. Expenditure is still rising and the April Budget looks very difficult instead of fairly easy. The cuts of £140 mn on Government expenditure in October seem a mockery, since the total is still rising.

Tuesday, January 31st

S.C. and a good many officials are in Paris and not having an easy time, though Hoffmann is most anxious not to embarrass anyone with the election coming up.

Bank Deposits Working Party.
Visit from J. Fischer Williams.
Lunch at *Economist* – Sumner Schlichter.
The Gallup Polls.
Future Economic Policy.
Jukes and Hemming on the Sterling Area.

I have written so little this month that I must try to give some account of developments, public and personal.

The Election. E.B. calls over the odds that most people would give at the 2nd Secretaries meeting every Tuesday. Most people began by giving from 5 to 4 to 5 to 1 against the Conservatives: N. Brook evens and S. Holmes taking 6 to 4. Since then the feeling has been slightly more favourable to them though I have been steady at 2 to 1. This morning we were told that the PM expected a majority of 50 or 60 and H. Morrison to lose by about the same amount. The Gallup polls have shown that Labour is gaining its lost ground rapidly. They were 10% down in November, only 2% a fortnight ago and 1½% up this Saturday. My own feeling really is that it will be a very close thing either way and that no one knows yet because there is no obvious issue. Tony Crosland seems very confident both about his own seat and the prospects. S.C. determined to give up office in any event. Today I see that John Anderson [Chancellor 1943–5], who was being tipped for Conservative Chancellor, is not going to stand at all. E.P. thinks that if Labour is in, the Chancellor will be Morrison or else Bevan will take the general economic portfolio with a minor Chancellor.

I have been working away at the note on future economic policy for Plowden (see Dec. 22nd–23rd). He got me to re-write it, then [Douglas] Allen did a re-write which is much worse, now I am at it again. I have come increasingly to the conclusion that we have only two real problems, both connected with inflation: (1) to get Government expenditure down, (2) to hold wages and profits steady in full employment. I think all the rest doesn't matter in the end. But we just cannot go on with taxes this way, which make everything else so unmanageable.

We now have the final estimates for 1950/51 and they show that Health is up nearly £130 mn on last year. The total excess of this year over last is more than that, even after allowing for £90 mn from the economies of October. Trend has been doing a forward look and this shows little further rise after 1951 but no one believes it. Meanwhile Bevan has tried to suspend the operation of the 1/- for prescriptions on the ground that he was making a review of all the health services. About time too. The October cuts will now seem rather derisory.

Nevertheless I think that the signs of the times are more deflationary than not and especially the food situation. All the shops are full of food and one certainly gets far better choice and service than since 1939. Today's *News Chronicle* had a story that the rations were not being taken up and I rang Frank Lee at once. He said that it was broadly not true but they felt very uncertain about how it would go later in the year. On the whole they feel that either a bit more supplies or a bit higher prices would nearly let them end rationing altogether. This may be partly the extra food from the Continental OGLs but I think it shows that we are nearer balance than anyone thinks. *The Economist* profit index has definitely stopped rising. I am going to talk over the food thing with MoF on Thursday – they have been wondering for a long time what they would do as supplies increase – the subsidy ceiling means that prices should rise. Their whole long-term organization depends on the future of rationing.

Last week I lunched at *The Economist* to meet Sumner Schlichter [an American economist]. Lionel Robbins, Austin Robinson and Roland Bird were there as well as Geoffrey and me. We talked mainly about the UN Report which *The Economist* was reviewing that week. Most of them thought that the idea of full employment was not practicable and that all the things in the report would not be adopted. Austin and I said that we thought public opinion would now *demand* full employment and that economists had done no work on it and had better state the conditions for success rather than the reasons why it cannot work. I said again that I thought wage restraint was the main condition.

Yesterday (30th) John Fischer Williams came to see me. He had been in Paris helping with the 2nd Interim Report. I had not met him before. He spoke mainly about the need for the US to get used to the idea that they would be discriminated against, as he did not think they would ever get used to importing on a large scale. We agreed pretty well about many things and he told me he had never believed the IMF would work and had often argued this with Keynes. But K. was so set on finishing the job he had begun that he would not see the snags. Now it was clear that the conditions of success – that everyone started in a position of equilibrium – were not present. So it *could* only work as long as the US were putting in dollars. We talked a bit about the future of the sterling area, which he thought was essential if world trade was to go smoothly. But he was not sure what was needed to restore sterling – we both agreed that in the end it was *first* internal stability, *second* some assurance that the holders of the sterling balances would be firm holders. He also spoke about the IEPS [Intra-European Payments Scheme] which is holding them up in Paris. But he was not clear what was wanted – neither was I.

We have been working on an EPC paper on the UN Report [EPC(50)27] – now called NIFE in Whitehall (National and International Measures for Full Employment).[11] I have been trying hard to get it a favourable welcome and rather unexpectedly have been backed by Otto. So it will go forward quite strongly pushed and I think that Ministers will be even warmer. We want to get it referred to Governments for the *next* ECOSOC [UN Economic and Social Council] to give us all time to think. But warmly welcomed subject to that. I feel sure that the UK is stuck with Full Employment anyway so we *can't* lose by it and if US would accept it it would be a great step forward. They probably won't, which brings us back to permanent discrimination as a policy. However no one feels strongly about this nowadays.

The Bank Deposits WP met again yesterday but it is hopeless. D. Jay means well but it is too complex for him; the Bank cover up all the time and Wilfrid Eady is slightly ga-ga. The deposits have risen very little over the year but this conceals a rise in advances and a fall in floating debt. Not good. However we always lose this battle and the only comfort is that if we keep on fighting, there is at least some attempt at moderation.

Jukes is back from Washington and has written a paper on the sterling balances suggesting that they are much less of a menace and that we ought to try to do new things.[12] Peggy H. has written a paper on the future of the sterling area. The Economic Section is doing rather better these days. Meanwhile we have a new Estab. Officer, Hewison, instead of Burgis who was always so nice and helpful. Hewison has been rather a nuisance and I am now having a battle with him about the salary of Economic Advisers. But I think I will win.

Wednesday, February 15th

Roffey last weekend. The main events recently:

Visit from O.S.F.
BC and Roffey.
Future Economic Policy Memorandum.
Sub-Committee on National Income.
The Survey.

The election seems to me to be causing very little stir and one has a strong impression that the electorate dislikes both parties and does not want to vote favourably on such issues as are before it. I think this is the result of the succession of crises and optimism. They have their doubts about everything except perhaps full employment.

Franks arrived from Washington on Saturday, Feb. 4th and went straight to Oxford. He came to see me on Sunday and stayed all the morning and to lunch. We talked mainly about current economic affairs and agreed generally that it was the high Government expenditure and the high taxes which were the main trouble. Otherwise things were fairly good. On the boat he had met a number of UK exporters all of whom were very optimistic about the business they were doing and could do. He said that the difficulties in Anglo-US relations were much exaggerated and thought we would be all right and get about $500 mn which would be enough. He was mainly concerned about getting something going on the sterling balances – SE Asian development front. The main problem was to get some form of presentation that would appeal to the Congress.

On Thursday I went to London and dined with him and Plowden, and we talked mainly on the same things. He was very keen on our needing to do more to push dollar exports. I emphasized again, as I had to Rowan, that it was no good expecting Ministers to do anything by administrative action because they could not bring themselves to discriminate, except against the rich which was nearly the opposite of what was needed here. It gets more and more of a bitter joke, that Ministers should believe so strongly in planning and be so anxious to do nothing about it that we have been gradually driven in despair to disinflation, to devaluation, and now are trying to get rid of controls to restore some semblance of competition.

We went to Roffey for the weekend of February 10th but as there were no Ministers there it was rather an idle journey. We all agreed that we could not produce an adequate Budget as taxation could go no further and Government expenditure went on rising. The only real taxes we discussed were more on petrol and a possible simplification, extension and lowering of purchase tax. We left to produce a sort of manifesto [BC(50)12] for the next Chancellor.

A number of people have been working intermittently on the Memorandum on Future Economic Policy and it is taking some sort of shape though I doubt if it is much better than the first draft I did.[13] It makes the three original points, that we need the BC, the IPC and the Programmes Committee. The main weapons are disinflation, investment control and import control. The main problem is balance of payments and the consequential one at home to keep costs etc. from rising, which runs into subsidy policy etc. There is little new or drastic. The BC paper from Roffey is to deal with Government expenditure and I am going to write a fresh note on wage policy alone – Downie is making a first draft.[14]

The Sub-Committee on National Income forecasts has written its report and the outlook is very gloomy.[15] There is a deficit on the capital account of £150 mn this year and about the same in 1951 and 1952. The growth of the National Income is mortgaged already to the needs of the foreign balance, the growth of investment, and the growth of Government expenditure: at least, over £600 mn of the expected £800 mn rise is needed and the growth in Government receipts will not cover this. So to be safe we would need *more* taxes in this period.[16] I saw the IPC on this and they did not like the prospect at all as they did not see either what could be cut without damage, or how the cuts could be made even if they were decided.

Wednesday, March 1st

The election came out more or less as most people expected, after Winston's remarks on Russia which probably gained some votes. But D. Jay and Crosland both told me that they and Labour were much surprised at the pattern, i.e. they won constituencies normally regarded as crucial and lost in places they ought to have won if they had won the crucial ones.

S.C. came straight from Saturday's Cabinet and ordered a BC meeting for Monday, and we are all busy on work arising. I spent three-quarters of an hour with him on Monday and he told me he was under the most severe pressure to make some concessions. He felt isolated as almost all his colleagues could not understand why he needed such big surpluses and indeed did not understand modern Budgetary methods at all. He was full of rather wild ideas and also thought the situation less inflationary than appeared in our note.

Thursday, March 2nd

I lunched with Crosland today, who had just been to the party meeting. He said it had gone fairly well, no severe criticism though S.C. told me later that there had been many suggestions for increased expenditure. That was when E.B. and I went to see him alone about the Budget. We did much better with a small party and he seemed much more reasonable though still not sure what to do. We want a standstill.

Friday, March 3rd

All this week has been intensely occupied with B. problems. S.C. is wrestling with himself and the pressure under which he is to make some concession. I wrote a long paper yesterday to show that productivity was not likely to increase by much more than 2½% p.a. and how much difference it would make if it did, and the troubles we were going to run into on engineering anyway. On Friday the first Cabinet meeting on the outlook took place and N. Brook gave us an account in the afternoon and various jobs to get ready for Monday. It seems to have gone better than we feared and at any rate no one is in favour of compressions of the general principle. H.D. [Dalton] said that if any concessions were made they should be balanced by increases. Everyone worried about wages.

But I am told that Tewson [TUC General Secretary] says that he can hold out a bit more: and some Ministers that they will rise, whatever is in the Budget.

Tuesday, March 7th

Gaitskell came in today.[17] We had from 12 to 1.10 with him, D.J., S.C. about the Budget but it went very well. P. and I are to see Tewson this morning to confirm (or not) that the changes will make no difference to wage claims.[18]

Thursday, March 9th

The days are so busy that I can hardly even put down what is happening. P. and I saw Tewson as arranged – he was extremely sensible and on the whole thought:

(a)   that the Budget position ought not to be compromised;
(b)   that any concessions would help;
(c)   that he thought wages would hold for a few months yet, but that *no* concessions could give any guarantee that they would do so.

He said that Trade Unions would not accept the idea of the social wage.

Yesterday we arranged the work for the Budget speech. I went to the Food Dist. Committee to discuss the end of points rationing and suggested that when the things left were very few they should go on allocation. Lunched with [Burton] Klein [Council of Economic Advisers] who said Harriman wanted to run for Governor of NY State – no one thought he had a chance but the [Democratic] Party owed him so much for putting up money.

Discussed work at 4.30 and with E.B., E.P., D.J. and H.G. The shape of the Budget at 5.15. Agreed more or less. This is a new line. S.C. obviously intends to use H.G. as a clearing agency.

I saw him (H.G.) alone afterwards to discuss his idea of getting some economist in regularly – I will write more of this later. (He wanted me to talk about current economic problems to a few economists who were strong Labour supporters, especially Kaldor and Balogh. I formed the impression that it was to stop them pestering him continually with ill-informed ideas. I managed to stave it off until the next election.)

Thursday, March 16th

A lot of discussions about budgetary policy etc. Lord Addison [Lord Privy Seal and Leader of the House of Lords] wrote to Stafford to say that he did not see why we needed a surplus at all, and the PM who had a copy wrote commending the letter. I had to write a rejoinder but H.G. thought it was too difficult and rewrote the middle part, leaving out all the argument.[19]

There have been various rows about the Health Service and Supplementaries. On Tuesday P. was in a very black mood as he said that the M. of Health had won all along the line. However Stafford's speech did not seem to me to be too bad – if they can really impose a ceiling it will be a good step. The trouble is that nothing which has happened so far gives any reason to think that it will in fact be imposed.

Wednesday, March 22nd

The final adjustments are being made to the Survey. I cannot say that I think the editing CEPS have done every year has made it very much better and it always irritates my people. In fact the only advantage is that it doesn't bother me so much. This year D. A. V. Allen took over from Downie, to shorten it and remove any so-called taint of politics. But the style now is very mediocre. There has been a lot of late adjusting and in particular Gaitskell has been consulted at every turn.

His position and behaviour is leading to a great deal of discussion among the 2nd Sec. levels of the Treasury etc. He has not been given a specific job so far and S.C. refers a great many things to him, always ad hoc. So he does not know where he is, does not always deal with the same issues, and it wastes officials' time in routing things through S.C. Personally I like him and think he has a very good and honest mind: though he is very much given to making drafting changes which are quite unnecessary, bad administration and irritating. At M/FP he was always holding us up because he would himself draft the bits for the Survey at every stage. I wouldn't mind it at the very end. Last week I did a paper for S.C. to circulate and he re-wrote it (see last entry). Then S.C. said he would not accept the re-draft unless I was happy. But by then it was too late. They [the Cabinet] took this paper on Friday and all agreed that the present policy was correct.

Tuesday, March 28th

One of the things we have been worried about lately was the question of the next approach to the US. Labouisse [State Department: British, Commonwealth and North European Affairs] really started it off in Washington where he told Leslie Rowan that a lot of people on their side had been thinking about some form of US–UK partnership. Trying to work out what to say led Otto to write a paper which became a milder form (after my criticisms) for a select ED(W) party. The line was that we had to make a move, though we were much stronger than we used to be: that we had rejected a two-world sterling–dollar division and that we were committed to convertibility but that how fast we could go depended on how the US actually behaved. We must never do things we couldn't carry through in return for a promise or a hope of more gifts or loans. We must keep discrimination much longer than non-convertibility.

While this was going on it became clear, in connection with the EPU discussions, that H.G. thought we should *never* return to convertibility and never offer anyone gold points. E.P. and I had a lot of reasoning with him on all this, last week. I think we made some progress and that if we had time we could convert him to all our ways of thought. This afternoon Wilson Smith had a meeting of himself, Bolton and Fisher of the Bank, Brittain, Clarke and I to discuss ways of proceeding. We all agreed on our moral case but it is clearly going to be hard to move towards convertibility – in fact many of the suggestions were really moves towards relaxation. We are going on with this.

I have begun to draft the Budget speech. S.C. came up today with an opening that said that Labour wanted to stay on the knife-edge but if she must fall she wanted to fall on the employment side rather than the deflation side. We all felt that this *in* the speech would be taken by the world as a declaration that he had abandoned his objectives. E.B. and I saw him this afternoon and talked him out of this. I gather that all the changes are now in hand. There won't be much, if any, of an overall deficit this year.

The Survey came out today. The last stages were *most* unsatisfactory as Jackson [CSO] did not produce the NI figures until about 4 p.m. when the final printers' deadline was 6 p.m. (last Wednesday). The final figures were very different from all the earlier ones and he had changed the form of the tables. No one at all had any chance to comment. They seem all right but there is bound to be criticism of the form and the whole thing discredits NI planning. E.P. is furious and wants to sack Campion but I don't suppose his wrath will continue.

T. Stone came to see me today. He wants to do some work on wages and stability and I encouraged him.

Thursday, April 13th

It is now only five days to the Budget, which was settled finally about a fortnight ago: everyone has been working on the speech and I spent most of today at it, though Downie did nearly all the work. The aim is really no change though one tax is well up and another equivalently down. A number of left-wing people have been arguing that there should be large concessions, and especially Seers, who wrote an article in *Tribune* which my people consider irresponsible to the point of dishonesty. One sometimes feels very isolated in this job because so many different views are held about what ought to be done that there is no comfort in advice. This is wrong, of course: I generally feel when I talk to other economists a good deal of sympathy and understanding.

The underlying tone of the British economy seems to me to be as strong as it has ever been today. The reserves rose beyond all expectations last quarter and this week was just as good. Exports are running away above targets, and production is still rising faster than we expect. The only clouds at all on the horizon are the movement of wages (they are bound to rise this year and that won't matter, but it will be much more serious if there is another round in 1951) and the amount of sterling still about, fed by capital exports. There is a fundamental incompatibility between sterling as a world currency, and a Socialist Government in England which keeps super-tax at 19/6 and death duties at 85–90%.

Monday, April 17th

I took Wilson Smith to the Domus Dinner in Trinity on Friday and it was a pleasant party. He and I are getting on much better than we used to, and Otto Clarke and I see almost eye to eye. This is partially because of our all having to argue with Gaitskell, who is very doubtful about whether we are right to want to go as far as we have been suggesting in our relations to convertibility in EPU and to the USA generally. He wants to see sterling inconvertible (except for strictly controlled trans-actions with the dollar area, and the dollar ration for the sterling area) – no gold settlements with anyone else and no relaxations at all at any rate until it is proved that there won't be a US slump. This would be an almost impossible starting point for any further talks with the US and would be regarded by them as a reversal of our policy up to date, which has been a factor in getting both the loan and ERP aid of which we made a point last August. It is difficult to start a new set of talks here with someone who doesn't share the background and general strategical plans on which we have been going.

The Budget is tomorrow. I had to come back on Saturday for meet-ings on it and to stay till Sunday morning to look at the next (and practically final) revise. It seems fairly clear that there will be an attack from the left on the ground that the whole approach is too austere and deflationary. Seers has an article in *Tribune*.

Friday, April 21st

The Speech was far too long but better received than I feared. The mood was obviously much more favourable than last year. There have been two days' debate, but no real criticism that was worth anything. Tony Crosland in a very good maiden speech said that the Chancellor had calculated all the figures too severely and also that he ought to have used the petrol money [from an increased duty on petrol] to help the cost of living, because wages were the worst problem.

I was rather gratified to be asked to go to the talks with the US next week. We have been looking at some FO papers and urging that our economy is so strained that we cannot afford even our present foreign policy. Both E.P. and W.S. wanted to go and compromised on me.

Tuesday, April 25th

The main debate on the Budget ended last night. Winston made a long speech but it was not very intelligible. He does not know any economics at all and says the most extraordinary things. I think we have got through very well and now we will see what happens to wages and to unemployment. My own guess is that exports will keep us going but that we will have an easier Budget next year.

Wednesday, April 26th

The talks with US officials began on Monday (24th) with a long dreary meeting in which we agreed that we both wanted to contain Russia and that China was a bad show (i.e. the coming to power of the Communists and expulsion of Chiang Kai Chek to Formosa (Taiwan)). There was little in it that would not have been heard at a second-rate intellectual after-dinner talk. Yesterday we did a bit better and began to touch on economic problems, which we are to explore today in a smaller group. They have Jessup, Perkins, Holmes, Labouisse, Stinebower [all State Dept]: and we Strang, [Gladwyn] Jebb, Makins, Hoyer Millar [all Foreign Office], Plowden and me. Jessup mentioned convertibility etc. and also said that we must not make viability a sacred cow to put before all else.[20]

Thursday, April 27th

Plowden and I and Makins saw Labouisse, Stinebower and Berger in the FO all yesterday morning. I explained our ideas about viability and our fears about being deflated by the US and said that this made us cautious but that we considered that it was in our best interests to get level and even if this led to domestic troubles for them, they must try to understand. They made a great deal of what they called 'the public relations job' implying that we must do things we didn't like to help in the process of educating US opinion. Afterwards we talked it over and felt that there was still a big gap between us and that they hadn't taken in what we said. Labouisse got nearest to it but he is very much worried about the effect on Congress of the deterioration of our relations and keeps on saying that we are in danger of losing more by ill-will than we gain by economies.

Friday, April 28th

Yesterday E.B. had a meeting to discuss a note I had drafted about wage policy. S.C. is to see the TUC again shortly and we wanted him to say that it was a problem but that it needed working out, and leave officials to try it first of all. It is interesting to see how conscious everyone has now become of the problem – once a thing gets really identified, before long everyone is talking about it. In the afternoon we had another go at explaining our position to the US people, and I gave them an account of the fiscal outlook to prove that we could not afford any more on defence. I doubt if they took in the views on viability. Meanwhile H.G. has persuaded Stafford to accept *his* version of the 'fundamentals' talks – and EPC is to take it next week.

Tuesday, May 2nd

I wrote a long minute to S.C. dissenting from the fundamentals paper [EPC(50)44] – and sent copies to H.G., also to R. Makins and Max Nicholson to help them brief the Foreign Secretary and the LP. Also spoke to Caplan who is briefing Wilson. I do not think this will do much good except for the Foreign Secretary. Everyone else is either too feeble to stand up to anything or inclined to think that a tough line would be just the thing for the Americans. It is really rather frightful that they should be allowed to play with dynamite like this and reverse our economic policy just for a whim of Gaitskell's, who has had little experience with the US anyway.

Meanwhile we are still talking to the officials.

Wednesday, May 17th

Last week the French launched their scheme for integrating their iron and steel industry with the Germans [the Schuman Plan]. This caused us great alarms and excursions and a paper was quickly done. Broadly the FO welcomed it, so did the Chiefs of Staff: while the economic departments were a little chilly. I argued that it was absurd to discuss it in itself: if they could carry it through it would change the face of Europe. Ministers apparently all thought it was a plot but argued at length about why it was hatched. However Attlee had had to give it a welcome in the House before the meeting took place, though he was not very warm.

Monnet came over that day and talked to Plowden at great length and yesterday P. saw me and we agreed that we ought to back it. Last night P. had me to dine with Monnet, Bridges, Rowlands [Perm. Sec., Ministry of Supply], Fergusson, also G. Crowther and R. A. Sinclair, [President, FBI].

The general discussion gradually got more favourable and by the end everyone had agreed that we ought to join if we could do so on suitable terms. This morning Bridges had a meeting and it was agreed to recommend to Ministers that we should participate in the first discussions, and that if possible we should agree to join if they met our conditions: or if we wouldn't do this, we should make it clear at once. I found this encouraging, especially the attitude of Rowlands. Fergusson is coming along slowly. [Stephen] Holmes representing Board of Trade very negative as usual.

Meanwhile Ministers had gone ahead, as at an EPC yesterday they had practically decided on the same line. So all the stern resolves of P. and I to see it through were hardly needed. But there is a great deal of work and fighting yet. Monnet makes it clear that he has no concrete ideas yet and indeed he wants a treaty agreeing to join the thing first, and then experts to work out the details later. This is part of his general belief that no real progress can be made in Europe without a high political act first – if you leave it to the working level you will always bog down, and then fail on detail. Plowden has had every meal with Monnet since he arrived and is getting weary of it.

I had to see the Chancellor this morning about buffer stocks, where the Economic Section has disagreed with everyone else about the price limits for the proposed tin agreement. He showed me a long paper Harold Wilson had written about future relations between Government and private industry: and P. and B. Gilbert and I discussed it with him in the House at 4.30. It was rather a weak paper as one would expect from that disappointing source. It said that direct controls were not making private industry efficient and went over various possibilities, ending with the idea of having a Government director on the board of all the key firms in GB.

S.C. obviously didn't think much of it. I don't know if they intended to discuss it at the Labour Party weekend at Dorking or not. It hadn't been seen by anyone at the Board of Trade.

On the buffer stocks, we held out and got the EPC to approve the paper but to hold out on the buffer stock question and the method of operation. It seemed to me that all Departments had forgotten the principles which had been agreed earlier from 1943 on. So the Economic Section is going to start to re-educate them again.[21]

Thursday, May 25th

Marjolin has been here all the week selling us his scheme for a new OEEC Report to cover the next 4/5 years and to show what is needed if Europe is to expand strongly in that period. He feels that this is essential politically and that only something of this kind can retain American interest in W. Europe to a sufficient extent. If it is properly done it should link up with the Gordon Gray Report on what the US needs to do to balance its payments.[22]

Gaitskell gave a lunch yesterday for Marjolin and I found myself next to Harold Wilson who has practically cut me since he became President of the Board of Trade which is very silly of him: and the fact that it could happen explains why his stock is falling and why he who was once thought to be the obvious next Chancellor, is not now so regarded. However we got on well enough then and talked a good deal about films.

Just before Monnet went, Uri[23] came to see me and told me that the

Monnet idea was primarily that there should be complete freedom of movement of steel and coal within the area of the participating countries, and that the main authority of the new central mechanism would be to ensure this. Otherwise it would be mainly a place for consultation though clearly any large new steel works would only be started if it could be fitted in. There would be no direct orders about individual plants – they would have to endure the market conditions and close down if they were not economical. In fact the new body would work rather like the BISF – a sort of cartel but based mainly on free trade and laissez–faire. The reconversion funds would come from a levy and be used *only* to help to modernize or convert plants that would fit in to the new conditions. *Not* to compensate those which they compelled to close down. On the wage question he was very indefinite. Later Plowden spoke to Monnet who was not nearly as clear as this and gave P. the impression that he disowned Uri.

Friday, May 26th

I am off to Washington tomorrow for about 10 days. Wilson Smith has gone already. It is mainly a refresher visit for us both but we want to talk a bit to the US Treasury people and especially to exchange ideas about next steps. Before we went we saw S.C. and H.G. and got rather looser instructions than we had thought previously. The main problem is that the reserves are rising quickly and it is likely both that the next ERP will be cut, and that there will be a good deal of pressure about Article 9 of the Loan Agreement. My own view is that we ought to decide the next steps jointly and choose the ones most likely to ease relations. It is absolutely essential that we should do nothing that would lead to another crisis of convertibility or anything else. But equally we don't want to exacerbate relations any more than we can help.

I had a talk to Plowden and he told me a number of things. That S.C. is likely to go in July as he is completely exhausted; that he will probably be succeeded by H.M. keeping H.G. where he is, to train on – he isn't ripe yet; that H.W. is teaming up with Nye B. because he feels he is losing ground as against H.G.: but that this won't do him any good.

While I was there a messenger arrived with a letter from Monnet, in which he explained his plan in more detail, exactly on the lines that Uri had put to me. It is a pity he didn't say so when he was here. I doubt if M. really understands it though I am sure that his deeper feelings are right. Strath has been put in charge of a working party to conduct the negotiations and to work out the implications for us.

Petrol rationing ended today. We accepted the Standard/NJ offer to supply all the petrol needed, or rather their share of it, at no dollar cost. Caltec did too. It will cost us about $8 mn for the marginal dollar cost of what the British companies will have to bring in.

Points rationing is gone too, so there isn't much left now except the basic foods.[24]

P. asked me to talk to Oliver about the defence problem which hasn't had much impact in the UK yet. I had taken Jo Alsop to dinner there a week ago and we had both tried to put a sense of urgency into him. The trouble is that we are so pre-occupied with the internal situation that we have been holding down tight on defence. Now it seems that there is much less time than we thought, because of China and the atom bomb: so we must change our priorities. But there isn't much feeling of urgency yet and in particular we don't know what we must do as part of getting the US to take the main load.[25]

Otherwise things are well in hand for the moment. The reserves are rising all too quickly. Exports are high. The cost of living has not risen nearly as fast as everyone but the Economic Section expected. Wages have been held down far better than anyone thought. Unemployment is still falling seasonally in spite of Seers and Crosland. In fact devaluation, the autumn cuts, and the Budget have all been as successful as anyone could have hoped. But to stop us being 'dizzy with success', there are a number of gloomy prospects for the future.

(a) The wages position may get out of hand. It seems clear that there will have to be modification anyway. The cost of living is bound to rise at least two points more before the end of the year.

(b) The first run-over of the Committee of Four makes it look as if the terms of trade will be far worse this year than we forecast.[26] The US boom, which is partly why the reserves are rising so well, is mainly responsible. But export prices are rising more slowly than we expected.

(c) We are almost bound to run into trouble with the capital goods industries expanding so fast and cannot yet see how to hold them down. So we are headed for a somewhat painful readjustment: though I do not mind very much if we can make it without causing too much of a fall in productivity.

(d) We are still overloaded in the sense that there is very little margin and nothing likely to give at all easily. The only things that would really help would be a big change in the terms of trade, or a big fall in the investment programme.

Tuesday, June 6th (British Embassy, Washington)

I am writing a few notes in Jukes' room while waiting to see O.S.F. and I hope a few other people. I am going to New York this afternoon and crossing to London tomorrow morning. W.S. went to Canada on Sunday and is crossing by sea on June 8th.

It has been a very interesting time. Jo Alsop lent me his house but I did not manage to entertain anyone there, or be in for anything but breakfast.

W.S. and I had several talks with Martin, Willis and Glendinning of the US Treasury. And I have seen Gordon Gray [Special Ass. to Pres.] Keyserling [Chairman, CEA], Ed Mason, Walter Salant and several other CEA people. I have not called officially on State or ECA and Paul

Nitze is the only man on that side I have seen at all to talk to. I've talked a good deal to Rowan, Jukes, Caine, Christelow and HE and been to a number of our UK meetings. W.S. was concerned mainly with immediate problems on ECA and the persistent rise of the reserves: he and I were both concerned about the future of the Loan Agreement, while I have been trying to find out about the state of business here and the outlook, and the whole Gordon Gray set-up. Everyone has been as hospitable as usual.

General Observations. These are also based on talks to Walter Lippmann and Stewart Alsop [American commentators]. The economic situation is at least for the moment of far less importance than it has been. The European recovery has made the atmosphere better and especially devaluation, which has removed a fruitful cause of suspicion and conflict and has in itself (so far) produced much better results than anyone expected. The combination of US recovery and European (especially UK) progress, with the more realistic American attitude, has produced an atmosphere in which our short-run economic problems ought to be quite capable of settlement. Further, the political situation is deteriorating, in that SE Asia is likely to go more against us than for us, and there is no confidence in Europe, particularly in France, Italy and W. Germany, that we can settle our defence well enough to give them a fair chance of survival. In each of these countries morale is low and the people concerned are anxious to know which side will win before they will select one. Thus the task of preparing for defence and strengthening the democracies will require all our energies and we should not allow ourselves to be distracted by economic issues, which are now minor ones. The main things are (a) to keep up the level of production, (b) to avoid strains, (c) to remove causes of irritation. (b) and (c) may come into conflict but it is the task of the statesman to remove the conflict.

Lippmann was still a bit concerned about sterling balances, on which he had made a stand. He was worried (so was Alsop) about our reaction to the Schuman Plan, mainly because it showed lack of leadership. He thought (and I agree) that whatever we might lose economically or in internal inconvenience was nothing to the possible gains. On the war front, he felt strongly with *The Economist* that we ought to say more about the fact that we were preserving peace than preparing for war.

Stewart Alsop developed a good deal the theme that this was a crisis of leadership. Truman with all his merits had no real vocation, otherwise he would not be able to say two (different) things at the same time so often. However I felt that the Alsops and Lippmann were closer together than one would have thought from recent columns.

O.S.F. is rather too cheerful. The UK recovery makes him think all our troubles are over. He wanted my views on where to go next on the Agreement etc., but didn't seem to think that we need worry too much. His idea is that nothing can happen on defence until October at the earliest and what is the good of worrying.

Leslie Rowan is almost in a demoralized state. He has a lovely house and a charming wife and he entertains very well but he is not quite the man for his job. He feels that he is not getting adequate instructions and yet he won't make any move to get better ones: and there is a constant feeling in his mind that he is not doing a proper job. He was upset because we talked fundamentals in London and somewhat upset that W.S. and I came to talk them here. There are really two troubles: (1) he is neither an economist nor has had the long background on their stuff to make him move easily. So he feels in his heart that their material is rather second-hand and maybe he doesn't know it too well. And (2) he is a very good civil servant in the sense that he is trained to carry out instructions rather rigidly even if he does not like them, and won't stick his neck out as some of us will.

It is a great dilemma. Obviously no civil servant should make policy because that is for Parliament. This *sounds* fine, but Parliament makes policy much worse if it isn't led and equally Ministers lead much worse if their experts don't help them. My own view is that there is no solution except to get men you can trust. That is why H.G.'s incursions have caused such confusion. He doesn't trust the Treasury or the Bank but he can't get a new set of chaps and when they feel that he is against their policy they feel hamstrung in carrying out either theirs or his.

S. Caine is very wise and sensible but no real fire in his belly. When we talk about the situation or the steps we should take I agree almost entirely with him. But when we are taking the steps he does not seem to have his heart in them. Christelow seems to me to get better and better. Jukes whom I lent to Rowan is good but shy and needs to know more people and also to open his mouth wider (literally). I get a little deafer as I get older and find both Jukes and Rowan speak far too softly especially if there are others in the room.

We talked a good deal both with the Treasury and the UKTD [Treasury Delegation] about the future of the Financial Agreement [of 1945]. Martin was very pleased by Stafford's reply to Snyder's letter, in effect asking for official consultations. The main problem is really that Articles 8 and 9 run out at Dec. 31st 1951 and Snyder will have to give an account of his stewardship to Congress before then. His letter was indeed mainly for the record. Martin feels, and I think Glendinning and Willis, that no one would expect us to get to full convertibility or non-discrimination by then: but that it is in our own interests that we should make some progress. I feel sure this is right myself and at a lunch one day tried to explain how we saw it and that we were alive to the dangers of getting the world economy distorted through paying too much for non-dollar supplies, for too long.

The first nine months after devaluation had gone well and it looked as if the United Kingdom would soon be able to dispense with external aid for the first time since the war and yet preserve full employment. The political situation on the other hand was deteriorating in Asia and Europe, morale was low and there was no confidence that Europe would be able to defend itself against Russian aggression.

In May and June three major issues arose more or less simultaneously. The first was the need to decide what to do about the Schuman Plan.

Ministers and officials were at first disposed to join but were unwilling to commit themselves without knowing what powers over the British coal and steel industries they would be surrendering. The government had already decided in October 1949 'not to involve themselves in the affairs of Europe beyond the point from which they could, if they wished, withdraw' (CP(49)203). A second issue was arrangements for a European Payments Union. These were coming to a head early in 1950. The British position, which had been a major obstacle to agreement, underwent a radical change in the first half of May and a settlement establishing the Union was reached early in July. A third issue was defence. On June 25th came the beginning of the Korean War, an event that brought on rearmament on the grand scale and dominated economic policy in 1950–1.

In assessing the economic impact and limits of rearmament, Hall played a major part: it was the Economic Section that prepared the key documents. When the initial moves were made, it was understood that the United States would underwrite any balance of payments difficulties. From this position the US retreated step by step. First it proposed instead a formula – named after Paul Nitze, an American official – for sharing the financial burden between the Allied powers; this involved an elaborate statistical exercise covering all the members of NATO. The formula was later interpreted to deny aid to countries whose reserves were increasing (as Britain's were in 1951). Meanwhile, under American pressure, the defence programme was expanded in January 1951 well beyond what had been said to be feasible in August 1950. To a programme of £780 million a year before Korea additions were made bringing the total planned expenditure in the three financial years 1951–3 first to £3,400 million in August, then to £3,600 million in September, and finally to £4,700 million in January 1951 (this excluded £450 million for the accumulation of stocks of key raw materials).

On top of this, rearmament in America pushed up the price of raw materials to record heights and created shortages of many of them. At first these high prices allowed the other members of the sterling area to pay dollars into the pool, causing both the reserves and sterling liabilities to grow. From the middle of 1951, however, the primary producing countries of the outer sterling area drew dollars from the pool to finance the additional imports they could now afford. At the same time the rearmament boom and the swing in the terms of trade produced a large deficit in the British balance of payments. The reserves drained away in the second half of 1951 faster than they had accumulated in the first half. A balance of payments crisis ensued that was as serious as the convertibility crisis of 1947.

Tuesday, June 20th

The main troubles since I have been back were with the Schuman Plan, the Labour Party Executive Statement on European integration, and EPU. Marcus, who got a CMG in the Birthday Honours, has been away with pneumonia and I have been away several days, so that yesterday was my first settled one. Strath had done a good but slightly inconclusive report on Schuman which we took yesterday morning at EPB [CP(50)128]. A small attendance and no great progress. The general feeling was that a consultative body, such as Strath proposed, could be useful but not one with complete powers. The biggest difficulty seems to me to be with a full employment economy – how can one keep this up if one has no power over the heavy industries. The talks open in Paris today but we don't expect them to come to much.

I had lunch with E.N.P. and he discussed the UK strength and how G. Crowther was so disappointed that there was no collapse that he had openly said in *The Economist* that we must *hope* for one. Both E.P. and I feel very disappointed about G. as two years ago we felt we saw eye to eye about everything.

Wednesday, June 21st

Things are fairly quiet and I managed to talk to a number of people yesterday. At 2/Secs. E.B. talked about next week's debate on Schuman and the spot the Government are in because of the document about Labour Policy and Europe.[27] We all felt that this might well be made a serious issue (because of the expression about Socialist Governments being able to co-operate only with one another) and wondered if the Government understood it. It is awkward to know where official duty lies in this case. We felt that some bits should be repudiated but this would be a vote of censure on Dalton and after 1947 this would not do the Government any good either. It is clear that we cannot advise Ministers to criticize one another.

Monday, June 26th

There was a meeting of the War Economy Committee last Wednesday.[28] It was rather depressing because all the civilians seemed to understand the problem very well and the soldiers, because they felt that if they made forecasts these would be unreliable, felt that forecasts were no use. They could not see that to a civilian planner, who needed up to 3 years to do anything, all one did implied a forecast and it might as well be looked at. A little point is lent to all this by the fact that fighting began in Korea on Sunday and I suppose it might bring on the war. Something will.

Wednesday, June 28th

At 2nd Secs. yesterday we discussed Korea. Everyone but I thought that the US would not be willing to do anything as it could have no effect (on the development in Korea itself). I felt sure that the US would not face the overthrow of their foreign policy. At 11.30 W.S. had a meeting on the Financial Agreement and I asked Berthoud [Ass. Under Secretary of State, FO] if the US were moving. He said no. But he called me at 3 p.m. to say that it had now been decided to give 100% support, and on the tape at 5.30 this was confirmed by the beginning of Truman's announcement. It is a very great relief and may well be a turning point in the history of this period. If it stops the USSR they will lose, and the US gain, a great deal of face. If not, we will have the war when on the whole I think we are relatively stronger now than we will be later.

Otherwise things are fairly quiet. Wages are going on gently with the TUC and I feel sure that HMG should make no pronouncement without consulting them. H.G. wants a Government policy and Kaldor has written a paper advocating an agreed total advance each year and also an ingenious scheme for having dividend limitation. The maximum to be the present rate or x% of the equity earnings whichever is greater.

Thursday, June 29th

Yesterday, E.P., Brittain, Otto and I saw S.C. and H.G. about the brief for the NIFE Report at ECOSOC.[29] N. Kaldor had been to see me about it previously and E.P. and I had told H.G. that we thought the brief fairly good but not warm enough. The meeting was a great success as far as I was concerned. The Chancellor said that Gaitskell must go to Geneva – this turned out well anyhow as Younger [Minister of State, Foreign Office] has to stay with Korea on and Bevin still away ill. Both Ministers wanted us to be much more enthusiastic, to press for follow-up action, and to try hard to get the US and other countries not only to accept the objectives but to report fairly soon on what they could do. H.G. was very anxious that I should go with him and I suppose I must. The timing is as awkward as can be: he must be in Paris for [final agreement to establish] EPU on Wednesday and Thursday and these are the days on which it is most likely that the report will be taken. Marcus is slowly recovering from pneumonia and can't go till late. I don't want to go at all.

After that E.P., B.G., H.W. S. and I saw H.G. about two papers the M/Food and BoT/M/Supply had put in to the Production Committee on the future of controls and bulk buying. I had been asked previously to put my views down and had said that there were no general principles, only certain considerations. The main thing was the future control of balance of payments; everything else could be managed either way and it depended on Government policy. H.G. said he wanted (a) Ministers to lay down the principles to be followed, (b) an inter-departmental Committee to report on all proposals for de-control. This is of course part of his general line: he doesn't want to give up any controls he can help and he doesn't want to give any discretion in this field to either other Ministers or Civil Servants. Nothing settled at the meeting.

In the morning we had had another go at the question of fundamentals and next steps, arising from a Rowan telegram about the first meeting with US Treasury on the Financial Agreement. It was the same old ground and the same obstacle namely H. G. himself. However a paper is to be put up.

In the afternoon the Defence Committee authorized the C.-in-C. Far East to put his fleet at MacArthur's disposal and agreed to urge all the Commonwealth to play along. It all seems wonderful to me and the whole situation is transformed. If the US stick to the line, they have gained the moral and the effective leadership of the West and we shall gain millions of those waiting to get on the band-wagon in Europe and the Far East. The USSR must put up or, not exactly shut up, but at least pipe down.

On Tuesday, I dined at the Tuesday Club. This time first at Brown's, and very nice though less wine. Hubert Henderson made a most extraordinary address about how we couldn't get back to international equilibrium without using the gold standard technique, i.e. deflate and raise interest rates when you lose gold. He ruled out devaluation: said nothing on unemployment but obviously hoped that it would produce very little. I was glad to find that most people disagreed with him. It is always a comfort at such gatherings to find how little outsiders have thought of that we haven't.

The TUC took off the wage freeze today. Still great discussions about the proper policy – I think we are all right as we are for the present.

The BC decided to recommend a new Royal Commission on the effect of direct taxes – mainly the effect on industry and incentive.[30]

Friday, June 30th

It was learned yesterday that the US Senate had not yet confirmed Lubin, their new ECOSOC representative, and they wanted the NIFE Report put off until July 17th. So I won't have to go. Weintraub came to see me on his way from Lake Success to Geneva and we had a long talk.

I had a busy day. First Burke Knapp who is trying to get staff for the Bank (IBRD). Then there was an urgent meeting held by Bridges because S.C. wanted to put out a new White Paper on wages to offset the TUC document – practically setting up a Central Council of guidance. Ince said this would be a national disaster and we agreed that the big job was to keep the TUC alive.

Roll and Hall-Patch lunched with me and told me that our lack of a foreign economic policy was very unfortunate – Schuman, Stikker [Dutch Foreign Minister, author of the Stikker Plan for sectoral integration], USA etc. Later Otto Clarke talked to me on the same lines and we agreed to try to write a paper. He gave me several bits he had written. His idea is that we are now in a position to lead all the non-US world and get even the US going in the way we want, but that the trouble with H.G. (he takes so long to persuade) will make us miss the boat. As usual, a good deal of sense and a lot of wild stuff.

Monday, July 3rd

S.C. made the wage statement today but it was a piece of luck that it did *not* contain proposals for a Central Body as he wanted to put them in. E.N.P. tried hard to persuade him but it was only after they brought in Vincent Tewson that he was fixed. No doubt he inclines to doctrinaire solutions and is encouraged in this by Gaitskell. This will just confirm the TUC in their idea that he does not understand the working class mind.

Wednesday, July 5th

At 2nd Secs. yesterday I urged the Kaldor view on dividend limitation and I think it may go. Long talk to Plowden. We think that we ought to spend something on re-armament and that if we put it on the engineering industries it can be stood.

Tuesday, July 11th

Yesterday E.P. and I visited Sir A. Rowlands at M/Supply – I had not been in Shell-Mex for years but it looks much the same, all the corridors that I saw blown down so often still in their temporary repairs. We put our point about re-armament – if possible without expanding, if possible without affecting the export trade – and on the whole he agreed and said he would set up a private working party to investigate. This morning at 2nd Secs. E.B. mentioned the strategic reserves and I took the opportunity to say that I thought we were mad to be running down stocks and that we ought to build them up. N. Brook said that nothing was being done except a CoS (Chiefs of Staff) appreciation of the new prospect: but he thought we should plan for the probable, which is thought to be intensification in Korea, Hong Kong, Malaya etc. I thought it was much more dangerous than this. The US was committed and would have to go on, so that USSR must back down or carry through. In the end we decided (a) to push on with strategic reserves – I got permission to talk to Fennelly, (b) to get an appreciation, (c) N.B. to have a meeting at which he would put the stocks point. As far as I can see only E.P. and I feel at all worried.

A good deal else going on in spite of my feeling that all is quiet. We had a Section meeting yesterday on the economic situation, where the retail stock position begins to look almost disinflationary. However we all agreed that there was no need to do anything yet, especially as unemployment falling normal for the season, and the need to keep exports up. The economic situation is really immensely good just now – devaluation paid off handsomely, wages still steady, prices not up much in spite of the worsening of the terms of trade, and exports booming. Downie is doing a preview for the Budget Committee [BC(50)17].

I have done a note on internal, and Otto on external policy for the 3rd

OEEC Report. The main problems are the amount and split of the national income, and whether any structural changes will be needed. Not much doubt that one of them will be in engineering. On the split, do we assume same or rising investment, what about taxes, what about the foreign balance? Otto and I have agreed that we must assume the necessary imports and take the right steps to get the exports. The big external problem is to decide what to say about convertibility. Meanwhile Otto has shown me privately a paper he has done on next steps with USA. The right lines, i.e. going for an expanding world with planned foreign trade. But the time-table is impossibly short. We *must* talk to the US first not as Otto suggests launch it on everyone at once. And that can't be done within the next three months.

Marcus is back and has revised Nita's draft for H.G. to deliver on the NIFE Report at Geneva next Monday. We are gradually getting quite a warm line into it. David Butt back from Australia and full of energy; Dow back from Paris ditto. No doubt this policy of sending people abroad is paying off handsomely: they all seem so much better when they come back.

Thursday, July 13th

Yesterday was quite interesting. In the morning Marcus and I saw H.G. about Geneva and more or less agreed a line. He said that HMG were thinking of introducing a Full Employment Bill for political reasons! and hence that it might be useful to accept more obligations than we otherwise might have done. The big problem is what to say on the external side: we can't promise to stabilize investment irrespective of all else. In the afternoon P. took a special meeting about the 3rd Report which went off quite amicably – it is very interesting that there should be so much agreement about planning, and about how to put things to Ministers in the hope that they won't take decisions too much against what officials consider the national interest. I must write something about this some day.

There is no doubt at all that in these days of no clear policy, no high official thinks that he is carrying out Government policy – he thinks his job is to cajole Ministers, or bully or cheat them, into doing the right thing. This is not to be wondered at since most Ministers try to cheat themselves and officials especially by the unscrupulous use of statistics. Fortunately we have the statisticians on our side: I don't know what we would do if we got a statistician as Chancellor. It is bad enough to have H.G. who is fairly well on to the figures, but who has at least some conscience in using them.

After that S.C. had a meeting in the House, where nearly all meetings with Ministers are now, of H.W.S., E.B., E.P. and me, with the three Treasury Ministers. They had just come from the Production Committee and I gathered that bulk purchase etc. had been settled on the lines of my note. I haven't seen the minutes yet. But they were all in a good humour. W.E. and Customs and I tried to get some more tobacco – the

Customs think we are substituting too fast and this is helping the decline in consumption. But needless to say we were turned down. However S.C. is much better and P. told me lately that he is not going to resign after all but take three months' leave. The PM persuaded him to this.

Tuesday, July 18th

Yesterday I went to a meeting of the Defence (T) Committee to hear an appraisal of the situation. This was given by Sir P. Dixon of the Foreign Office and was very carefully balanced so that anything might happen. However the view seemed to be that the most likely was on a limited scale, e.g. Korea and bits and pieces of pressure on Hong Kong, Malaya, Persia etc. The Permanent Secs. had little to say on this except that it would be easier to do anything with some warning. It was decided to put up a paper with some recommendations, probably on strategic materials and making a start on production, for which the CoS are to make a list. I had a talk with E.P., J. H. Woods and N.B. after and they agreed that the Chancellor's remarks at EPC (we had discussed this with him on Thursday) were enough even to submit a programme on a tonnage basis. I dined with Fennelly at the Union later and told him to push on fast with the strategic materials and make early recommendations – and to start at once on a general import survey, any ton as good as another except that the longer the haul the better. He as always is absolutely first rate at this and will go straight ahead. I offered to lend him a man if he needed one and hope he will accept.

This morning saw L. Rowan at 2nd Secs., just here on a short trip from Washington. He confirmed that US thinking was now dominated by Korea and that we had a good chance to be treated as partners if we did our stuff. O. had asked him to say that now was our chance to earn a lot of dollars. I pointed out that we could only do this if we found something to earn them with.

Later on E.B. had a meeting on wages. There had been one the previous week and after it was over I wrote a long Minute to him saying that I thought the White Paper HMG wants to issue should be on Employment Policy, with the wage issue in that context, rather than on wages as such. It was HMG's duty to explain to the public (a) its policy, (b) what it thought might be done in any year. B.G. revised his paper on the lines suggested. I felt a little annoyed to find the whole thing recast, largely in my words, without any reference to me at all. However I suppose one should be content if one's policy is accepted.

Thursday, July 20th

Colin Clark came to see me on Tuesday evening. I had not seen him for years and found him very stimulating, but fuller than ever of wild ideas. He began by saying that we would have to export 10% of the GNP by 1950 as capital exports – he didn't say why. He also said we could not stand present tax rates without inflation, that wages were getting out of hand so that we would have to devalue again, and that the terms of trade were bound to get much worse before long. I did not have much trouble with any of these points except the last with which I am inclined to agree. But on the whole I felt that he was not aware of what was going on in England at all, and took no notice either of the productivity increases or of the general policy on wages and dividends.

S.C. had a meeting yesterday on the 3rd Report, which EPC is taking today. As H.G. was still away, we managed to get accepted the doctrine of limited convertibility based on continued discrimination and parallel dollar austerity. Campion is very much disturbed that we are taking the 4% productivity hypothesis but the Chancellor is determined to have it and I must say that this year's experience supports him.[31] It is really rather epoch-making, if Ministers accept it, that we have got back to a workable convertibility doctrine. But a great deal of persuasion will be needed to get the US and indeed other countries to accept it. I think we could do it if we linked it very closely to the dollars which they would allow us to earn.

Thursday, August 31st

I have been on leave for three of the last six weeks and have written nothing. Meanwhile there has been a revolution in our interests and pre-occupations. At the end of July, while I was in France, the US asked us what we would do to prepare to defend ourselves and how much more we could do if they helped us. We replied that we could go from £780 mn a year to £950 mn on our own, and could add physically up to about £1,110 mn if they would find the difference. But after that Ministers decided to spend £70 mn a year on service pay. Everything is now in a state of extreme confusion, in two main respects: (1) where do we stand as to orders actually placed, authority to commit, and what assurances, if any, have we got from the US; (2) where are these matters being discussed, and what is the seat of authority? There is the Tripartite organization in Washington, ECA, who say that they have the authority to administer Mutual Aid Defense Funds and who still operate to some extent in Paris; the NATO deputies who are in London; and all sorts of conversations on the side.

Monday, September 4th

P. back today. I worked all the weekend at the economic effects of the defence programme. The picture has come out only too well – for the US aspect. The main burden is taken by reducing our exports on the one hand and letting rising import costs affect the standard of living on the other.

Meanwhile the US have thrown almost a bombshell since Spofford announced on Saturday that US aid to NATO, of about $4 bn was nearly all for the supply of finished items from the US. Only about $475 mn was for direct aid, mainly materials and components from the US, and even this was conditional on the European powers spending $3½ bn which is much less than they have announced so far, i.e. the most one can get is less than one-sixth of the total. This is so different from our thinking that it has produced a crisis; and in a minor way made it almost impossible to write the speech on economic effects for the debate next week.

Tuesday, September 5th

We saw the ECA Americans in the afternoon and confirmed that they couldn't do much for us. They were clearly disturbed at the situation and have been trying to get something out of Washington. Afterwards Bridges had a meeting about the debate etc. I said I did not know what could be said in the speech and Leslie was turned on to write it. We are between the horns of two dilemmas: (a) If we say we can't get anything out of the US it will be bad for relations. But if we don't, we can't explain to the House or the country the lacunae in our preparations; (b) If we say that the impact is small it will not help us in our case to the US. If we say it is severe it will spread alarm and despondency among the Government supporters here, who are already being squeezed by rising prices and will be squeezed worse.

Everything is in frightful confusion in our thoughts, in our actions and in our organization. However it does not matter at all (unless there is a war this year when it would be changed anyway) for the underlying economic position is very good.

Thursday, September 7th

Spent most of yesterday drafting a paper for Ministers about defence. It recommends (a) going on with next slice (but I think Shinwell is doing that anyway), (b) telling US that we must have more help than seems likely on their current formula, (c) but that we think we can get on with £350 mn instead of £550 mn.[32] It will be taken by ED [W?] this afternoon [EPB(50)16].

Friday, September 8th

We had a lot of anxiety about the paper because of the difficulty of showing that £350 mn was the right amount. P. in a flap, largely because we had let the overall balance go. Gaitskell took it in the afternoon and upbraided us for the same reason. It was very refreshing to find a Minister telling us that we were not doing enough for once. Worked on the speech also. It keeps on being shifted back and forth but the present idea is that the PM should open.

Tuesday, September 12th

Friday's Cabinet took the same line, that officials were being wildly optimistic and not caring for the balance of payments. I had to stay all day Saturday. In the morning to discuss the speech H.G. was to make and also various points arising. In the afternoon discussed with P. and Strath the line G. was to take in NY. Ministers decided someone should go and brief Bevin on economic questions, and Strath flew off last night. He is very good.

I wrote various bits for H.G.'s speech at the weekend but he didn't seem too pleased by them yesterday afternoon when we talked to him. A weekend of work altered him a great deal. On Friday he was fresh and vigorous but yesterday already seemed tired and less clear. 2nd Secs. was yesterday morning (Monday instead of Tuesday), very unusual. In the afternoon after H.G., N. Brook had a meeting about stockpiling etc. How to discuss with the US and conceal it from the French.

Friday, September 15th

The debate went off all right and H.G. took a very firm line against inflation, though P. and I urged him only to do so if he was prepared to stick to it and reminded him how often his colleagues had run away.[33] Unfortunately all this is rather marred by the decision to go on with steel nationalization. I gathered that only Attlee and Morrison were against it. It does seem folly at this time to do something no one really wants, and when the industry itself is beating all records.

A ridiculous 'bus strike going on against employing more women – a very good example of the monopolistic tendencies of workers.

Wednesday, September 20th

Still a great deal of confusion about what is going on. E.B. had a meeting on Friday to agree the new organization – a new Ministerial Committee (P.M., L.P., C.E., F.S., M.D.) – then a new Steering Committee, Bridges, Plowden, Brook, Hall, Makins, Rowlands, Woods, Parker, Ince, to take over from ED. Then a new Committee under Hitch to be called the Mutual Aid Committee. Secretariat all from Cabinet Office: and under this what is left of London Committee. Various strings out to AO Committee, JWPC, Strategic Materials, Economy in a Future War. The great thing is to get the Secretariat to see all the papers. Meanwhile we are dealing very blindly from day to day with major issues. The US have suggested that common defence efforts should be shared after some national income investigation.

Tuesday, September 26th

On Monday morning came a flood of telegrams from Washington and Bridges had a meeting about them at 11.15. We saw Gaitskell at 12.30. The purport was that they couldn't give us £550 mn or any fixed sum but would try hard to find us sums on account by various procedures, and have a general National Income investigation of all the countries in NATO including themselves, about the cost. Gaitskell approved this and seems to have squared the PM. It seems to me an important matter on which to reverse the Cabinet (from the idea of a fixed sum in advance) without consulting them.[34]

Plowden and I are going to Washington on October 3rd, W.S. on the 4th and H.G. on the 6th. We three had a meeting about it last night. He (H.G.) is very keen to appear as an economist and perhaps settle the formula by which contributions to NATO will be assessed. But there is no one anywhere near his level in Washington who understands these things and one of our problems is to stop him committing HMG to people too low in the hierarchy to be able to commit the US. Otherwise we thought it would be useful if he had a talk on fundamentals.

3rd Report. Great confusion about this because the NATO exercise will be the same for the NATO countries. Bissell wants to keep Marjolin in the picture. I probably have to go to Paris tomorrow to try to see Bissell about this.

My main concern on all this is that the UK should not commit itself on the prospects until the end of the year. I sent a Minute to Gaitskell which he accepted making this point and we have told Paris. And we did another on the Survey, arguing that we did not want to reach any decision before December at earliest and that we should then put a skeleton (i.e. mainly statistical) survey to Ministers. No balance of payments recommendations until then.

Wednesday, September 27th

Max Nicholson called this morning. He said that Nye B. was trying to split the Labour Party by arguing that defence could only be financed by reduced social services or by a capital levy or other drastic tax. Was this right? If not, the LP should be told before the Party Conference at Margate (next week? – I haven't read the papers). I said I thought that we would not need any drastic Budget though we would probably need to be a bit more austere or accept a bit more inflationary pressure. I have to do the LP a note for this afternoon. Later I had a long talk with D.J. who hinted at the same thing, said he thought Nye wanted an early election and probably a Labour defeat, as this would improve his chances of leadership later on. He asked various questions about possible new taxes, should these be wanted – oil again, the perennial profits [tax] etc. I said I did not want to suggest anything yet. We then talked a bit about wages and I think I persuaded him that a new White Paper was what was really needed.

Then saw P. for a bit, mainly on when (if ever) we should put the points to H.G. about National Income and how tricky it was. I haven't sent a cable to Strath yet as I had promised.

In the afternoon was a great press of business. First a BC about dividend limitation. Both HF and Revenue considered that any scheme except freezing where the dividends were in a base year was unworkable. I felt unhappy about this but it is hard to tell the practical people their job. They suggest increasing profits tax and freeing dividends which I do not like.

Then saw Hitch about Paris and whether to keep or kill OEEC. Finally a long session with H.G. about our paper on wages policy. He pressed for action but in the end very mild action, a National Advisory Panel which would have to be consulted (but not obeyed) during all wage negotiations. He agreed to have a White Paper on Employment Policy and we all hope it will be a real State paper. I will put (I think) Downie to make the first draft.

Sunday, October 8th

I am writing this in Washington but have been to Paris since the last entry. I went there on Friday, Sept. 29th, the visit being postponed because Bissell was delayed. Geoffrey Wilson [Treasury] went with me. We got there for a late (and magnificent) lunch with H.P. and Roll, and then I spent most of the afternoon at the Economic Committee. Bissell spoke a good deal. In the evening H.P. gave a dinner for selected Americans, Marjolin, and some chaps from NATO countries. Bissell spoke a lot more. The upshot was that he wanted an immediate OEEC exercise on 3rd Report lines but one purpose of which would be to help ECA to take decisions on the 3rd Appropriation, since the Snoy–Marjolin formula was out of date.[35] He said he had an open mind on the question of OEEC–NATO relations, but in fact all he said was an impassioned plea for OEEC. This was warmly welcomed by the other NATO country people who seemed to resent all that had just been done in New York about which they knew very little. They mostly said OEEC was a going concern; they had no staff who could do this international economic stuff in London as well as in Paris; and anyway it would squeeze out Switzerland, Sweden and W. Germany if NATO were supported and OEEC allowed to wither and die. Bissell also suggested that the US [*sic*] resented the bilateral talks taking place between US and UK in Washington, both on the Nitze formula and on interim help for our defence programme.

I suppose that H.P. and Roll had been first hinting at this and then saying a good deal of it. But London regards them as interested parties, and H.P. and R. Makins have got across one another anyhow, so it was all new to London. And it was difficult to know whether Bissell was speaking for himself, or ECA, or for the US, especially as they have tended to tell us rather different things.

I got back late on Saturday and spent a fair amount of Monday talking about it all: we changed our line a bit but there was so much confusion about what the US really thought (since there were parallel talks going on in Washington), that it was hard to know what was right. However broadly speaking we accepted Marjolin's plan for an early study of urgent economic problems; and agreed that some work must be done on the 3rd Report: but that NATO and not OEEC must do all the work on sharing the defence burden. Meanwhile H.G. was pressing for a formula on that and Campion and Fleming produced something which he quite liked. He still does not understand that no formula can be worked out to give a predetermined result unless you know what quantities are to be put into it.

On Tuesday night, Oct. 3rd, Plowden and I set off for Washington. We had a very broken journey as first we went out to the runway, then had to come back and unload, and finally we did not get off till 9.30 a.m. on Oct. 4th. Then there were headwinds, and we stopped at Shannon, Keflavik and Gander, and only reached New York at 2.30 a.m. There was the admirable Mr Jones and he took us to a hotel and next day we got the 10.45 'plane. Rowan met us, also Jukes and Pat Young and Strath and we went to the Embassy where we stayed several days. I am now at the Shoreham and E.P. with Leslie Rowan. Gaitskell came late on Sunday night.

On Thursday, 5th, Oliver had a dinner for us: Strath, Rowan, Caine, Finletter, Labouisse, Martin, Nitze, Gordon and Bissell. In the after-noon he had cross-questioned E.P. and me about the UK economy and in his usual manner he led off after dinner with a potted version of what I had said. Then he asked what the probable size of the US defence programme would be and what its impact. The answers were very interesting but not illuminating: it seemed clear that the Services and many officials wanted to go up to $50 or $60 bn from the present about $30 bn. This would give a big jolt to the economy and probably need quite severe controls. But it could not be done until Congress was ready to approve and this would take a long time and might be difficult with the taxes and controls involved. Later talks have confirmed all this and in general I have the impression that this is very much a transitional period. They are setting up new agencies rapidly but are not sure what they will do; while we have been here they have appointed a Price Stabilizer, Valentine, and a Wage Stabilizer, Ching. Meanwhile ECA is to be made into a new Agency, like FEA was, but called OEC.[36] And I gather that it is to have wider functions and that everyone there is busy marking out a new job for himself.

On Friday night Leslie Rowan had a dinner for the same UK people plus H.W.S. who had come but there was no general talk. P. told me on the plane that W.S. was leaving at the end of this year to go to Powell Duffryn and that Leslie was to take his place. Oliver also told me and he and I had a long talk about the need to have a successor and generally to keep an adequate staff in Washington. I could only think of Helsby as a successor but I think Oliver will ask for him and refuse flatly to have S. Caine whom Bridges will want to send.

My own feeling on the UK economic position is that the effect of all this on our balance of payments is much exaggerated. Exports are keeping up extremely well, and the September figures are not so much worse than those of August. It is true that we haven't felt the full impact of the price rises yet but neither has the consumer: and my own feeling is that by now there is a real pull from the export market. Thus I would expect there to be some inflation at home but not of a kind that has very serious consequences, since the forces making for wage increases generally, or the forces holding them down, are stronger than the 'gap' is likely to be. If I am right, the most serious headache for us will be the rising cost of living, and the greatest threat to our economy actual shortages of material. Already the US have announced a large cut in exports of cotton and if this is persisted in we will soon have unemployment in Lancashire and all our hard work will be undone.

Thursday, October 12th

I have been writing this in a desultory way. Gaitskell has now been here three full days and he leaves for Canada this afternoon. He is very good with the Americans except that he *will* talk too much about things beneath his dignity, as if he were an Assistant Secretary. Yesterday, for instance, we went to see Foster and Bissell [ECA Administrator and Deputy Administrator] and he and Bissell talked for hours about the procedure on the Deputies, and the problems of assessing fair shares under the Nitze Plan; Foster obviously did not feel that he knew, or should know, enough about this to be able to join in, so he just sat there bored.

The main work here was to discuss with H.G. on the UK side, the line we should take about defence finance. We had a long meeting on Tuesday, H.G., O., W.S., E.P., Rowan and me. O. led off, I think quite unnecessarily, on the probable burden on the UK – putting the points I had made, and explaining his political thesis as in his memo to the PM etc. about getting out of the debt payments, which we had all turned down. Then we went round the table. H.G. did not accept our optimism about the balance of payments though he was interested, and of course a bit shaken by the idea that the home consumer was going to be the one to get it in the neck this time. However he accepted the main thesis, that we should let our request for £550 mn or any prior sum lapse, get any sums we could on account as the exercises went on, and wait for the result of the Nitze exercises themselves.

I suggested that we should try to get some ERP kept on in the meantime – they are talking of cutting it all off at Christmas – and we thought we might do this but I doubt if they will give us any. The rise in the gold reserves is too awkward for them and indeed we are suffering from our reluctance to spend dollars to keep them from rising. Later when H.G. saw Foster and Bissell they said that they wanted to discuss this with us, and gave us the impression that there would certainly be a cut-off at Christmas.

Thursday, October 19th

I got back last Saturday (14th) and have since then been talking about defence, raw material shortages, and the rising cost of living. Yesterday Shaw (one of the Chancellor's PS's) came to tell me that S.C. was resigning. It is to be announced tomorrow and I am to see him this morning. I feel very sorry indeed and think he has been one of the great Chancellors: it is only in the last few months, when he has not been here, that one is fully conscious of his stature.

The new machinery for dealing with Mutual Aid etc. is at last set up, after a great deal of agitation, and N. Brook had a meeting of the Cabinet Office staff last night to explain it. There is no Ministerial Committee yet, and I gather that the PM is thinking of doing it at EPC + M. of Defence – some of the junior EPC people. This seems a silly way of reaching the result but would keep Nye in the set-up.

H.P. gave a small dinner last night at which were Roll, me, Bissell, [Arne] Skaug (Norway) and [Hans] Hirschfeld (Holland) – to talk about the arrangements for the economic side of defence. He wants a quick exercise to be done, mainly in Paris and mainly using the material needed for the 3rd Report. But we all agreed that the defence estimates used, which would have to be hypothetical until the Nitze exercise is done, would have to be of the right order of magnitude. We also agreed that the security problem did not matter much in this context as no details were wanted.

Friday, October 20th

At 10.10 yesterday I saw the Chancellor to say good-bye. He looked very old and his hair had lost all its colour. He is resigning his seat and taking a year off. Gaitskell is to succeed him and L. J. Edwards, whom I do not know, to succeed Gaitskell [but as Economic Secretary]. S.C. and I talked a bit about how successful the new experiments had been and he particularly said that we must not go back to having the Ch./Exch. separated from overriding control in the economic field. I think he will be one of the great Chancellors, and certainly the first to plan in peacetime in the sense in which we have done it.

In the evening I saw D.J. in the HC. He is worried as I am about the rumours of what the soldiers want to spend. Shinwell has put up an estimate of £3.7 to £3.8 bn over 3 years instead of the £3.6 bn which was to be our maximum but I am told they would really like £6 bn. Meanwhile they have put in an estimated bid of £1 bn for US direct arms, though they told us this couldn't be done when we were planning our own programme. He wants me to see H.G. with him this evening. P. and H.G. are due back today, also W.S. (who is leaving the Treasury for Powell Duffryn – E.B. is very angry. They want to bring T.L.R. back from Washington to succeed W.S.).

Saturday, October 21st

P., W.S., H.G. all back yesterday and I saw the first two at a meeting on Defence Finance in the afternoon. This was mainly to discuss a paper H.G. had written in New York to put the issue of whether to go on with the £3,600 mn programme on the Nitze formula or not. I have worried a good deal about this as the Cabinet decision was to do it only against *advance* promises of US help. However H.G. thinks he cleared it in principle with the PM and Foreign Sec. before he went to Washington. There was a good deal of talk about the probable cost of the Medium Term Defence Plan, which will, everyone thinks, cost *us* much more than the £3.6 bn. And we all felt that Shinwell must have firm instructions before he goes above the limit which Ministers think the UK economy can take.

Thursday, October 26th

I had to stay up on Saturday to finish drafting the paper for the Defence Committee.[37] H.G. was quite good. Later he and Plowden saw Bissell about the ending of ERP which has been under discussion for some time now – the US side have been suggesting that this must happen for some time but have been very erratic about the steps, varying from Foster telling us in Washington a fortnight ago that they wanted to discuss it all, to ECA [H.E.] Linder telling us last week that we had been given a total for 1950/51 of $175 mn and this was absolutely all.

I have been worrying a good deal about the raw material supplies for next year and finally got P. to join me in a paper to the new Economic Steering Committee on the gloomy prospects ['Materials in short supply' ES(50)4]. All our calculations on the burden of defence will turn out quite wrong if, as now seems likely, we go short of materials and production ceases to increase.

Monday, November 20th

This is a very long interval and I must make notes of topics.

1. *The Chancellor* – it has been a worrying time as he is not yet nearly so easy a man to work with as was S.C. He likes to talk about economics and uses up a lot of time that way. But he has two great defects at present. First he wants to go into too much detail himself – more like an U/Sec. than a Minister. There isn't time for this and he *must* trust his staff even if they are very bad. In fact they are very good and he ought not to waste his or their time on details. Second he has an unfortunate manner of putting things in a critical or imperative tone and this antagonizes senior civil servants. He has several times reduced Plowden to complete rage but everyone feels it more or less, though I must say he is on the whole extremely nice to me. But E.P. is certainly nearer to

resigning than he has ever been and he has gone so far as to ask E.B. to give him a date. This is partly because he has been attacked several times in the Beaverbrook press, part I think of their general campaign.

2. *ERP.* H.G. and Batt [Chief, MSA Mission to UK] are negotiating the end of this. I still feel afraid that we are holding out for too much and if we don't settle before Nov. 27th we may lose the pipe-line which is worth at least $200 mn. The US elections have clearly made all this much more urgent.

3. *Budget etc.* Dow did a first run for the BC [BC(50)25] and this showed that we might get by without more taxes – I feel sure this is the right line. We are working on a report to Ministers which can be the basis of the OEEC Report and the Survey. The problems for 1951 seem to me to be first raw material supplies and next the cost of living, but I hope that the latter will be kept in check (I hear the complaints) by increases in wages. I don't think the balance of payments need worry us at all – it is running very well indeed just now and though there will be increases in import prices, exports have been consistently strong and I doubt if there will be much shortfall because of defence. In fact I feel sure that at last the external pull on our imports is stronger than the interest to consume them here. Deflation has kept on very nicely and there is no doubt that we hit it off well in the Budget, if there is really the sort of connection we like to think. Next year will be more difficult because of defence which will probably show at least £300 mn up on this year.

4. *Wages White Paper etc.*[38] This has made very slow progress. The concept of a paper on wages set in the context of a full employment economy which I first got accepted, has become more and more about employment and less and less about wages. It is complicated by the Full Employment and Planning Powers Bill or whatever it will eventually be called: and by the ECOSOC resolution to which we are supposed to reply in January. The more H.G. thinks about it the more doubt he feels about wages and the more he wants to put in about other things. And we both lose time and add complexity. P. and I saw him about this to try to tell him how difficult the time-table was but I got the feeling that he was not taking it in. He also wants to mention credit policy and when I warned him that the B/E was very hard to move he said to leave them to him.

5. Meanwhile the B/E has actually gone so far as to prepare to increase the Bank Rate. They wanted to do this at the time of devaluation but were not successful. Now they think it would be useful as one of the counter-inflation measures. We had a funny meeting between Eady, Trend and me and Mynors, Beale and Peppiatt at which Wilfrid put a whole series of arguments, mostly contradictory of one another, against it and I argued strongly for the Bank who were themselves pretty dumb. I don't suppose anything will come of it as the Labour Party's views are so much the other way on the practical issues – dearer houses, more interest on debt, more income for the City etc. – whatever their theorists may think.

6. *NATO, OEEC, Nitze etc.* The main problem here has been the

£3.6 bn and how fast to get on with the orders, against the needs of the medium-term plan which would cost us about £6 bn over the three years. We have been resisting strongly any exercise however hypothetical over £3.6 bn because it would certainly manoeuvre us into a position in which we were partly committed to it.

Thursday, November 30th

The Chancellor had a great meeting [of the Budget Committee] on Tuesday to go through all outstanding points, mainly in connection with the Budget. He talked a great deal about my note on wages and the terms of trade and wanted me to say what rise in wages was (a) right for the terms of trade, (b) safe having regard to our future competitive position. But when I pointed out that it was impossible to give that sort of answer and that we ought to be very pleased that the rise likely to take place this year would not do us much damage, I think he saw how silly such questions were. It was an amusing meeting in a way – one could not help feeling that everyone was being called up in turn by the Chief Examiner and given a mark. Edward Bridges did not do well on the question of what economies could be made in Government expenditure – the Chancellor had asked him to look at what might be done and he brought up a list and pointed out that to go any further would involve changes in major policy. But the Chancellor finding the total unsatisfactory, asserted that he had wanted an examination *inside* the Treasury of major policy changes that might be made.

On the whole very little was settled but I suppose that he was pleased as he could feel he had stirred things up. It is still very hard to know what to think about him, or to balance his good against his bad qualities: but I feel that he is not the sort of firm rock that Stafford was and that he is in real danger, not of being easily swayed by difficulties, but of a mind inconstant as it plays over the changing circumstances or toys with intellectual processes. There is almost a whimsical quality, something like Keynes had but without Keynes' immense force of character.

Friday, December 8th (Washington, DC)

On Thursday evening last, Nov. 30th, during a debate on Foreign Affairs, there was a revolt of back-bench Labour members against UK foreign policy. This was touched off by a much exaggerated report of something Truman had said about the atomic bomb. Attlee decided at once to go to US to see Truman – I think he was being heavily pressed to do so – and announced this, with very little idea of what he would say except on China policy. It was almost universally felt in England that MacArthur had provoked the Chinese attack in N. Korea and that if he had stayed further south, as we had urged, the new phase would have been avoided. On Thursday afternoon there had been a meeting of the

ES Committee at which N. Brook said the Cabinet wanted an immediate appraisal of the effects in all fields of war with China, and I had to do the economic bit.[39] R. Makins had a meeting in his room on Friday to discuss this but as he was called to a Cabinet Plowden took the chair. While we were talking Bridges arrived and called Plowden out and in a few minutes P. returned and said that he and I had to go to Washington with the PM. It was not very clear why because there was really no agenda but it was felt vaguely that economic affairs might be discussed and better that I should be along. They had suggested Strath too but P. thought *he* would sooner go as he would be tougher.

I spent most of Friday and Saturday trying to adapt the bit on China to be a brief but it suffered badly from its start. However it mainly made the point that we were likely to be hit by raw material shortages, that the US must behave properly, and that in imposing cuts our export interests would be respected. The whole brief was taken in the Cabinet Room at No. 10 at 5 p.m. on Sunday – PM, Bevin and H.G. who had returned from Paris on Saturday to read the economic bit and held a Treasury meeting to consider it – he approved it fortunately. The No. 10 meeting was very depressing as B. in a state of great perplexity and gave no lead and the PM appeared to think that times had not changed and that our great object was to get £550 mn from the US over 3 years and that it was their plain duty to give it. As there was no mention of money at all in the brief this made it a bit awkward but it was passed.

We left Heathrow at 9.30 p.m. in a certain amount of splendour – I had got so used to travel *and* to Ministers that I didn't quite realize that it is a State occasion when the PM travels. We had a very good journey and got to Washington about 9.40 a.m. on Monday and were met by the President and Oliver and Dean Acheson and a lot of others. Then whisked away – we had been billeted on various members of the Embassy staff and I was at the Empsons with David Butt whom I had brought along.

During the flight and the talks the Korean situation got very much worse and the political and military side has dominated the situation. My own impression is that we both agreed on the analysis, and on the broadest lines of what we should do – don't take our eyes off the West, don't get bogged down in China *but* try to maintain your resolution and prestige. But that it is extremely hard to translate these precepts into a plan of action.

However we have had quite a bit to do on the economic side, entirely connected with raw materials, and I have found it an exhausting trip. We talked around on Monday and wrote a brief on Tuesday which we discussed with the PM. This asked for quick help on zinc, sulphur, cotton and cotton linters, and a proper set-up to deal with all these questions in the future, not putting UK (or US) in a special position but recognizing that if they did not take the lead nothing would be done. The PM agreed on the whole. We had wanted to be a bit more forthcoming about defence and what more we might do, but he did not like this, and I pressed both Oliver and P. to make sure that at least he realized that there was a difference between us and the US on this – it seemed to me to be frightful if he should be here and this, which was the worst difficulty about our present relations, not brought into the open.

We had a meeting at the President's Executive Offices with him and the PM on Wednesday morning. He spoke moderately from his piece and the President then said that at last night's Cabinet he had instructed his people to get ahead on the whole problem of world raw materials. Dean Acheson [Sec. of State] spoke saying that we must not dominate and in any case had no navicerts; a number of priorities were needed. He stressed increases in supply but said that in giving priority to defence the health of the civilian economies must be kept: also that we must try to keep critical materials from our enemies. The whole thing was remitted to a meeting at 2.30 and Dean Acheson was careful to insist on *all* the affected US Agencies going.

Apparently they hadn't all been in a room together before, as we suspected. Plowden reiterated what the PM had said about our exports being vital.

The afternoon meeting was mainly notable for the people there – [Stuart] Symington [Chairman, National Security Resources Board] in the chair, Snyder, Sawyer [Secretary for Commerce], Harriman, General Harrison, Bissell (for Foster), Willard Thorp [State Department], a man called Larsen who it appears is now their main buyer – he is head of a thing called the General Services Administration but it seems to be a mixture of RFC, Treasury Procurement and a Secret Service Fund, i.e. to be able to exercise powers involving spending money over a wide field. We produced our list and they told us the story – mainly their difficulty is with zinc. They want us to control rubber completely – apparently Larsen has just been appointed sole buyer and they are going to close the NY rubber market. He said they were ready to make contracts for *all* the Malayan output. They obviously felt deeply about this and were rather cross when P. said that it would not keep rubber from China and Russia (one of their objects) to close the Singapore market alone. Sawyer said that we ought to match action on zinc and sulphur against action by us on rubber. Symington was very nice indeed and made one very helpful remark, that the US were going to have to reduce their living standards heavily. He did not want to let them think that it was because of any Anglo/US agreement.

We hadn't got far with the general question, though Plowden and I had opened it to Bissell on Monday, so we got Lincoln Gordon to dinner at Leslie Rowan's that night and after dinner I explained the problem as I saw it and Lincoln agreed and this later became the Anglo/US agreement: about the quickest bit of backstage work I have ever known. But as in all cases when this is done it is the facts and the sensible course that leads to the agreement and it would be folly to think that two private people could do much more than get it given one twist rather than another. However it was a ripe moment with the PM and the President together and forced to think about materials, and we ought to have some credit for seizing our moment.

What I suggested was a small group, say UK, US and France with as few others as possible, to take the initiative and do the staff work, and call commodity committees, *not* conferences, to deal with the critical commodities. The problem was really to get the 'top hat' under which it would all be done, which wasn't either NATO or OEEC. And to supply that authority with proper technical advice.

I told Leslie exactly what to say at a meeting at 9.45 on Thursday and we met again at 10.30 in the Exec. Offices. He made his speech and Symington said their ideas were exactly the same – Lincoln and I smiled at one another here – and that they had dictated a piece about it. We had a bit of talk about how many charter members and on the whole it seemed as if the fewer the better and three was best; it would arouse more anger than it calmed to put someone else down, e.g. Brazil to speak for Latin America.

Then we asked about spelling out the priorities, maintaining the civil economy, altering stockpiling policy, stating that UK exports were essential and so on. But they were all insistent that in the present state of affairs, Congress so irritable and the Senate so evenly balanced, that it would be madness to write these things down. Congress would get wind of them and would tie up their freedom much more than if we stuck to general principles. I felt quite sure they were right but we felt very sad about exports – however Harriman who was very good said that we had made the point, they had not demurred, and this was the best we could hope for. Snyder incidentally has been extraordinarily friendly all the time and indeed the whole atmosphere was very good. Sawyer seems and I suppose is far the worst but the others said that, for him, he was also being as helpful as he could.

During the rest of the day we talked at various parties about our immediate needs and what they wanted us to do on their things, especially tin, rubber and wool, where they want some kind of international control and allocation at once. Rubber as above – tin to revive the International Tin Allocation Committee – wool not clear, except that they don't like the price and don't think they can get all they want. They also mentioned a lot of old favourites and in many ways it was just like the old CRMB days – asbestos, Rhodesian copper including coal and the Port of Beira, Gold Coast manganese, Rhodesian cobalt. It seemed completely clear that they were in a very bad way about zinc but Larsen said he would try very hard to get 20–25,000 tons, by reducing the intake for the stockpile, subject to a strong case and to an ECA reservation about OEEC countries. We are to get a quick ship of sulphur and Tom Blaisdell promised us that they would settle their international allocation very soon and that we would get a fair bit. Not much on cotton linters. Cotton rather difficult as Trigg their man maintains that we are being treated much better than anyone else. We met again at 5 to report progress and settle the general statement on allocation and international machinery and got on fairly well. Plowden is very temperamental and kept on saying we would get nothing at all. But I think we have made some progress on our urgent needs and quite a lot on the long-term one, since we had got something like a joint Anglo/US Secretariat and something like a continuing organization. On Friday morning there was a final meeting of the PM and Truman to which I did not go. We had done a lot of work on a statement for the PM which inter alia was to make it quite clear that we would be in trouble unless they did more on raw materials. But P. told me that the PM mumbled it so and said it so badly that Truman said 'Well that seems very satisfactory' – it reminds me of the Collection at Magdalen where all the tutors spoke severely about a man and the President (Warren) said 'Well Mr. —, I am glad to hear such good reports of you – please remember me to your father'.

On Thursday night the PM, P. and O.S.F. had seen Harriman who had put strongly the point that unless we did a good deal more on defence we would get very little in money or materials from the US. Harriman had said that at the 5 p.m. meeting but it was no good saying it to us. I gather the PM said 'Humph! We are doing a great deal already'.

The whole trip has been very scrappy and unsatisfactory though I think we have done pretty well on our side and indeed that it will be our own fault from now on if we can't get on an equal footing on raw materials. I haven't had time to read cables or hear reports on the other side but as the communiqué makes clear, we disagreed on the correct tactics and indeed policy towards China: I don't know what the outcome will be on public opinion. Essentially, the US feel that to countenance China in any way after her intervention in Korea is to accept a plain disaster to the UN. And *we* feel that as we have no resources to spare in the East and want to try to keep the Chinese quiet if we can, we ought to avoid empty but provocative gestures. I fear that the US are probably right and that though our tactics may be correct, it is a frightful mistake to think that any appeasement of China will do any good. They are xenophobes certainly but they are Communists too.

Sunday, December 10th (Ottawa)

We left Washington on Friday about 3.10 p.m. and flew to New York where the PM walked about the Lake Success corridors and said a few words. There was a frightful mess on the luggage and poor Mr Jones, who is always so very cheerful and efficient, was in despair. But it was our fault as we had not labelled anything. I was told that 36 pieces were labelled 'Inspector Buswell' – the PM's detective. I was worn out and went early to bed but they kept on waking me up with telephone calls to say that the Canadian pilot wanted us to leave early. However we didn't: left Essex House about 9.20 but with a police escort had a quick run to Idlewild and got on a Canadian North Star 'plane and flew very quickly to Ottawa where we arrived at 11.45 as scheduled. It is nice to be here, partly to be in Canada at all where they are all very nice indeed and partly to be in a hotel again after the slight strain, much too much against the general strain, of being a guest in a strange house. We are palatially housed in the Chateau Laurier as guests of the Canadian Government.

Shannon (the Deputy to the High Commissioner Alex Clutterbuck) took P. and me to lunch and we gave him a preliminary run over what had been done on raw materials. It is obviously an awkward one as they may think that we and the US are ganging up and excluding them. We saw the PM immediately after lunch to discuss this with him and he seemed quite aware of the point for once and used the word 'initiatory' for the UK/US/French action, which I thought was just right. We didn't do much after that but went for a drink with Clutterbuck about 6.15. He told us that when the PM met the Canadian Cabinet he had said his piece about raw materials etc. but that the Cabinet was so much more interested in other things that this had passed by.

He said that it was a great help to have Slim there as when the PM dried up Slim was able to talk with authority about the military position which the Canadians found very interesting. I had only met Slim once before this trip, when he was Head of the Imperial Defence College. He seems to me to be a very good sort of man for the job, calm and solid, obviously ready to do his duty but not to push himself: and when I have talked to him he was quite able. He gave a most interesting sketch of various Armies in the car on Saturday going to Idlewild. Said the Germans were plainly the best soldiers in the world. Compared the rigid obedience of orders in the US Army with the 'basis of discussion' order in the UK. Said the US was much better on the lower levels (I suspect he meant battalions) because the Commander knew where he was and this was worth the losses caused by mistakes. Higher up he was not so sure. The US give complete power to the Commander in the field, hence much of the trouble with [General] MacArthur. He gave us a good account of the Russian Commissar system and said it worked much better than we might think. They chose good soliders as Commissars and it was a great relief to the soldier to be able to hand all 'political' decisions in the field, e.g. how to treat civilians, to another man on the spot. Also all welfare, educational, chaplaincy questions.

Clutterbuck, whom I used to know very well in 1940 and 1941 when he represented CRO at inter-departmental meetings, and whom we all thought a very stupid man, has done extremely well here and is obviously highly thought of. At the dinner given by the Canadian PM on Saturday night he went out of his way to pay him a tribute. P. agrees that he is stupid but says, and I am sure this is right, that his transparent honesty and goodness of character is worth a great deal more than being too clever and that we only used the word stupid in comparison to a rather select band – in those days the people going to such meetings were men like Caine, Max Nicholson, Roger Makins, F. G. Lee.

The PM made an extremely good speech at dinner – a much lighter and defter touch than I had expected at the beginning – I was so exhausted that I went to sleep in the middle and had to be wakened by Max Mackenzie who very smoothly thrust a cigarette case under my nose as I began to nod. This has been by far the most exhausting and unpleasant trip I have ever made, though I feel sure that we have done pretty well on our own narrow front.

Monday, December 11th

We are leaving this afternoon, home for breakfast tomorrow, D.V., W.P. etc. I feel a bit better now; it is an enormous relief to stay in a hotel and go to bed and get up and breakfast in as morose or detached a mood as one wishes. We had an easy morning, read the first telegrams from London – obviously Leslie Rowan is working fast in Washington and London seems to approve. Max Mackenzie gave a lunch at the Country Club for Plowden, Makins, Rickett and me – N. Robertson [Cabinet Secretary], Graham Towers [Governor of the Bank of Canada], Plumptre were there. After lunch we explained in detail the proposed raw material arrangement and they took them very well, didn't raise at all the question of why Canada was not on the Central Group and were mainly concerned about whether anything sensible could be done by really large international commodity committees. I think they are anxious that there should be prior consultation among those mainly concerned before any big gatherings are called.

Afterwards Mackenzie took P. and I to see C. P. Howe [Canadian Minister of Trade and Commerce and Defence Production] and we discussed the current situation. Jephson had told us that Howe was very cross with Symington and the US generally and that this had made our path a bit smoother, though as Howe pointed out, our behaviour to them has been very bad as we always turn to them in a jam and cut off purchases when we can get them anywhere else. We discussed various materials, especially zinc for us and steel for them – the US have practically cut off steel exports to Canada. They also suggested that we might make long-term contracts for copper and aluminium. I feel sure that this is what we ought to do. Howe said that next year's wheat outlook was very poor – Canada had a bad crop last year and the US winter wheat did not look well.

We sent some cables later, and dined with the GG [Governor-General] at Government House. I was too tired to enjoy it much especially as we couldn't leave until the two Prime Ministers had finished a game of bridge. I sat next to Heeney, Deputy Minister of External Affairs, a nice man. The dinner was good except for a horrible savoury made of frozen Camembert mousse which perplexed and dismayed everyone.

We saw George Bateman at 6 p.m. and he came to lunch today. This was an extremely useful contact as he had been deeply concerned with allocations especially of NF Metals, during the CRMB days and is now in a dominant position as adviser to the Government *and* to the companies on base metal. He was the only one to make the point that Canada didn't want anyone to dispose of *her* affairs without her concurrence – we tried to reassure him. But he was mainly concerned that whatever was decided should be workable and wanted preliminary discussions on a small group basis as early as possible and certainly before any international bodies met. P. urged him to go to Washington again and to see Rowan as soon as possible. If he goes it will be very good for Rowan as he has had no experience at all in this field.

A cable from Rowan came in this morning giving suggested terms of reference for the Central Group – we thought it had too much of a flavour of dictation and cabled to say so. We are now (2.20 p.m.) at the Airport and in the 'plane and just taking off for New York where we are to tranship to our Boeing. Montreal is closed in. If all goes well we should be in London about 9 a.m. tomorrow.

Misc. Notes. Wilson Smith is leaving in about a fortnight and it is still not clear whether Rowan is to replace him or not. P. thinks it would be a grave error to take him away now and this is probably right in the context of possible successors. Who should replace Wilson Smith is a frightful problem. D. Rickett is suggested by H.G. but I doubt if he could do it or is the man for it. P. thinks Hitchman might but I doubt it. *I* think they ought to get F. G. Lee but everyone else is against him. It is really extraordinary that we should be so short-handed.

Linc. Gordon rang me on Friday just before lunch and we both felt sorry that we hadn't been able to exchange ideas about the UK general economic position. I told him that our real worries were the growth of production and the cost of living, not the balance of payments or inflation. I said I would write to him and he said he would do the same for me about the US outlook.

Tuesday, December 19th

When we got back we found that H.G. had been making a fuss about the Economic Outlook paper [EPB(50)20], mainly because it showed an overall balance and he wanted a surplus. My people were rather cross and so was I as we had taken a good deal of trouble to give him the maximum room for manoeuvre. He was also doubtful about it going to the EPB or ES Committee and all this made P. so cross that he made an impassioned speech to him about how well planning had gone and how he was ruining it and he offered to resign. H.G. very upset but couldn't see at all what P. was after.

The US is running out on our raw material agreement already and wants to increase the numbers of the first Group to 7. Meanwhile the feelings of the OEEC delegation have been very much hurt and so no doubt will the feelings of the OEEC countries be.

We are now having a look at adding another £300 mn or so a year to the defence programme as Acheson in Brussels is said to be urging that all pre-Korea expenditure be doubled. Rowan wrote to the same effect. But I doubt if Ministers feel any sense of urgency and they seem to be muddled in their own minds between doing something for our own safety and doing it because the US want us to. Since the Chinese intervention in Korea, the whole thing has seemed much more urgent to me: and I think that 1951 is the most dangerous year.

Thursday, December 21st

Yesterday the Chancellor had a meeting about Bank Rate. He was against any increase. He is as out of date in his beliefs about how the money system is controlled as I was two years ago, and talks glibly of changing reserve ratios, directing the banks to put up overdraft rates etc. P. and I were much in favour of the change though personally I think that if we add £300 mn to the defence programme we shall perforce have to control investment closely and therefore less need to give the market a shock. However, P thinks that control of private investment is very difficult with full powers and bound to be very corrupt in administration so feels this is all to the good. Cob. came to urge us to help; he is to see H.G. in the New Year but I am sure he won't be able to explain himself. No one who understands it is coherent, so I perforce am the nearest. But H.G. doesn't think it worth the high political price.

Monday, January 8th 1951

Several discussions on Bank Rate: the Governor brought Mynors and Peppiatt and Beale along but they were all dumb or yes-men and H.G. said I put the Bank case much better than they did. P. and I both wanted it moved as we cannot see how to hold investment down unless we use every weapon available. We shall probably try to do something about the initial allowance.

Tuesday, January 16th

The Chancellor has turned down the Bank Rate and written a long letter [to the Governor] to say so but to suggest 'other measures', e.g. restriction of credit. I don't suppose much will come of it.

Downie finished the first draft on the economic impact of the new [defence] programme last night [CP(51)20]. It rises too slowly, £1,250 mn this (1951/52) year, £1,550 next, ? £1,750 in 1953/54.[40] Something on this for civil defence and stockpiling (i.e. building up imported stocks). We have been trying hard to get the Chancellor to go along with us as we went and are to see him this morning.

Wednesday, January 17th

He made more or less the same comments as we made last night at the preliminary meeting: and found it all read a bit too easily – he said that the last thing he had expected when he came to the Treasury was to find things presented *less* sharply than he would like but this was the third time he had done so. It seems to me a very good technique to put in the severe bits late on the Chancellor's instructions. A long and useless meeting of the D(T) Committee in the afternoon to look at the measures for accelerating Civil Defence. Bridges and Padmore and I also had a meeting with Jay on wages as applied to the Civil Service – Jay rather out of touch I thought – it is Ministers who are dragging their feet just now.

Thursday, January 18th

The Defence paper was rewritten on Wednesday night and yesterday and is, I think, a very good paper indeed though almost too severe. The CoS [Chiefs of Staff] paper [CP(51)16] is sound and the two fit in quite well except that the Chiefs want something like absolute priority and the Chancellor of course insists on alterations and consultation. After we had read the draft in the evening, I had a talk to P. who had been having tests for suspected appendicitis all day but won't know till Friday if it is this, or a gastric ulcer, or nothing. He has been feeling very ill for weeks he said. We both agreed that it was an admirable paper and that it could not have been written so well or in so short a time three years ago. I had been much impressed by the collaboration of Downie, Saunders and Allen.

P. also said that he had been feeling very discouraged generally, partly because we were unable to reap the fruits of our labours now, partly because Stafford has gone, partly because he feels that H.G. does not trust or appreciate him. He also asked if we (he and I) were still entirely of one mind – this was because I had not felt as strongly as he about stressing the gloomy side of the Defence picture. He is acutely sensitive to what I think and is always fearing he may have said something silly. But his general judgment is quite good though he is too quick and passionate in expressing his views – a good thing for a man of action but not in this highly technical field.

Friday, January 19th

Spent most of yesterday at the Planning Board and the ES Committee on the impact. The Chancellor had given us his comments early in the morning: they were few, mostly drafting, but so illegible that it took a typist 2½ hours to decipher them. The reception was very easy: mostly small points but a lot of argument about Labour Direction and Control of Engagement.

Tuesday, January 23rd

The paper was finally done and sent to the printer by 10 a.m. on Friday. The Defence Committee is taking it and about five others today, and Cabinet on Thursday. We had a bit of a session with H.G. last night to go over it again: his main trouble was with a paragraph on the real effect on consumption, which he had had put in himself. But he was quite good, I think because only P. and I and three junior economists were there. It still doesn't look unbearable though the Budget estimates now coming round look a bit grim at first sight. However they can be managed. The other papers are the CoS one, several on Civil Defence and two on the Z class call-up. The Defence Ministers, quite mistakenly I think, consider that the three months' call-up would be a political mistake and they buttress their views with very feeble arguments. This is the last straw to P.

The weather has been mild and there may not be a coal crisis. It has not shown up Noel-Baker [Minister of Fuel and Power] at all well – he reached a nadir with a proposal to stop broadcasting after 11 p.m. and save 50 tons a week: but the PM still keeps him.

There was a good deal of talk last week about the Isaacs to Marquand to Bevan to Isaacs move:[41] it was all right as far as it went, and is a double advantage in that B. both leaves Health *and* goes to Labour. But the Foreign Secretary and the Defence Ministers are in their various ways quite wrong, especially Bevin who is almost dead.

Kaldor came to see Jay on Thursday on his proposal on dividends which the Inland Revenue has been so much against. I was asked to go but told that it was on wages so was ill prepared. It was *not* a good meeting as Jay hadn't really got either K.'s proposal or the Inland Revenue objections: and as I quite agreed with Nicky it was no good having me there.

P. says his doctors have said he is fit. No appendix, no st. ulcer, no colitis.

Wednesday, January 24th

Very gloomy 2nd Secs. yesterday as everyone considers that Ministers are being extremely feeble about defence and instead of arousing the country to a sense of urgency, they are doing their best to hide the difficulties from themselves. They are turning down 3 months for the Z reservists but will probably take everything else. I suppose that better results are got by feeble Ministers who are hounded along by officials than by strong but evil ones. *Evil* being what the officials think and *better* what they think good for the country.

I went to a meeting of the official Coal Committee to talk about increasing charges. D. Fergusson was there – he has only one gear and must say his piece in his own way – it is not bad when it is out but he can't be interrupted. It is hard to see how some of the Permanent Secretaries rose to their great eminence but I suppose that often they have burned themselves out on the way. In my time I have seen a number of very doubtful 2nd Secretaries made but no permanent ones: and the 2nd Secretaries I thought badly of for a variety of reasons. Hutchinson [Board of Trade] was completely negative, Bowyer [Ministry of Supply] is a defeatist, Calder [Board of Trade] a cypher, Stephen Holmes [Board of Trade] in quite the wrong place etc., etc.

Long talk with P. and Strath in the afternoon about the Survey. It will probably come out on April 3rd, a week before the Budget: we will do it for publication straight away and save a bit of trouble. Butt will be Editor but we hope to borrow Wright from [S. C.] Leslie's EIU (now IDT) to write the prose. P. thinks Butt a bad draughtsman – it is a typical bad judgment by P. on poor grounds, just like a business man.

We also talked about the Budget problem and how little time we had.

Tuesday, January 30th

After a terrific struggle the Chancellor got the Cabinet to agree to the new plan except for the 3 months for the Z class. Bevin and Shinwell who ought to have done all the work were both away ill and so was P. Gordon Walker [Sec. of State for Commonwealth Relations] who was in favour. So H.G. had only the LP to help him – he must have done a very good job indeed and P. and I think much more highly of him. There was a flap on Friday about the statement the PM had to make yesterday – I had to draft the 'impact' bit, but it got done all right.

Wednesday, January 31st

At 2nd Secs. yesterday N. Brook very cross because the typist at No. 10 had left out a paragraph – the one dealing with directions to manufac-turers – in doing the type for the PM's actual statement, which is done on special paper like all speeches to make it easy to handle. As it was in the roneo'd statement given to the Press before, it made it a bit awkward. But apparently the PM did not mind a bit and said he would put it right in Hansard and say it was inadvertence on his part.

P. and I saw H.G. in the afternoon about the Budget. It looks as if it will be quite manageable, at the most we shall want another £100 mn. This will surprise everyone as it is not generally understood what progress we made in 1950. We also discussed the problem of pensioners etc. – H.G. repeated what we have often been told, that there are no votes in family allowances and the TUC really dislike them. We went over the whole field and were very much of a mind, including initial allowances and profits tax. Dividends are becoming a bad headache.

Friday, February 2nd

BC today: Dow has done quite a good paper [BC(51)16] making the present gap about £75 mn. I think this is on the low side but there will be economies though perhaps also other expenses, e.g. pensions. P. and I had another talk to H.G. yesterday, to pick up a few points that we did not look at. He also mentioned Prospero, rather to my surprise.[42] He has read Kaldor's paper on it. Fortunately Nita [Watts] has done one for us so I was able to say so – though I have in fact been considering it for at least 6 months. It depends a good deal on whether the US goes on inflating at its present pace.

Later Nye Bevan came in with Myrddin-Evans [Deputy Secretary, Ministry of Labour] to discuss the talk he and the Chancellor are having with the TUC about wages next Tuesday. They agreed to go rather slowly: Nye said he was on intimate terms with them all and would have no trouble. He talked about the need to control dividends and H.G. gave him some idea of how we had been thinking. I had not met Nye since P. and I and Geoffrey Crowther had had him to dinner at Brown's a long while ago. There was some talk of the US and Nye said 'we were tied to the tail of a Kilkenny cat': he went on a little later to use the same expression of some engineering firms which were paying more than agreement wages. I felt strongly that he regarded order as a great good and was against competition if it led to disorder – the planning instinct – though it is fair to say that at other times he has shown some comprehension of the virtues of competition.

Monday, February 5th

The BC went off fairly smoothly although most of the Committees were a bit horrified at what they regarded as economic gymnastics in turning a budget swing of over £700 mn into one of about £70 mn. Dow had done a very good paper. The main features were (a) stockpiling £150 mn, (b) other changes from the traditional to the alternative classification, (c) changes from the latter to the Survey. Of course the real differences are that this year we get £250 mn more revenue, at least £100 mn more in company reserves, and let the balance of payments go by £175 mn. Total £525 mn against increased expenditure of £600 mn. Everyone felt that we were being too optimistic but only by £75–£100 mn or so. Dow was there at first and was much amused by E.B. having a secret ballot on the amount to write up our £75 mn deficiency. 3 of £100, 3 of £200, 3 of £150, 3 of £125 – average about £145 – a write-up of £70 mn. We talked a bit about various odds and ends.[43]

During the weekend I read Roy Harrod's life of Keynes and enjoyed it very much. It is written with great distinction – Harrod must be one of the few people who could appreciate from his own education and experience so many of the facets of Keynes' nature. Several passages – a comparison with Churchill, and an extract from Lionel Robbins' diary expressing his wonder at the extreme virtuosity of a performance at (I think) Bretton Woods – with both of these I agreed completely. I wrote a longish letter to Roy to say how pleased I was – my only criticism was that he did not allow enough for the ill effect of Keynes' rudeness and arrogance with the Americans. I felt at the time and still do that it was very irresponsible of Keynes where his own position was so much stronger than that of the country he was representing.

Lucius Thompson-McCausland gave me lunch today – he had been a sort of p.a. to Keynes on several of the US trips. He told me that Keynes was extremely kind when he had the attitude of a pupil but that if he tried to argue as an equal Keynes was very overbearing. He also said that he thought Keynes had very poor ideas on money! I am afraid I think Lucius has very poor ones and when I argued with him two years ago about central banking policy I thought he was very bad, like everyone in the Bank.

Most of our talk today was about commodity policy and the proposed rubber and tin agreements which are to be the first of the new commodity attempts. L. was mainly concerned to keep the London markets open – I don't quite see how this is consistent with an allocation scheme – and also that we should not get stuck with a bad agreement on prices. I suggested a reconsideration clause if MS prices moved more than by some agreed amount. Incidentally L. told me that *he* personally was in favour of a strong exchange rate and the Bank not so much against it as they had been during devaluation. Nita has re-written her Prospero paper and it seems to me very good. Butt showed me his first chapter for the new Survey. On the whole the office is quieter than it has been for months.

(John Fischer Williams came to see me about Jan. 25th – just about a year since his last visit. He didn't say much – nearly all on my views of the current situation.)

Tuesday, February 13th

The Budget season is now in full force. Just before the meeting on Friday Dow handed me a paper to say that his calculations now increase the shortage by £80 mn. As the Committee had already made their covering note as fierce as they could, they were rather shaken at this. Yesterday he had reduced it by £40 mn. Once all this gave me fits but I am tougher now – no doubt that one needs a strong stomach to make Budgets. The Committee has had a good look at possible taxes and likes none of them so has called sternly for economies. But I do not suppose they will amount to much. Armstrong came to see me yesterday to hurry up Prospero a bit. It was discussed at a Section meeting on Thursday and now must go publicly to a pigeon-hole.

Saturday, February 17th (at Roffey)

This has been a busy week: a good deal of it on G.'s speech on defence which he made on Thursday. In the morning T. J. Bligh [PS to Bridges] told me that the whips expected to lose the division because there was so much 'flu': in the end there was a big majority (21) but I think nearly all of the difference was the Liberal vote. In the speech he followed the Cab. paper quite closely, and in the end left all the comparison with the US, which he had wanted to make, to Bevan.

Otherwise a good deal on the B. I did him a note on the White Paper – now that they are dropping the Full Employment Bill and can make no progress with the Unions on wages, he is inclined to drop the Paper.

There are a lot of things it would be nice to say about 6 years of full employment, but too many holes in the policy, especially on wages, money, dividends. We are in an awkward position both with ECOSOC and [The Council of Europe in] Strasbourg as we took the lead in both places in stirring up full employment. Now we shall fall down with the answers. But quite apart from our own policy troubles, the world has changed and is now pre-occupied with the special problem of re-armament inflation.

Tuesday, February 20th

The Chancellor had a talk yesterday with E.B., E.P. and me about my Prospero note. He agreed on the whole with the conclusion that the time was not ripe and that we ought to see what happened in US before reaching any final decision. He wants a very small working party of me, O.F. and Bank to look at it and also to see about the possibility of a float. Must write about Roffey when I have a little more time.

Later. Roffey was not too bad. I had the usual uncomfortable time at the beginning because the Chancellor had not really understood the relation between the three classifications – the figures had altered at the last moment and in trying to get them right we all got deeply involved.[44] However apart from the incorrigible attempts, always made by D.J., to prove that we need do much less than we said, it was generally accepted; and John Edwards was very good indeed. H.G. had a sort of poll at the end to agree a figure and himself chose about the same as the BC had before. Then we went all through the list: adopting the planning changes, partly put forward by E.P. and partly already foreshadowed in the House. But there was a good deal of discussion about the rest, mainly on what if anything to do in the Income Tax field – I was in favour of reducing the second band. We are suffering deeply now from the poll tax nature of the reductions of recent years – the corollary of giving all the money to the lower levels is that that is where you have to get it now.

Thursday, March 1st

This is a bad time in all sorts of ways. It is always difficult with the Budget having to be finalized and the Survey under way: and this year we got such a late start because of defence. But in the last two weeks the information coming in has been mostly rather bad, particularly on steel where the Ministry of Supply allege that last year nearly 700,000 tons of stocks were used and they have only just found out about it.

Wednesday, March 21st

These three weeks have been hectic and difficult. It has been the worst year for the Budget calculations I have ever had and makes me feel again how very chancy the whole thing is. The price increase in imports in December and January seems to have been overlooked until lately and this upset all the balance of payments calculations and the gap.[45] By contrast, the Survey has had rather an easy run mainly because no one was much interested. Fuel and Power have been almost worse this year than ever before, but it is on the whole a bad and uninformative Survey and partly reflects the dying Government. H.G. told me that there would probably be an election in the autumn – they did not want to go through another winter.

At a meeting between H.G. and Nye it was decided to drop the idea of linking wages and cost of living. Nye was very sensible. He called me Robert – sometimes he appears never to have seen me before.

O.S.F. has been here – he came to see me immediately he arrived to get the latest gossip: and he lunched with me yesterday. He thinks E.P. will probably stay on after December in spite of what has been arranged. He asked me how his stock was here. I told him it was high in Whitehall but that there was press gossip against him, to the effect that he was hardly known in the US. Several stories of that sort have been put out, and P. suspects that someone in the FO has been passing them to leading Opposition members.

Saturday, April 7th

This is being written in a 'plane on the way back from the US. At the end of last week, a cable from Oliver said that the US were not going to recommend that we should get *any* aid in the next fiscal year, and suggested that I should go out to talk to their people to see if we were taking the same view as they of our prospects. On the form for Nitze, we can't tell whether we should need any help or not until we have compared the various submissions. But if the US go into the exercise with their position made firm in advance because of what they have said to Congress, it is hardly an impartial exercise, and our Ministers who only took on the £4.7 bn defence programme because they thought we had an insurance policy in the Nitze exercise, are certain to be very angry indeed.

H.G. did not want me to go as he was anxious that I should be there for editing the Budget speech. But P. persuaded him that I could get it all done by Monday evening and ought to go then. Meanwhile Otto Clarke went on Sunday. We had a meeting on the speech all Saturday morning and I worked all the weekend on the passages that needed adjusting: had them done on Monday but could not see the Chancellor. However I went through them with Leslie who is going to take on the editing, and laid on Dow and Downie to see all subsequent versions. So finally got away, feeling very exhausted, as the calculations kept on changing up to the last minute and my nerves had practically given out. The Survey was due on the Tuesday.

I slept very well and though there was a four hour delay we got to

New York about 12.30 and I was whisked through and over to La
Guardia and was in Washington by 4.20. Jukes met me and we had a
meeting at once with Oliver, Leslie Rowan and Otto to discuss strategy
for a meeting with the US side which was fixed for Wednesday morning.
I thought Oliver was a bit shaken and much less confident than usual –
I suppose he feels particularly that Ministers may blow up about this.

On Wednesday morning we had a talk with Bissell, Perkins, Willis
and Lincoln Gordon and a lot of their satellites. On our side Leslie
Rowan, Otto and I, Christelow and Jukes. We exchanged views a bit
and they undertook to let us see their figures on which they had arrived
at the view that we should get no aid. I said that we felt our position to
be rather precarious, partly because of raw material shortages and
partly because of the change in the terms of trade. We didn't get very
far, and in the afternoon met the ECA technicians and got from them
their figures of what they expected our position to be in the coming year.
We took these away to study them, having given them our own Nitze
submissions. On looking at them, it seemed as if their N. Inc. calculations were quite like ours but that they showed a lower level of
international trade – Otto thought this might be inconsistent with the NI
they have assumed.

On Thursday afternoon we had a talk with Bissell and the ECA
people alone, about the principles which they thought should govern the
whole operation. He said that, since burden-sharing involved transfers,
it would be necessary to reduce the result of the exercises to balance
of payments deficits to be financed by the transfers. For example, a
country doing too much, but where it was decided that it should not cut
its programme, would import more or export less than it would have
needed for balance [and so would qualify for aid]. Consequently
payments would not be made that would cause a country's reserves to
rise, since this would mean that the real result was not being achieved.
He was aware that the sterling area presented a special problem but they
could not depart from this view (a) because they would not be able to
persuade Congress to give us anything when our reserves were rising,
(b) in any case they felt that the RSA should make some contribution to
the defence of the West and it was rough justice that this should be
done.

He said that they would try to get the allocation of funds as flexible as
possible so that the fact that they showed no probable allocation to the
UK did not mean that they would be unable to give us anything. But the
principle just set out might prevent us from getting anything whatever
the exercise showed.

This, of course, was an extremely serious bit of news for us. It is a
quite new principle and it will certainly upset Ministers very much. They
took on the original £3.6 bn programme on what they took to be a
definite promise of US aid and when this was turned down they went to
£4.7 bn on the clear understanding that there would be an equitable
sharing of the burden. If they had known that there would be this
arbitrary rule, which as far as the UK is concerned may mean that we
can *never* get any help, they might well think twice. The trouble is that

we probably needed to arm for our own defence: and that it is quite likely that we can afford what we are doing, even having regard to the terms of trade. However it seems to me to be quite outrageous to behave in this way and I am entirely at a loss, at the moment, to know what line we ought to take. The obvious one is to contract out of the Nitze exercise, since why should we go through the motions when the result can have no interest for us? But what good would this do? I must say that I tremble to think of what the Ministerial reactions will be.

We had a more formal meeting with ECA, State and Treasury on Friday and they confirmed the two points, (a) that funds would be flexible, (b) that they would not transfer if this meant rising reserves. We did not say much in the face of this as I think we were all bewildered and regarded it as too serious to argue much about without taking thought.

Afterwards I had a bit of a private talk to Bissell, mainly about the future of EPU and about the raw materials outlook. On EPU, he said that they were trying to think of some way under which the UK [then in substantial surplus with other members] would get better quality assets – perhaps the US would arrange that the really weak countries should pay 100% in gold, and that even Germany should pay and the UK get about 75%. I was expecting something like this, as we are very much tempted to break EPU up altogether on present trends.

On the raw materials side; I had already discussed the organization with our people in the Embassy, especially Murray MacDougall, Hooper and Nancy Fisher. They were not running very smoothly yet and felt that there would not be any satisfactory alteration on this round. Thus they all felt discouraged, and were inclined to be critical of one another. I gathered that Knollys [UK representative on the IMC] was also discouraged as he had started off at top speed and gradually got nowhere. This was a good deal because of the great disorganization in Washington.

Bissell and I agreed that the outlook for raw materials was probably the gravest one before us, and he said that the present organization (the one we set up when I was in Washington with the PM in December) was not doing any good. I said that I thought this was inevitable. At the early stages of any international organization, it gave the impression of ineffectiveness but it needed time for the staff to get used to one another and the job. As for allocations, the Governments concerned including our own were not taking the problem seriously enough yet. But it *was* serious and by the end of this year it was likely that the whole effort would be threatened by material difficulties. We were not going to let this happen and destroy the defence of the West just because we couldn't allocate materials. Hence the organization would be needed later and it ought to get going now. He agreed and we then talked about sanctions for allocations. Nothing much can be done unless the UK and the US agree to take a common line and we thought that if they did this there could be some form of sanction through making available or with-holding of scarce export goods. I mentioned this talk to Rowan yesterday and he was anxious that the UK should reach agreement with

Commonwealth countries before trying to do so with the US.

That is about all for this trip, which has been too hurried to organize properly and where I have seen many less people than usual. All the ones I know well on the US side are very much afraid of inflation, do not think that any drastic steps will be taken, and also feel that the administration is in bad shape for dealing in an orderly way with its problems. I have had no proper talk with O.S.F. Rowan is due back in May but his successor has not been agreed on. He talked to me at some length about Treasury organization, largely on the theme that we were now too centralized. I do not know how he thinks this can be undone, consistently with getting on with our problems. But we agreed that the top level of Treasury officials is very weak and that if Eady and Gilbert, who are shortly due to go, are replaced by stronger people it might be easier. But where are they?

(I see that in the confusion of recent weeks I have made no comment on any of the Ministerial changes and indeed I have been little affected by them. It is better to have a strong man at the Ministry of Labour and it is much better that Nye is no longer responsible for housing or health. I don't think H.M. [Morrison] will be a good Foreign Secretary. He had almost ceased to do anything about economics though Max Nicholson continued to write briefs for him and on important issues E.P. would get him to support the C/E's line. I suppose he will be more affected by R. Makins now.)[46]

On the political side, H.G. told me about 3 weeks ago that the Government would hold on until the autumn if they could, but that he did not think they would try another winter. Several people have said that the Labour members with safe seats are very tired of having to be on hand to vote all the time and that in any case it would be more congenial to them in times like these to be in opposition.

E.P. has definitely arranged to leave on Dec. 31st. He was being pressed by his firm, Tennants, to return or stay. He got a message to the opposition leaders asking if he would be fired if they came back. On Winston's orders, the reply was non-committal. So he decided to go – said he would be ruined if he were sacked by the Tories. Now the decision is taken, he is unhappy about it. O.S.F. thinks that he won't go in the end. I think T.L.R. would like him to go – many permanents, though they value him, regard the CEPS as an anomaly really.

Tuesday, April 24th

A great deal has happened since I got back. E. Bevin is dead, the Budget is out, Nye Bevan and Wilson have resigned: Gaitskell is now the most powerful of the economic Ministers and near the top anyhow: Plowden is the most powerful economic civil servant and altogether our faction very much in the ascendant, but I do not suppose it will endure.

I got back on Monday [16th] and found the B. speech much improved and everyone fed up with the constant re-writing of it: not much more on the gap or the outlines. But on Monday night and Tuesday morning there was a frightful row as Nye who had accepted the whole thing a fortnight before, now objected to the Health charges and wanted them withdrawn. H.G. at that late stage had no option but to stand firm, did so and was supported: and Nye in spite of his threats, did not resign.

The Budget itself had a reasonably good reception in the House – we had tried to shorten the speech and H.G.'s manner was much more conciliatory than S.C.'s. Also everyone expected worse than they got. This was repeated in the country and during the weekend members found that it had produced a very good impression. T. Crosland told me that the only thing anyone minded was the idea that Public Assistance scales might be cut down for the old age pensioners whose pensions had been increased. But this was put right.

Nye was criticized a great deal because he had said in a speech before the Budget that he would not remain a member of a Government that imposed health charges. Judged in the light of subsequent developments, it seems as if his initial acceptance of the charges and his not resigning before Budget Day were only tactical moves. Anyhow he made another demand that the charges be dropped at the end of last week, when the Bill imposing them was coming up. He refused any compromise and in the end Morrison and Whiteley [Labour Chief Whip] got so fed up that they told him he had better accept Cabinet decisions or resign. He could not believe they meant it but by now they were determined and got Attlee to write to Nye and this so enraged him that he resigned over the weekend.

He put his resignation on much wider grounds, rather clever ones on the whole. The real substance was that the UK would not be able, because of material shortages, to bear the burden of re-armament. He said a lot of other things that were easy to refute or that did him no good. But I thought that if we got into trouble, as we probably shall, all this would be forgotten and people would only remember that he had prophesied less re-armament and hard times and he was right. The fact that the Government had also thought these things probable might be forgotten. I thought it very important that this should be pointed out now and that he should be publicly accused of doing (what he is doing), that is running away from responsibility because reality looks unpleasant. Wilson took the same line the next day but much more cleverly.

However it has all gone quite well. The Party meeting on Tuesday was a triumph for H.G. and I gather that Nye behaved like a maniac and made the worst possible impression. At one stage he said 'I won't have it! I won't have it' and everyone shouted 'I? I?'. The general reaction in the country was good and the TUC and the Party National Executive both supported the Government strongly. The Chancellor was most anxious to make a public speech as soon as possible but was restrained. He is giving one in Scotland on Saturday, on which we have been working.

Meanwhile the raw material crisis has reached its height and a new Department is being set up. This is a complete victory for Gaitskell and

Plowden and a defeat for Wilson and Helmore, who has been the bitterest enemy of a new Department. Norman Brook had a good deal to do with it also.

Monday, April 30th

H.G. is still very much taken up with what Plowden calls his 'career'. He made a long speech in Scotland on Saturday but did not get a very good press and he left out the parts S.C. Leslie and I had put in about those who resigned being unwilling to face reality. Meanwhile Nye made quite good speeches at Ebbw Vale at the weekend, taking a more restrained line. The general effect of all this seems to have been to make the US more willing to give us materials. Wilson (i.e. the American Charlie Wilson) [Director, Office of Defense Mobilization] is coming to London on Wednesday – he is at present staying with Eisenhower who is himself concerned about raw materials because he feels that economic difficulties will lower European morale. E.P. has laid on a good deal for Wilson – I have been urging that we should not ask him for anything, just tell him our story and hope that his attitude when he gets back will be benevolent.

Stokes has been made Lord Privy Seal and Minister of Materials and E.P. has persuaded E.B. to make Hitchman his Permanent Secretary. I am glad that Hitchman has been promoted so fast – he is a sound, virtuous and hard-working man, also a friend of mine and I think an admirer. He has several times said that the events of the last few years have shown that the economists (i.e. me) have been right and the pure Civil Servants wrong. I rather hope he will take Bretherton who has been more than any one man responsible for there being a new Department since he pressed Turnbull [Planning Staff] and me and we pressed E.P. Also I think B. has served his turn in the Economic Section. He is very good but not as an economist and embarrasses me at times because his economics is a bit shaky. Though what I will do without him I don't know.

Saw P. tonight. He was reading an essay by N. Brook for the Machinery of Government Committee on central departments and (to some extent) economic. He said N.B. had very wild ideas and wanted CEPS in the Cabinet Office. I fear this may be partly due to something I said to Brook last Friday when I was feeling nervous about the victory over Nye. N.B. is obviously thinking about organization after the Tories come in, on present view about next October: and he thinks CEPS should probably be abolished and the Treasury re-organized. I was very anxious that the Central Departments should not do or try to do the work of the Departments themselves. Otto Clarke thinks we are much too centralized.

A good example of all this is the Defence Programme about which there is now such a row. It was done mainly by Downie (Economic Section) with some help from CEPS and CSO and a very little from OF. The Ministry of Defence agreed or perhaps put forward the £4.7 bn figure. Supply and Trade more or less reluctantly went along. The Chancellor with a little help from the PM and the Foreign Secretary and Morrison pushed it through largely on a belief in the Nitze exercise. But in a sense it all went back to Plowden and I being convinced by Jo Alsop that we needed to re-arm, about last April.

Of course I know that two civil servants could not push the country into anything – it is international affairs and Korea and American pressure and so on. Yet if we hadn't said we could stand it it might have been £3.7 or a smaller figure, and if we had not pushed the 4% productivity idea or had said it was all going to be disastrous, I doubt if it would have gone nearly as far. I think we were quite right, naturally enough. And Ministers have said over and over again that we must re-arm and they seem to believe it. But yet it is true that if we had taken different views the outcome would almost certainly be quite different. Just as, if I said that we ought to revalue today, we probably would.

However, one could not have all this influence unless one were (a) fairly steady, (b) made out a case that would stand up. In fact it is events that dictate the solution if one is an expert – it is one's own interpretation of them but it has to be an interpretation they will bear. One could get away with one imposition of oneself, just as if you are known to tell the truth you can get away with one big lie if no one can prove it wrong. But no more than that. However, all this is really meant to establish that the present defence programme was largely pushed on to the Departments and the Cabinet and the public by a few people and it is hard to believe that they really believe in it. A great deal will now depend on how production goes – it is a bit shaky at present but is still compatible with 4%. It may go lower. There may even be unemployment. If neither goes badly wrong, Nye will be proved wrong and we right.

Sunday, May 6th

I am on a 'plane again, on the way to Washington. Plowden and Makins left last night. He (P.) had been going for some time and in the end wanted me to go along, mainly just to look round but we may take the opportunity to talk about the long-term outlook for raw materials, and I hope also to talk about War Finance, picking up where Otto left off on our previous trip.

The last few days have had several interesting features besides the fact that the Festival of Britain opened and took all the top people away for two days. Charles Wilson was here on Wednesday – he saw Ministers in the morning. P. said it was a bad show and made him want to sink under the floor – and in the afternoon Bill Batt brought him to see P., me, Rowlands, John Henry [Woods], Harold Parker [Ministry of Defence] and Roger Makins. We had a pleasant time. I liked him very much. He was very anxious that raw materials should be shared fairly and also that the RM Conference should work properly. He said that until this trip he hardly knew about the effect of RM shortage on Europe, or about RMC at all. But he was going back to stir it up. I only hope we can put some decent staff there. He was worried about the US inflation but hoped to be able to stop the cost of living from rising much more and with that to put a real ceiling on wages. My view is that they will have much more trouble than they think: but I want to find out more of that on this trip.

US are now placing orders at $4/5 bn a month, deliveries are about $2 bn. By the end of the year they expect deliveries to rise to 4. If they have this and their present investment boom they will probably be unable to fit it all in without a good deal of inflation.

Monday, May 28th

Plowden and I were in Washington from May 6th to 16th. I had the best flights I have ever had but P. was much delayed on the way out.

We saw a great many people: no one would believe that we had only come to look round. I was very much struck by the extremely friendly manner of all the officials – the most marked for 4 years or more. This is partly because of the end of ERP. The main conclusions I reached were that the raw materials thing is much further forward than it was a month ago: and that their inflation has reached a temporary halt and may not turn out as badly as we expected. There was really a mild recession on while I was there and it has been followed by this curious price war at the banning of Resale Price Maintenance. Incidentally the new President of the Board of Trade [Hartley Shawcross] is just putting forward the White Paper on this: but his own attitude is very luke-warm.[47]

Wednesday, June 27th

Nothing has been written about home events since before I went to Washington. Most of the time since we came back has been spent in discussing economic policy: whether we should revalue, should we do anything about wages, credit, price control, dividends and so on. The Chancellor put a paper on all this to EPC last night [EPC(51)65] – I did a great deal of the drafting and am I suppose responsible for a good deal of the ideas.[48]

After a good deal of anxious thought I decided against RV [revaluation]. Needless to say the Bank and all Treasury officials were against it on instinctive rather than rational grounds. The Chancellor very much the other way but it was hard for him to go it alone. He wanted me to consult some other economists and himself suggested Kahn and Meade. Whether independently, or because of my arguments, they were both against it so that made it easier.

Our present policy is based on the view that the US had got commodity prices under control and that if they fall, or stop rising, we can reach a new equilibrium later this year or early next. I have been urging strongly that we should try to agree with the US to keep [commodity] prices down and the Chancellor has now taken this up strongly [EPC(51)68]; I am probably going to Washington next week for preliminary talks and he and Stokes will follow. I wish Ministers were not going as it is a very delicate job.

Prices. I have been suggesting that the Government ought to give the impression that the big price rises are nearly over for the time being.

Wages. They should repeat moderation and point out that wage increases will bring price increases now that production won't rise.

Dividends. They should really take action if the increase goes on.

Credit. There has been a great discussion on this. The B/E still want to put up the Bank Rate but the C. has refused and wants them to get the banks to go in for selective credit restriction.

Thursday, July 5th

W. [Washington?] refused to have Ministers on the price talks but said they would see Muir [Ministry of Materials] and me. I thought we were going this week so got out of Paris and Otto Clarke presented the UK case on Nitze. I gather that the Europeans spent most of the time trying to prove that we couldn't do it without foreign aid. I have been doing a variety of things – partly getting ready for Washington – we go on Tuesday 10th – partly discussing a speech the C. wants to make, probably at OEEC, against high raw material prices, partly the speech he wants to make here about the economic situation and the rise in the cost of living.

Last week H.P. and Marjolin saw Stikker who wanted to give a lead to Europe, which he said was getting demoralized. Marjolin was told off to draft a plan of action and we asked him to come and talk to us. He came yesterday and we have seen something of him. P. had a meeting yesterday. M. said that Europe was feeling very discouraged; they felt that re-armament was preventing any chance of improvement in social conditions. M. thought that this was too gloomy and that if only new impetus could be given it could be possible to re-arm then and later improve things generally. We all agreed with this.

The economic side is fairly easy – we can say how much coal, steel etc. is needed to permit a steady increase in production. My own view is that there is no fundamental difficulty about getting the production needed. But how to get the political impetus? The French and Italian elections have shaken everyone because after four years' recovery the Communist vote is increased. M. said that better tax systems and a fight against inflation were needed. But who is to give a lead to Europe on things like this? None of our Ministers, nor I think on the Continent. R. Makins said that only Winston and de Gaulle in Europe can give any lead. However we all felt that the first step was to assert confidently the economic possibilities but that we couldn't be ready before September.

Today the C. had to lunch in the House of Commons, Marjolin, H.P., Plowden, Makins and me. On the whole a very influential gathering, since what P., M. and I jointly advise in almost any wide field is likely to be done if it is a political starter at all. No one can do much, events and the momentum of the situation mean that whatever policy is adopted is not so different from what would have been adopted with different advisers or a different set of Ministers or party in power. Though I think that over some years the policy is important. The ship of state is very sluggish but it answers to the rudder or engine gradually. However I suspect that the longer one delays using a particular rudder, the more certain it is that it would have been used. This is all determinist, probably too much so. I have set the Budget figures for four years: I fought almost alone for devaluation and in the end got it: P. and I are really responsible for the two re-armament programmes. But if we hadn't been here, would we not have come to deflationary policies, to revaluation, to rearmament just the same. And how much difference would the delay have made?

At lunch we talked on the same general thesis; it was quite interesting. H.G. seemed in very good form; he must recover quickly as he has taken a bad beating over the Finance Act, now at last through. P. said that he was living on benzedrine and sleeping pills. Both very good occasionally, but not as a steady diet. Anyway we agreed to a talk at OEEC next week with a view to more of a demonstration in September. Also to the Chancellor making his speech against raw material prices, which I have changed into a plea for world economic stability. But didn't say much about the deeper problems.

Meanwhile [Robert] Neild, who has come to me from ECE strongly recommended by Kaldor, has been put on to making a study of Germany, which we have neglected too long. He went to Germany last week and has written me a horrifying note about the economic advice given by the UK advisers. He says they are all in favour of all the old laissez-faire remedies we have abandoned in the UK. I can well believe this.

Later Marjolin rang me and asked if we could have a drink and I took him to the Travellers. We talked a bit about the work he would do before September, stating physical targets and so on – we had all agreed earlier that it would be very ill-judged to bid for US help. Then he opened up on the state of Europe and we got on very well together – I was in a mood to see things broadly I suppose. He said that unless France, Italy and Germany could reform their tax systems, get inflation under control, and introduce social reforms, they would eventually move right or left again. He did not quite see how it could be done though he felt that the US had been far too weak – they ought for example to have forced land reform on Italy. Anyhow I was so much interested that I felt it was worth doing something.

M. was I thought not hard-boiled enough about *how* to do things. For instance he thought Crowther would help, whereas I don't think the influence of *The Economist* gets much done at all. What you want is to see that the right advice is given to Ministers at the critical moments. However we agreed to pursue this and I think I will do so.

However the question is can I fulfil in hours of gloom tasks in hours of insight willed. At the moment I do believe that we ought to try to save Europe, which I think is on the way down. I did not think this during

ERP; on the whole it clearly was not. Nor at the start of re-armament; I thought NATO was doing the job somehow. But since Nitze began all the Europeans are trying to show the US that they needn't do any more and ought to be greatly helped all the same. And now these elections. However . . .

Friday, July 13th

I am writing this in Washington where I have come to talk about raw material prices and whether we and the Americans can get them down by concerted action, or rather by agreeing at IMC [International Materials Conference] and elsewhere to act in such a way that they might fall. In the end we got very little instruction – EPC only talked about the paper on wool [EPC(51)71] and after I waited a long time to see H.G. he only spoke to me for two minutes and said I was to remember that tin and rubber earn dollars! Otto had just done an exercise on sterling area dollar earnings which showed that we actually gained from high rubber and tin prices. But high wool prices cost us very much more in sterling than the dollars coming to the reserve. Muir [Ministry of Materials] is with me. He and Hitchman had lunch with Stokes (the Lord Privy Seal and new Minister of Materials) just before they left and Stokes was all for much lower prices for almost everything but non-ferrous metals.

The Ministry of Materials came into formal and actual being this week and the staffs are now being moved. They have done much better with staff than I expected and both the Board of Trade and Ministry of Supply behaved very well in the end. Bretherton is going from me – I am sorry to lose him and cannot think of a successor but I am sure it is right: and anyhow he is much more of an administrator than an economist now and doesn't think internationally on the lines of most of the Section.

Thursday, July 19th

We have been talking prices most of the last week. The US views seem to be almost exactly the same as ours: that we want prices to be lower but fairly stable; that on the whole any general discussion had better be in IMC; that when a commodity was scarce it was difficult to control prices except by allocation; that in any case the whole operation we had in mind was a very difficult one; and that our means of carrying it out were not very good. On Friday last we had a first round: H.E. came and made a good speech from my notes and there wasn't a great deal of discussion. On Monday we had a long talk on techniques without H.E. and it was then that we found there was so much identity of view. Gibson (the chief US man on IMC work) was obviously regarding IMC as his child already and was mainly concerned that we should not overload it too easily or hurt its feelings too much. On Tuesday we talked mainly about wool and copper and on Thursday we had a concluding meeting.

Friday, July 20th

On Friday we had a short meeting to tell the Commonwealth people in Washington what had happened and we got the 1 p.m. 'plane to Idlewild and the 4.30 BOAC to London and I am writing this in that 'plane on Saturday morning.

Eric Johnston [Administrator of the Economic Stabilization Agency] had us and Knollys to lunch on Thursday: Fleischmann [DPA Administrator] was there, also Thorp [State Dept], Keyserling [CEA] and Griff Johnson [Agency Staff]. He had been talking to Howe about copper and wanted a meeting between US, UK and Canada to fix the price of a great deal of the world's copper which Howe thought the three of us could manage. This is of course almost exactly what I had had it in mind to do, as the next stage after allocation. We sent a cable to London and got a tentative approval yesterday.

The only thing we could not quite agree with the Americans about was on publicity. The Chancellor wanted to make a statement in the House to include a statement that the US and ourselves had agreed on the next steps to be taken and on the objectives. The US people felt that this would cause a lot of alarm and prejudice future operations. However the Chancellor gave way in the end, just as well: my own sympathies were on the US side.

I had a number of talks with Caine and Christelow. Caine is worried about the succession in Washington. Rowan has gone, Caine is going, Rowe-Dutton [Exec. Director, World Bank] going also: most of the UK TSD [Treasury and Supply Delegation] staff have been engaged quite recently. If (as I had suggested) Christelow went to Knollys it would mean that there was hardly anyone left who knew anything at all about the long and complicated story of UK/US financial and economic relations since 1940. I was much impressed by this: it is perfectly true and in my view it is the most important single thing in the UK economic picture. We have had, according to Christelow, an average of over a billion dollars a year one way and another since 1946 and of course under Lend/Lease we had a great deal more. In fact our whole economic life has been propped up in this way. This is no shame to us but it does mean that we ought to have good people there. In fact we are rather in a mood of penny pinching just now. I was a little indignant myself that the Grade I allowance for visitors was cut down from $16 to $14. It seemed so odd when prices have risen so fast lately, and considering that devaluation has reduced the value of transferred pay so much.

Christelow has written a memo on the functions and organization of a supply delegation in Washington which made inter alia the points about importance and penny pinching. I went to a meeting to talk about this and naturally was much in sympathy with the whole thing. The biggest trouble is not the money but the lack of any organization in London to act as a co-ordinator of the work there corresponding to all that is done in Washington. Rowan is very hot on all this and I had already made some suggestions to E.B. on a memo he sent.

Friday, July 27th

I got back on Saturday and Hitchman met me at Heathrow, an unusual attention for me – he was very nice and mainly wanted to hear how we had got on which I told him on the drive into London.

This week has been catching up a few odd bits and working at the Chancellor's speech. I thought it would all have been done when I got back but though Leslie had sent the Chancellor a draft, he had said he wanted to write his own first draft and done nothing when I got in on Monday. He began to work on it on Monday and most of the bits came out in the course of Tuesday. They were not very good and he himself didn't think they were. We all made suggestions and did some re-drafts, then he re-drafted again and at 9 last night he had a meeting in the House of Commons for final editing. Edwards and D. Jay, Eady, Gilbert, me, Armstrong (the PS) and Wright from IDT. H.G. kept us all waiting half an hour – it is a very bad habit of his and he really ought not to do this for senior officials. Then we talked interminably, he himself rather tired and not at all clear what he wanted. This went on till 11.45 and then most of us had to sit up another hour or so re-drafting. All very unsatisfactory.

I talked to William Armstrong about it this afternoon but he said and I agree that nothing will make H.G. efficient in this respect. He cannot leave it to others, he won't start till it is too late, and he cannot make it plain what he wants done in a draft. William also said that he felt that no Chancellor these times could afford to dine out as much as H.G. does: and that he made too many trivial and too few important appointments in the day. I feel very cross with him just now but much of it may be the late night.

I did not hear the speech but gather it went down well with the party. The general line was the one I had originally suggested, i.e. that we were nearly through with the rise in import prices and if the Government took a few steps in price control, credit policy etc. it would show it was being active. Subsidies were firmly rejected although the TUC had I think been pleading for them. The big feature was a freeze on dividends – this had been only a threat when I went to Washington but was fully settled, to my surprise, when I got back, and a White Paper ready. Inland Revenue had prevailed over economics in the form, which is a freeze at the average of the last two years' results. No nonsense about rewarding the enterprising or those who have behaved well. H.G. got in a bit about tightening credit which goes no further than I would have expected, though it says plainly that he won't have any rise in the Government short rate.

Not much else has been happening. J. H. Woods' resignation announced today and Frank Lee to succeed as Permanent Secretary to the Board of Trade – I am delighted. There has been a big battle against Helmore and it had reached a point at which it was just as well for the planners etc. that he should lose, since if he had won he would have won in bitterness. I hope now that he becomes P. Sec. of some peripheral Department out of harm's way. However the main reason I am pleased is because I really believe that the Board of Trade wants pulling together and I don't think Helmore is the man to do it. Frank Lee believes in all we are trying to do and I feel sure that he will collaborate.

Planning Board this morning to look at the state of the economy and the defence programme. Most of the worries were about the shortage of man-power for the new programme. But I complained bitterly that we ought to be trying to get labour for the coal mines. In the afternoon there was a Steering Committee to take a report by the Ministry of Defence on the defence programme [ES(51)49]. In this case it was because they had now worked it out in more detail and wanted to show that the impact was no heavier than had been expected in January. I suspect that they were putting over some increase but the people who argued this did not make a good case. The main points that emerged were:

(1) The economy is weaker than it was in January. This is mainly steel in my opinion.

(2) The programme is a bit bigger but it will slip a bit so over 3 years may be as it was in January. But it will taper off very slowly after that. The idea that Ministers and the country have, that there will be a big fall after 3 years, is nonsense if the Ministry of Defence get their way. This isn't generally realized.

(3) The Ministry of Defence have made *no* allowances for US end-items as part of this programme. Anything they get from US will be extra – we will be more armed than if it hadn't come. I don't believe Ministers understand this, or that they understand that the US ideas are probably similar, i.e. we can't get any economic help, only help to an increased programme.

I ought to write the whole history of the defence programme some time, going back to the dinner Joe Alsop and I had with E.P. late in April or early May last year [entry for May 26th 1950]. I feel quite sure myself that if we hadn't changed our minds then, we wouldn't now be doing nearly as much as we are. The most interesting point however is that no one has ever come really clean. The US gave Ministers the impression that we would be helped a good deal whereas we probably won't be helped at all. The economists and planners decided more or less arbitrarily what the country could stand and then slanted the figures to show that we could stand it. Since then the terms of trade are much worse and the steel outlook much worse, so if we could just stand it then, we can't bear it now. The soldiers played hard to get as much as they could, both on US aid and on the home programme itself. Ministers have never been convinced in their hearts that the programme was a good thing but they have been bounced along by everyone else and on the whole I think they have allowed themselves to believe only too easily that it would come out all right. It is rather a sad story.

Personally I think that the situation required that we should do about what we have done and that everyone must do what he can even if he is being a bit political or disingenuous if he really believes that the survival of his country is at stake. But it is a dangerous way to proceed and would disrupt all our system, the relations of Ministers to officials and of the planners to Departments, if we went on too' much like this. It is unfortunately a result of weak Ministers that officials get driven to acting like this but it is a very unhappy situation for the officials themselves.

Tuesday, August 28th

Plowden's resignation was officially announced early this month, and that N. Brook was to succeed him [as Chief Planning Officer]. P. is rather sad now that he has actually seen his successor's name in print. I had lunch with N. Brook but we did not get really intimate in our discussion; he admitted he knew very little about it. He wanted to know if I thought Campion was too much out – he *is* rather out of things but by his own desire, as the CSO itself is very much involved in planning. But I think that Campion's personality is the root cause – partly he does not explain himself, or speak, well or forward looking, and partly that he really does not want the CSO to be a forecasting office; in fact I don't think he is, or would regard himself as, a good economist as distinct from a good statistician. Saunders who does nearly all the forward looking for him is quite a different man.

N. Brook is to be succeeded by Padmore. Compton has taken Hitchman's job as Chairman of ONC, MAC etc.; not a strong man nor (I think) a good choice. Alec Johnston is going to the Treasury [as Third Secretary], where Leslie Rowan is just installed as head of OF. Eady is going some time this year but not likely to be replaced. It is said also that Ince is going from Ministry of Labour and Fergusson from Fuel and Power: while Bridges is due to leave next year some time. Altogether a tremendous change among these great powers in the economic sphere, and practically a new set of men. I will know nearly all the new ones quite well and in most cases I think the changes are actually very good ones: quite different from the feeling one sometimes has that the giants are going and only men to succeed them. Partly I have been working on a level with the old lot and they don't have the gigantic appearance that they have from a lower height. But partly that I think some at least of these who are going are not much good, they must have been once but are burnt out now: the dreadful life of the higher civil servant especially since 1937 or so has been too much for them.

Wednesday, August 29th

A good deal of work has gone on over the last month on the Nitze exercise and burden-sharing and European defence generally. The Economic Section (mainly Downie) has been mainly responsible for the work, through Roll on the drafting Committee and Licence whom I lent temporarily to the FEB Secretariat. Last week Strath had some meetings with the US side in London and achieved a great triumph as they agreed to say that '95% of the burden of defence would fall on UK, US and France, and that if each carried out its plans there was no reason to suppose that any was carrying a load much out of line with the others'. If this is admitted we are a long way forward.

Meanwhile however there has been something like a bomb-shell as Spofford introduced a paper to the NATO Deputies at the end of last week. This said that NATO must now concentrate on the Medium Term Defence Plan (which costs a good deal more than present commitments), and that no more help can be expected from the US than is at present likely from 1952–54, i.e. about the present foreign aid vote for 3 years. But there is plenty of room for more effort in Europe and what is needed is a plan to make all this, to fill the gap. This must be done as soon as the US have to go to Congress in January for next year's appropriation, and they can't hope to get the money unless their European partners are showing a satisfactory amount of keenness and energy.

This document coming just when the Nitze exercise, on which we set so much store, was nearly ending its first interim report, so different in tone, caused great surprise. It was written in the language of an official communication from the US G. [Govt]: at least it spoke of 'the US G.'s' and the 'US Administration's' intentions in categorical tones. If true it means almost a reversal of US policy and might well break up NATO: but I suppose it is not likely to be anything so drastic as this. The Americans who are not in the State Dept are very ignorant of the doctrine of when and how you commit your Government. There was a good deal of to-do about all this. It seems clear however that there is a great deal of difference of view between the various NATO countries about what each can do: at one extreme the US thinking that they are the only ones who are trying and that everyone else can do a great deal more: at the other some of the Europeans who don't really want to do anything except at US expense. It is quite clear that we cannot do much if any more – we are in a bad enough jam already. Otto and OF Stats. have done a brief for the Chancellor to take to Washington about our balance of payments outlook and it is intensely gloomy.

Thursday, August 31st [30th?]

Plowden came back yesterday and we lunched together at the Travellers. He is obviously very sad indeed to be going and said he had spent a good deal of his leave thinking that he ought to have become a Permanent Civil Servant. He had turned this down before partly on financial grounds and partly because he could get no guarantee that he would not be moved, if times changed, to some Ministry like Pensions or Civil Aviation. But now he feels that any work that he gets will be dull compared to the present and that he can hardly bear to see others sitting in his seat. As I think I have noted earlier, the reason he gave me for actually resigning was his fear that a Tory Government might arrive soon and organize his job out of existence and him out of the Civil Service. As he could get no informal assurances from Winston he thought it safer to go and I felt bound to agree.

I have been working on the speech the Chancellor is to make to the TU Congress on September 4th. He wants to talk about profit, dividends and wages in the hope that this will encourage moderation in the coming round of wage claims. It is very unsatisfactory to work on his speeches. Before he went on leave I agreed an outline with him, but this was no sooner done than he began to draft new bits. However we worked them all in and sent him an agreed draft last week: he has just sent back a quite new, and to my mind inconsequent version, and I am at a loss to know where to start. He is always like this with his speeches and does not seem to have, as most people do, a fairly clear idea at the start of the main ideas he wants to put across and the order of their development.

He, Plowden, Rowan and Leslie are going to Washington ostensibly for the IMF meeting, early next week. But they want to talk about many other things. And I hope very much that the Chancellor will decide not to claim the Waiver this year.[49] We have had a great deal of talk about it and all officials are firmly against this.

Friday, August 31st

I am going on leave today. Most people have tried harder this year than usual to get a proper amount. There has been no evident crisis, and as far as can be seen the war is much less likely than we had expected – at any rate the soldiers do not seem to be alarmed.

Leslie and I saw the Chancellor about his speech: he was very nice about his changes of mind but I had lost a great deal of interest by then.

E.P. came to see me to ask whether we would not have to cut the defence programme. I said we couldn't be sure yet and that a great deal depended on coal and steel which were under our own control. He wanted to know what line they should take in Washington.

Friday, September 21st

I came back from leave on the 14th. Gaitskell, Plowden, Rowan and Leslie still away. Otto Clarke has been working up a great atmosphere of balance of payments crisis while I was away, and Strath and Downie came to see me almost as soon as I returned, to discuss this. I had been very anxious that it should be done as a general exercise. There is something very odd in the situation, as imports and production both seem to be higher than consumption investment and exports warrant. I think almost certainly we have been importing stuff that has gone into consumers' stocks, work in progress etc., i.e. investment in stock.[50]

This was all somewhat put in the shade by the announcement of the general election. I suppose to some extent because I had been away, I had no idea at all that this was coming. I had of course been told earlier by H.G. that the Government was unlikely to go through the winter, but the form had been gradually looking more and more as if they would go on and dividend limitation seemed to be based on the assumption that the legislation would go through. I suppose P. will be able to give me the news when he comes back next week. I am very sorry that Retail Price Maintenance will be lost but on most grounds can't regret it a great deal (this is all assuming as everyone does that the Conservatives will be returned).

Friday, September 28th

The Washington people all back this week. They pitched a very gloomy story there and gave all the US people a great shock, though they ought to have been prepared for it. Nothing at all conclusive happened. I have seen quite a lot of E.P. who is even sadder than before to be going. N. Brook came to a meeting P. called to review progress; he made a bad impression on me as he was too ready to make generalizations, which showed how little he knew about it all.

They decided in Ottawa to set up four 'Wise Men' – after the OEEC precedent – to look at the problems of armament and economic capacity. H.G. wants to be the UK representative and after a lot of thought E.P. decided not to be the working deputy but to recommend N. Brook. However I suppose the election will make anything we say a bit restricted. The Chancellor has been getting drafts for the Mansion House speech on Wednesday [3 October].

Monday, October 1st

The Cabinet wanted another Minister to be G.'s Deputy for 'Wise Men', and he tried to get Pakenham who knows a little economics and is fairly sensible and being in the Lords not so tied up with the Election. However, P. said his health was too bad; and after some to-ing and fro-ing between N.B. and E.P., P. was told by the Chancellor that he must do it. He is going to Paris tomorrow to have a chat with Monnet, who with Harriman [and Plowden] will be the Wise Men. I don't think there is to be a fourth though somehow everyone talks as if there were, combined ignorance of scripture and of what is going on.

Meanwhile we have a big exercise going on arising from the balance of payments but designed to look at the whole economic system; Downie is doing most of the work. So I put Butt on the Wise Men working party and Neild to act as Secretary. Between these two we ought to keep the whole exercise together.

There is profound gloom about the balance of payments especially as we lost so much gold this quarter. I don't feel that it is as bad as all that but there are certainly some troubles around. Coal is the worst. Fuel and Power have produced a paper showing that we are badly out of balance over the next 3 years. On their forecasts we ought to import 7 million tons of coal a year. This costs about £50 mn in buying (from US) and freight. If we don't buy we cannot get various things from N. Europe by bilaterals. What makes all this so bad is that European Recovery depends to a large extent on getting coal and we are one of the obvious sources. How can we ask for help from others when we are quite unable to help ourselves?[51]

Monday, October 15th

The Programmes Committee have forecast the overall deficit next year at £515 mn which after allowing for stockpiling is about £400 mn more than we expected earlier. Abadan and other oil costs £100 mn. Coal perhaps £50 mn. Increased consumption, including imports for defence, about £150 mn. The rest is within the margin of error and in any case I doubt if it will be so bad, though I must say that we have not allowed enough in our calculations for steel.

Otto wants to make all sorts of import cuts and to go back on all the liberalization measures. He is also forecasting a very severe drain of gold, about £700 mn at least, because the RSA will also be in dollar deficit.[52] It is true that they are still spending the big wool profits of last year and that they are not getting them now. Otto Clarke seems to be able to prove that we suffer whatever happens, e.g. to wool. He is confusing various elements. In any period high prices for tin and rubber suit us. But high wool prices cause us to increase sterling liabilities very fast, and gold reserves not so fast, and the result when wool prices are falling is that we tend to have to pay in gold for our borrowing.

There is almost feverish activity in Whitehall owing to the combined effects of the bad economic outlook, the Wise Men operation in Paris, and the prospect of a change of Government. There has been a drift since 1945 and nothing since last year to have much effect on it. And now it looks as if Abadan and perhaps Egypt will offset some of the recovery that usually takes place in Labour votes as soon as an actual election is announced.[53] I have a feeling that the majority for the Tories will be 80–100. Last week I thought 50–80. It might even be bigger as so small a change is needed to produce a big result.

Norman Brook especially has been preparing whole flocks of papers on every conceivable subject including all the major things foreshadowed in the manifesto. The dossier will include a paper largely by Plowden on the Central Planning Machinery, one by me on the new

Budgetary methods, and one by me (I hope) on the actual experiences of control. But whether Lyttleton [Conservative MP], if he is the new Chancellor, will read any of this I do not know. He is generally said to be able, lazy and somewhat unscrupulous. I met him occasionally as the first NFM Controller, and later as Minister of Production in the war. He seemed to me to be the first RM Controller who really understood the problem of distributing a scarce material and the horrors of priority systems. We all felt that he did very well [as President] at the Board of Trade when somehow or other between him and Richard Kahn and all the officials between they introduced clothes rationing, utility schemes and concentration. But neither he nor anyone else who might do it will much like what he finds.

I went to Paris on Oct. 7th and spent Monday 8th there. Plowden in a state of high activity. I got the feel of the beginning of the exercise quite well but we made little progress that day because P. and Harriman quarrelled with Monnet all day. Ostensibly this was about the form of the exercise. H. supported by P. wanted it primarily to close the 'gap' between present plan and mid-1954 requirements as upped by Ike and to be cut down by a screening Committee under General McNarney. Monnet wanted to spend most of the time looking at the present situation and how to build on that, the 'gap' to be a very secondary consideration. As it could not be as simple as that, everyone was speculating about what M. really had in mind. It might have been that all the French plans were on paper and he wanted to cut them down by a realistic exercise (he said this quite often). Or he might have felt, only too rightly, that the US needed to be stopped straight away from setting the sights at a level Europe could not reach.

However, the Americans said they would sooner go home than do it Monnet's way. Harriman was said to have lost his temper with Monnet at lunch, not that Monnet minded. He has weathered more storms than that. However he came round about 11 p.m. – when we were all sitting worn out at the Bristol. Linc. Gordon telephoned to say he was all right now and it was all a misunderstanding. Obviously M. is not the man to misunderstand anything: so it is all a mystery. However I must say that later work suggests that as far as Europe is concerned his way might have been better, since their plans for post-1952 are all said to be as non-existent in any operative sense as those of the French.

Eric Johnston, ex-Head of the MPA and now Price Stabilizer, was here last week. F. Lee took a meeting to talk to him on Wednesday, and Stokes gave a lunch for him afterwards. S. talked quite amusingly about his time in Persia during lunch, where he was between Johnston and the American Ambassador. I thought it was not a very good idea. On Friday Leslie Rowan had been to lunch with Otto Clarke and me and his adviser, Griff Johnson, who used to be Bureau of the Budget and then helped Walter Salant to write the Gray Report.

I thought Johnston a very able man, who never spoke without considering what the effect of his words would be. I also think he is probably very unscrupulous. He was interested mainly in raw material prices and especially wool. Hitch has just gone to Washington and will

talk about it there – we have agreed that no use starting it up again in
IMC unless UK and US have agreed a line. But J. thinks we will run out
on it if the Australians protest enough. He may be right. Wool prices
were very jumpy all last week.

III

The first six months of Conservative government,

24 October 1951 to 11 April 1952

The new Chancellor turned out to be Butler and not, as generally expected, Lyttelton. His freedom of action, like that of other departmental ministers in the new administration, was limited by the appointment of a number of elderly peers as super-ministers, including the Lord President, Woolton, the Chancellor of the Duchy of Lancaster, Swinton, and Leathers, the Secretary of State for the Co-ordination of Transport, Fuel and Power. Butler had also to contend with the forays into Treasury affairs of the Prime Minister, Churchill.

Butler was a capable but indecisive and not very forceful minister. He lent a more willing ear than Labour Chancellors to the Bank of England in reviving the use of monetary instruments of policy and in seeking an early return to convertibility of the pound. Tighter money, in Conservative thinking, was preferable to higher taxation even if it meant a higher interest burden. The Conservatives also wanted to 'free the pound' by letting market forces govern the rate of exchange and hoped in this way to remove obstacles to the conversion of sterling into other currencies.

When Butler took over, unemployment was under 1 per cent – a peacetime low – and prices and wages were increasing fast. There was an acute shortage of labour and a growing shortage of raw materials and fuel. The balance of payments was in very heavy deficit and the reserves were plunging downwards, nearly $1 bn draining away in the fourth quarter of 1951 (entries for September 21st, October 1st and 15th). The economic situation reflected the impact of the re-armament programme, the sharp rise in import prices, massive stockbuilding, and special factors such as the take-over of the large Abadan oil-refinery by Iran.

Wednesday, October 24th 1951

Polling Day tomorrow. All the opinion polls suggest that feeling has been coming back to Labour and that the Tory majority will be smaller than had been expected until a week ago. It seems as if the feeling on foreign affairs reached its strongest over Iran and that we feel better because we are being tough in Egypt.

An enormous set of papers on the economic position has been prepared and the main one, by the Strath Working Party, is like a small economic survey: it will be taken by the Steering Committee tomorrow.[1] The OF people get gloomier every day about the balance of payments, largely because the drain on the dollar reserves has been much more than was expected, every week so far of this quarter. It seems quite impossible to stop these fairly big capital movements though I cannot quite see why they should be bigger now than they were just before devaluation.

At 2nd Secs. yesterday we had a rather long discussion about what we should say to Ministers and in particular whether we should press for a supplementary Budget. My own view was against it. The studies we had made show that we were not far out in our April calculations, and that the main error was on the balance of payments, partly because OF forecast the invisibles wrong and partly because the Programmes Committee forecast the volume of imports too low. If we had got both these right, the Budget might have been £100–£150 mn stiffer. But I don't think it would have made things very different. And what is needed now is not budgetary action of the kind we have had over the last 4 years, but something new.

In a way, I have come to the conclusion that this particular experiment in full employment has been almost a failure. Early in 1950 I thought it had been a success because it looked for a while as if we could get taxes down, and that would have provided an opportunity for taking a little of the strain off the system. If things had seemed to be getting easier we might have persuaded the workers that wage restraint was a regular part of the bargain instead of a temporary expedient. And at that time it looked as if we could get more people into the coal mines. But Korea and re-armament and the rise in import prices have brought out all the strains and rigidities, and it does not look (at the moment) as if they can be cured by the methods we have been using.

The worst single thing is coal. The labour force drops steadily, so far as we can see because of the boom in investment industries. We could export all the coal we could dig to Europe, save them dollars direct, and ease our supply problems and our EPU ones. But for all our planning we cannot get 0.1 of 1% of the labour force to move. So we will have to try either much higher wages, or unemployment. Coal itself has been one of the main factors in getting steel, since the iron ore programme was wrecked by last winter's coal imports from US, and if we had more coal we could get more good ore from Sweden. And the shortage of steel has ruined all our plans for taking the load off re-armament. Labour is also very short on the railways and there may be a transport crisis this winter. In short, all the critics who said that labour was maldistributed have become right, though the numbers involved are not large. The steel shortage has also led to a good deal of hoarding of labour as firms expect to be able to do more work than there will in fact be steel to permit for the aggregate of the engineering industry. There is something like an investment boom, though on the consumer goods side things are fairly easy.

My deduction from all this is that a Budget alone will do very little good and that its influence will be mainly psychological at this time: and it may produce a sharp upward wage movement, which we do not want.

I thought E.B. was much too optimistic about the speed with which we could make new Ministers, if they are Conservative, take painful decisions. They are very nearly pledged to do little about the social services, they certainly do not want to produce much unemployment, and they cannot really start by making taxes much more regressive. What I should like would be a cut in imports, an increase in Bank Rate, and a real attempt to deal with coal, steel and the railways. If these were done we could I think let the Budget wait. And I believe that the capital outflow which alarms OF so much would be much lessened by the combination of a Tory Government and Bank Rate.

Thursday, October 25th

Polling Day. The sky is quite clear at 7 a.m. and this ought to help
Labour. We had several very interesting meetings yesterday. First about
coal where Harriman has been trying to get a Superman appointed to
co-ordinate European efforts and wanted Spaak [Belgian Prime Minister 1948–51] to do it. Min. of Fuel and Power began by saying that there
was nothing anyone could do to help us increase output: then FO said
that in any case it was politically out of the question to have a European
come here to make remarks about our coal policy. Strath and I were
rather heated by this and pointed out that we wouldn't expect others to
help us if we couldn't help ourselves on coal and that the consequences
of refusing to play might be that other countries especially US would
refuse to play with us, on IMC and in many other ways. It all calmed
down after this and we agreed that Harriman and Stikker could
approach OEEC in any way they liked but that we could only sound
sympathetic till after the election.

In the afternoon Norman Brook had a meeting of Cabinet Office
Secretaries to tell them all about the constitutional difficulties of a real
change of Government. They say that it hasn't arisen since 1929, as all
Governments after that were regarded as successor Governments to
their predecessors. The turning point is whether the PM was a member
of the previous Administration and except for a very short period in
1945 it is true that there has been continuity. All Cabinet papers are
called in from Ministerial offices and it is the duty of officials not to show
any they retain to their new masters. And all official Committee papers,
files etc. are to be inspected to try to remove direct references to
Ministerial proceedings, other than decisions which have to be stated to
explain the position. The object is to prevent new Ministers from being
able to refer to secret matters such as dissensions in the Cabinet, refusal
to accept advice and so on.

Then E.B. had a meeting on the things we should say to new
Ministers, following the talks at 2nd Secs. N.B. and I got our way on
everything. E. and Leslie Rowan wanted to come out with a full
programme of all the things to be done, in the King's Speech on Nov.
7th. If time was too short for this, they should put off the speech till
Nov. 14th and say this was because they were getting a full programme
ready. We said that we would not be able to bully our new masters as
fast as this.

Monday, October 29th

It did not turn out quite so well as E.B. had another meeting on the 25th
and they had a new and fiercer draft done by Leslie Rowan. It called for
as much as possible on the 7th and the rest on the 14th, including some
policy changes in public expenditure. I objected to this and said the
crisis wasn't all that bad – we still had $3,000 mn in the reserves against

$1,500 mn in 1949, when I could not get O.F. to do anything. And I felt that it would be very bad if officials put Ministers in a panic and got them to do bitterly controversial things. Indeed I began to be nervous lest this was what would be done. However they took out the references to policy cuts, and the immediate measures were left at Bank Rate, import cuts, a halt on new building starts, a review of investment and of public expenditure, both *not* to be spelt out. There is not much in there (except Bank Rate) any different from what Labour has done and would have to do.

Today was spent on farewells and alarms. I saw H.G. at 11.30 to take leave – he was very nice and extremely complimentary, and we talked a bit about the election and the future. We both felt that the result was much better for Labour than could have been expected, and that this meant that no right wing Government would come in except after very unusual events. (NB E.N.P. later said flatly that it was a vote against Winston and that but for him the Tories would have done much better.) He said he would have to earn some money but wanted to write on Socialist Planning. Edwards and Jay both said they must earn some money too. Edwards rather pleased as he increased his majority. He said he might go to PEP, but would give up his Union, as he thought it would be rather wrong to start negotiating on the staff side when so fresh from the Treasury.

The alarms were all about Winston wanting to reduce the Chancellor to a tax-collector and make Anderson [wartime Lord President and Chancellor of the Exchequer] Chairman of EPC and the Production Committee. Apparently Plowden spent nearly all of yesterday with R. A. Butler, the new Chancellor, and told him that if W. had his way the Chancellor would necessarily play a very much smaller part – R.A.B. hadn't of course grasped this. P. was rather bitter about Winston and said as above. R.A.B. asked him if he would stay and I gather that he made a qualified affirmative. He wants to stay but has to save his face and not annoy E.B. and N.B.

Wednesday, October 31st

Yesterday at 2nd Secs. E.B. told us that there would be no change in the Chancellor's position, at any rate at present. He was obviously under very heavy pressure and he and N.B. were getting on very slowly with Winston, mostly I think persuading him out of ideas they felt sure would not work. E.N.P. in his usual way of pressing his own problems, pointed out that he *must* get a decision on whether he should go back to Paris (i.e. remain in effect the UK wise man) or not; and what our line should be. E.B. said that P. wanted to lay the foundations of far too many houses; if he did, hardly any would be built. We were told the names of a number of new Ministers: Salter was said to be coming to the Treasury as Fin. or Ec. Sec. Swinton to do Materials, including Allocation, as a help to Butler on that specialized side. Winston won't commit himself on the future of the Ministry.[2]

From 10.30 to 12.30 we had a meeting with the new Chancellor, my first. All the Treasury 2nd Secs. and me. The Chancellor, like Cripps, looks much less attractive in pictures than in the flesh. He was almost pathetically anxious to stand well with his officials but showed enough firmness when it was necessary: and enough ability to follow most of the arguments. I don't think he will be quite tough enough for the time but certainly it was a reasonably good first impression. We ran right through all the recommendations and it was rather sad to see how difficult it will be for the Tories to do what is needed without breaking most of their election pledges. He was in favour of Bank Rate but not convinced by Trend's paper – quite penetrating as Trend wasn't convinced either. And afraid he would be heavily criticized for a banker's ramp. It is a weakness, though it should be a strength, of the Tories that they want to placate their opponents while Labour on the whole wants to appear to treat theirs as badly as possible. One might almost say that Labour would like to conceal pro-Capitalist measures under a cloak of anti-Capitalism and the Tories to conceal anti-Labour measures under a cloak of benevolence.

Monday, November 5th

Donald MacDougall rang up last Tuesday to say that Cherwell was re-constituting the PM's statistical section and wanted him to head the economic and statistical side.[3] Could he come and talk to me urgently? He came up on Wednesday (31st but I had not time to put it down above) and we had a long talk. He obviously wanted to do it very much but was afraid I would be offended. I told him that it would be regarded in Whitehall as a retrograde step, on a par with the attempt to reduce the Chancellor to a tax-collector; but that I personally welcomed it because I did not want the Economic Section to have to spend all its time working for the private whims of the PM, but would nevertheless be very glad that someone was keeping him straight, or at least trying, as long as I could work with that someone. I think this is practically true though one can't be sure of one's own feelings in a matter so close at hand. At any rate it is clear that W. wants a staff and I certainly don't want to provide it, and better MacDougall whom I know so well and who wants to keep in with me than someone who wouldn't or who was a wild man. I saw Plowden and told him that on the whole we ought to welcome it and we sent messages to Brook and Bridges to that effect. They were much relieved as they were worn out from fighting W. on much bigger issues and did not want to start again on this, as they might have had to do if it had been someone I couldn't get on with.

He took me to see Cherwell in Christ Church on Sunday and we talked the economic situation over. C. has a pocket slide rule which he constantly brings out to do little sums: it is a mannerism as he did the only one we wanted much in his head or rather orally. He didn't seem to be very much on top of things and was deeply worried about the inadequacy of the measures we had proposed, in relation to the July visible trade gap: inclined to say there was no point in cutting food and doing so little and losing votes. I tried to explain that this particular gap was not the most significant, especially judged against July 1950 which he was doing. But McD. says he is quite good on some things, and of course in principle it is much better to have a PM who makes a row over important things than one like A. who never stirred a finger.

There has been a constant to-do about the measures to be taken, and the speech the Chancellor is to make on Wednesday [7 November]. It was to be Thursday but Cobbold practically refused to change the Bank Rate at any other time than noon on Thursday, and as we all felt that it would be a bad start for the Government if the first announcement came from the Bank, Butler is now to announce it after business closes on Wednesday and the Court will make the changes at the historical time. B. is in favour: Salter very vague and I have had several goes at him to try to explain it.

Today there was a meeting at 11.30 to run over the speech: B. very good, though still far too punctilious to his officials: however there is some *fortiter in re* as well as *suaviter in modo*. But I can't see him sending his colleagues weeping away because he has refused to let them spend money. Most of his suggestions for the speech showed good sense and political judgment. His colleagues have all been difficult about the measures but I think all came round now.

After the meeting Salter sent for me to ask about bank rate, full employment etc. Bridges had an official meeting at 4.30 to look at the re-drafts and when I got back at 6 there were two rather elementary essays by Salter, one on the evils of inflation and one on the present situation, which he wanted to send to the Chancellor that night. There were a number of errors which I mentioned to him; but the main trouble was that he has to do this sort of thing at all. I do wish he could get some work and not just attempt to think.

Wednesday, November 7th

Winston got a statement in the King's Speech that the Home Guard was to be restored. He did not say whether it was inside, or extra to, the £4.7 mn programme. In a good many ways he seems to be acting as if it were 1945 again and that everything we had or did then must be better than anything that has been changed. Otherwise the Speech not very controversial and at the last minute they left out the University seats.

A good deal more talk yesterday about Butler's speech and who else might speak. The 2nd Secs. meeting thinks less than nothing of Salter – I asked if he couldn't be given some work and E.B. said he was going soon to do all that the Ec. Sec. had done.

In the afternoon Rowan had a meeting about briefing himself and me for next week when we are to be examined by the wise men. The US are sending a very exalted team led by Charles Wilson so we are now trying to get the Chancellor. I saw MacDougall later on: he seems to be full of ideas for saving us and went into Bank Rate and selective credit control.

It is very hard to know what impact they will make but both Prof. and he clearly want to earn their keep and wield the instruments of power. David Butt has been doing a great deal to put McD. in the picture and will I hope keep on with it.

My own staff problems don't change much. Licence was going to replace Jukes in Washington but at the last moment we found that Rickett's staff are on UKTSD allowances instead of FO, so that L. would be half as well off as J. As he had meanwhile fallen in love with an American lady in Paris, he took this excuse to cry off Washington. He wants to stay on with FEB.

Thursday, November 8th

The [Chancellor's] speech yesterday was a great success – I had a few words with E.B. just after and he was obviously delighted, a most unusual compliment. I heard some of it and some of Gaitskell, who did very well but it sounded strange to hear him speaking with us not having prepared it. The Labour Party are very resentful at Winston's use of the word 'disclosure' in the King's Speech and feel that the Tories made all sorts of wild promises, refusing to look at the facts. Butler himself was very honest and referred to G.'s speeches.

It is a great thing to have got so far safely, told Ministers the worst and got them to tell the country and adopt some remedies. The crisis is so like several we have had in the past that I don't think anyone minds much. There is a run on tinned meat. Bank Rate went off calmly enough and the stock exchange actually improved. One of the evening papers said it was because it (the Stock Exchange) discounts all sorts of fears and the truth is never so bad.

There has been a rapid crystallization of feeling in Whitehall lately that the US has let us down over burden-sharing and that we cannot carry out the defence programme without help, and should say so plainly. Of course it has been expected for a long time that we would get something but the latest form makes this uncertain: and at the same time it seems clearer and clearer that our plans are too ambitious, as things have turned out (in my view as coal and steel have turned out, worsened by Abadan). I do not feel any qualms about our decision but I am sure we would not have made it if we had not been clearly given to understand that we would be in the burden-sharing exercise.

Tuesday, November 13th

I am going to Paris today with Leslie Rowan to be cross-examined tomorrow by the 'wise men'. The Chancellor has also agreed to come which is a relief. I have spent a good deal of time trying to get a few Ministers briefed about the whole exercise – I am sure that none of them understand it. I had a long talk to MacDougall on Thursday and Cherwell on Sunday. Also did some work on the Chancellor and even gave a private brief to Armstrong. All this because I feel that Compton who is responsible for all this, is incapable of grasping the essentials much less of stating them. To my horror, the Chancellor read my brief to Armstrong at a meeting yesterday and said 'This is all the Cabinet needs'. It was really, but of course said much less than the official brief had done. It only proves that we cannot do much by backstairs methods unless you know the people *very* well – or are prepared to act unscrupulously by giving hints and so on.

Friday, November 16th

Leslie Rowan and I went to Paris on Tuesday evening, with Goldman and Downie. We dined with Plowden and Eric Roll. The exercise is not making much sense so far and P. very frustrated. The French had been examined on Monday, a lot of Ministers had gone but had not answered any questions, only made speeches. The French economic situation is desperate and they had told Harriman that they would have to cut imports heavily and set the whole system back unless they were given immediate promise of help. P. said Harriman was so alarmed that he promised them $600 mn at once; they all spoke of this as blackmail but all my staff in Paris say that French morale is very low indeed and that whether they ought to collect the taxes or not, they cannot in fact do it.

We were examined on Wednesday. [Maurice] Dean [then Deputy Secretary, Ministry of Defence] and the soldiers did quite well in the morning, though it would have been a very dull affair but for General McNarney, who is running the TCS and who asked all the intelligent questions after Harriman had put the main ones.[4] The Chancellor arrived about 11.45 but just slipped into his seat. We were given lunch by M. Réné Mayer, the Minister of Finance, at the Café Laurent – a most opulent meal. Guindey and Clermont Tonnerre [French Ministry of Finance] were there. Mayer very cheerful and he and the Chancellor chatted away in French. Guindey and I talked about the organization of economic co-ordination – he had a Council of Ministers but practically no inter-Departmental co-ordination below that level and could not get any. C. Tonnerre told me how difficult Monnet was, with direct access to the PM and refusing to listen to anyone but his own advisers. He gets an idea and drives it hard to the exclusion of all else – I must say that we could do with some of that, instead of giving everything equal priority irrespective of its importance.

In the afternoon we had the economic examination. The Chancellor made an opening speech in which he mainly expressed our determination to do the defence programme even if it ruined us! But of course if we were it would do no one any good so we needed help now. However the firmness of the resolution made a very good impression. The rest of the examination seemed very perfunctory to me, and it was difficult to think that Harriman or anyone else was interested in the replies. The only real stir was on coal where we were very properly attacked by Harriman and Monnet and a Belgian who was attending as the representative of the 9 NATO countries not on the Executive. We had agreed beforehand that Plowden should stir them up to attack us on coal and that we should not try to defend our record. The Chancellor said that the Government had determined to do its best. I must say I thought Monnet went a bit too far as he suggested that it was the most important single problem for Europe. However much coal we dig up, the French will still have a financial collapse because they cannot collect their taxes.

After the main talk there was a much smaller private session where the Chancellor asked explicitly for $600 mn before June 30th and 1½ mn tons of steel in 1952: and they pressed us again on coal. The Chancellor dined with Harriman who told him he couldn't manage more than $300 mn. This was as much as I had expected and no doubt we will manage on that. Roll gave a dinner for us; Gordon, Tasca, [Etienne] Hirsch and [Pierre] Uri were there but we did not get anywhere. It seems a long way to getting the report written, and P. says that Monnet and Harriman both want to concentrate on 1952 because the prospect after that is so obscure.

Monday, November 19th

The Chancellor has put his Monday meeting at 10.30 so I was able to go today, almost the first time. He has now got quite steamed up about coal which is something. I was amused when he said that the PM also considered it the first priority, and that this showed how intelligent the PM was. The first fruits of the MacDougall, Cherwell chain: which is now working smoothly, and indeed MacDougall is now being got at by Strath and Rowan as well as the Economic Section. Strath and I thought there should be a small Ministerial Committee under Leathers [Sec. of State for the Co-ordination of Transport, Fuel and Power] and an official Committee under CEPS to deal with coal. This is the first step that gives any cause for comfort.

I was rather embarrassed on Sunday. On Friday B. had said that Salter was doing a paper on inflation and that I was to vet it, and Salter asked me to see him at All Souls on Sunday morning. He proceeded to give me his own calculation of the inflationary gap – the method would have raised the collective hair of the NIFWP and in particular he neglected the income effect of price changes and the price effect of income changes which seemed a bit elementary. It was a relief to find that he put the 'gap' nevertheless about where I did, say at £100 mn plus £150 mn for luck. And he returned to the old problem that caused Stafford so much worry, how to increase productivity and to keep wages from rising faster than this. S. C. Leslie had written E.B. a paper on the wage problem, and we are going to have an official meeting about it on Wednesday. It is not the demand inflation that we need to worry about.

I had a meeting of the NIFWP in my room on Friday to get their views on what we ought to do. There was general agreement that we couldn't deflate enough to hold wages but Downie thought we ought to try a bit more than we have done so far and I think he is right. The prescriptions were (apart from this) as one might expect. Most people wanted a bit more monetary tightness, a tax on steel and investment goods, direct checks on investment and so on. The big difference was between those who wanted prices to rise as soon as wages did, to show the link and to check the demand inflation; and those who still wanted as much price stability as we could get in the hope that this would give wage stability.

Wednesday, November 21st

Not much at 2nd Secs. yesterday – it seems a different place with Frank Lee instead of John Henry [Woods] – he is full of ideas of the most general kind. Hitch is a source of strength. N.B. can hardly ever come now and is I suppose at No. 10 nearly all the time. In the afternoon Strath and I had a meeting to lay on a paper for Ministers about the burden of armament now. MacDougall came. Downie was given a first draft to do.

Thursday, November 22nd

Salter produced his draft paper on Inflation yesterday and E.B. insisted on seeing a copy for a meeting of officials at 11.30. The paper was very rough indeed in its calculations and very vague in its remedies so I was put down to write a competitor, mainly about the wages problem. In the afternoon I saw Salter at the House about his paper. He seemed very ready to accept changes when I suggested them but not really to take them in; in fact I felt that he just wanted to get his paper finished because of the statesmanlike treatment of the problem – he had ended up with a lot of general stuff about more production and getting the co-operation of the trade unions, which was worse than either Stafford or Gaitskell on the same subject. Fortunately two of his constituents arrived and he was so anxious to talk to them that all the last of my remarks were accepted en bloc and I was almost hustled away.

Friday, November 23rd

P. came back from Paris yesterday for the Planning Board. The Chancellor went for ten minutes and said the right things. He also announced that P. was going to stay on; I think no one knew though I was expecting it. P. told me afterwards that the PM had agreed without enthusiasm. N.B. had a briefing meeting to which McD. came. It was agreed that I should start my briefs again, sending them through Norman. Norman was rather upset because the M. of Labour had put in a paper recommending a Control of Engagements order and we all supported it. He said 'I suppose this is a good Conservative measure' but I pointed out that they had accepted both the arms programme *and* full employment and this was one of the consequences. P. and I lunched together – he is very pleased that he is staying and wants to get back to London as he finds the whole Paris exercise very wearing.

The Planning Board meeting took the paper on the economic situation ['Report on the economic outlook for 1952', EPB(51)15] which had been shown to Ministers, and I thought it one of the best meetings we had ever had. We talked nearly all the time about coal. Vincent Tewson was the only TUC man there, and perhaps because of that he really said what he thought. Godfrey Ince was very good too, indeed I felt that in the course of the meeting he came round from the view he seemed to hold before, that really what was needed was more discipline for the miners and a new NCB, and was thinking in terms of anything that might be suggested. Graham Cunningham put forward the idea that the food subsidies might be abolished and the money used for the lower ranges of income tax but there was a lot of doubt and Tewson especially said that it would lead to equivalent wage demands. Nobody came out with any startling new suggestions for the coal problem but they all agreed that it was the most urgent one and that Ministers should be told so.

Ministers themselves haven't done anything about it so far and Strath is rather despairing. We thought it was all laid up for the Cabinet that took the question of the current wage increase – the Chancellor had promised to speak and Cherwell was said to have squared the PM and it was not necessary to do any more propaganda. But apparently Leathers refused to listen to anything else till he had the wages settled. As we had thought the wage settlement itself could be used as a contribution, this was bad news. But the worst was that there was no Ministerial Committee, no special attention to suggestions, no nothing. A month of the new Government lost already.

The Conservative government's measures to deal with the economic situation began with a rise in Bank Rate from 2 to 2½ per cent on 7 November. This apparently minor change heralded the reactivation of monetary policy, Bank Rate having remained at 2 per cent since 1932 apart from a short blip at the outbreak of war. It was followed by a series of cuts in the import programme in November, January and March, adding up to £600 mn, which were expected to wipe out the deficit in the balance of payments by the second half of the year. Public expenditure, including defence expenditure, was pruned in December and hire purchase restrictions were introduced in January.

The Treasury wanted a severe budget as soon as possible and proposed a cut of £200 million in food subsidies which the Economic Section thought would add four points to the cost of living index, and still more to wages, unless offset in some way. Hall argued that there were already some signs of disinflation, with consumer spending lower than a year before. In these circumstances it seemed useless to depress purchasing power by a severe budget in order to stimulate exports. There was capacity to spare for supplying foreign markets with consumer goods, particularly textiles, and re-armament prevented any substantial diversion of capital goods to export markets.

Debate on the action to be taken in the budget continued over the winter but before it was introduced on 11 March (and proved to be unexpectedly mild) the Treasury came forward in alliance with the Bank, with drastic proposals for a change in exchange rate policy, arguing that the fall in reserves was bound to continue and lead to a crisis of confidence in sterling that would make it impossible to maintain the parity.

Tuesday, November 27th

At 2nd Secs. this morning Edward Bridges suddenly said that we were going bankrupt rapidly, that the Governor (of the Bank) had just been to see him and said that the gold drain would continue until the Government showed that it meant business, and that this meant cutting Government expenditure firmly. The only thing that would help would be the food subsidies. At this Rowan, N. Brook, Hitchman, Frank Lee all chimed in with (I thought) fiendish glee to say yes that was the only thing to do. Eady said that Bank Rate would be more effective, Strath and I that we thought any crisis measures should be aimed at the crisis and to be shown that they were, and B. Gilbert took more or less the same line. But E.B. seemed determined to railroad it through and soon brought the meeting to an end, commissioning Rowan and Gilbert to do a paper to be given to the Chancellor that evening. I did not even see the paper before it went in.

The whole incident was very disturbing and shows how silly some of them are. If they are not careful it will be 1931 and another Bankers' ramp. But there is much more economics on the labour side, and much more confidence and militancy on the TUC side, now than then. I cannot see that labour will meekly accept the view that because the experts say this will restore confidence the workers must accept a large cut in their standard of living as a result, and not ask for more wages, which is what they will certainly do.

Thursday, November 29th

Yesterday was an interesting one. I got the memo at 9.30 and found it had been toned down a good deal but still asked for urgent action including food subsidies. The Chancellor told us at the morning meeting about his trip to Rome. He describes these things very well, making them seem funny and yet giving the main substance. He had gone mainly to see Snyder and inter alia had talked about the loan and the waiver. Snyder had advised him to pay and said that a preliminary look by the IMF had suggested that we would not be eligible for the waiver.

He said, what we had always expected, that in the middle West a man with a grocer's bill always paid it before asking for more credit. Nevertheless, if we wanted the waiver he would do what he could to smooth our path. He had also suggested a letter on Articles 8 and 9 – I did not see it but the Chancellor thought it very satisfactory. On all this, the Chancellor thought it better to pay the interest – Leslie Rowan and I were strongly in favour, Bridges more doubtful. It is an enormous relief to me – for all sorts of reasons, real and psychological. I have been convinced that we ought to strain every effort to make this first payment in full.

We then spent from 10.30 to 1.30 and from 4.20 to 5.30 discussing the memo and the crisis. However I got my way on everything and I think the food subsidy idea, as a rush measure and now, is pretty well dead. Strath helped a great deal but Butler and Boyd-Carpenter [Financial Secretary] were both anxious not to do it unless it was inevitable and I think they were much relieved that I was against it. In the morning we went over the whole ground and B. then lunched with the PM. In the afternoon he told us what had happened. Salter made a speech in the House lately threatening all sorts of vague cuts and this has embarrassed the Government a great deal. The PM told B. that he had not meant S. to make any speeches, just to think. He said 'You must keep him in the warren'. This was too much for us – it seemed frightfully funny and we were all reduced to helplessness, most unusual. Though I must say B. is a much pleasanter person than Stafford or H.G. and conducts business almost facetiously.

A great deal of the time was spent on the economies so far suggested to or by the Treasury. The big ones are on health – dentists' charges for all work except on children, pay beds in hospitals, and a charge for prescriptions as put forward by the last Government but dropped on pressure from Nye. On the food subsidies, I said that I had always been in favour of reducing them but had thought this should be done on merits and probably as a combined packet of higher pensions, tax reductions and so on, and not as a panic measure because of balance of payments considerations. They would not help very much here and might easily lead to further wage increases, which we did *not* want, and to industrial unrest. B. was clearly sympathetic to this and the others just sat and felt frustrated – I felt as if I had killed it single-handed. However the most important thing was that Butler himself was against making rush decisions, and he also urged strongly that since Parliament had objected violently to being sent away early, it would be out of the question now to keep them on for a fortnight. As I had been very frightened that officials would be bouncing Ministers into measures of political suicide by alleging that there was a real reserve crisis, I was deeply thankful. It would have meant charges of another 1931 and with the reserves even at $2,400 and the last six months with a build-up of imported stocks of £240 mn, we simply could not have got away with it. MacDougall has picked up the stocks point and told Cherwell (whom everyone calls Prof. and so will I) about it and he has made the point already.

The PM called a Cabinet for 6. He was against saying anything before January, on Parliamentary grounds.

Saturday, December 1st

Cabinet decided to have a statement on January 22nd, that is to get Parliament back a week early. They left the details to be worked out by a Sub-Committee of EPC and this will start work next week. The defence-engineering paper that Strath got finally agreed [EA(E)(51)1] is to go there for the civil cuts proposed – £60 mn off metal consumer goods and £100 mn off home investment.[5]

Wednesday, December 5th

The EPC had a meeting about coal on Friday – it was only partially successful. They refused to provide any imports as yet and they fixed the export at 8.5 mn tons for bilateral negotiations. But measures to produce more were left to Lloyd and Leathers, consulting other Ministers as needed. We had hoped that a Special Committee would be started. Cherwell was helpful. Butler told me on Monday evening that he would get his way with Leathers in the end, but he had to play him along now. He also said that Geoffrey Lloyd [Minister of Fuel and Power] had told him that he was already nothing but an Under Secretary to Leathers, but he was willing to do this if it helped the situation.

The EPC Sub-Committee had its first meeting on Monday. In the evening B. asked Eddy Playfair and me to dinner to talk about cuts in expenditure and their economic effects. If felt odd to sit in a room with three impressionist paintings I had often seen in exhibitions and worth very large sums each. Mrs B. was a Courtauld and B. and Playfair gossiped a good deal about making her a Tate Trustee. They were against it while B. was Chancellor. All this was well above my head. Afterwards we had a somewhat frustrating conversation about the main subject. Both B. and P. hopped about all over the place like birds and I like to finish the subject before going to another. However we agreed that most reductions in expenditure helped to reduce demand inflation – all except dismissals of the elderly – and that cutting transfer payments might add to cost inflation, especially food subsidies. The Chancellor's instincts are the same as mine, and he does not want a Budget in January if he can help it. He is a bit concerned however lest he be accused of making too many bites at the cherry and doesn't seem to realize that we left his last speech [on 7 November?] so that both January *and* the Budget are regarded as continuations.

After P. left he talked a good deal about personalities which I found embarrassing. It is clear that he thinks Leslie Rowan is panicking too much, as I did. Cherwell is plugging his point about stocks all the while and I think Leslie would be well advised to admit it instead of leaving it out altogether in his presentations.

Thursday, December 6th

A lot of meetings today. The Chancellor at 10, where he told us that Cabinet had refused to bring Parliament back on the 22nd and it would be the 29th as arranged. B. the only man for the change – his colleagues apparently (a) thought the less they saw of Parliament in its present mood the better, (b) could not think of any reason except the real one to give; and no one thought it wise to give the real one. E.B. and L.R. protested that it might be necessary, if a run developed after the figures were published on January 7th, to have an emergency meeting. I doubt it. The gold loss last week was the smallest for the quarter though at 44 still uncomfortable.

Monday, December 10th

I have written a note for the Chancellor to circulate to his EPC Sub-Committee about inflation and the wages problem [EA(E)(51)13]. Downie has done a first draft of the proposed White Paper.[6] Rowan and Clarke are more and more alarmed about the balance of payments every time I see them and keep on saying that the statement on January 29th must 'restore confidence', though it is not at all clear what they mean or expect. A big slice off the food subsidies would not do that.

Tuesday, December 11th

The draft TCC report [of the 'wise men'] arrived today. It is quite a good job but it skates very lightly over the fact that the US contribution will do them very little damage whereas for many other countries the recommended effort will be very painful. No increase is recommended for the US, UK or Portugal. All the rest are pushed up. The conditions needed to make the recommended efforts are stated fairly enough but there is too much protection by qualification and too little plain statement. It is just assumed as a fact that Congress will do nothing more. All this may be realistic, in the sense that Congress *is* the governing factor and that the European countries *can* be bullied or cajoled by the US. But it makes nonsense of the burden-sharing concept.

The talks on US aid to the UK began today in London between Batt and Compton with teams. The whole process ever since we were asked to go in for a defence programme in July 1950 has been most disillusioning. I thought then that we would be fools to trust the US but allowed myself to forget it. Not that I think it was wrong, even with the most complete hind-sight, to go in for the £4.7 programme. At that time it seemed to us that war was a very real threat and it was necessary for our own defence, and to encourage the US momentum in Europe, to do what seemed a lot and to take risks. But I think we allowed ourselves to rely much more on the Nitze exercise than we ought to have done.

The US have really behaved very badly indeed and not only annoyed all their friends in official circles here but have let down Attlee and Gaitskell and strengthened Nye Bevan. For some obscure reason Winston told Nye in the House that he was right when he said we could not carry out the disarmament programme, though for the wrong reasons. But all the Bevanites are arguing that he was completely right and H.G. completely wrong. I lunched with D. Jay today and he said Nye was now almost off his head with rage and megalomania and was demanding Gaitskell's resignation; from the post of ex-Chancellor I suppose. Tony Crosland is very much upset also as he has backed H.G. and the defence programme from the first and says now that he looks a complete idiot. They have all got perfectly good defences and in particular what we always said, that if the programme wasn't carried out it was all the more reason for the cut in the health service, is right. But Bevan keeps on saying that Gaitskell split the Labour Party for a few million pounds when it was clear that the defence programme would fall short by much more than this.

Thursday, January 3rd 1952

Keflavik, Iceland. I am on my way to Washington to be around during the PM's talks, though I am not officially one of the party We are stuck in Iceland for the time as one of the engines went wrong. Both Plowden and the Chancellor wanted me to go but it was thought that the PM was determined to keep the numbers down and so I was not on the official list. As Cherwell was going and taking D. MacDougall, they felt embarrassed and said it was ridiculous that the PM should be thought to be against it. And in fact B. told him about a week ago. However I am very glad I am going by air as the party on the QM had a lot of delays and probably very bad weather too.

The last three weeks have been busy ones, with the TCC Report ending, all the briefs for Washington to be got ready, and a rush of Ministerial meetings to take decisions about the cuts on investment and Government spending to be announced on the 29th. And everyone tried to get some Christmas holiday too.

The main things have been:

Cuts. The general effect is to get the Civil Estimates *below* last year's total, which is a great triumph if it sticks, since prices have risen about 11%. There are to be charges for prescriptions, a good deal of the dental work, and ceilings on some other bits in health. Also some rather small charges in education. Nothing else major. Nothing decided on the subsidies yet.

Budget. Arising from this, there has been a certain amount of preliminary talk about the Budget. Cherwell and Salter are talking about an above the line surplus of £1,000 mn for next year [it was in fact £88 mn]. I doubt if it will be as much as this, but this year's surplus will be much more than we expected [in fact, £380 mn], a combination of less spending and higher tax receipts. Next year defence will be up quite a bit but the holding down of civil expenditure plus rising revenues may give quite a good surplus. Also we have stopped stockpiling. Salter got hold of me yesterday to give me a long lecture on the probable surplus and what we ought to do with it. It is too early to spend what we are not yet sure of having but I have got the NIFWP to do a Final Budget in the next 10 days. A great uncertainty is the Investment Programme.

On this (*IP*) Eccles [Minister of Works] and Macmillan [Minister of Housing] have been making an attack to get the housing targets settled as 230, 260, 300,000 over the next 3 years. This increase is flat against the general requirement to cut investment but of course the Tory Party went a long way out on a limb on this. P. and I agreed to it as long as the total building labour force was not increased. Partly for this, but mainly for steel, there is going to be a savage cut in industrial building. The PM has agreed to scale down the building and civil engineering sector of defence, which had jumped up a great deal since the original £4.7 component.

The biggest headache in investment, however, is the plant and machinery. In order to expand engineering exports, against steady or falling steel supplies, the stated demands which are in any case bigger than available capacity, need to be cut heavily. And we cannot quite see how to do this. Strath has had some meetings which concluded that direct controls were not likely to be very effective. Now they are looking at fiscal measures but these will be politically unpopular.

Balance of payments. The gold loss in the end [in the fourth quarter] was about $935 mn. This includes the principal and interest on the US and Canadian loans. I think the UK is in overall balance already, with the import cuts, exports holding up well, and the decisions (if they can be implemented) on exports of coal and engineering goods. The black prospect next year, according to OF Stats., is that the RSA will draw down the reserves by nearly £500 mn and their balances more or less equivalently. But this depends on what is settled at the Commonwealth Finance Ministers Conference in a fortnight. I think it is quite certain that the RSA won't force us to bust the sterling area system, as they would do if they drew enough of their balances to run the reserves out. OF want to put a great deal of stress on internal measures but this will need careful handling.

White Paper. Downie did a first draft before Christmas and I sent it to Ince. He did not like it to be about full employment and wanted it to be called 'Inflation'. Probably it is right to say that the workers will object to a Tory Government publishing anything on full employment as they will think it is a preparation for an attack on it. However we recast the paper slightly to make it seem more on inflation, while keeping our three central points:

(1)   Balance of payments.
(2)   Distribution of labour.
(3)   Cost and Price Inflation.

While I am away B. Gilbert is taking charge, with Myrddin-Evans. The time-table needs to be pretty tight as both Cabinet and NJAC will have to approve it before it is mentioned by the Chancellor on the 29th. I have been more anxious to get this out than almost anything else. Now I am wondering if it will be as good or effective as I had hoped. I have not had nearly as much to do with the drafting as I intended. The constant pressure of other work and of trying to keep something of one's private life means that there is a great gap between one's ideas beforehand and the reality. In prospect, it seems that if a thing is really important one can drop everything else and concentrate on it alone. But however important, it gets into the machine and only the man who is put onto it as his main job can really concentrate. Meanwhile the process of official and Ministerial criticism whittles away the vision, that has not in any case taken the shape of one's dream.

Of course I am always having this, a sort of artistic frustration to which I am well accustomed. But I somehow felt that on this White Paper – where full employment is so important that the Government has a duty to explain to everyone what it will cost them – I would make a real effort and since it was my own idea that we should do it, it should also largely be my own drafting and management. Now quite apart from other things I will be in the US for ten of the important days. The only consolation is that Downie's drafting is entirely on the lines of my instructions, and I suppose these lines will persist.

Survey. Ministers don't want a survey that makes too many forecasts this year. I doubt if they can get away with it. However there is to be one. D. A. V. Allen and Wright have rather jumped the gun on the writing of it and persuaded Strath to put a draft round to the Economic Section and the CSO before we had had a first meeting. I don't care at all – the main decisions were taken on the basis of the documents prepared for after the election, and this might as well be written direct for the public. But Butt is annoyed. However he is always annoyed about something or other.

I went to Paris for a few days before Christmas, mainly to settle about Keane, Licence and Neild. Keane is to stay in Paris for 6 months or so, then he wants if possible to go to Administrative work. Licence is to be left with NATO for a year or more, and this will please him and allow me to get my staff down as needed by the intention on economy. Neild is to come back at once but be lost to Plowden for analysing the replies to the TCC Report which are needed before the Lisbon meeting (of NATO] in early February. I saw H. P. Rowan wants him to go to Washington to do the Fund and the Bank: but he feels this is a demotion (as indeed it would be) and wants to see what is to happen on our European interests. I think it is almost certain that NATO will be moved to Paris, in spite of the FO determination to keep it in London: and the Deputies will also be the heads of the OEEC Missions. But I fear H.P. is losing – it is a pity as he is really very good and faithful and the main tragedy is that he and Roger Makins did not hit it off. Oliver Franks got a GCMG in the New Years honours and presumably this is a pay off and he won't be renewed in May. However he will tell me all about this if I get a chance to see him tomorrow.

I had a long afternoon yesterday before I left. Swinton wanted to give me a message: it amounted to keeping the PM off all raw materials except tin and steel, because S. wanted to go to W. himself later to settle them. I doubt if anything will keep the PM off anything but S. hopes that Ismay [Sec. of State for Commonwealth Relations] and Cherwell and N. Brook and Knollys [UK representative on IMC] may be able to. However we had quite an agreeable interview.

Then I had the talk with Salter about the Budget mentioned above: and finally nearly an hour with the Chancellor, whom I like more and more, presumably because of his personal charm as I cannot really make out what he thinks. He purported to want to find out if I approved of how he, and our affairs, were shaping. I *do* approve on the whole. He told me that Eccles was campaigning against him which was very silly as it was all reported back to him at once. Eccles has been saying that the Treasury were just as Socialist under B. as under S.C. or H.G. But I do not see how they can get on without controls unless they use much more severe monetary measures than they could afford politically. In any case B. is just as keen on high employment as his predecessors. I think he is much cleverer, both intellectually and politically, than he thinks. And he has really got everything from his colleagues that he had set his heart on. I told him that all these difficulties were nothing compared to what we would have if we were not bloody now, and that he would get all the raps at Budget time if he did not make his colleagues take a few now.

I feel extremely uncertain about what the PM wants to do and what he will get on this visit. There are lots of briefs but he did not inspire any of them and we just can't say what he will play. However, all this will no doubt come out in the wash.

Frank Lee had lunch with me on Monday. He says that he is almost ready to get rid of Calder, his very ineffective Dep. Sec. He wanted Watkinson [Deputy Secretary of] Fuel and Power but I doubt if he will go as I suspect that D. Fergusson will be moved before long. He ought to retire in October anyway but wants to serve a bit longer to qualify for the higher pension arising from the Chorley increases. It is a frightful scandal if the retiring age, designed to guard against being stuck for too long with a bad senior official, is waived for the man more responsible for our troubles on coal and electricity, and hence on a great deal else, than any other man. Things have reached such a pass that all his own officials give information behind his back to other Departments. Frank Lee is doing well and Thorneycroft is, I think, making a good start as President [of the Board of Trade].

Campion is back from a great tour and came to see me yesterday. He wanted to hear the latest gossip. I told him that I wanted Saunders as Dep. Director – he was less opposed to it than I had expected.

Saturday, January 5th

Washington. It was not a bad flight: though I was practically a day late, it fell so that I could sleep most of the time. Eventually I got to Washington at 10.15 yesterday, travelling from New York with Taylor of the RM Mission who had in fact been on the 'plane from England, and who told me all about the non-ferrous situation on IMC while we were at Keflavik. He is a dull man but very competent and honest at the principal level and gets on well at IMC: is in fact Chairman of two of the Committees. He confirmed what the M/Materials brief had said, that the US were very worried about their supplies of copper and zinc and thought we had been buying what used to be their supplies at higher than their ceiling prices, and that they felt this did not square with the Muir/Hall talks. But we had not really been getting their supplies, and were mainly doing well because we had made long-term contracts. This shows how sensible we were to get the M/Materials going: our position is much better than it seemed a year ago.

I was met by Miss de Freitas of the UKTSD and am glad to be back under their wing: came to the Shoreham, and had lunch with Oliver and Barbara Franks. O. was in a rush as he had to go to New York that afternoon to be ready to meet WSC [Churchill] today. We talked briefly about the UK situation and he agrees with me that it is much better than seems likely from the gold figures alone. He feels that it is a run on the bank and a question of seeing it through. It isn't *exactly* that, since the current account transactions are nearly enough in themselves. But the RSA drawings must have a good deal of anticipation in them, just because of the Fin. Ministers' Conference. And the UK has taken measures to stop the drain from our own point of view. I discussed all this at greater length after lunch, with Denis Rickett. He made some quite acute observations though I think he is naturally very dilettante. He asked what I would do and I said that steps were in train to deal with nearly all the problems, and that if the Finance Ministers' Conference was a success it would be mainly a question of holding out – I would be willing to raise a loan on the RFC securities, if everything else done seemed satisfactory. He also asked about wages and said that these seemed the worst problem to him: I told him about the White Paper. Oliver and I had also discussed the C. [Churchill] visit – he is no clearer than I am about what will be the points for settlement and had had a letter from Roger Makins just before they sailed to say that this went for the political as well as the economic side. I think we have all been too concerned about an agenda and not ready enough to accept the truth, that W. just wants to re-open relations. As far as I can see, the people in the US are very glad C. is coming and hope somehow that he will give them a lead: but the Administration are nervous. There are no plans beyond today's, and a first business meeting on Monday.

Later I called on Knollys and delivered Swinton's message, that everything must be done to keep the 'package' deal to steel and tin. Knollys said that it now looked as if this might be done. The US side had wanted to include copper and probably zinc, as well as aluminium and tin. But they were now convinced that we couldn't do anything except be co-operative on copper and zinc, while he (K.) had already authority to lend some more aluminium. So it may be that we can give all that will be asked without going beyond existing instructions. K. brought in Waite the new man acting as his Deputy: he has only been on this for

3 months having been in Cairo and Burma on Treasury work before. He said he still felt very bewildered. I saw N.K.F. [Nancy Fisher, Counsellor, British Embassy] later and she said he wasn't doing too well as he never told the staff what K. was doing, and did not so far have any ideas of his own. I think she is very disappointed about him.

It seems fairly clear from the *Washington Post* this morning that C. is still a great figure. Apart from other references, the Hecht Co. have a welcome on the whole back page and Drew Pearson his whole column. Both the *Post* and Pearson plug the need for UK to join in European unity, the latest panacea here.

Monday, January 7th

The party arrived on time on Saturday and Leslie Rowan had a meeting in the afternoon about the economic side, which added very little. They had mostly spent the time on the boat reducing the briefs to single sheets of paper. I was surprised to see [Richard] Powell (M/Defence) there – he had been told to come at the last minute. We had another meeting yesterday afternoon to run over the ground finally, and then Norman Brook had a more general one. Nothing at all to report. I think I am going to the first meeting at the Exec. Offices this morning.

I had lunch with Allan Christelow on Saturday and quite a long talk with him in the morning. He is very disgruntled about Washington and the Treasury, and thinks that many of the recent appointments have been bad. I agree on the whole. The organization here has not developed at all and there is still very little co-ordination in spite of Leslie Rowan's efforts. Oliver has taken hardly any interest in this. I gathered that both S. Caine and Christelow himself are fed up about the treatment of Caine and especially that Rickett instead of C. replaced Rowan. I don't think R. a good appointment but am not sure that I would have thought C. one either. He is able enough but too detached and too prone to treat things purely academically. However Frank Lee thought very highly of him and indeed offered him the 2nd Sec. job at the Board of Trade.

Tuesday, January 8th

The first plenary yesterday morning in the Exec. offices; it was just like when Attlee was here. The President between Acheson [State] and Snyder [Treasury], with Lovett [Defense], Bradley [Chief of Staff], Harriman, Wilson and Fleischmann. Churchill between Eden and Leslie Rowan, with Cherwell, Ismay, Franks, N. Brook, [Field Marshal] Slim [CIGS], Roger Makins and me. The PM was very bad indeed on the economic side and I thought on other things too. He was deaf and constantly cupped his hand to his ear, and he was on most things not very clear in his thoughts. He was probably pre-occupied with the problem of saying we did not want help for ourselves but we did want it for defence, which I thought he need not have said. And he was pretty uncertain about dollars and steel. Eden was a bit better and Cherwell spoke once or twice but not well. Altogether a poor show on our side. It was at once clear that they wanted a number of materials in return for steel, as in fact we knew already from Knollys' conversations with Fleischmann. It was decided to have a Working Group on that in the afternoon – and Snyder is to give a lunch today at which, it is alleged, we will talk about finance. Eden mentioned NATO organization, both our desire for Paris and our doubts if it would be wise to have a permanent D/G as Chairman but that was left for a talk also.

Knollys had a buffet lunch to talk about the afternoon; Mike Wheeler [Jt Man. Dir., Guest Keen] had just arrived and I was glad to see him – now I have renewed acquaintance with three of my old steel friends. We agreed that Senior was to do all the talking on steel, and Knollys if possible on the others. At 2.30 we met Wilson and Fleischmann in the Exec. Offices with Harriman, Bissell, Willard Thorp and Ticoulat [?] who is Chief of the US side on IMC. We began on steel and to my surprise they said they could probably meet our needs, or nearly so. The types were difficult at first but they could promise that as the year went on, we would get more, and a better selection. This was a great relief as it had always seemed very important indeed that we should get something like this – in many ways it should put us on the right road again.

We then went on to their things. On tin they wanted 25,000 tons at $1^{12} instead of our offer of 20,000 at $1^{25}. They were mainly if not entirely troubled by the politics and I think felt they could not break so sharply with the present policy, especially perhaps as Symington is just going. In the end Fleischmann, who seems to me a very good and a very helpful person, suggested $1^{18} for the first half and to negotiate the second half price when we saw about the first. They begged us for copper, which is a very awkward one for us: and they were very cross about our offer of aluminium, where Fleischmann is much upset because their takings from Canada are falling while ours are going up. F. said that he could not face getting only the 7,000 tons we suggested. We were very stiff on most of this and I thought a bit ungracious in the face of their steel offer. Afterwards we had a frightful time sending a cable and I was exhausted by evening.

Wednesday, January 9th

A quiet morning yesterday. Before lunch I saw Charlie Hitch [ex-Fellow of Queen's College, Oxford], now Chief Economist to the Rand Corporation, which is a US Air Force organization for academic research into Air Force problems. I am trying to find out if we ought not to do the same sort of thing but Charlie wouldn't talk about it much. Of course there is a big security point. In any case I have, I hope, started an approach to the Defense Department to get some advice.

Snyder gave a big lunch at the Treasury to Cherwell and the economic members of the PM's party. I sat between Glendinning and someone I couldn't place called Graham. After lunch there was a short talk. Snyder as usual said practically nothing except that it would help a good deal with Congress if we would make an expression of intent about our long-term ideals on convertibility and non-disc. Cherwell was quite good on our economic position and Harriman very helpful indeed. Prof. tended to blame the last Government for our troubles on re-armament but Harriman said we had acted very honourably in putting up the programme and acting on it and he reminded Snyder that the TCC Report said we couldn't manage the defence programme unless our dollar deficit was covered. Snyder suggested a group to look at long-term problems and asked Willis to get it moving. I had a word afterwards with Glendinning and Thorp and I think their ideas of organizing it, to be quite informal but continuing, and meeting as occasion served, are just what I have in mind, i.e. it won't consist of the UK Washington people, *nor* of visiting firemen on the occasion of their visits. But there will be a US group in Washington and a UK group in London and we will exchange ideas, and have meetings when any of us are available.

In the afternoon a difficult and painful but in the end satisfactory meeting with the US people about the steel/raw materials deal. We told them what we could do, more or less their minimum requirements, on tin and aluminium. But when we came to steel and tried to finalize it, it seemed that Fleischmann had not understood what we wanted or had been given a different set of calculations from his own people. Prof. took this very hard and said how disappointed he was and pressed strongly for an agreement to be reported at 5 to the President and PM. I felt that Fleischmann thought we were trying to put a fast one over on him and that he was being reasonable in asking for at least a meeting to try to reconcile the figures. However in the end under pressure from Wilson he agreed to a formula which sounded all right. However I think there was a real danger there. It all arose because instead of cross-examining us about our needs, they said they thought they could meet them, first off. And apparently thought they knew exactly what these were, but it is doubtful whether they had grasped what either the PM or Prof. had said they were.

After the meeting both Senior and Knollys saw him and he seemed quite happy, so perhaps I was wrong. But it was quite uncomfortable for a while.

Friday, January 11th

There have been some ups and downs on materials. On steel, Senior and Wheeler saw the US people on Wednesday and got a most satisfactory agreement, which to our great astonishment included a request that we should take care of their export markets in certain cases.

As we had been terrified lest they should question the large exports we wanted to make, and say that we could not adopt an easier policy than them, this was a big change. I don't know why they have unless it is that they want us to take a lot of ingots and hence that they are short of mill capacity. It suits us very well to have ingots.

The big surprise has come on tin. Harriman wrote to the PM on Tuesday night asking us to give them the second 10,000 tons at 1^{18} firm because they were disappointed at the little we could do on aluminium. The PM accepted over the telephone without consulting anyone, a most admirable decision from all points of view though it must be annoying when one doesn't agree with the decision. However yesterday there were signs of great distress and it transpired during the day that Symington, whom I had understood from several people to approve the whole transaction, was very much against it. I could not make out whether he had been consulted during the negotiations or not. But apparently he now argues that we have been buying tin at under $\$1^{18}$ and will make a profit and that he could have got it for less. As we originally offered to let them have it at cost or $\$1^{25}$ whichever was the cheaper, and they preferred 1^{18} firm, we feel a bit disgruntled. Last night Charlie Wilson was proposing to drop the tin deal altogether and I gather that Harriman told N. Brook to let it go on our side to give Symington a chance to buy if he could. I knew of course that it was very much mixed up with politics but did not realize that it was as bad as this. Symington is resigning next week and we know they are very short of tin and have been afraid to enter the market because it would push the price up. But now there is a chance for us to take the risk and save their faces, and he (Symington) is playing it for a break purely because he feels that he will seem to have been consistent right to the end.

On Wednesday George Willis had a meeting in the Treasury on long-term objectives. Bissell and Thorp and Stinebower were there, and for us Leslie Rowan, Rickett and MacDougall and me. Willis very cautious and on the whole implied that the problem was entirely how to manage the UK and the RSA efficiently. Bissell of course ready to examine all the possibilities. He says he is really going now but I don't know. The end of the meeting was an agreement to study the problem independently both in Washington and in London but to keep in touch. This is probably better than to use the tripartite organization machinery, which did not work at all. But I don't know if this will either.

Thursday, January 24th

I returned to find OF even more gloomy about the gold reserve prospects for the next six months. The only really adverse factor or rather sign was the $75 mn gold payment to EPU in the third week but I suppose that as each of their successive forecasts has been so much worse than the one before, they have decided to be professional bears in all they say and do.

The Commonwealth Conference has come and gone. It was a

moderate success but they did not offer to dollar ration. E.P. had Doug Abbott [Canadian Minister of Finance] to dine on Tuesday 22nd with John Deutsch, Frank Lee and me. He was quite interesting, mainly because he thought the RSA was a great weight round our necks. Like everyone else, he was against the Food Subsidies. OF have persuaded R.A.B. to have a March budget to take them away, as they think this will restore confidence.

Monday, January 28th

A good deal of Friday was spent in drafting the statement to be made in the House tomorrow. Armstrong negotiated with Gaitskell and he suggested a statement so that the Labour Party could have a meeting that evening and not begin the debate till Wednesday. He hoped in that way to make the debate constructive rather than bitter, though the cuts in social services, small though they be, will stir up a few troubles.

We have been working on the consequences of the early Budget if it is agreed (the final decision is for Cabinet tomorrow). I had a meeting of the Ec. Survey WP on Friday and we agreed that neither the balance of payments nor the Nat. Income figures could be ready by Feb. 20th which would be the last day for a Survey to be published March 4th. It would be rather pointless to have one with no figures in it. We recommended having one in April as we felt the Government would be very much criticized if it dropped it altogether. Today I had a meeting with Trend about the Alternative Classification etc. My working party on this has just finished its report and decided to recommend a definitive one to be called the Economic Classification. However it is too late to agree on this now so we decided to have the Alt. again this year.[7]

The Budget will have to rest more than ever on the Chancellor's judgment. The NIFWP is working at this year's objective but it looks very uncertain. If anything deflationary, more because we cannot sell the exports than anything else. The problem is undoubtedly to divert engineering output to export. Jukes has just written a long paper on all this [EC(S)(52)5].

E.P. has to go to Paris on Thursday for the second round of Wise Men. Then he is supposed to go to Lisbon for the NATO meeting. He hates to go just now with all the Budget decisions to make, especially as he thinks that he and I are the only people capable of giving the Chancellor a clear picture. I must say I think he is right. E.B. only wants to decide *something* and Leslie Rowan is in a state all the time, and will be until the reserves stop falling. The 3rd week was bad because of $75 million for the December EPU settlement. The 4th week started badly but ended quietly. I still do not believe it is as bad as it seems. Met Muir and Bretherton today – they have just sold the US 25,000 tons of our stockpile of rubber and it is a good deal, as they can replace it cheaper. They are almost ready to start the tin and are on the point of selling 30,000 tons of lead – all this should bring in quite a lot of dollars: going on for $100 million.

Wednesday, January 30th

I went to the House yesterday to hear R.A.B.'s statement. It was very full and before it Winston was arguing with Attlee in a friendly way about his statement next week on the US visit; and Eden made a statement about the Ismailia police and the Cairo riots. On the whole the House was very much with him though several Labour members asked questions about notice, the size of weapons and so on. The Chancellor's statement was a bit too long on the general considerations, and sounded very unconvincing on the import cuts. I was glad to hear Labour members protesting at claiming the use of stocks as an economy. The rest of the speech was better and was well received, Labour almost disappointed that the social service cuts were not more savage; and everyone startled about the early Budget. I am a bit nervous about this because it looks as if we are moving into a deflationary situation. However we must push at exports; and we can always get the tax incentives better and plug that line; the trouble is that Butler insisted on giving the idea that it would be a savage Budget in spite of advice to the contrary. I felt that he did not really know what he was talking about in the speech, and E.P. told me yesterday that he did not really know what the current position was or have the feeling. No wonder, poor man.

Thursday, January 31st

I had nearly an hour with the Chancellor yesterday. E.B. saw me first – even after this long time he feels that he ought to know exactly what goes on, I suppose quite rightly. The Chancellor wanted mainly to find out how I thought things were going and what should be done about the Budget and so on. I told him that I thought he had had a very good press. He said somewhat wistfully that he did not think he had yet attained Stafford's stature – he was younger and had had less experience, but he hoped he was growing in the public eye, not for himself but because a Chancellor should do that. I feel all this is genuine really and that he *does* want to do his duty. On the B., I told him that we probably ought to get in a little more but where could we get it? He wants more also, and suggested wine and tobacco – I am a bit against either. I tried to warn him that we were running into some unemployment, and after all this was a bit surprised when he asked what could we do about inflation, as if it were a new subject. I thought he was rather relieved when I said he couldn't very well be criticized for unemployment *and* inflation at the same time.

Later I discussed things with Plowden who was just going to Paris for the next TCC exercise. He had been to a meeting of Treasury 2nd Secs. to discuss top positions. Compton was down to go as 3rd Sec. to HF to do the work Eady gives up on retirement. I have known him a long time and am quite sure that he is a man of no real mental capacity and somewhat doubtful honesty with himself, though I think he is very assiduous in writing minutes and so on and of course well above corruption in the ordinary sense. P. has seen a lot of him lately as he was the London end of the exercise being Chairman of MAC, ONC etc.: and P. has gradually come to share my view. But when he said this, N. Brook and L. Rowan were scandalized. The Chancellor apparently said we ought to get someone who understood finance and banking from the City to take Eady's place, and they were scandalized at this too. The Trade Union in action. I must say that I don't look forward with any optimism to the time when these two are the top men. L.R. is very good in some ways but 'the top economic job is too much for him, and I can't think N.B.'s judgment of men is any good if he thinks Compton and Campion so good. The CSO think Campion does practically nothing and are not sure how much he understands. But I think he constantly consults N.B., as Compton does too – maybe this is the high test, i.e. in N.B.'s eyes, of merit.

Monday, February 4th

The BC took our paper on the prospects for 1952 [BC(52)8] on Friday and agreed without much talk that there was not much to be gained from further straight austerity. The system was spotty and the un-employment that would be caused by this would be a heavy price to pay for a bit more exports. The problem was really to expand the engineering exports. The rest of the time was spent on possible ways of giving back anything that came in from food subsidies. We sent up a selection to get the Chancellor's reactions. Croft made a passionate plea for less indirect taxation but no one else wanted it. On beer and tobacco, where it would be sensible, it is almost out this year politically. I was asked to re-draft the paper a bit for R.A.B. ['The budget prospects', 4 February 1952].

Tuesday, February 5th

The Chancellor had a meeting yesterday about the wretched White Paper on wages etc. It has already been re-drafted about six times. He and Monckton [Minister of Labour] have very sensibly decided that it is no good putting it out before March 4th since that would seem something between special pleading and a bad joke. But they will meet in a day or so to discuss the draft in the hope that we can agree the form and ideas so that if it is later decided to issue it, all the first agonies will be over. S.C.L. [Leslie] wants him to meet leading Trade Unionists, at dinner or elsewhere, in the near future to explain Government policy on wages, social service cuts etc. We all feel a bit nervous.

In the afternoon Strath and Campion and I had a meeting about the Survey and agreed to write it first and get the Chancellor's ideas after. The decision to issue it after the Budget makes it essential that it should at the least give an account of policy. Departments are to be asked for material at once. Butt and Dow were rather annoyed because CEPS have been grabbing the drafting from Ec. Sect. Butt at least deserves no pity as when he writes it he fills the air with protests to the effect that it is humiliating for an economist to do such prostitution.

Hopkin came to see me – he is tempted by the Directorship of the NIESR [National Institute of Economic and Social Research] but would sooner research *inside* the Government. Rather than lose him, Campion is prepared to make such a job for him. I hope this goes through – he wants to work on Nat. Income statistics and these are disgracefully bad, considering that the Budget rests on them.

In the evening the Chancellor asked me to dinner to discuss the Budget prospects paper. He was very amusing and intelligent, and I enjoyed the evening very much – he is, unfortunately perhaps, the sort of man who persuades one to talk freely and afterwards one wonders if one has been indiscreet. He always tells a few stories about Winston – last night he said he has no sense of honour in the way ordinary people understand it. Drive, enthusiasm, patriotism and so on: but not honour as between gentlemen. He also said 'He loves cads. Can't keep away from them. It is the most disturbing thing about him'.

Winston keeps prowling round looking for surpluses the Chancellor can give away: the Chancellor really understands he can't do this but keeps on asking wistfully.

Wednesday, February 6th

The Chancellor had a meeting at 10 this morning to go through the BC papers. At 10.30 William Armstrong brought in a slip of paper and he said 'It looks very bad', and told us that there was a Cabinet called for 11.30. At 10.45 William came with another slip and he (the Chancellor) said 'The King is dead'. We were all startled of course. It had just come over the tape. The King [George VI] died in the night but it was kept very dark: I am quite sure that neither R.A.B. nor E.B. knew until then, and I heard later that Mountbatten [uncle of Prince Philip] had not known at 10.20.

We are to meet again at 2 but there was another Cabinet until nearly 4, so we continued then: at 4.50 the Chancellor had to leave to go to the Accession Privy Council. I suppose the Accession will be announced tomorrow. I think everyone without exception will be very sorry and will recognize, what indeed we all feel, that he was a very good King, who was not expecting to have that arduous and exposed position but who did his best when his duty called him to it. It must have been agony to have to speak to the world when one has a bad stutter. I cannot help feeling that it is a good omen to have another Queen called Elizabeth. Tony Crosland lunched with me and said that Attlee brought the news to an acrimonious meeting of the Parl. Party where someone (? Fenner Brockway) was making a violent speech against the bipartisan foreign policy here. The meeting adjourned at once, which all felt to be a commentary on the speech. Tony feels very blue as the row with Bevan is very high and likely to continue.

We argued a bit about Butler's measures and I felt that Tony's main objection to them was not that they did not suit the situation, but that they helped Bevan. I told him I felt annoyed that he and H.G. had been arguing that there was no connection between social service cuts and the balance of payments though there were cases where it would be slow to work. I think I have now briefed five Ministers on this subject, the Chancellor, the Financial Secretary [Boyd-Carpenter], the President of the Board of Trade [Thorneycroft], Lord Swinton, Crookshank [Minister of Health]. It shows how little the leaders of the Tory Party understood the policies of the Labour Chancellors.

At the two BC meetings the Chancellor showed a good deal of doubt about whether it was wise or expedient to have so mild a Budget, and in the afternoon Leslie Rowan and Frank Lee argued strongly in the same sense. I agreed that if we could get a better balance of payments by a more severe one we ought to do so: but I felt I *must* pose the question of the unemployment level that we wanted. It was left that we should try to collect a bit more and give away a bit less.

Friday, February 8th

Yesterday afternoon we met again, and B.G. produced a paper on the food changes and the reliefs to children and pensions. The latter cost more than we had expected and the Chancellor and Ministers were rather alarmed at the large addition on bread. The atmosphere was therefore becoming very dejected, that of doing things that cause a lot of trouble for very little good, when suddenly Cockfield [Director, Statistics and Intelligence, Inland Revenue] produced a scheme for putting a tax of £1 on coal and thus getting a great deal more to give away. This electrified the atmosphere. Rowan, Lee and I were all very enthusiastic; the others more doubtful about buying so large a pig without trying to open the poke a bit. However the more we looked into it the better it seemed and for once I went away in almost light spirits.

Later on went to L. Rowan's meeting, which I had been to the day before also, on what we would do if the reserves went on falling. Otto Clarke is now in favour of devaluation and I am not. The main problem was the steps we would have to take on the sterling area. It is difficult for most people to envisage the end of so many options, that when there are no reserves a number of courses *cannot* be chosen because you have not the means to choose them.

Tuesday, February 12th

Plowden was back over the weekend. The Chancellor had a BC meeting at 11, after 2nd Secs., and Armstrong, E.P., Strath and I had a long discussion at 4.30. The situation is still very undecided, as Leathers does not like the coal tax at all, while the Chancellor is a bit nervous about food. Armstrong argued strongly at the later meeting that there would be a great deal of bitterness, in the present mood of the Opposition, and that the best thing of all would be to do coal, plus minimum compensation, and keep the proceeds. Then if there is too much unemployment later, we can have another Budget in the autumn to give something back. I thought this was attractive – I had never liked the food [proposal] much because of the political bitterness it might cause, and the wages aspect.

Friday, February 15th

These few days have been publicly taken up by the funeral arrangements, and privately the most violent shifts about what will be in the Budget. Now 18 days away and 20 major decisions taken. However the issues are (a) will Winston get any of the surplus, (b) coal or subsidies, or both or neither.

R.A.B. lunched with Winston on Wednesday and they spent 4½ hours on it and even tried to read the Ec. Section paper on the gap [BC(52)22]. But gave up in despair. Leathers doesn't actually block coal and Houldsworth [NCB] has argued for [a tax for] 1 year, but there seems no point in it for so short a time. D. Fergusson has made all sorts of difficulties and is now concentrating on the alleged effect on the NUM. As he has been wrong in all his judgments for years I don't see why anyone should listen to him on this.

The Bank plan, first mentioned in the entry for February 16th, and later christened Robot, was devised in the expectation that the reserves would fall to a level at which it was no longer possible to peg the rate of exchange. The Bank, supported enthusiastically by OF, was in favour of letting the pound float at once, within a defined range, blocking 80 per cent or more of the sterling balances held by other countries, and making current earnings of sterling by non-residents of the sterling area (and such balances as were not blocked) freely convertible into gold or dollars. This would have flouted IMF rules against variable exchange rates, put an end to the European Payments Union, and provided Britain's trading partners with a strong motive to discriminate against the purchase of imports from Britain so as to be left with more sterling for conversion into dollars. The only alternatives to Robot that were suggested – for example, an Atlantic Payments Union or an enlargement of the sterling area to include members of EPU – were unlikely starters or suffered from serious drawbacks. If, however, the Bank was mistaken in predicting a collapse of sterling, no radical changes might be necessary.

The scheme had been brewing for some weeks but Hall first heard of it only on 16 February and was taken aback to discover four days later that it was intended to give effect to it in the Budget on 4 March. Although at first willing to consider the plan (entry for February 20th) he became strongly opposed to it and took a leading part in mobilizing opinion against it.

At meetings of the Cabinet on 28 and 29 February, the plan was shelved, thanks largely to the opposition of Cherwell, the Paymaster-General, whom Churchill had brought in as a personal adviser, and it was again turned down, without going to Cabinet, at the end of June. What survived was a modified plan for combining early convertibility with a floating pound provided a number of conditions were met, notably financial support from the United States and the IMF. This plan, to be implemented in association with continental countries, was called 'the collective approach to convertibility'. It took shape in the later stages of the preparation of a report by a working party on convertibility, chaired first by Hitchman and then by Brittain, and was debated at a conference of Commonwealth officials in October 1952 and a second conference, of Commonwealth Prime Ministers, two months later. When it was at last put before the United States government in March 1953 by a mission led by Churchill it was dismissed as 'premature'. As will be seen from the diary, however, life in the Treasury in 1952–3 was dominated by plans for early convertibility.

Meanwhile other members of the EPU were on tenterhooks to know what was going on and were strongly opposed to the central idea of letting the pound float. Efforts were made to work out some link between European currencies that might be introduced after convertibility was achieved. It was not until 1955, however, that the conflict between British and continental ideas came to a head and not until the end of 1958 that convertibility of European currencies, including sterling, was finally established.

There are various published accounts of Robot including Cairncross (1985), MacDougall (1987) and Plowden (1989). The Bank of England side of the story and the later history of 'the collective approach' are in Fforde (forthcoming). For a European perspective on the long struggle to reach convertibility, see J. J. Kaplan and G. Schleiminger, The European Payments Union *(forthcoming).*

Saturday, February 16th

Downie re-did the NI calculations yesterday but they came out much the same as before. We have however put the export target up and consequently the figure for personal saving required, to something like last year's estimate. This does not alter the picture of course as we will still get unemployment instead of exports if the Board of Trade forecasts are right.

Most people went to the funeral yesterday so there wasn't much business and I managed to write, or get Dow to write, my drafts for the speech including a convincing case for a coal tax. But the whole speech may have to be re-done as the major decisions are not taken, and indeed we are meeting all day today instead of [at] Roffey.

Yesterday L. Rowan showed me a paper from the Governor advocating a most drastic operation on the sterling balances, to be followed by 'limited convertibility' whatever that means, at a range round a rate. It sounds wonderful but I suspect he needs to use budgetary and monetary policy, i.e. variations in employment, to keep within his band. No Government would accept this at present.

We are doing better in EPU this month but the reserves took a big knock this week from the Jan. settlement – over $90 mn. The January trade returns were good except that dollar earnings so low. It looks as if the world hasn't really begun to solve its dollar problem.

Tuesday, February 19th

We spent most of Sat. on the B.: still a good deal of uncertainty. Yesterday afternoon there was first a meeting to look at the first draft of the speech, then Leslie Rowan had one with George Bolton, E.N.P., Otto, Lucius Thompson-McCausland, Parsons [Bank], Flett [Treasury] and I to discuss the Bank scheme. Then the Chancellor had a meeting from 5.30 till 7.15 to go on with the B. Very exhausting.

I feel rather pessimistic about everything, an unusual state of mind for me. The details of the B. are nearly settled now, though they may come unstuck: but at least we have got the candidates done and probably the range of each. But I do not feel very much at one with anyone about either its appropriateness to the situation, or its political impact. It may well set off a big round of wage increases and cause a good deal of disturbance industrially.

The Feb. unemployment is thought by Ince to be up on the Jan. figure and if so it will be the highest for a very long time. My feeling is that we are more or less in overall balance at the moment, and if so and if the RSA are going to make heavy cuts on their imports from us, we are probably running into less employment still. But underlying all this is the feeling that the country is approaching a political crisis, in which the dilemma between the ideas of egalitarian socialism and of middle-of-the-road planners are going to clash violently.

Wednesday, February 20th

Meetings all day yesterday. The Chancellor had a BC instead of the morning meeting. He is very much against putting up the standard rate and it was practically decided to do one of the schemes which spend about £200 mn and give progressive ease up to £2,500. There is a meeting today at No. 10 of the inner group to discuss the main features. MacDougall came to see me in the afternoon to say what he had been telling Prof. – it squared surprisingly well with what we are in fact intending, which was a relief. The Chancellor had previously said he was apprehensive about what Prof. might say.

After the BC we had a talk about Bank Rate where views were still somewhat divided, and then I had a chat with E.P. who was very gloomy and felt that if only he had not been in Paris we might not have done the food subsidies which he and I both feel are probably a bad bet. However I said that we were only too likely to have a big change because the reserves were still moving out and that this would lose the food subsidies in the general commotion. As for industrial unrest, it will follow from the unions' unwillingness to accept a Tory Government and not from any particular measures.

I took Armstrong to lunch and discussed the whole situation and sketched a plan if it were even at this last hour decided to drop food. It is lucky we have coal in the picture. In the afternoon, three meetings about the Bank plan, which now seems more attractive to me. One with Rowan and Bolton etc., one with Rowan and Bridges, the last with officials and Salter and the Chancellor. It certainly looks a great deal better when one thinks of alternatives. It seems to me very likely that Maurice Allen thought of it as it is much too clever for George B.

Friday, February 22nd

On Wednesday afternoon there was another meeting with Rowan, Bolton etc. at which it was proposed to do the new operation, if at all, on March 4th. This was the result of a dinner the PM had, with Rab., Cob. [Cobbold] and Crookshank the previous night, at which Cob. had propounded his scheme and the PM had said it would be dishonest to introduce a Budget without disclosing all your intentions. I was very much taken aback as I had never supposed that there would not be time to have a good look at so revolutionary a scheme. We saw the Chancellor later and got authority to look at it with the Departments most concerned. I took MacDougall to dinner and we talked a bit about the B., since Prof. now knows the story. However I also gave him a hint of what was in the wind and found him very much opposed to the floating rate or to any move from the present one. There is no doubt that the critical effects will be very adverse.

Yesterday Maurice Allen [chief economist, Bank of England] came to see me in an agitated state and I found that he also was opposed to the move. I wrote a Minute to Bridges first thing, protesting against this very precipitate action, and later saw the Chancellor and he agreed and (I think) it is put off a week. But it is still most alarming.

Saturday, February 23rd

Yesterday was given over to what might almost be called intrigue. On Thursday there had been a meeting of Permanent Secs. of the Departments mostly concerned, taken by Leslie Rowan, who explained what was in the wind and asked them to give preliminary opinions *that day* about how it affected their Departments. (It was from this meeting that I was extracted to see the Chancellor.) There was no comment at that stage. Allen saw me at 12 and I took Frank Lee to lunch and told him how much alarmed I felt. I also said that Plowden should be brought back [from Lisbon]. In the afternoon the morning meeting was resumed – everyone but Frank Lee and Strath (to whom I had spoken) was stunned and the FO especially merely said that if they had to tell other countries this they would have to – they made *no* comment on the political repercussions. Lee, Strath and I all raised objections but were not given much chance to speak. Then we saw the Chancellor and to my horror he said he fully appreciated all that this meant, that it would end the Conservative Party, but that it had to be done. Salter was much weaker. Meanwhile Otto had written a draft paper for the Chancellor to put to his colleagues on Friday morning. It was a most able document and set out the issues very fairly though it did not try to quantify the results.

Yesterday morning I saw the Chancellor early and asked that Plowden should come at once and repeated my fears that we were acting blindly. Then I saw MacDougall who said that he could guarantee that Prof. would hold it up. Then I went to a small meeting in the Board of Trade to discuss alternatives – I found Helmore, Caplan and Cohen [all Board of Trade] more against it almost than I was. In the afternoon I saw Prof. and MacDougall and at 7 p.m. the Chancellor who was very depressed as he had had a bad Cabinet.

Friday, February 29th

There was supposed to be a Cabinet at 10 p.m. last night but unless it reached a decision, the issue is still open. On the whole the party in favour of the Bank and OF scheme is in the ascendant. Cherwell, Salter (who has been very good) and Swinton against, Butler and Lyttleton and Thorneycroft for. Other Ministers have been brought in slowly and the whole thing conducted, in my view, with the greatest impropriety, since issues of fundamental importance to the UK and the western world are being rushed through without any attempt to analyse them. P. came back on Sunday night and has been fighting nobly but no one will listen to him or me now as we are regarded as sentimental defeatists.

Tuesday, March 4th

Apparently the Thursday evening Cabinet was left very even, as Eden had swung towards our side. On Friday morning they met again and practically decided not to go on with the scheme, at any rate for the time being. R.A.B. was exceedingly distressed as he had regarded the thing as his own child to save the country – he called a meeting (I was not there) and practically upbraided Salter and Plowden. In the afternoon they accepted the alternative we had suggested, or some of it, and at 5 there was a BC. By then the Chancellor was in better balance and L. Rowan behaving like a good civil servant. But I think there is probably a good deal of bitterness left.

Yesterday at 2nd Secs. Hitch asked what had happened to the plan and I took the opportunity to say that I thought the events of the previous week were distressing and ought not to have taken place. N. Brook said that it was not the different views held among officials that mattered, but that Cob. should have known about them. In the afternoon I saw E.P. who was very angry as he assumed that this referred to him. He said also that E.B. was very cross with him and thought he had behaved badly in intriguing against the Chancellor. I said I felt strongly that it was the officials in favour of the plan who had behaved so irresponsibly, in allowing the Chancellor to put forward something so drastic at short notice. He talked about resigning as soon as a decent interval had elapsed and so on, but I suppose it is only another storm.

Wednesday, March 5th

I saw E.P. first thing and said that it would only be running away from our enemies if he resigned (I had previously said that we might not be forgiven and ought perhaps to take the opportunity to clear the field of them!). He was in any case a good deal calmer and arranged to see N.B. later and try to make an agreement with him. This he did at 3 p.m. At 4.15 we had a talk with Strath and MacDougall about what ought to be done next but did not think of anything new though I felt that we ought to have a good look at the problem of frustrated exports.

E. told me he had had a friendly talk with N.B. I saw him myself at 6 and he told me that Prof. had made a great deal of play with the fact that E.P. and I were both against the scheme. He did not *blame* either of us or hold us responsible but he thought Prof. had no business to quote officials by name, though he admitted that my position was different from Edwin's, and that I had a responsibility to the Cabinet as a whole. I told him that I had been very worried over the whole episode not for those reasons but because I did not believe Ministers were being given a chance to understand the thing and he said that several of them shared this view – the papers had been quite inadequate. I regretted that I had not consulted him – looking back I certainly should have told him how alarmed I was – and he regretted that he had taken no part in how it was handled: he said that until a late hour he thought of it as 'Budget' which he tried to avoid. It was a useful talk and he was very nice and sensible about it. I can never quite make up my mind about him.

Friday, March 7th

No sooner had I sat down on Wednesday (March 5th) than William Armstrong came to talk about the speech and while we were talking E.P. burst in. As soon as William had gone he said he had been offered the NATO job which Oliver had turned down; Monnet had suggested him and the FO had indicated that they would not object. The Chancellor wanted him to go. However much more agitating than this, William had told him that the Chancellor had lost confidence in him 'because he had changed his mind so often'. He was devastated by this as he had always supposed that R.A.B., like Stafford and Hugh, had more confidence in him than anyone else. He did not know what to do. I said I thought he would not be happy in the NATO job as he would find it very frustrating.

Later I saw the Chancellor who was very frank, said he thought E. ought to go to NATO as it was a wonderful opening. The Treasury would have to be re-organized anyway and though there would be a place for E. it would not be at the top. In any case he could not see E. as a permanent Civil Servant. I was very cautious and told him that I had said to E. that *I* thought NATO would not suit him: I reserved my views on the Treasury. I do not believe the Chancellor understands anything about what the Treasury does or how CEPS runs or the economic system as a whole. His main trouble with E. is that the latter has been away nearly all the time since the election. If he stuck around a bit now he could soon be restored to favour. Later E. said that the Chancellor thought we had changed our mind very much about the blocking of the balances during the several bits of alternative suggestions we had made. But he said *I* was restored to favour and not him. It may be, of course, that the Chancellor feels that E. is very temperamental and unsure of himself, as indeed he is. But no one else in the Treasury gives any advice worth much on main policy questions, and none of them have any administrative drive at all.

Yesterday E. told me he had decided to turn the job down because the Chancellor wanted to get rid of him and he wouldn't go in those circumstances – it would be running from a fight. However it was clear that he had to leave in the next 12 months anyway as all the Civil Servants had come to that conclusion.

Worked most of the day on the speech. It is coming round. Dow and Downie are towers of strength. The decisions are not yet taken, it is a very late hour.

Had a long talk on Wednesday to N.B. and Padmore about Ec. Sect. staff. Agreed that I *must* get a Deputy from a University. But could probably promote Dow and Downie now. I had been rather annoyed as N.B. had kept me waiting for 6 months for this talk. He was very apologetic and said he was little more than an extra PS to the PM now so could not call his time his own.

In the budget on 11 March Bank Rate was raised to 4 per cent; food subsidies were reduced from £450 mn to £250 mn a year; the duty on petrol was increased; an Excess Profits Levy was introduced; and initial (depreciation) allowances were withdrawn. On the other hand, reductions in income tax were made that roughly offset the impact on consumer incomes of other tax and subsidy changes. The net effect of the budget on consumer demand was quite small but it was intended to exercise a damping effect on domestic investment.

Tuesday, March 11th

As I write this the Chancellor is making his [budget] speech. It really only just got written in time. The final decisions can hardly be said to have been taken before Sat. lunch when he lunched with the PM, though by then it was mainly a question of £50 mn more off the food subsidies, or petrol, or the surplus. To the last the PM wanted to raid the surplus or at least put it in a 'suspense account' as he did in 1927.

On Friday night the Chancellor rang me up at Oxford about 10.30 and talked about the Budget on an open line, it is true in rather cryptic terms. He was mainly worried because a telegram had come in from Australia announcing the big import cuts and he said this was what I had been predicting all along and did I think we ought to have a less surplus. Of course I said no. It is so funny that ten days ago he and O.F. wanted to cancel 80–90% of all the sterling balances of everyone and now one country acts as if they have only small balances and they get alarmed. R.A.B. rang me again on Saturday morning to ask if he was right to leave the taxpayer in the same position – just the opposite of the night before. I said we had to because it would do little good to make him worse but we were cutting investment instead. He said he had now seen it for the first time.

All the same, Bridges decided at 12 that I would have to go up so I did – the Chancellor had asked Eady of all people to re-write the section on the economic objective. Plowden and Downie and I laboured on Eady's draft and cleared it with the Chancellor. On Monday the whole thing was re-drafted by Salter to leave out nearly all the calculations. I re-drafted it again and put them back and took the opportunity to make it quite plain that we were not producing more austerity because we did not think it would do any good. This draft got by – at midnight Armstrong was still working with Eady, Trend, Downie, Jenkyns (the 2nd PS) and I in the room. By then I felt that the speech was really becoming a good or at least a lucid one.

This morning I got the final draft for checking but while Downie was still working at it I was told to go at once to the Chancellor and found Bridges and Armstrong with him. He wanted the calculations about the effect of keeping taxation unchanged (net) on the inflationary position to be reduced almost to nothing. As it was 11.45 and the speech had to be duplicated at 12 it seemed hardly worth struggling further. So Bridges and I re-did it on instruction. I expect it will baffle the critics as it is hardly a calculation at all.

At the end Armstrong said that all this re-writing and cutting out was due to the Tory belief that it was 'Socialist planning' to make forecasts at all: and that Salter had been working away at the Chancellor on this line. Hence all the troubles. I never knew a Budget speech to be left so late, or for that matter the main decisions. But it is partly because of the frightful struggle about the overseas sterling etc. which took up ten days or so at a vital time. Armstrong says that the Chancellor is determined to come back to his plan at the end of the month. I would expect this to depend on how the reserves react. I suspect that the Budget will have a good effect, as Bank rate and food subsidies together will look pretty fierce. It seems to me very likely that unemployment will get a good deal worse this year: we shall have to see if the demand in the engineering industry keeps up.

Thursday, March 13th

I did not go to hear the speech, perhaps partly from pique that there was no room in the box – I let Dow and Downie toss for my seat in the gallery. About 5.40 E.N.P. came in and said it had pleased the Conservatives very much and that the Labour Party were disappointed because they had expected it to be fierce. I took Dow and Downie to dine at the Travellers, as a sort of gesture after all their work: and I enjoyed the evening. I am sure they ought to be promoted: no other Principals in the whole service are asked to take anything like their responsibility.

The papers yesterday gave the Chancellor as good a press as we could have hoped and a better one than we expected. They were a bit surprised that more was not needed, because they did not understand the combined effect of the import cuts and the need to export more engineering goods. In the afternoon H.G. opened for the Opposition and he also broadcast at night. He made quite a good point, that if no net addition to taxes were needed why was the Budget advanced? There is no real answer to this except that OF and the Bank were convinced that a strong Budget was needed to give us any chance of restoring confidence. They felt that food subsidies and incentives, plus Bank Rate (which need not have been at Budget time) would be the best assortment. G. also criticized the transfer effect of the tax changes as redistributive against the poor, and he made some play with the obscurity of the statistics. No one else made much of a speech and Salter not at all strong to wind up. However the Government came out of the debate all right so far.

Friday, March 14th

Yesterday was mostly on the Ec. Survey. Planning Board in the morning and Steering Committee at night. A great deal of the heat is out of it, partly because it avoids forecasts wherever possible and partly because the Budget is over. It makes the Nat. Inc. section very much easier to write and in any case the tables are being omitted. B. Gilbert thinks Ministers will still jib at it. In the morning Vincent Tewson asked for a fuller account of what was happening and I was able to put the economic diagnosis behind the Budget much more clearly.

In the afternoon I had a Section meeting to prepare more material against ESP [External Sterling Plan, i.e. ROBOT]. The week has been a bad one for dollars, and so very disappointing, and to that extent bringing the plan closer.[8] On the other hand the country seems upset by Australian action against UK imports, for that is what it really is.

Tuesday, March 18th

Nearly all of yesterday on the winding-up speech. It is very hair-raising as the Chancellor does not really understand a thing about it, though he is a good politician. He was very dejected because *The Economist* and *The Observer* had said he was too weak, and several of his colleagues had said the same – that they could not understand why consumption need not be cut. E.P. was in a flap about the same thing. It adds very much to my trials at this time to have all these cowardly backward looks at things that were fully agreed. The Chancellor also feels hurt because he got the best advice but his critics think he has been playing politics. He forgets as all Chancellors do at this time, what a compromise economic policy is between good principles, the practical difficulties of what the country will stand, and the cowardice of Ministers. All the cuts in stock-building and especially the stock run-down is bad, but Ministers flatly refuse to cut rations or much else that might hurt.

I sent E.B. a note last week on current problems: (a) the dollar scarcity, (b) how to get more exports, (c) unemployment, (d) wages. He had a chat with T.L.R., E.N.P. and me in the afternoon. Rowan said they were working over ESP again and would be circulating a paper. The talk was quite amicable and some of the bad feelings are dying down. We decided to talk to M/Labour about (c) and (d)

Wednesday, March 19th

I had a quiet morning yesterday and sat by my fire for an hour reading the last days' Debate on the Budget. The Chancellor made a very good debating reply to his critics and I think had another personal success. MacDougall came to see me in the afternoon and rather alarmed me by saying that he thought the Chancellor wanted to put ESP into operation on Good Friday and that the PM had been much impressed by the deputation of Cobbold's stooges which he had brought along after the Cabinet turned the plan down for the first time. I saw E.N.P. later and told him this and he was inclined to believe it. If this is true and known to E.B. and T.L.R., they were a bit disingenuous at the talk on Monday. E.P. said that we must fight it again but that if we defeated the Chancellor again we could not expect to go on working long for HMG. I must start some more opposition. R. Makins is back and he mistrusts both Rowan and Bolton so he will be a great help, though it is extraordinary how much Berthoud did last time.

At 6 p.m. E.B. had a meeting with Gould [Chief Industrial Commissioner] and Myrddin-Evans from M/L, with me and E.P. and Gilbert. They were quite sensible: they thought the Chancellor should see the TUC as soon as possible, before their opinion crystallized. I urged that the Budget as a whole should be fully regarded in all wage negotiations, and they said it would be useful to publish a White Paper which at least the independent members would look at in negotiations. They thought we could at least indicate the question of the sliding scale agreements though there was no clear way to abrogate those already in existence. On unemployment, they said their transfer arrangements were already very efficient (which I am sure is correct). They did not have any views as to when we should intervene.

Sandys [Minister of Supply] has put a paper to EPC *already* [EPC(52)32], with the Budget debate still on (i.e. on Monday) asking about frustrated exports and unemployment in the car industry. We told the Chancellor that if he agreed to do anything here, his position on the Budget would be impossible.

Friday, March 21st

Yesterday morning Rowan sent round a paper expounding the new sterling plan, now called ROBOT. It suggested April 1st or April 27th for it. I don't think he and Bridges were being disingenuous on Monday. The main features were as before but some attention given to maintaining the level of trade in the non-dollar world, though it is not made clear how this was to be done. E.P. had decided to go in the morning to the Leonardo Exhibition and E.B. sent for me to ask how it ought to be handled. He has clearly made up his mind to do it as amicably as possible. I suggested a '2nd reading' talk at 5.30, after the Steering Committee. The Steering Committee took a paper on investment in 1953, and everyone agreed that the housing programme was too large, and that it was a contradiction to want a big diversion in the export trades and to shut down so violently on factory building at the same time.

At 5.30 E.B. took a meeting of E.P., R.L.H., T.L.R., B.G. and Herbert Brittain. We had quite a friendly discussion in which they all tried to be reasonable and were clearly trying to persuade P. and me to go along with them. P. had been very worried during the afternoon and kept on coming to me when I was trying to absorb the new plan. I cannot think at all quickly about these very complex things. We are to see the Chancellor at 10.30 and I think he is lunching with the PM at Chartwell today to talk about the same thing. The Ec. Section has worked out an alternative plan and I may have to put this forward. It would go for less convertibility rather than more.

Tuesday, March 25th

The Chancellor had a short meeting on Friday and I said once more what I disliked about the new plan and said that it was too violent a plunge towards one world and that the alternative was to go more towards two: I suggested that we might give up convertibility altogether except for UK and Colonial authorized transactions. L. Rowan reacted very violently. It is a comment on how muddled and emotional we all are, that he said that this would finally antagonize the US although in general he is himself violently against any policy that assumes any US help or good-will in any practical sense. But all through this battle both sides are tending to put forward foreign and Commonwealth reactions as against their opponents' plan but as trivial matters when urged against their own. I got the Ec. Section to work on a paper, to be finished by Monday morning.

MacDougall came to see me and was somewhat horrified by our ideas which I think he thought were almost worse than those of the Bank. I got him to talk to Butt: I did not feel at all well and indeed am somewhat exhausted by the continuous nervous tension of the Budget, then by the first consideration of this, then the final Budget, now this again. It is very unpleasant to be dealing with important issues in an atmosphere in which the degree of technical expertise differs so much. In the end it is all a practical judgment but argument is difficult when the background is so ill assorted. This is worst with the Chancellor, but even with E.N.P. I find it a handicap – he is so much inclined to identify himself with my views and push them along without fully seeing why I hold them.

Yesterday I read the Section paper and suggested some changes. MacDougall was sent a copy and came up in great alarm. We tried a few more changes to meet him but he wanted it so watered down that it would have spoiled it. Our plan is to work for a non-dollar trading area with *no* gold settlements but wide credit margins. At 5 p.m. Rowan had a meeting with Makins, Lee, Holmes, Poynton [Colonial Office], Bolton, E.N.P. and me to have a first (wider) talk. Everyone but Poynton against it but no one with very constructive alternatives. My paper still being revised.

Wednesday, March 26th

Spent most of yesterday on revising the Section paper, which Butt had already revised to try to meet MacDougall.[9] I also had Plowden's comments and a final crop direct from MacDougall. The result was run off in the afternoon but when I went to talk about it to P. he was very despondent and thought it was not clear enough either about the objections to the Bank plan (ROBOT) or the merits of our own. He had not taken the paper in at all and I did not take any of this too seriously. He says he has never been so worried since he became Chief Planning Officer – I think this is partly because of the great blow dealt to his self-esteem when he learned that R.A.B. had no confidence in his judgment and E.B. was very cross because he spoke to Eden against the Bank plan last month. When I got back I found Downie, Neild and Hemming and Miss Watts all rather angry about the final version, mostly the bits David had put in to meet MacDougall. I let them make a few changes and hope to get it round this morning.

Strath told me he had been to a meeting Frank Lee had held, about the trade side of the plan and that Otto Clarke when pressed indicated that the most arbitrary measures would be needed to keep up 'soft' trade against the probability of discrimination by everyone to earn dollars. The Board of Trade had urged that no tests could be found for deciding whether a country was justified in what it was doing, and Otto proposed to take retaliatory action pretty well on his own hunch.

Thursday, March 27th

I circulated my paper yesterday morning and there is a meeting to discuss it this afternoon. Plowden is more cheerful. We had a meeting with the Chancellor in the afternoon but did not make much progress, though he seemed to be less in favour of ROBOT than before. My views were left over until today. The atmosphere is very unpleasant whenever OF people are there. Leslie Rowan will hardly speak to Plowden or me and Otto Clarke and Brittain are apparently afraid to show signs of friendliness. It is a dreadful thing to have our overseas finances in the hands of an emotional man with a stomach ulcer, and one who prefers to carry out instructions loyally rather than to take policy decisions himself. He is at present completely in Otto Clarke's hands. Otto himself is of course open to argument in spite of his instability. But Leslie gets angry at any signs of opposition. Later on E.P. and I talked to R. Makins who was extremely sane and sensible and at least realized the frightful risks we would run with ROBOT.

Friday, March 28th

In the afternoon a note by OF (Otto) came round replying to my paper. It was a very dishonest reply as might be expected from both the author and the occasion. There were some misstatements of fact and otherwise it was mostly expressions of opinion. But there were statements such as that imports (of the world) from USA were not mainly 'essentials', and that my scheme called for 'limitless' credits, which were much more polemical than academic.

At 5.15 there was another meeting with the previous lot minus Copleston [Treasury] but plus Downie, whom I took, and Hancock [Perm. Sec., Ministry of Food] and Hitchman. It was a reasonably satisfactory meeting from the point of view of stopping ROBOT but not from any other as it is almost impossible to have a rational conversation with Leslie and George Bolton. In discussion, Otto is a model of sweet reasonableness compared to them. Leslie especially tries to behave like a very biased judge, snatching up anything that seems to be on his side and passing over with a sort of grunt anything on the other. Frank Lee was the most outspoken, saying he entirely agreed with my destructive analysis but not with my constructive suggestions. It was fairly clear however that in its most extreme form it will not be very acceptable to anyone; and the middle opinion seemed to be that as both courses suggested were so awful that we ought to try once more to get Ministers to take the internal steps they ought to.

Tuesday, April 1st

On Friday, L. Rowan tried to put together a draft paper for the Chancellor but he made very little progress. I sent in a piece on the Ec.

Sect. ideas and Plowden another, agreed with Makins, on the internal and other steps which in their view would give us a good chance of getting through till the middle of 1953, when Eisenhower would probably be President, the US settled down, and a chance of getting our mutual ideas straight. By yesterday the OF draft was still unfinished.

The Chancellor had a meeting to tell us about his trip to Paris and to take stock on the ROBOT plan. Apparently he and Cobbold saw the French Minister of Finance and Baumgartner, the Governor of the Bank of France: they hinted darkly that they were going to do great things but not till the end of June, and they didn't want us to do anything till then either, and especially that we should consult them before making a major move. There was a long chat about H.P. – all the foreign Finance Ministers asked R.A.B. to keep him in Paris – it was a striking tribute. But we felt that the FO were so much against him that it was not any good to keep on.

On ROBOT, I thought the Chancellor was less harried. All the Ministers he saw were very pleased by the Budget and told him he had saved the £. Last week gave a big gold inflow, the first since about last July, so that helped. It was funny to see the ill-concealed distaste with which Rowan told us about this.

In the afternoon we had a talk with the Minister of Labour [Monckton] and the Chancellor about the interview with the TUC today. It was a very desultory conversation, running uneasily over the same old ideas. Then we talked about the Investment programme. The Chancellor is sound enough on the merits of building factories instead of houses but of course it is politically the worst of all.

The PM is really no good at any of this and seems to think entirely in terms of popularity. Not that he does not want to do his duty but these facts of economic life are too much for him – E.P. thinks that we have no real hope until he goes: if Eden and Butler were running it, we should have a chance. E. thinks that they ought to have an election before any new drastic steps, an election to get rid of their promises, which in so many respects are mill-stones now.

Wednesday, April 2nd

I had practically nothing to do yesterday: it is a very long time since this happened. I used the time to read Duncan Hall's *History of North American Supply* which I had in draft. I was much more impressed than I had expected. He worked for me for nearly two years at BRMM in Washington and was practically useless as an administrator, but as a historian he is both thorough and imaginative.

Friday, April 4th

The last few days have seen a great stir about unemployment in the textile trades. The PM is pressing that something should be done because it will look bad if the Government permits unemployment. Thorneycroft has proposed lifting purchase tax for 3 months, so bogus a suggestion as to be almost dishonest – Helmore supports it. Strath has had a working party and E. Bridges has called high level meetings from time to time.

It seems to me to be appalling that they should be so alarmed at such a small thing, so soon after the Budget. But I am told that 'there are too many marginal seats in Lancashire'. It would be better to do something nearer to an election – if they do anything now it seems likely to make things worse later. The Chancellor is moderately sound – he is very much of a politician, a term I had never properly understood before – I think it means a man who thinks of things primarily in terms of votes, seats, divisions in the House, and who is not at all worried by minor inconsistencies in policy if they conflict with political desiderata. I don't mean that he has no principles but that he thinks *first* in these terms and not as Dons do, first in terms of logical consistency.

ROBOT is now rearing its ugly head again. OF has at last drafted a paper to submit to the Chancellor – it is a very partial document indeed.

Tuesday, April 8th

There were continual troubles about textiles [CP(52)103] but in the end the Chancellor stuck out for doing no more than spending £20 mn or so on service orders in the worst places. We had a bad time holding them off on purchase tax. The Government are in a bad way, not only Churchill but some Ministers and some back-benchers. Eccles and Macmillan objected even to facing the dilemma on building and it was sent back to IPC practically with an instruction to cook the forecasts. It is very common for Ministers to close their eyes to unpleasant facts but actually to direct officials to change them is going too far.

On Friday we had a look at the OF paper. Rowan was as conciliatory as possible and we let it go forward as a statement of OF views and of the counter-arguments. It was then sent forward to the Chancellor and at the same time I gave him a summary of the opposing views which had been prepared in the Ec. Section and which I thought would make it a bit easier for him to find his way round.

Wednesday, April 9th

Yesterday the Chancellor decided to put in only a short paper [CP(52)111] to Cabinet before Easter: saying (a) there was likely to be a dollar shortage, (b) our own position though a bit better was not good and the chances of getting through '52, much less '53, on present policies, small, (c) work was going on on new policies and he would be making a submission before long, (d) meanwhile extravagances at home were quite out of order.

We did a note for the Chancellor who is to see the BEC today, on the same lines as for the TUC. We all felt that he ought somehow to urge them to resist wage increases though he couldn't say it very plainly.

N.B. sent me a note of a talk he had had with Lionel Robbins about a Deputy Director, and a note from Winnifrith (Treasury Estab. Officer) about the suggestion that we should promote Dow and Downie. The latter note annoyed me a good deal as it suggested that they were too young and offered seven alternatives, three of whom had been promoted at 32 and one at 35 and one at 36. In any case they were all very mediocre people or not economists. I find the attitude of the Cabinet Office and the Treasury very irritating indeed.

Thursday, April 10th

Ministers are going off tonight for the Easter Recess and I am hoping to take the week off and so is Plowden. I don't think they could possibly write a paper on ESP and get Ministers together and the thing through in that time. Indeed the Chancellor has put in an interim note which says practically nothing.

I feel rather more alarmed about the UK situation than I have ever done before. I feel sure that the world dollar position is getting tighter and US aid getting less and the US economy likely to have a bit of a recession in 1953 and the power to have a big one any time defence spending slackens. This is a poor outlook with the reserves so low.

But meanwhile our own Ministers seem to me to be much worse than their predecessors. I really feel very much shaken by this textile incident, combined with the decision on housing which will if carried through cause a serious jam and perhaps an expansion of the industry.

The same thing is shown in the incident about railway fares. The Transport Commission has to go through a more circuitous proceeding to have its charges increased than the other nationalized bodies; in essence it is still the old Railway Rates Tribunal procedure, set up long ago to protect the public from monopoly. But like the other nationalized industries it has a statutory duty to pay its way.

Nevertheless there was a storm about the new fares and after the results of the local election the PM got very heated and finally took the rash act of announcing that a direction had been given to suspend the increases. This was done in defiance not only of the principles of the Budget but also of the very procedure which had been established to safeguard the public: and he asserted that it was in the name of Parliament and its rights and duties. It seems to me certain that they will get themselves into a bad mess as there is no decent way out.

Friday, April 11th

The Chancellor apparently was hardly consulted at all and he rang Downie today to try to find out from him (he was Duty Officer) what the PM's meeting had decided. He was so worried about his position that he launched into a defence of himself and how hard he had to work and that he was doing his best against his colleagues – this over an open line to a principal in the Cabinet Office. He is a very sweet character and the strongest man they have on the economic side, but not very strong at that.

IV

Convertibility after Robot,
24 April 1952 to 30 December 1953

For the next year economic policy continued to be dominated by the issue of convertibility. Although the Cabinet was unwilling to sanction immediate action it had left open the possibility of later acceptance of the Robot proposals. The argument among officials continued. Towards the end of June the Governor of the Bank of England warned the Chancellor once again of impending disaster if the proposals were not adopted immediately. At an informal meeting of ministers on 30 June, Lyttleton alone offered support to the Chancellor and the idea of re-submitting the proposals to the Cabinet was abandoned. One reason for their rejection was that, on the initiative of the Australian Prime Minister, Mr Menzies, it had just been agreed to call a Commonwealth Economic Conference and it was judged desirable to put the proposals to the Conference before coming to a decision.

Thursday, April 24th 1952

I was away last week. My return has been clouded by a disagreement with N. Brook about my staff. I had been trying to get Downie and Dow promoted and had been led to think that he would agree but on Monday we had an interview in which he gave me the impression that he had no confidence in the way I was recruiting. This although he had himself agreed to the view that we had to get people through training them ourselves, because they could not be got from the universities. We agreed that I should make strong efforts to get a Deputy from outside but he wanted me also to get the next layer from there and almost implied that it would be a mistake to promote people within the Section. I feel that this attitude is very unfair to the ones I have got already.

Friday, April 25th

The Government economic policy can hardly be said to exist. R.A.B. made import cuts, put up the Bank Rate, and reduced the food subsidies on advice from officials but I don't think either he or his colleagues are very clear about how these measures affect the situation and I am very much alarmed at various signs that they have no clear plan or purpose. We talked about it at 2nd Secs. on Tuesday and E.B., E.N.P., Leslie Rowan and I had a talk about it to the Chancellor yesterday. He obviously felt the need for a policy but he did not know exactly what to put in it. E.N.P. offered him a four-year plan which I thought a mistake and so did he and E.B. In the end I was left to draft a paper.

Yesterday I did the draft for the Cabinet paper on economic policy [CP(52)166] and discussed it with Plowden and Rowan.[1] The latter was very helpful and for the time being good relations are almost restored. I think he is much happier because the gold reserves are falling so much more slowly – the latest forecast is much better than the ones before that. US help is coming in faster also.

I have been very much upset by the interview with N. Brook and yesterday wrote and offered to resign if, as it appeared, he had no confidence in my handling of the staff problem.

Tuesday, April 29th

N.B. sent for me to see him on Friday (25th) at 3 p.m. Just before I went down E.P. appeared and told me that he was much upset by my letter and would ask me to withdraw it. Fortified by this I went down in a cheerful mood and we had a pleasant talk – he apologized for his offensive remarks but said he had not intended them to be so, that he did *not* think that my staff were inferior to academic economists but that he was quite ready to treat them all on their merits, and that he had full confidence in my conduct of the Section. He knew I agreed with him (as of course I did – there had never been any difference) about the desirability of getting in outsiders from the universities if we could get them. He also admitted that he had taken a long time to deal with my suggestions. At the end he asked if he could tear the letter up – I gathered lately from E.N.P. that he went at once to him and tore it up then and there! – a little theatrical. However I was glad that it all ended amicably. He is quite right in thinking that it is high time more effort was made to deal with the staff problems. And it has in fact stimulated me a good deal and made me give it more priority, so it is a good intervention.

We have all been upset by Stafford Cripps' death. He was one of the great men of our time: I hardly knew Winston in the war, the greatest of them. I knew Keynes a bit and always thought he was the most distinguished brain in the country. But I worked closely with Stafford from late 1947 until he retired in 1950 and I thought he was in almost all respects an outstanding character. From the time Bevin began to break up until he retired, Stafford was by far the strongest and most respected man in the Cabinet. He commanded almost uncritical respect among senior civil servants, which is very unusual in my experience. He was a wonderful man to work for especially if he respected you: once he was convinced he made much more of one's arguments than one could oneself, and he was almost over-loyal to his subordinates: not only would he take their faults on himself but he tended to think more of them because he was defending them. This, like his advocacy of his brief, was partly due to his experience as a barrister. He did not really understand the basis of economic planning as we developed it under his regime, but he was entirely responsible for its development. It is true that Dalton introduced a deflationary Budget in November 1947 – the one Cripps took over – but it was not part of a plan and Dalton himself had done a good deal to stoke the fires of inflation. Cripps from the first thought that the problems should be treated as a whole, as is clear from the opening words of his own first Budget speech. He brought in Edwin Plowden, and it was under him that the main instruments – the Programmes Committee for imports, the IPC for Investment and the NIF Working Party leading to the Budget, were developed. If he could be convinced, he would in most cases carry it through.

His weakness was really his emotional belief in Socialism, which allowed Nye Bevan to defeat him on several crucial matters. In my view, it was the constant tendency of Government expenditure to rise which was the great handicap of the Government from 1946 to 1951 and Nye was the main force behind this, not only on health but on the extravagant housing and in his general pressure. Stafford would never stand up to him in the end and that was why Nye said that (in effect) he had out-manoeuvred him on several occasions. This was because Stafford's conscience was against him.

R.A.B. asked me to take him to lunch on Monday, which I did at the Travellers. He is very indiscreet in the things he discusses in public. He said that Robot was doubtful now, perhaps June, perhaps November. He was in a hurry for something for Cabinet on Economic Policy. He brought up again the question of the cost of living and doesn't seem to grasp it. I think he wants E.P. to go and fears that Leslie Rowan will break up. I said that Strath and F. Lee would be a very good team and he seemed to agree. But one never knows.

Thursday, May 1st

GATT Revision: Ec. Policy papers: TCC and OEEC exercises. (These were the week's activities for me.) The President of the Board of Trade put a paper to Cabinet about six or seven weeks ago asking that Committees of Ministers and officials should be appointed to look into the fundamentals behind ITO, IMF, GATT etc. with a view to deciding whether we should take a new line especially in the GATT talks.[2] I have long thought that this was needed but there never seems to have been time to do it. As the inquiry treads completely on the Robot toes, no one quite knew what to do (Cabinet agreed the paper) and there have been somewhat agitated talks between E.B., T.L.R., E.P. and Frank Lee. However it was finally decided to let it loose and Lee had a meeting on Tuesday for a first look. He asked the Economic Section to write some preliminary papers, which pleased me as the Section had so much to do with all this under Robbins who was deeply involved in IMF and Meade who did so much of the work on ITO.

The work on the Chancellor's Economic Policy paper is going haltingly. I did a note, then we agreed an outline, then I put together bits from various hands. Today Bridges said it was too long and he is going to do a new draft himself. It is supposed to cover a number of fundamental points but I don't know how it will end up. It is hard enough to get officials to agree and impossible to know how to write on such topics, to strike the Ministerial mind.

Tuesday, May 6th

At the weekend I talked to Hicks and Champernowne [in Oxford] about the staff problem, but they did not have much to suggest. However, Champernowne is rather keen on getting Downie as the new Research Fellow [at Nuffield College] and this would suit me very well so I encouraged him, and later saw the Warden, Loveday. I also mentioned him to [Norman] Chester [of Nuffield] whom I met at the MacDougalls' on Sunday: he seemed favourable. I gather that [Philip] Andrews [Fellow of Nuffield] is against Downie – his own Fellowship ought to expire soon; I never thought he was up to it and I still don't. I will be very sorry to lose Downie for a few years but it will be very suitable.

The Chancellor thought E.B.'s draft was too short and wanted a lot of the bigger one brought in so I did some of this. I find Plowden rather a trial at present: he wants to fit in with the Ministers' ideas but is not very good at expressing himself or even formulating his own ideas and he seems to me to be much less agile in the new situation. I cannot quite make out why and I feel very sorry about it but I can well see why R.A.B. and E.B. both think he would do better to go later this year. Leslie Rowan has become much less difficult and offensive for the time being, perhaps because we are losing much less gold.

Wednesday, May 7th

Marjolin and Lintott [Dep. Sec.-General] of OEEC called on me yesterday. We talked about the prospects for world trade and agreed that the dollar outlook was very bad and that there was a real danger of progressive restriction. He wants a new approach to the US (a) to get them to spend more on off-shore purchases, primary products etc. and also a better tariff policy, (b) to set up a World Payments Union more or less on the lines of EPU. I did not quite see who would do this or whether it could be done at all before the new President has settled down. I agree of course with the basic idea but am a bit disillusioned about its chances.

P. came to see me and asked if I thought he was losing his grip. I did not know what to say as I think he is but I doubt if it would do any good to tell him. I did not discourage him from the idea of leaving soon. E.B. is weakening a bit, I expect he knows there must be a Plannery and fears that if P. goes it will be disbanded and Ministers still ask that the work should be done.

In the afternoon we discussed the CEPS paper on the Defence programme for '53–'55.[3] It looks very gloomy because it is assumed that we get neither German contribution, nor US aid, after June 1953. This gives a sudden new load against a rising programme. It was not well drafted and I made a lot of suggestions. But Allen who was doing it is very stubborn in drafting, as he tends to be in economics too.

Friday, May 9th

The failure to agree about Robot is leading the Bank and the Treasury, and the Economic Section, into a number of conflicts which are rather unpleasant. The latest is on the EPU where the Belgians are well over their quota and are, in effect, demanding gold for the surplus. If it had been known that they were going to do this it would have probably meant quite different arrangements at the time. The Section is arguing that to give a country 100% gold is to encourage it to earn gold and that EPU was not meant to do this. The Chancellor and Salter saw the Belgians last week and encouraged them to borrow on the security of their EPU credit. As they wanted to pledge this with the Bank with gold guarantees from the debtors, and short redemptions, this was very much on the anti-Section line.

I sent the Chancellor a note of disagreement and this rather shook him. Today Leslie Rowan sent me a very silly Minute – I had seen some people from the US Embassy with Strath – they were bringing round the new man on the 'UK desk' who is here to look at his bailiwick. And I sent a note of the meeting to various people including Otto. He showed it to Leslie Rowan who picked up two points, one wrong and one very stupid (i.e. *he* was (a) wrong, (b) stupid). I had said that among the burdens we were bearing or having to bear we feared we might have added German costs. Leslie said that as Ministers had said we would not pay, this was giving our case away. He has got morbidly sensitive lately – he was bad enough in Washington but no doubt Otto exacerbates him.

Wednesday, May 14th

Yesterday E. Roll was here and took P. and me to lunch at the Union. We talked mainly about various facets of Marjolin's idea for an approach to the US next year. P. wants UK to be Chairman of the Council of Ministers because he thinks we would do better at the head of Europe than alone. Roll more doubtful (partly because this brings OEEC back and he is now NATO), partly because it is the opposite of the orthodox line.

Bridges has now given up drafting the paper on Economic Policy and P. has taken over. The Chancellor did not like B.'s pleas for something short and vague. P. told me that the Chancellor is now at odds with the Governor and has no use for T.L.R. So the Robot camp is disrupted. All very unpleasant but in the right direction.

Thursday, May 15th

Went to Cambridge yesterday to talk about staff questions, and had lunch with Richard Kahn and Austin Robinson. Austin forgot to come and had to be telephoned. Richard said 'Joan [Robinson] says now whenever anyone telephones to ask for Austin "He is a Professor now and thinks Professors ought to be absent-minded"'.

It was a useful talk. They both felt that it was too much of a sacrifice to ask a young man to come because he would not get back again at all easily – his contemporaries would have gone on with research, teaching, writing and it would be too much of a gamble to take him on. They said they would help at Cambridge in getting it established that we should take people for two years or so.

They thought it would be quite attractive for someone more established to take a Senior or Deputy post.

I came back by car to go to a meeting the Chancellor had at No. 11 to consider the 7th draft of his paper on Economic Policy. Besides the 2nd Secs. were F. G. Lee and R. Makins, and Salter. It was not a bad meeting and at the end I thought the paper would be tolerable. But there is still a conflict between directness and truth, and not over alarming or antagonizing Ministers. Especially on housing.

I took William Armstrong to dine afterwards at the Travellers and we had a general talk. He confirmed that the Chancellor is now much more doubtful about Robot, and that he has lost confidence in Leslie Rowan's judgment. He says the Chancellor is 'perplexed and distressed' and does not feel that he gets any really good advice. He says no one warned him that there was a depression coming up in Lancashire. We also talked about Treasury organization, where William and/or the Chancellor want to make some big changes, to try to bring it into line with its new responsibilities and to make it a unity. I promised to write him a note on my ideas. The main trouble from my point of view is the split between OF and CEPS, which is of course all Otto's doing.

Friday, May 16th

Planning Board yesterday. We took the CEPS paper on defence but it was a bit too much for them. The gloomy outlook, and the combined effect of such a serious defence production cut and the bad prospects of selling all the metal goods put down to be exported, needed a lot more digestion.

In the afternoon the Chancellor made his long-awaited statement on wages to the NJAC. Downie had drafted most of it, either at one remove (because the Ministry of Labour draft had been cribbed from his draft White Paper) or direct. He went along but told me afterwards that it was disappointing as there were barely any questions.

Friday, May 23rd

I have had a fairly busy week. The general Economic Policy paper was circulated on Monday and taken yesterday [CP(52)166]. I saw Prof. on Monday afternoon about it and afterwards N.B. to discuss the brief for the PM. In the end I also did the Chancellor's brief. I told N.B. that things were very difficult between the Section and OF – he said 'is it OF or Leslie Rowan' and that gave an opening to discuss the whole problem of Leslie's health and Otto's determination to run the show. He was already seriously concerned and gave me to understand that relations between himself and L. were very strained. But he did not quite know what to do.

On Tuesday (20th) I took Frank Lee to lunch at the Travellers and it happened that our table was next to R. Makins. Frank and Roger immediately began to talk about T.L.R. in almost an extreme way so I had little to do; but I mentioned it after lunch again and Frank said he would talk to N. Brook. He also asked me who should succeed Leslie and was plainly relieved when I said *he* should – he said he was up to it: and we then moved a few other people in our minds, including Hitch who is ear-marked for Fuel and Power but we thought should go to Trade. All this is no doubt very much in the air and E.B. may well blench, even if persuaded. Frank later sent me a note to say he had seen N.B. who fully agreed.

Tuesday, May 27th

On Friday E.P. said that he thought Robot was afoot again, owing to the fall in the NY rate: the Governor had been pressing for it. He (E.P.) wanted to put up Bank Rate – I said I did not think it would help much and might harm. I am getting rather alarmed about the onset of depression here. The reports from the Board of Trade and M/L are not depressing but a number of people have told me that they expect trouble in the engineering industry too. Betty Ackroyd [Ministry of Supply] for instance said that a few months ago they couldn't persuade anyone to take defence orders and now they were faced with queues looking for them. It looks as if we may be facing the classical problem of unemployment accompanied by balance of payments difficulties. I saw R. Kahn at the weekend (we had Samuelson to stay and a lot of people came in to see him – R. had been to Faringdon to a Fabian Research Group meeting) and he said he was very nervous about the same problem.

Yesterday T.L.R. showed me a brief he had done for the Chancellor to talk to Menzies [Australian Prime Minister] about Robot. It was a very biased brief and I did a note on it. I fear M. may not grasp what is being suggested to him: his chief adviser Roland Wilson is a difficult person, he was frustrated as a D.Phil. student in Oxford and has never recovered.

Wednesday, May 28th

D. MacDougall took me to dine last night. We talked a bit more about Robot. He has been sent for several times lately by T.L.R. in order to discuss points Prof. made in submissions to the Chancellor. He thinks L.R. is much less sure of himself and trying to be conciliatory; but as his arguments are so bad it doesn't get far. OF showed me yesterday a paper on Robot and EPU which I could not understand – it is a scheme for keeping EPU alive at the cost of making our debt there convertible but I could not see the attractions.

There are now a great many papers about the economic situation in front of Ministers and they are to be looked at today. Besides the original one on policy generally, which has only been half discussed, there is one on the balance of payments which is just repeating arguments already in the others, one on exports by the President of the Board of Trade, one on defence and metal goods, one on coal, one on food.[4]

The coal situation is fantastic. Stocks are 4 mn tons higher than last year, labour is well above and the NCB are being difficult about taking on more men, it is constantly said that we are in danger of having to close pits because we can't clear supplies away, but Leathers is determined not to export more than another 1.5 mn tons above the previously agreed level and mostly rubbish at that. Everyone is against him except D. Fergusson, who having been alone in the country (with Shinwell) in 1947 in saying there would be no crisis, is now determined to be alone in the country (with Leathers) in saying that there will be one. He has been consistently the most difficult, wrong-headed and uncooperative of the Permanent Secretaries ever since I have known him. But it is apparently impossible to get rid of him and indeed he is staying beyond the retiring age to qualify for a higher pension (because of the rise under the Chorley scheme).

Thorneycroft's paper [CP(52)175] is rather woolly in the early part and reverts to the idea of Commonwealth unity later on. It is queer that this idea, so popular with the country, should be held also by those keen on Robot. But it is clear that Ministers generally have no integrated view of economic problems.

Thursday, May 29th

E.P. and I saw Sir Cuthbert Clegg [Chairman of the Cotton Spinners' and Manufacturers' Association] yesterday. He is a member of EPB and has just ceased to be President of the BEC [British Employers' Confederation]. We wanted to know whether it was likely that employers would oppose the current round of wages claims. He said he thought they would: in some trades, e.g. cotton, they were in difficulties and might even press for decreases. He thought it important that the Government should not appear to be egging the employers on or that the employers should even seem to be having a common front. It was quite a useful talk. The cotton export trade is still very dead.

In the afternoon there was a BC about the form of Budget accounts, the long paper we spent so much time on last year. The Treasury officials including E.P. very cautious about publishing anything. Hopkin of CSO was rather upset because they did not even want him to use our suggested economic classification in the Nat. Income White Paper. Since E.P. was frightened by the idea that the Chancellor was against him, he has become very orthodox in places which don't affect him much.

I did a draft note on the increase in unemployment – it is hoped that this will allay Ministers' fears.

The Chancellor is very upset because the ECE Bulletin criticizes the Budget. He has had a rough time in the House over the Finance Bill, and stood it very well but his nerves are frayed. The Bulletin is very mild and he would only make a fool of himself if he tried to make anything of it.

Friday, May 30th

I wrote a long minute about ECE which R.A.B. accepted – he wrote 'tant pis' across it. He has now finished the Finance Bill with an all-night sitting but this so exhausted him that I gather he was almost incoherent at the Cabinet which took all the economic papers.

E.B., B.G., E.P. and I talked to Ince yesterday about wages – how often we have done this before. He said that the Chancellor's speech was a great success and made a deep impression on both sides at NJAC. He was fairly hopeful that we would get by with a small rise.

Friday, June 6th

I went to Paris on Tuesday afternoon to lead the UK Del. to the expert OEEC Committee on Internal Financial Stability. This was set up by the Council no doubt at Marjolin's instigation and in imitation of the [J. M.] Clark and [J. W.] Angell UN Committees. The change in tone lately led to it being made up of very old-fashioned sound money economists. Lionel Robbins in the Chair, who is an ideal man for this job but who is temperamentally anti-Keynes and for the strong use of money. The others were Bresciani-Turroni [Italy] who was very sweet but backing up and holding the simplest quantity theory: Rueff [France] who is nice but muddled and essentially a money man: a Belgian called Masoin who clearly had instructions to support his country's rigid lines: Lindahl [Sweden], who seemed old and unenergetic: Schneider [Germany] who said very little: and Marget of the FRB [Federal Reserve Board] who was very able and on the whole nice though strongly in favour of a tight money policy.

They were all charmed that we had [Leslie] O'Brien and Maurice Allen from the Bank and charmed that we were in fact adopting a tighter monetary policy. O'Brien gave an account of how the Bank controlled the volume of money which sounded just like a text-book but which delighted them all. On the basis of this conversion to right views, as they felt, we got by fairly easily though they were all very much anti-planning, anti-full-employment and anti-direct controls. Sam Goldman [OF Stats.] was there too: he was a bit too voluble but clearly knew what he was talking about.

Tuesday, June 10th

R.A.B. had a meeting on Economic Policy generally at 4.30 yesterday. It was a good idea to have a run over the ground still under discussion by his colleagues. He has the right views about the need for progressing but doesn't know exactly how to get it done, or grasp the limitations on action by officials if they do not trust the resolution of Ministers. No concrete decisions have been taken yet on defence, on priority for exports, on housing or investment or coal. The balance of payments is better for the time being and this quarter should show little if any loss of gold. OF still gloomy about the next half year.

Frank Lee had a meeting on Commercial Policy in the afternoon before that. It is a huge subject and we can't see how we can get it done with no really competent staff to put on it whole time. Before ITO etc., Meade and Liesching did little else for several years and then it was quite simple, with agreement about the world they thought they could make, and no present to embarrass them. Now there will be great differences of view about what is desirable and what is likely. Conservatives are extremely vague about it all and have little but an emotional view about the Empire.

Wednesday, June 11th

Yesterday was fairly quiet. Leslie Rowan is much more polite than he was and E.P. told me that he had been spoken to. Nothing much at 2nd Secs. Then I talked to Clem Leslie who has been on leave in Switzerland and told me how easily one can have a fortnight on £25 [the tourist allowance]. I wondered if he had a bad conscience. He wanted as usual my appraisal of the outlook. I feel more confident than six weeks ago but of course it is precarious with reserves so low. They will run nearly level over the present quarter, partly because a good deal of MSA [Mutual Security Aid] has been received.

In the afternoon long talk to E.P. who is in an aimless and somewhat defeatist mood. The combination of Ministers who do not know where they are and won't really take advice, the precarious balance of payments situation, and the unresolved quarrel about Robot, are too much for him. He gave me a long and rather dramatic, obviously rehearsed, oration about how little attention we paid to the balance of payments and how much to all other claims. But he didn't really want anything but a firm policy.

Thursday, June 12th

Hall-Patch was here and I took him to lunch. Mostly to talk about Robot, where his view is very much on the right lines. In the morning Playfair had had a meeting about this year's NATO Review, based on a letter Butt had induced me to write which asked what line we should take and what we expected to happen. It was quite a satisfactory meeting and we all seemed to be agreed.

Neild and P. Hemming have done papers for the Commercial Policy Review – quite good ones. I gave them to Otto to read before circulating them.[5]

Friday, June 13th

I took Maurice Green (City Ed. of *The Times*) to lunch yesterday hoping to persuade him to write a leading article on wages. But I don't know if I shall succeed – he seemed to think that restraint was against human nature and thought unemployment should vary between 2 and 8%. He seemed to know all about Robot and asked me which side I was on. It is perfectly clear that the top people at the Bank have been talking about it. Lionel Robbins told me in Paris that Marget and Rueff had both heard about it from Frère, Governor of the Bank of Belgium, who was in favour of it and told them that 'very high' quarters in London were also. I told E.B. this and he said he would speak to the Governor but I do not suppose he will. After devaluation, George Bolton told several of my friends that the Bank had been in favour of it a long time and had wanted a floating rate. Both statements are exactly the opposite of the truth. The Governor's opposition is shown in the Annex to Stafford's Cabinet paper [EPC(49)72]: and it was the Bank which opposed Edwin P. and I who wanted to float.

Friday, June 20th

I went to Bristol on Monday to see a man called [Miles] Fleming whom Ronnie Tress [Professor at Bristol] had recommended. He is 32 and the senior economics lecturer there: had got a 1st at Belfast and worked with Hicks at Manchester. I liked him and his interests seemed right and Ronnie not only recommended him but was willing to let him go.

On Sunday I had dined in Trinity and Ian Little [Crosland's successor] told me he was leaving to go to Nuffield so I asked him if he would come as Deputy Director for 2 years and he said he would if Nuffield would let him go. I put these names to Norman Brook and also that of C. R. Ross, a Fellow of Hertford, who was recommended to me by several people there. Norman approved so I wrote to tell Tress that I would be taking Fleming. In the afternoon Ross himself turned up and said he was really rather keen to come and thought that if we approached Hertford at once they might agree: so I wrote off to Murphy, the Principal. This makes the whole thing look a good deal more promising – if I get Fleming and Ross it will be a good start and if I get Little too I will be in a strong position. Once one starts a movement of this kind it will be fairly easy to keep it up: in a few years people will be trying hard to come. It is a great relief after all my worries – of course if I had tried this two year secondment idea earlier it would no doubt have worked then. Everyone says that economists are now getting a good deal more plentiful.

I lunched yesterday with N. Kaldor who had Hal Lary his successor in ECE and also Robert Neild who used to work there and now works for me. Nicki seems a little happier about the Royal Commission (on Taxation) but I think he is a very unpopular member of it. He has a great scheme for revolutionizing the whole thing by an expenditure tax but it is a nice point as to whether it comes in the terms of reference or not.

Lary called on me later, mainly to ask how I felt about a world economic conference about the dollar problem. He thought it needed (a) strong Congressional representation, (b) first class documentation by experts. I told him I thought it would come to nothing unless there was a lot of hard preliminary work by Governments, strong leadership, and if possible some prior agreement, e.g. between US and UK. Everyone seems to be talking about a world economic conference now and it looks as if Lary and Marjolin are trying to beat one another to it.

Meanwhile our work on commercial policy etc. has had to be very much accelerated as Menzies agreed with Ministers here on Tuesday to try to have a Commonwealth Conference on this, at the PM level, about Nov. 19th. This caused the greatest alarm among officials here and I must find time to write down the week's developments.

Tuesday, July 1st

The gist of what happened was that E.B. had a meeting at which it was agreed that (a) it was practically impossible to study the subject properly and to educate Ministers in it, in the time available, (b) it was no good saying this and we had better do our best. We agreed therefore to put some people full-time on to the job. After a few days' thought we met again and OF tried to get the whole thing into their hands by proposing that they should write a paper by June 25th on the problem – E.B. should have a meeting on their paper on June 30th – which would instruct a drafting group – this group would place the alternatives before Ministers by July 14th – and Ministers should choose what they wanted among alternatives – the working party should then proceed on the basis of their instructions, in order to present a clear case to Commonwealth Ministers.

This was all in order to prejudge the issue by getting Robot and nothing else. However all but OF at the meeting showed some alarm until it was proposed that Hitchman should come from Materials to be Chairman of the Working Group to take over after June 25th and until the Conference. Such was the confidence of Permanent Secretaries in

Hitchman that they felt that no other precautions against OF were really needed. The Group will be Morland, representing FO, Snelling of CRO, Leckie of the Board of Trade, MacDougall representing me as well as him and helped by Dow, who will in fact be a full member and represent the Economic Section. Meanwhile the PM sent off an agreed telegram.

On Monday, June 23rd, the Chancellor summoned his chief advisers, E.B., Gilbert, Rowan, Salter, Plowden and me, and showed us a letter from Cobbold, which said that the measures so far taken had been insufficient and confidence in sterling would soon be lost and there would probably be a crisis about the end of August unless we carried out his plan. The letter was quite formal and of course needed to be taken very seriously. The Chancellor accordingly proposed to put Robot before his colleagues again. There was no argument and none expected really though I said I was still against it.

That night William Armstrong told E.P. that our silence was taken as consent, however reluctant, and that the Chancellor would now rush it through. He wrote a short paper on Tuesday asking a lot of questions, and I drafted a memo against it that night which I finished on Wednesday after showing it to Downie and Butt. It was a very good memo. The Chancellor had gone to Oxford to get a degree at the Encaenia. He read the memo on Thursday. I gave copies to F. Lee and R. Makins and I think they showed it to their bosses. Makins said that from a political point of view it was not so objectionable as before owing to the fact that the Bank had told so many people about it! so they would not be shocked. Also there was much more provision for consultation. Economically he was as much against it as ever. Plowden was very despondent and said that the Chancellor had made up his mind to go ahead and that our advice was biased. However W.A. told me on Friday that the memos from Salter, E.P. and me had shaken him and he was undecided.

On Sunday Prof. sent for me and showed me a paper he had written against Robot – it was somewhat intemperate but the argument very good, indeed as I had given MacDougall a copy of my memo some of it was based on my arguments.

Last night, June 30th, the PM had a meeting of Ministers mainly concerned and they were *all* against it except the Chancellor and Lyttleton. N.B. told me this afternoon that it was practically dead now until the Commonwealth Conference. All the Ministers thought it was very wrong to get the PM to call such a conference and less than a week after he had sent the telegram to propose crash action which would compromise the whole situation.[6]

This episode has been very unpleasant. The Bank has done its best to cause a run on sterling by telling everyone that we would be ruined unless we did Robot. In addition to what Robbins told me, I myself have been asked directly by Maurice Green where I stood, and by Denny Marris. Bob Brand has written to Salter and Makins to say that the Bank have done this. Wilfred King was told all about it and wrote it up in an article in *The Banker*.[7]

It is astonishing to me that this should pass with so little protest. It is also extraordinary that the pound should stand up so well against these rumours. We only lost $15 mn in the second quarter – one of the arguments used against the Bank was that they (or OF – they are all one in this context) forecast a loss of $375 mn this quarter. Apparently they now say it was a good forecast because it was ± $150 mn and they got $100 mn more MSA than expected. Therefore their forecast was really $125 mn! The loss was $15 mn so they were only $100 mn out – which is very good. All this quite overlooking that they have been trying hard to get emergency action based on the $375 mn figure.

Meanwhile relations between CEPS, the Economic Section on the one hand and OF on the other, are as bad as they can be.

Otto wrote his paper for June 25th; it was a great tour de force and by leaving out all mention of the need for, at any rate the political pressure for, stability, he managed to make it seem that Robot was the only course and that it was nothing but perversity which led to the troubles of the past. He propounded at the end a series of questions which I think Ministers would refuse to answer as they were too much in black and white. We had a meeting about this paper yesterday and made a few strong comments. It is now turned over to Hitchman and his party.

[Peter] Vinter has succeeded Goldman as the head of OF Stats. – Goldman has replaced Copeman [Estimates Clerk], who is ill, as the incipient HF statistician who will be able to do the Budget accounts in the end.

N. Brook has agreed that Downie should go to OEEC. We both think that Nuffield is driving too hard a bargain in asking us to pay his salary while he is a Research Fellow. I will try to get Dow promoted and let Butt go – he is having a bad time as he has one of his vertebrae cracked but they cannot find which it is. Both the Paks. and the Ceylon people are toying with the idea of taking him on as an economic adviser.

Plowden has lost quite a bit of his nerve and all this now with OF and the mistrust the Chancellor feels about him is not doing him any good. I think probably we ought to be more aggressive from now on.

By the beginning of July preparations for the Commonwealth Economic Conference were in full swing. A committee on external economic policy was meeting under Hitchman and organizing, on the basis of a draft by Otto Clarke (Gen 412/1), the preparation of papers for submission to a Ministerial Committee on Preparations for the Commonwealth Economic Conference (PEC). Hitchman soon disappeared from the official committee and the chair was taken in succession by Edward Bridges (on 18 and 21 July), Arnold France (on several occasions) and Maurice Dean (at the final meeting on 11 September). Nearly fifty papers were circulated, many of them prepared by special working parties on development policy, commodity policy, the US tariff, imperial preference and so on, under Dean, France and others. Convertibility was dealt with by a separate working party under a Treasury Third Secretary, Brittain ('Steps towards Convertibility'). This issued a lengthy report (or 'Statement of conflicting views') on 1 September (WPSC(52)9 and PEC(52)18).

The Ministerial Committee was thus flooded with paper, including some by Ministers themselves (entry for August 8th). Several papers were circulated by Cherwell, starting with one on an Atlantic Payments Union (PEC(52)7) on 1 August (see entries for May 7th and July 16th). This envisaged something on the lines of the European Payments Union but enlarged to include Canada and the United States and permitting discrimination against the United States by other members. Hall had little use for this proposal, which he thought almost as objectionable as Robot, but felt that he had to keep it alive. It was the subject of two critical reports by officials, PEC (52)17 on 1 September and WPSC(52)10 on 11 September.

A revised plan for early convertibility was put forward by OF under which the main European countries would all go convertible together with the help of a large exchange stabilization fund (entries for September 2nd, 4th and 5th). This proposal for a 'collective approach' was put to the preparatory conference of Commonwealth officials ending on 15 October and met with little enthusiasm. The reactions at the conference did not, however, deter ministers from submitting the new plan to the Conference of Commonwealth Prime Ministers in December (entry for November 5th).

The papers of the official committee on external economic policy are in PRO CAB 130/78, most of those of the ministerial committee are in PRO T 236/3071 and others will be found in PRO T 236/3072–5 and T 230/220.

Friday, July 4th

After all these storms the rest of the week has been extremely quiet and I have practically cleared my desk and indeed my private correspondence and some staff matters. Ministers are now back at the various papers asking for decisions on defence, investment, import cuts and so on. Macmillan [Minister of Housing] and Eccles [Minister of Works] who continue to act as if building of all kinds has got the highest priority, have put in a paper in which they ask (a) that the production of building materials and their import shall not be restricted, (b) that building for nationalized industries etc. be held down by credit control, (c) that limits be placed on the number of subsidized houses, (d) that, except in congested areas, there should be no control over anyone else who wants to build. This is a great programme for inflation.

Tuesday, July 8th

Still quiet. Hitchman's party is working away industriously and sitting up half the night, to get a submission for Ministers on our policy to be put before the Commonwealth Conference. Otto Clarke is attending and he is at odds with MacDougall and Dow. Dow saw me yesterday to say that he was afraid the documents would be rather tendentious unless he made a fuss. But I had seen MacDougall on Sunday and found that he was prepared for a minority report if necessary and I told Dow that I would support this. However this morning he seemed much happier as they had worked late and as Otto had had a dinner engagement, they had made a lot of progress in his absence and now Dow was doing the drafting.

Plowden seems worried about all this but he is always worried about something. I feel that we are doing quite well, first to have Robot postponed, now to get a rather vague report instead of the clear call for convertibility OF have been trying for. Ministers don't want any of the things that are possible and I can't help feeling that once they see the horrors the Bank and OF have in store, they will run away.

Macm. has just put round *another* paper [CP(52)226], which begins by rehearsing all the past errors of judgment of the Bank, and goes on to attack the Chancellor. I must say I felt some *Schadenfreude* at the opening though I didn't think he should have attacked the Chancellor, especially as his general line is inflationary and he thinks a bold course would be our best chance, meaning by boldness that we should not economise especially on houses. P. had dinner with him last night but I have not heard the outcome.

We lost $18 mn in the first 5 days but it was mostly a capital payment to Canada. The £ was very strong today, rising from 2–78¼ to 2–79¼. My own feeling is that the news has got round that Ministers have turned Robot down and all the people who have been selling sterling on the Bank's advice have had to cover. Tim Bligh said his theory was that George Bolton had been withdrawn from the cheap sterling market!

Unemployment fell in May but I do not think it means anything – it was all seasonal and the position in manufactures got easier. It is surprising how little fuss there has been about what I thought would be considered a big increase.

The Agricultural Wages Board today recommended 5/- a week for the increase; this is better than we were hoping for. For weeks now everyone has been intriguing to persuade the Board that it was in the public interest to make only a small increase but no one has dared to speak to anyone. The Chancellor wrote to the M/Agr. asking him to see Doughty, the Chairman. But the M/Agr. refused. I was told to see Ashby, the Director of the Oxford Agricultural Ec. Institute. But I couldn't find anyone who knew him at all well and B. Gilbert said that as he was a member of the Board, I must go very carefully. And so on. However, either someone got through, or they are not so insensitive to the public interest as we had supposed. With this increase, the other main negotiations ought to be settled for very small sums also.

Figgins of the NUR is talking of strikes and Horner [of the NUM] of all sorts of desperate measures, but I think this is only the first move or rather *a* move in the whole negotiation. Nye Bevan actually said yesterday that *he* didn't see where higher real wages were coming from unless productivity went up.

I had lunch with Tony Crosland in the House on Thursday, mostly to be told about his matrimonial troubles (he got engaged on Friday) but he also talked at some length about Ian Little whom I am trying to get as Deputy Director. He was afraid Ian was much too academic for the job and would not be happy here, because he was expecting much more of a back-room job. However on Sat. Ian came to see me in Oxford to tell me that he was alarmed by Tony's moves as he wanted to come badly and he was afraid Tony might have put me off. I also talked to D. MacDougall but I found that he did not share Tony's doubts. As I was reasonably confident myself, I don't think I need take any notice. Ian is clearly desperately anxious to come which is in itself a good sign.

With so little to do, one first clears up one's desk and then gets restless and wonders if one is doing a good job. The thing one ought to do – a little solid reading – is the hardest. I have commissioned a lot of papers from the Section about whether a slump is impending or not but I can hardly bear to look at them.[8] Downie did a summary of the outcome and it seems to me that it proves that one cannot *forecast* a slump at all – the first quarter figures of world trade are practically a record, and yet we know that everyone is getting short of sterling. All he could do was to point to the hesitations in production now going on in many countries. It is mostly hunch and half one's hunches are wrong.

'Do we do any good?' as Plowden says whenever he feels at all gloomy. He says that he has lost the confidence of E.B. ever since the row over Robot in March because E.B. thinks he intrigued against the Chancellor. This only shows how easily E.B. deceives himself. For (a) there has been no operation in my time carried out so improperly by OF as this – a major change and no chance to discuss it or attempt to do so, (b) E.B. himself intrigues against Ministers if he thinks it is in the public interest to do so. The whole thing continues to disgust me – the one man I felt was completely incorruptible has been swept away by his confidence in T.L.R. which in turn is based in confidence in Otto, the most notoriously temperamental man in the Treasury.

The Chancellor told G. Crowther all about Robot and E.P. and I were to dine with him to discuss it tonight – it has been put off. Meanwhile G.C. went to see Lionel R. and I got a long urgent Top Secret letter from L.R. this morning relating the conversation between himself and G. Lionel is the most correct individual possible, one cannot help liking and admiring him and after all, even if his theoretical writings or his abstractions on current events are a bit too laissez-faire, he really does see the political and humanitarian side of things. He has been extraordinarily nice and co-operative both about all this and about his Report on Internal Fin. Stability.

On this, by the way, there is going to be quite a stir. It suggests that the last Government was all wrong and righteousness began with this one and the Bank Rate. But L. did not mean or expect it to be published. However someone (no doubt Rueff) gave it to *Le Monde* which has published large extracts from it. Now it looks as if the US and probably other countries will press for publication. Rueff is said to be coming, with some Americans, to see the Chancellor about it all on Friday. It all sounds incredibly confused.

Saturday, July 12th

Ministers have been struggling all the week with the mass of papers about economic questions, nearly all for reducing the load on us. The Chancellor has had little help from any of them and shown little stomach to fight himself. In fact it has been an extreme form of the familiar spectacle of officials in the Treasury, with a little help from officials elsewhere, trying to bully and cajole Ministers into courses they find unpleasant because in the short-run politically unpopular.

Monday, July 14th

[W. H.] Draper, the US Ambassador to OEEC in Paris, came on Friday with Bill Batt, the London head of MSA [Mutual Security Agency], and Rueff and Marget who had been on Lionel Robbins' Working Party. Salter saw them with Lionel, E. Playfair (acting Chairman of MAC – Mutual Aid Committee), Copleston of OF and me. As we had been told, Rueff wanted us to make a splash for convertibility and had got Draper's ear. Draper, who seemed a very able and nice man – I had not met him before – said he wanted to do whatever would help us. I think Marget had been completely sold on the Bank's plan (Robot) – we knew that Frère, Governor of the Bank of Belgium, had told him all about it – and he actually told us how much it would help if we became convertible and suggested that the Fund should let us float, although against the Articles. I found this almost impertinent.

I had to go early to see the Chancellor who was appearing on a television programme that night and wanted to discuss the line he might take on various things. He seemed to me to be very good and I left with some respect for him. Meanwhile most of the Section were feeling that C. Dow was betraying them by his weak attitude on Hitchman's Working Party which has been spending very long hours on arguing about their Report to Ministers. Otto and Lucius Thompson want to make it tendentious towards Robot and MacDougall and Dow have been struggling. I wrote a note to Hitch and in the afternoon sent him a paper which Neild and Jukes had written. Christopher told me today he had not wanted this and I felt cross with the others who assured me that he would not mind. However I think it worked, as Hitch told me today that he was trying to adopt my suggestion of asking Ministers for authority to explore *two* lines – immediate and gradual convertibility – instead of the one that they had been going to be asked to select and which I thought was a ridiculous choice with Ministers so little educated.

The Chancellor gave a luncheon at No. 11 for Draper, Rueff etc. – Plowden and Makins also there. Lionel said that the US people had tried to be as helpful as possible but that we had been very discouraging because we had no policy. There was some talk after lunch and it was suggested that the countries named in the Report (UK, US, France and Belgium) should be invited to make further observations about progress, in consultation with anyone they liked including the Fund. I said I thought we all agreed that convertibility was desirable but that many conditions needed to be satisfied (as the Report said) before it would be possible: and that I thought that the changes to be made by all countries, including the US, would be worth studying. The Chancellor said this was a good idea and everyone else did too and we worked on these lines in the afternoon and reached full agreement *ad referendum*. It seemed to me that a study of the conditions of convertibility in which the US participated would be a good thing and pave the way for the Chancellor's visit in spring, if he makes one.

Today, however, there was quite a row. When L. Rowan heard of this he was furious at anyone negotiating about his affairs as he regards them, although Copleston had been there, without him. He wrote an angry Minute and this led to an even angrier one from Salter, saying that if the Rowan line were adopted someone else would have to go to Paris to negotiate, for *he* would not. I saw Rowan's Minute today and thought it a very silly one: he quite misrepresented the proposal, and said that the talks would be with the wrong Americans and that he or the Chancellor could do all that was needed or useful when in Washington in December. E. Playfair told me that he was extremely upset and accused the others of not asking him to the lunch on Friday. It was found that he *was* asked and his Secretary refused as he was busy. When this was pointed out he just said 'One can't go to everything'. He continues to antagonize everyone.

Wednesday, July 16th

Yesterday H.P. asked me to lunch with L. Rowan to talk to Robert Triffin, who used to be in MSA Paris and is now back at Yale but still advises both MSA and the Fund. Most of the time Triffin tried to persuade us about Marjolin's idea of an Atlantic Payments Union on EPU lines. It would be fine if the US could come in and there were rules against extreme creditors. L. Rowan was quite nice, but I suppose he had to be at lunch. I wrote a piece about our Friday talks and sent it round – this was done at Playfair's request. In the afternoon Compton asked me to do a note on the increase in the fiduciary issue which is now necessary. He seemed to think this was inflationary and was a bit surprised when I said that the demand for notes was a function of other things rather than a cause.

H. Morrison sent for me on Monday to ask me to help him with the chapter on Economic Planning in the book he is writing.[9] Plowden had done something but he did not like it. I don't suppose mine will be any better but it is an interesting subject.

Yesterday afternoon Plowden and I had one of our usual long talks, mainly about himself in relation to current issues and personalities. His latest trouble is that the Chancellor has asked O. Franks to come in as joint head of the Treasury with N. Brook, after E.B. leaves. N.B. to do the Establishment and O.F. the economics. I said I felt sure O.F. would not come – he had been offered a similar job in 1947 and refused. Why should he take it now? The Chancellor blows very hot and cold about E., who won't become a Permanent Civil Servant and yet won't make up his mind to go.

I have now lost most of my respect for the Chancellor though I still like him and think he is good at some things. But he is a weak man fundamentally. I feel stronger than he is and as he is not a very good instrument, one tends to discount him. So why should E.P. care what he thinks. E. told me also that the Governor has said that if the reserves fall to $1,500 mn, the Government must do Robot, or devalue, or he will resign. His resignation would do more to strengthen sterling than either of the other courses. But I don't suppose Ministers would see that, although several of them, notably Macmillan and Cherwell, do not at all approve of him.

Thursday, July 17th

Rather a quiet day yesterday. N. Brook who has been consulting me much more recently, had a long talk about the Investment Programme which Cabinet is taking this afternoon. The differences, though still violent, have narrowed a good deal and largely amount to how many houses we should try to build and say we are trying, out of a fixed amount of resources. No doubt beneath it all is a struggle – Eccles and Macmillan want to build at least 300,000 houses a year to advance their own careers, and Butler, urged somewhat unwillingly by Plowden, feels that this is very bad for the country – which M. and E. probably recognize also. But on paper there is little between them, and I did a brief saying so.

Salter has somewhat repudiated me after I wrote my paper at E. Playfair's insistence – it was all due to a final paragraph which was not in my first draft and which Eddie asked me to insert – I did not feel comfortable about it as it dealt too much with substance (though in fact Salter's alternative is very like one of my points). I suppose one only remembers the occasions when one acts on advice against one's judgment and it turns out wrong, and forgets all the occasions when someone else has saved one.

The PM in answering a question in the House about the economic debate yesterday, said that they would be discussing grave and far-reaching decisions affecting every aspect of our national life. This was about as bad a thing as he could have said in the circumstances, since the Cabinet have pretty well rejected every proposal for a grave and far-reaching decision and they are at their wits' end to know what to say in the Debate, which will be at the end of next week. The Government has been in trouble several times already over the difference between what it says the situation requires and what it does to deal with it. S. C. Leslie was in a great state as all the papers were after him at once: and it was very hard to avoid a repetition of the 'trap-door' speeches a little earlier when everyone accused the PM and the Chancellor of saying different things.

Friday, July 18th

William Armstrong dined with me last night and told me the PM had summoned R.A.B. at midnight to apologize for his rash remark. The PM apparently thinks that the fact that Cabinet has been talking about such serious matters is itself very serious and he quite forgot that they had turned everything down. William says that he loves arguing across the floor and thinks he has no equal at this – he stores up witticisms etc. to get off, and feels convinced he is having triumphs even when, as on Wednesday, he causes his own party a lot of trouble.

They turned down altogether any reduction in the Housing Programme. Meanwhile the Defence Ministers have produced a paper showing that defence will cost nearly £1,800 mn in 1953/54 and rising after that. This is the result of all the work designed to reduce it. They have taken some of the load off the metal-using industries but heaped up much heavier ones elsewhere.[10]

The Chancellor had an emergency meeting about both of them at 6 p.m. and decided to put in a paper on investment [in 1953] proposing either no control altogether, or sharp cuts everywhere else to keep within the ceiling [CP(52)249]. The hope is that this will make his colleagues realize what they are doing. I discussed with William the changed note in the Eccles paper and he said that E. and Macm. were parting company. I said that although I did not trust E., and had refused to convey his message to the Chancellor given at the Tuesday Club after the election, I now thought that Cabinet was so short of brains and Rab. so short of allies, that he might consider a rapprochement with E. just to get some support. As this would involve a break with Macm., it might give some chance of loyalty. E. must know that the PM could not last much longer and where would he be then with Rab. and Eden in control? William rather agreed and said that Cabinet had now reached its nadir, with a large collection of people whose only hope lay in the PM himself, and the elderly peers who knew nothing about either facts or politics. He said the Chief Whip was acting mainly as a sort of Gestapo for the PM, reporting every rumour and incidentally demanding concessions for every back-bencher who showed signs of disaffection.

Wednesday, August 6th

I was on leave from July 18th to August 5th. Ministers appear to have taken no decisions at all and the Debate on the economic situation is generally agreed to have been a ridiculous mouse after the PM's heaving of mountains. A paper is being prepared to try to educate the Chancellor once more about simple national income economics: the feeling is quite rightly, that part of his weakness comes from his not understanding it. However I fear that, as usual, the paper (we have done several before) will be ruined by having too many changes made by E.B. and everyone else.

The WP on the Commonwealth Conference has not made much

progress but Cherwell has put in a paper, by Donald MacDougall, proposing a sort of Atlantic Payments Union on the Marjolin model but with progressive penalties for extreme debtors and creditors. This seems to me to be very much what we would like though not very much what the US might take. But I wrote a note to the Chancellor asking that at least it should be studied by officials.

E.P. had Lincoln Evans [Gen. Sec., Iron and Steel Trades' Confederation] to lunch, mainly to find out how the TU Congress might go and whether HMG would help or hinder before then. He was reasonably confident and said, what is evident, that most of the heat had gone out of the Budget events. They had all been very upset when Monckton [Minister of Labour] referred back all the Trade Board decisions but this was blowing over too. They had seen the PM about this and were much amused when he said, quite early on, 'I have always been a warm friend of the labouring masses'.

He was very interesting about current and past Labour politics. Thought Nye had very little TU support and would probably be beaten. That Gaitskell would rise to great heights if he would stand up and fight Nye now and would get a little more 'fire in his belly'. That Attlee should never have been PM – he was all that was available with Lansbury [Leader of the Labour Party 1931–5] after the wreckage of 1931. And having been Deputy he became Deputy PM in the Coalition because they felt this was proper. But that Bevin ought to have been PM in 1945 and probably would have been if Harold Laski had not tried to arrange it and in a way that put Bevin's back up.

Friday, August 8th

We saw the Chancellor on Wednesday evening to discuss three papers on the Commonwealth Conference to be taken by the Ministerial Committee the next day. One by Swinton [PEC(52)9] and one by Macmillan [PEC(52)11], both arguing for more preference, continued discrimination till the reserves reached a pre-determined level, and an active investment policy. The third the one by Prof. already mentioned.

The Chancellor gave a lamentable performance. I suppose he is tired and also discouraged by his defeats: he clearly did not understand the subjects at all and had no ideas but wanted to put up a façade so that we would not see this. As we were all more or less experts this was a complete failure. E.B. and E.P. are trying to stop him going to the IMF Conference in Mexico City and he was very disappointed, almost petulant, about it. I felt less enthusiastic about him than I have ever done before. E.P. reduced to despair.

He (P.) came to see me yesterday and we had a long talk. He wants me to take a much more active part in the Commonwealth preparations than I have done so far, and I said I would. There is need, as they are now being handled by [Maurice] Dean and [Arnold] France, [both Treasury Under Secretaries].

A number of Perm. Sec. changes were announced today, really all to the good. Fergusson is at last going from F. and P., an enormous relief. He has done untold damage to his country by obstinacy, arrogance and stupidity. It is astonishing that the Nationalized Industries have not collapsed more completely. But under his regime we had a coal crisis in 1947, which he was the last person in England to admit: we imported a lot of US coal. We failed to get enough miners, largely because he was afraid we would have too many. We ruined our best export chances this year. We lost Abadan. We got the power station programme into a frightful mess and still have load shedding, after 6 years of investment priority to the BEA. He gave us more trouble on the Economic Surveys than anyone else except OF, more than all other Departments and OF put together. I dance on his grave.

He is to be succeeded by John Maud who is rather bogus but at any rate has none of Fergusson's dreadful qualities. The other changes are very good, and I am delighted about Helmore [now Permanent Secretary, Ministry of Materials] who has behaved irreproachably since his defeat over the Min./Materials and supplanting by Frank Lee. It must have been a bitter blow to him with John Henry Woods pressing him strongly: and I know that he thought very hard about leaving the Civil Service. I have wanted him to be made a Permanent Secretary for some time, if only to smooth over this period – since he is clearly quite able enough.

Tuesday, August 12th

After several others had tried their hands, I did a draft synopsis of the paper on Economic Policy which is to educate the Chancellor: and it was agreed. Now I must write it up and prevent it being bowdlerized. P. went on leave on Friday and will be away three weeks. R.A.B. has agreed *not* to go to Mexico City for the Fund and Bank meetings but to stay and prepare for the Commonwealth Conference. I do not know what L. Rowan will think of having to go with Salter. Rowan is on leave and was when the decision was taken and I fear that the contemplation of this did not prevent P. from urging the change!

Cherwell sent for me on Sunday to beg me to go to the meetings of the Convertibility WP under Brittain at which his scheme was to be considered. Ministers asked that it be looked at 'with a view to finding out how to do it rather than why not to do it' or words to that effect – this was the final phrase in my brief to the Chancellor and I gather that the Foreign Secretary took this line.

The first meeting was yesterday afternoon. The Bank of England (Lucius Thompson[-McCausland]) spent nearly three hours making a violent attack on it, with a little support from Snelling and a great deal from Brittain. Frank Figgures argued at great length, mostly the other way – it is lucky Otto and L. Rowan are both on leave, but Frank showed a refreshing independence.[11] I suppose if Rowan were in favour of something I wanted and Figgures argued warmly against it, I would feel that he had no right to take an independent line. But I will say that I do not impose any doctrinal views on my own staff! After three hours we got nowhere though I think the Bank were a bit shaken because we argued that they were speaking as if the present position were perfect. We are to meet again today as MacDougall is going on leave tonight.

Marcus Fleming is in London and came to see me. He looked almost like Redvers Opie which put me off a bit as Redvers has deteriorated a great deal – both he and Marcus seem to have a shifty look, though I can hardly believe that Marcus would go the same sort of way.

The other Fleming is coming at the end of August and Ross at the end of September. I have not made any further progress about Ian Little.

Thursday, August 14th

Harlan Cleveland of MSA/ECA was here for a few days this week to talk about the new submission to Congress, and the new NATO Report with which it will have to square. I took him to lunch at the Garrick on Wednesday – the Travellers is closed. He said they were doing large studies on all aspects of current policy so that either [Adlai] Stevenson or Eisenhower [Presidential candidates] would be perfectly briefed on where he started. He thought Truman would have a Budget all ready and that the new President would send this to Congress and then amend it. This was really inevitable on the time-table.

He told me that he thought both the UK and the US Treasury were quite mad about convertibility, which he said was the sign of a state, not a measure to be adopted in its own right. Of course I feel exactly the same.

Saturday, August 16th

Bill Batt and Julius Holmes gave a lunch at Claridges on Thursday to some visiting American Senators. It was interesting to meet Senator Connolly who is just retiring and obviously high time. I talked to Senator Long of Mississippi, a son of the great Huey. He was very keen on cartel legislation and seemed a nice modest sort of man. It was a pleasant lunch but I don't suppose it meant anything.

Thursday, August 21st

The Convertibility Working Party has been meeting for three hours every day. It is a most unsatisfactory party. After a long series of meetings (attended by Dow not me) they had a report drafted by Figgures, and all this week we have been trying to agree this Report. But since the fundamental objectives, and much of the thinking, of the different members is so diverse, it is almost impossible to get agreement. What has happened so far is that Brittain, the Chairman, asks Figgures to do a new draft which we do not see. I am afraid that by the time the new draft is ready there will be little time to see it.

Thursday, August 28th

The Convertibility Working Party was supposed to have finished some time on the night of the 26th. But it is still going on and will produce a very bad report, showing complete disagreement at almost all important points. The main troubles are (1) that the Bank and OF are quite opposed to the Economic Section and MacDougall and their representatives are under instructions: I do not think ours are but we have been driven by constantly meeting what we think to be closed minds into some rigidity ourselves; (2) the Chairman and the Secretary are partisans of one point of view, and though Figgures has tried to be fair, his drafts have often been badly slanted. I doubt if Brittain has even tried to be fair; (3) the representatives of other Departments do not really understand the issues involved and hence take no consistent position and do not even remain convinced of a particular point after they have thought they were; (4) the subject is much too complicated to handle in the time available.

Tuesday, September 2nd

The Report was finished in the end on the evening of Friday, August 29th. A good deal of it is a statement of conflicting views, drafted by each side as neither could trust the other. During the later stages, when we were discussing Trade Policy, Cohen of the BoT said that it was important that other countries should not be able to impose q.r.s [quantitative import restrictions] on us after we became convertible. We were not strong enough to offer them now that *we* would give it up but if we became so and could make a deal all round, it would very much reduce the risks of a contracting spiral of world trade. The Treasury leaped at this in the hope that they could bring round the Board of Trade and the FO, and worked up a plan for an approach to France, Germany, Benelux, Canada and US on the basis that we should all go convertible together, all give up q.r.s except against the US who would agree to everyone discriminating against her (including Canada) and who would put up an exchange stabilization fund of $5 bn. This scheme, which was not at all clear at first, was put in during the final drafting stages and became the recommendation of the majority, which they endeavoured to contrast against the Paymaster-General's Atlantic Payments Union, which had been found full of technical snags by the Bank of England. I had a great deal of difficulty over the APU as my people thought it wouldn't work; but [J. S.] Fforde representing MacDougall had to keep it alive and we could not split our ranks.

Thursday, September 4th

The Chancellor had several meetings yesterday about the papers and the series of Ministerial meetings which begin today. He is a bit doubtful about the new scheme and gave Plowden and me every chance to speak against it. He is quite clear that he wants it discussed by Commonwealth officials but no Ministerial commitment at this stage, so that they need not decide until they have heard what Commonwealth officials think. I hope this means that it can be discussed fully, with pros and cons. Plowden says that the FO are fully committed to this scheme, and consider that Robot is dead. His idea is to give it a run making clear the conditions needed if it is to be successful and the price we shall have to pay. He thinks that if we keep on merely opposing it we shall become a complete minority. I feel that the most important thing is that it should be carefully examined; the Paymaster-General will I think insist on this.

In the afternoon we talked about the internal measures needed if convertibility is to be successful, and tried to explain to the Chancellor. Later the Convertibility Working Party took the Economic Section paper on the need to strengthen sterling area arrangements. I managed to keep the temperature down and got it agreed that it was at any rate an important topic, though opinions differed as to whether anything could be done. I was asked to draft a note which might be sent to the Chancellor. [Jasper] Rootham of the Bank wanted to make the discussion acrimonious, as I suppose it must have been in the early stages of the Convertibility Working Party but I managed to stop him. However I doubt whether anything will come of the paper: it was written by Robert Neild.

Downie has now heard definitely that he has a job with ECE, and is going off for some years – he will be a very great loss. Fleming began on Monday. Ross is coming on Oct. 1st. The Treasury have decided to stop the scheme for making Economists in the Economic Section into Administrators. This is mainly because they are trying to keep down the total numbers (owing to present policy) and are using any device to help. It is very annoying and disturbing. As always, staff questions and the attitude of the Treasury to them cause me more worry and anxiety than much more important matters.

Friday, September 5th

Strath had a meeting yesterday to discuss a report which Turnbull (a CEPS man and Chairman of the IPC) had been writing for the Chancellor on alternative forms of investment control. Macmillan and Eccles are so much annoyed by CEPS efforts to curb the housing programme, that they have been attacking investment control altogether. They began by saying that building output was kept down by putting ceilings on it, since this led to programming below the capacity of the existing resources and builders couldn't build more than they had licences for even if they had the time. This is in general quite wrong when one considers that there are always more licences out than builders available, hence the necessity for the rigid starting date procedure. From this they went on to argue broadly that physical controls were against Conservative philosophy and that HMG should only control the public sector and use money and credit for the rest. Turnbull's paper was an attempt to work this out.

During the discussion we all thought that *some* decision about the level of investment would be essential unless credit policy were pushed to lengths which will add very much to the cost of the debt. And that if IPC did not do it (as now) on the advice of the B. [Budget] Committee, then the B. Committee would have to do it direct. The real trouble is of course that Ministers don't like being held down in fields that they think are politically important and this covers nearly the whole area.

In the afternoon Plowden drove me to Farnborough to see the SBAC Air Display. It was exceedingly interesting to see these 'planes which have given us such a lead over other countries and done so much to maintain British morale. We have been trying to push M/Supply to expand the industry to do exports and defence as well. The most startling one was of course the big delta wing Avro bomber which has only just begun to fly at all. After the conventional shapes it looks very much out of Jules Verne or H. G. Wells. The two-rotor helicopter also looked very odd – it seemed to have solved all the problems of poise and movement in any direction as well as straight up and down.

When I got back D. MacDougall was waiting in a highly excited state to say that Ministers had more or less turned down the 'collective approach' to convertibility and only the Chancellor and Lyttelton were for it. The others seemed almost to prefer APU! Anyway it was all being referred to officials. Dow told me that Donald was so pleased that he was now looking at all sorts of other schemes – I hope they will be more practical than APU which was a serious embarrassment to me. The fact is that I feel very suspicious of *all* great new plans to set the world right – not that we don't need them, but they each need six months' examination.

Friday, October 10th

I was on leave from Sept. 6th–22nd. When I came back I found that Ministers had decided to have the 'collective approach' put to the Conference of Commonwealth officials, but without commitment, and on the understanding that all the safeguards should be regarded as integral parts. A good deal of trouble has since come on the interpretation of this stipulation, which OF want to whittle down and MacDougall to stiffen. It seems likely that the Chancellor gave a different interpretation of what was meant by this to Rowan and to Plowden.

Anyway I have spent almost the whole of the last three weeks at the Conference of officials and have not found it very pleasant owing to the atmosphere of passion and prejudice. Leslie Rowan, who has expounded the UK case, has been scrupulously fair: Frank Lee who has been Chairman of the Conference, and who is not as keen as Leslie on Robot or this plan, started off very well but his fighting instincts have overcome him and he has gradually identified himself with the UK exposition and now rushes to its defence. I have had to sit in a back row but on several occasions have been asked to speak to give me a chance of putting views opposite to the plan. Nevertheless, one cannot but feel that it is all done in haste and passion: the best brains on the Empire side are from Canada, which naturally wants fast progress, and Melville of Australia who is very near someone like Lionel Robbins, in wanting convertibility based on whether deflation is necessary.

Tuesday, October 14th

The Conference is almost over and the final stages have not gone too badly from my point of view. No Deleg. likes the whole of the UK scheme and I think four of them (the Crowns and S. Rhodesia) are against it. The Australians like most of it but are much against the floating rate. The Canadians like it all but the safeguards. S. Africa likes the floating rate best. New Zealand is on the whole prepared to do what the UK wishes. The Report is a cautious document which certainly cannot be said to give enthusiastic support. The next struggle will be what the UK Del. says to our Ministers. I cannot at this stage say exactly what the other Departments especially Treasury and Bank of England will say but I doubt if they are overjoyed. Frank Lee said one day that *we* must consider what to do next and Leslie Rowan rather snubbed him and said *OF* must consider what to do next.

Most of the Economic Section think that we are in much too deflationary a situation and are losing much more output than is justified by the extra mobility of labour. I have had to quiet them, since the Chancellor is now struggling to get Government expenditure down. The whole situation is somewhat unlike anything we have had for a considerable time, certainly unlike anything post-war or that I have experienced while myself interested in policy. The balance of payments is running a surplus which is expected on present form to continue. But exports are increasingly difficult, mainly I think because the old soft destinations are short of sterling. Unemployment at home is well up on last year and activity is contracting slightly in most sectors. This includes a good part of the engineering field.

I have had long talks with Plowden to try to see that he gives such advice to the Chancellor as will let him out if we turn out to need a soft Budget. The line is that we *must* lower taxation and that we can only do this if we keep public expenditure down. The Treasury have been saying that the danger was a higher income tax, but I do not think myself that this is likely.

Wednesday, October 15th

At a cocktail party given by HMG for the Commonwealth officials, I managed to have a long talk to William Armstrong on the above lines. He is always chatting to the Chancellor and it is important that he should have the right slant. I mentioned the matter at 2nd Secs. also, to warn them that we may be attacked by the Opposition for unemployment and by the Government supporters for taxes too high. In fact everyone is longing to spend money if we give them the slightest chance.

The Conference has done all its work and closes today. The Development Report is a very good one. The one on Convertibility is not good professionally – many questions are ill-explored and the economics doubtful – and I don't know what the outcome will be. D. MacDougall wants to prepare an alternative course for Ministers, beginning with my idea of the economics of the cold war being the dominant theme.

He told me that although he had been extended for one more term, the PM had asked for Cherwell to be extended another year and if this were given he would be asked for himself. The Warden of Nuffield is annoyed because he thinks HMG are treating the loan of MacDougall too lightly, and this has made him look coldly on the request for Ian Little as Deputy Director. However I still hope that it may go through.

Thursday, October 16th

The Conference ended formally yesterday, with many well-deserved tributes to Frank Lee and the Secretariat. The standard of reporting has been extraordinarily high for such technical discussions.[12]

We have had several preliminary talks about the form of the UK Delegation Report and are to consider a draft this morning. It is difficult to know just what a fair report will be – [Arnold] France showed me a draft yesterday which in my view is too favourable to the UK plan, but D. MacDougall wants to exaggerate the feelings against it. Frank Lee and M. Dean both feel that Ministers will feel bound to put the plan to the Prime Ministers because they will look such fools otherwise.

Wednesday, October 22nd

On the Commonwealth front, OF have prepared a paper which they want the Chancellor to put to Ministers, which goes a long way towards meeting Commonwealth criticisms but at the cost of removing most of the safeguards previously prepared. The RSA is to be offered freedom to spend dollars on machinery, we are *all* to treat q.r. as something quite exceptional, including the US. The Nuclear Group is to go in favour of a vague Committee of the IMF and the Fund. And instead of a US exchange support fund administered by the group, we are to have a bilateral credit of $2 bn, half from the IMF and half directly borrowed. In fact it is much nearer to full convertibility and non-discrimination, without frills and with little but the floating rate to change it from the gold standard days. Meanwhile the doctrine is put forward that internal measures are *worse* with non-convertibility than with convertibility.

Yesterday evening Prof. sent for me to show me a paper he is thinking of circulating to Ministers as a first blast in the opposite direction – it introduces my idea, that the real problem is to live through the cold war, not convertibility or anything like that.

Had a long talk with Plowden about his future. He has refused to be P. Sec. of the M/Supply and has been offered the Economic Headship of the Treasury under the P. Sec. who would thus do mainly general civil service work while the Ec. Deputy would be a sort of over-lord over all the other 2nd Secs. He seemed to be hesitating, but I thought he was mad – after all our battles to be offered what was in effect a clear win and then not to take it! In the end he agreed though he felt, quite naturally, that he would have trouble with Leslie Rowan. I thought that as long as he made it clear to N. Brook that he would never stand in his way for Bridges' job, he could smooth him over: it was inherent in the situation that he would get across Leslie since that was the main struggle.

He wanted three stipulations: (a) that if a Labour Government came in he would be free to go (I persuaded him not to say that he *would* go); (b) that if he were offered the 'perfect job' outside they would be sympathetic; (c) that though he would carry out the Chancellor's clear instructions he would be free to oppose him on Robot etc. I think it is a most extraordinary thing considering that only in March the Chancellor wanted to get rid of him and E.B. was furious with him on the ground that he had intrigued with the Foreign Secretary against the Chancellor.

E.B. had a meeting about whether a slump was coming – we agreed that the Chancellor ought to stand fast until the Budget but that he would have a tough time. It seems to me ridiculous to think they would endure convertibility when they won't (as I'm sure they won't) even endure this much deflation.

Had a talk to Strath about Agricultural Policy and also about the Ec. Survey. Neither of us thinks that there is any chance of an improved Survey this year; it will still be the problem to have one at all and although the Section will be unhappy, I think that it will be better for the whole thing that CEPS should edit it.

On Agric. Policy (mainly milk at present) it is hard to see what one can usefully say, since it is all politics and no economics. The Milk Marketing Board are pressing for the restoration of most of their pre-war powers: I think it would be quite all right to do this as long as Ministers would give them clear policy directions.

Thursday, October 23rd

Yesterday I took John Maud to lunch, who has just gone to Fuel and Power. He was naturally overwhelmed with so much of importance, especially Persia [i.e. Abadan] which is pressing, and next year's coal Budget. I used to know him well when we were both young Dons but have seen very little of him since he went to Education just after the war. We had a long talk over the whole field, mainly because he is collecting views and wanted to add mine to them. On Persia, I said I thought it did not matter much what line we took – as between ours and the US – because it was impossible to know which, or whether either, would hold the situation. I preferred ours because there was less appeasement in it. He had had some long talks with Paul Nitze who is just going there and wants to appease a bit more. I told him I liked Paul but didn't think he was very tough, and that the words 'Nitze Plan' were very ill-omened in Great George St.

On F. and P. generally, I told him just what I had thought of Fergusson and of all the rows we had had – he said Fergusson had said the same though not blaming people! but of course from his side. We also discussed investment control in relation to the Nationalized Industries – apparently at Education, the Ministry knew all about the plans of the Local Authorities and there was complete co-ordination on building. But at MFP there is nothing, the Ministry have no idea about the make-up or the progress of the investment, only the alleged totals put in to IPC. Anyway John will certainly be a great advance on Fergusson though there is so much room that one can't say what that will be.

E.P. had a meeting at 3, of CEPS and Economic Section, to discuss the economic prospects. The main question we discussed was whether we should abandon building control, as Eccles is urging. CEPS have discovered that there will be well over 300,000 houses building by the end of the year and that if there is no jam, we might build well over 300,000 next year against the target of 260,000.

I am still trying to prevent my people from making too much of the coming slump.

Friday, October 24th

Yesterday took Tony Crosland to lunch. He had just come from the Parliamentary Labour Party meeting and was reasonably pleased by the results, a good deal due to a speech by H. Morrison. However, he seemed a bit depressed on the whole. He is to be married on Nov. 7th. We had some talk about convertibility etc.

This morning E.B. had a meeting – the Chancellor was dismayed to get the Minutes of dissent from E.P. and me, as he thought the draft paper sent him by OF was the agreed Treasury line! It just shows how little he knows about it that he could even think that I was in favour of all these courses. E.B. seemed a bit cross – he doesn't know much about it either and keeps on hoping that there will be a party line. However we narrowed the issues a good deal and I am to write a note on the difference in internal policy needed with, and without, convertibility. E.P. as usual hopes for great things from this – it is curious how in spite of all reverses he still believes in the power of a written argument.

Wednesday, October 29th

During the weekend the Chancellor circulated 'notes' about the modifications he wants in the collective approach. Eden had persuaded Prof.

to hold back his paper on the understanding that R.A.B. would hold back his. Prof. was very angry and felt he had been cheated on a technicality. He wanted the meeting postponed but they had the first one on Monday afternoon, and spent most of the time evading the issue. However at the end they got on to it and apparently everyone but Prof. was in favour of going on, those who were nervous thinking that there were quite enough safeguards.[13]

MacDougall is very depressed. I do not feel so much so as I still think events will make it difficult to go as fast as OF want. From predicting the loss of all the reserves in March, June and September, they now predict the next strain on these for *next* September. However my own view is that unemployment and a shrinking of world trade is likely to lead to great pressure before we have gone far with the talks to Europeans or Americans.

The Chancellor had a meeting on all this yesterday. It is impossible to know whether he understands anything at all about it, or not. He has a lot of conversational points which usually counteract one another, so that one feels he knows nothing at all about the real arguments. But this may be going too far. His policy has given the country a feeling that he is a strong man and our best hope of salvation. To me he seems a weak man driven to take some measures by the whims of his officials, who has also been lucky in that he has inherited the reversal of the stock-building and terms of trade which made 1951 look so disastrous a year.

I dined with the Tuesday Club last night to consider Crowther's suggestion that it be wound up. No one wanted this but N. F. Hall [Director of the Henley Administrative Staff College], whom no one takes any notice of – he is a Ben Gunn sort of character. Sigi Waley [a former Treasury Third Secretary] offered to take Crowther's place as Secretary and it was agreed to go on, but to try to widen the scope and the depth of the discussions. I did not belong to it before the war, when (apparently) it was regarded as a much grander body than now. I suppose everyone is much busier and that economic problems now seem more intelligible and less soluble. Bob Brand who was in the Chair would not agree with this view – he thinks we still know far too little and could do much more by reason. This seems to me very sentimental in terms of our present situation. We need to convince political leaders that it would pay to educate the country: and we cannot do that by reason.

Friday, October 31st

Yesterday was a bit quieter. I had a talk to Plowden who had seen the Chancellor and was dumbfounded – instead of being asked to be a real Deputy to E.B., as he had been told, R.A.B. told him that he was trying to get Oliver and in any case did not want any structural changes: he made E.P. feel that he was being kept on out of kindness because he could not get a job anywhere else. E. was in a bad temper and talked of resigning but he will soon forget about it.

Wednesday, November 5th

The PEC and yesterday [November 3rd *not* 4th] the Cabinet have decided to go ahead with the Collective Approach, but as Norman Brook says, without belief let alone enthusiasm, only because they cannot think of anything else. Cherwell opposed it to the end and a number of his colleagues were very nervous on employment aspects. On paper it has been a good deal watered down, in that a final decision will not be taken till we see what are the conditions which are changed during negotiation, and what the economic conditions are like at the time. At any rate Robot is out of the way for the present, and as the reserves are rising at present it may stay out. OF have shifted their gloom to the second half of 1953.

Meanwhile there have been more struggles over the Defence Programme: these seem to have been going on almost since the Budget, and the UK submission to NATO is held up long after it should be in. We will be last instead of first as we have usually been in these Paris exercises. The Chancellor and all his colleagues have got into such a mental state that they argue about things like defence, housing and so on in terms of the extra taxes that may be needed – and as there is now so much latitude in the system, it is a dangerous line for the Chancellor. I have been trying to persuade him to talk to his colleagues in terms of the other things we want to do – more exports, more investment, less taxes. But he is very woolly. Yesterday Wilfred King, Editor of *The Banker*, took me to lunch and I tried to persuade him to write an article for *The Economist* this week, so that it could influence the debate on the Opposition Amendment to the Address, to the same effect. They haven't taken much notice of the fall in production yet but the Opposition will bring it well to the foreground. Whether the Chancellor realizes that we warned him of this, I don't know – he certainly has forgotten that we warned him at Budget time that it was likely.

Thursday, November 6th

There was a Planning Board yesterday, at which Helmore and Maud, the new Permanent Secs. of Materials and Fuel/Power, attended for the first time. We talked about the demand for steel over the next 5 years [EPB(52)8]. It was a most discouraging meeting. Jukes had had a big battle on the Working Party to provide enough steel for the expansion of the engineering industry which was possible, if all went well. The result was a compromise but it at least allowed enough for a reasonable steady increase of production. At EPB however, the bulk of opinion was that we could not hope to sell the exports needed for our targets of debt repayment, Commonwealth investment, and increased imports; and that it would be extravagant to invest so much in the steel industry as to provide for so unlikely a contingency. Only Plowden, Strath, Cunningham, Rowlands and I were in favour of expansion. However

Plowden managed to bully them into a qualified approval of the Report, quite against the sense of the majority.

Defence with R.A.B. again in the afternoon. He reached a new low: his colleagues had been telling him that there would be unemployment in the engineering industry unless he increased defence expenditure and he was prepared to accept the argument. The idea that we now had no hope except to make employment by increased arms spending was almost too much for Plowden and me. However we recovered, with E.B. very firm and sensible as he sometimes can be on critical occasions – and went painfully again through all the Tory Party objectives to try to convince R.A.B. once more that if there was any slack he had better uses for it than his colleagues thought. I doubt if we did much good.

Friday, November 7th

I took Nicki Kaldor to lunch yesterday. He is pre-occupied with a problem about his Tax Commission [RC on Taxation of Income and Profits]. He wants it to discuss the problem of taxing expenditure instead of income, he being a passionate believer in this. The Chairman ruled this out of the terms of reference which referred to income, and the Chancellor supported the Chairman. He wonders if he can defeat this by putting his ideas in a minority Report. Otherwise he could clearly publish his views, since if they are out of the competence of the Royal Commission, it cannot affect them if a member publishes them. He would say in his article that he would have put them to the Commission but was told they were irrelevant. Then the Labour Party would probably make a row. However he does not want to be unnecessarily difficult and is still trying to proceed with the Chairman's benevolence. I could not think of anything sensible to say but advised him to play it long and do what he could to stay on good terms with the Chairman.

He has to give a lecture shortly to the Institute of Bankers about convertibility and so on, and we talked at length about floating rates. I find him a very sensible man on actual current problems: he had a good deal to do with converting H.G. to devaluation in 1949.

No progress anywhere else. E.P. is still very angry at the incompetence and vacillation of the Chancellor. B.W.G. told him he thought he was the weakest since John Simon [Chancellor in 1937–40], who had no standing in the National Government and whom his colleagues would have been glad to lose if he had stood up to them at all. It is very sad, and one cannot help liking R.A.B. in many ways and looked at objectively he has not done at all badly – I mean judged by events.

Tuesday, November 11th

The Government have done quite well so far in the Debate on the Address. We have all had a good deal of work on R.A.B.'s speech which he makes this afternoon. He writes his own version of prepared drafts, more often revised than Stafford's but much less than Gaitskell's. I re-wrote over the weekend a draft the CEPS had done on measures against unemployment. I felt a bit angry at their having done one without even consulting me, especially as we had previously agreed on a line at the small Budget Group. This paper was really a sort of shopping list and not nearly enough addressed to the actual situation.

Lady Cripps has been trying to get a biographer for Stafford and I have been consulted from time to time. She has been urged to choose Colin Cooke, the Bursar of Magdalen whom I have never met, so far as I remember. However I asked several people about him this weekend and they were generally favourable, though Worswick thought he would not really understand Stafford's 'Messianic' qualities. I am generally in favour of having a biography written soon after a man dies, when many people can remember him. It will not be the final one because you can't get the historical perspective: but it will give everyone a chance to criticize the facts and the interpretation. I have tried to persuade Lionel Robbins, and Frank Lee and Redvers Opie to write critical accounts of Keynes' later period now that Roy has produced a biography. However they have not been very co-operative even to leaving stuff with the British Museum. Roy has no conception of the damage Keynes did us in the US by his arrogance.

Tuesday, November 18th

I went yesterday to a meeting to clear the briefs for the Commonwealth talks. They have been altered a bit from what was put to Ministers, though I don't think very much. The talks with the USA are now to *precede* the approach to Europe. D. MacDougall says that this is because OF have realized how much the Continent is afraid of an early move. But it is sensible in itself if one wills the end at all. I have been trying to stay on the side-lines as the Chancellor has persuaded his colleagues to go on with it and I must accept with as good a grace as I can. I suspect, however, that the Chancellor himself is not so enthusias-tic as he was. I saw him on Friday to talk about the current situation and he said I had always misjudged him and thought he wanted to move faster and more rashly than he did. This is palpably untrue, since he twice tried to panic his colleagues: but it shows how he would now like to interpret the past.

E.N.P. is very fed up with all the re-organization talk. I don't know if he will really go – he has cried 'wolf' ad nauseam. But it is discouraging to deal with someone who does not know his own mind. I gathered from E.P. that there is some idea of getting an academic economist in the Treasury at the 3rd Sec. level, under him but in daily personal touch with R.A.B. This would be useful if he were sensible as he would no doubt command his ear. But it would make my own position look very odd and I do not think I could stomach it. However all this is very nebulous so far. E.B. is said to be completely undecided and also to want to overlap with N.B. for a year, which the latter could not bear. It all makes one think that there should be an earlier, not a later, retiring age – if everyone else behaves like this, presumably one does oneself but no one will tell one.

Joe Alsop is here – I dined with him in Oxford at the Chilvers on Sat. and he is dining with me tonight.

Wednesday, November 19th

The Chancellor suddenly decided to have a morning meeting yesterday, which we had after the 2nd Secs. He wanted a general run-round which we did fairly inconclusively. He seemed anxious to placate me as he constantly asked for my views.

In the afternoon N.B. had a meeting to clear more Commonwealth briefs. This included one on the communiqué and later steps. It seemed to me that we were in serious trouble on all this. Unless there is a fairly full communiqué it won't seem to have been a good Conference. But if there is, the Europeans will learn all about it. In any case there will have to be a Debate early in the New Year. It will be impossible to get much to the US until Jan. 20th and very doubtful if they will want to talk for several months. But the Chancellor cannot leave in March or April and the PM is not likely to want to leave in May. So it may well turn out that by the time we talk to the US the whole thing will have had several airings, the Europeans will have taken up positions and may want to come too, and both in the UK and the US a great deal will have been said to prejudice the discussions. Rowan thinks that the US talks can be earlier but he is not used to this situation (between election and inauguration). None of us are either but all our friends, as well as common sense, tell us that they won't do much on so difficult a subject till they have had time to consider.

Alsop and I discussed Butler's character. I still find this baffling, and since E.P. told me that R.A.B. had had some ideas about getting an economic adviser in the Treasury as well as in the Cabinet office, I have had a direct personal interest which always concentrates one's thoughts. Joe said he was a 'sharp' man by which he meant that he was alert and intelligent in matters that might affect him, even though not a profound thinker who might be very able intellectually but a fool in affairs. He thought, as William Armstrong does, that the Chancellor is not nearly as ignorant as he seems. Joe also thought that he regarded everyone else as a 'boob' and did not expect them to see the inconsistency in what he said, or care anyhow if they did. I think there is a sort of truth in this, that the Chancellor regards himself as manipulating other people and thinks it easier to do this if they think he is rather a fool – and if this were so it would give him a feeling of triumph that others should think him stupid. It seems rather a peasant's outlook, however, and I don't think he has that in other ways!

Thursday, November 27th

All the papers for the Commonwealth talks were agreed officially last week and approved by Ministers on Monday. Cherwell put in a paper at the last minute pointing out how far the present proposals departed from the ones first approved and how much worse they were. But the other Ministers all supported R.A.B. who himself said that we were in no way committed. Frank Lee told us at 2nd Secs. on Tuesday that there was a very marked lack of enthusiasm among Ministers nevertheless, and that they supported R.A.B. because they had gone so far already and not because they liked where they had got to. The first meeting of the Conference took place this afternoon but I have not heard what happened at it.

This has been a very quiet week for me but E.N.P. has been worrying a good deal about his future. After our previous talks on this subject, I managed to have a chat with William Armstrong and he indicated that E.N.P. could not become the chief co-ordinator in the Treasury because T.L.R. and B. Gilbert refused to be co-ordinated by him: and indeed I wonder if T.L.R. would allow himself to be co-ordinated by anyone without a struggle, while Otto is still with him. The more I think about it the more I regard Otto as the fundamental difficulty based on his unwillingness to be driven anywhere when he is not driving – though I don't think he would mind much where he went if he were.

William said that the Chancellor did not want me to go and that he valued my advice though he thought it was given from a 'left' point of view in social outlook, though not in terms of political parties. However he considered that he would now get some 'right' advice from Maudling who has just been made Economic Sec. and William says entirely at the behest of the Chancellor (who is now feeling himself much stronger in relation to the PM than he used to) and will be very much in his pocket as his career depends on this. I have not met Maudling yet; Frank Lee says he is very good, i.e. very efficient as a junior Minister. Apparently he was a temporary during the war and was in the Conservative Central Office during the Labour Government – someone (? who) said the propaganda was all right from there but too much Eden and Maudling [Eton and Magdalen], a joke I never heard before, in fact I never heard in any way that registered of Maudling.

Anyhow William said that I stood all right with R.A.B. and he suggested that E.N.P. did also but could not become the head man on the economic side because of the other 2nd Secs., though from the way William spoke I got the impression which E.N.P. himself has, that R.A.B. would not mind losing him if this could be managed in a friendly way.

Tonight Edwin came to see me and said he had again been pressed by E.B. to go to the M/Supply as they could not get anyone suitable and would otherwise have to try to persuade Eric Speed [formerly Perm. Sec., War Office] back from Lazards. He said he had refused to go because he would regard this as accepting and indeed endorsing his defeat in the Treasury. He did not really mind if he were beaten but he would mind if he stopped fighting. I think he is quite right to feel like this but that he ought to have a plan for his subsequent fighting, which he has not got at present. Neither have I. I must try to think of something: I don't feel that I have had the situation properly in my mind so far and indeed it has been so uncomfortable that I would be quite glad to go myself, if something I liked turned up.

Wednesday, December 3rd

The Commonwealth Conference began on Thursday with formalities. On Friday and yesterday they had four meetings at which everyone made long and dreary opening speeches about their economic position, general attitude towards the 'collective approach', development and commodity policy. Today they are meeting under R.A.B. (instead of Eden) to try to get down to business on the collective approach. My impression is that they will all say that they are in favour of convertibility and all that. They see great risks in it but that it is up to the UK whose currency it is, to take the lead and the decision. The more I think about it the more I think how incredible it is that we have gone so far on a road wanted by neither political party, approved by no economist, and by no other OEEC country. The sinister influence of the Bank of England in this is more like reality than myth.

The EPU Managing Board have been working on a report on convertibility and they practically produced one saying how dangerous it would be to move soon and in general very nervous about any move by the UK. The Bank and the Treasury OF disapproved of this and tried to get our delegate to come out much less solidly. Then Cobbold went to Basle [to the BIS] and harangued the Central Bankers there and they all went back and worked on their Governments and got them to instruct their representatives to take a much less committed attitude. The object of all this is to prevent there being too much evidence here that OEEC countries are against the Bank's plans.

Sunday, December 14th (Washington, DC)

I did not have much to do with the Conference and left London on December 9th for a short visit to Washington where I now am. The Conference did not seem to me to be a great success, on the whole they accepted the general lines of the UK paper on convertibility etc., which was the main subject. But the same doubts and misgivings were expressed about timing and the main details, as had been done at the official talks. And I don't think anyone was enthusiastic or thought it was a heaven-sent solution. There was also some sharp division about rate policy which nearly led to a disagreement, while Australia was more interested in getting free access to the London money market than in anything else.

The final communiqué was issued on Thursday night but no text is available in Washington yet! I gather that the transmission was interrupted and no one in London noticed! though I do not understand the system used which could have given this result – however this is what Paul Gore-Booth [Director, British Information Services in US] told me. It is clear from the summaries, and from speeches by Eden and Butler which have been reported, that the main lines stayed as they were but that the final decision has been left, if possible, less fixed in time and substance than ever, and dependent on negotiations with Europe and USA. Fortunately I have not been much questioned here about it although R.A.B. told me I could discuss in general terms if I wanted to.

Although the 'collective approach' received a rather lukewarm response from the Prime Ministers, it was decided to proceed with it and sound out the Americans before disclosing the details of the plan to the Europeans. A group led by Churchill and including Butler and Cherwell went to Washington at the beginning of March 1953 (i.e. as soon as possible after Eisenhower had taken office as President). The Americans, however, offered no encouragement and dismissed the proposal for sterling convertibility as 'premature' (entries for March 9th and 11th and June 25th). The Europeans, who disliked being kept in the dark when matters of importance to them were under discussion in Washington with another member of OEEC, were also discouraging, particularly as convertibility meant putting an end to the European Payments Union (entry for June 25th). At the end of 1953 convertibility still seemed a long way off.

Wednesday, January 14th 1953

A month has passed by and I must try to summarize it. I was in Washington from early morning of Dec. 11th to Dec. 17th, then two days in New York and flew to England to arrive late on Dec. 19th. I stayed with Joe Alsop in Washington and saw a good many people – he and Walter Lippmann, Bill Martin [now Chairman of the Board of Governors] and Win Riefler of the Federal Reserve Board, the Nat. Income economists at the Council of Economic Advisers, some Dept of Commerce economists, Tom Finletter, Justice Felix Frankfurter, Chip Bohlen [Counsellor, State Dept], Dick Bissell and many of the British – though Oliver had gone. Both Rickett and Hall-Patch were in London and I saw them before I left. But Washington was naturally rather dead: however I got a clear idea that economic activity would stay up for 6–8 months and that there was a good deal of nervousness after that.

In New York I saw John Williams [Professor of Economics at Harvard], Elliot Bell, editor of *Business Week*, Lew Douglas [former Ambassador to the UK] and a very interesting man called Gabriel Hauge who has been made special assistant for economics to Eisenhower. He had been a student of Williams and had then worked on

Business Week and been lent to Ike for the campaign – hence the job. I found all the New York people very sensible or at any rate very much the same in their ideas as the ones I had got on with before. Lew Douglas had a lot of ideas about what the new Administration would do, especially on the price of gold and on a support fund for convertibility, which seemed very queer. He had given some of them before to Geoffrey Crowther who had passed them on to R.A.B.

I was mostly on leave between Dec. 24th and the end of the year and everything has been very quiet in Whitehall until recently. The PM decided unexpectedly to go to Jamaica and to stop and see Ike on the way – this was regarded as rather naughty but no one dared to say so, and in fact it seems to have turned out well. There was a lot of fuss in drafting a note about the Collective Approach, from which he might speak, but I don't think it was delivered in the end. He cannot have said very much about economic questions, which is just as well – it seemed clear to me when I was there that they were anxious not to commit themselves to anything until they had had time to settle in Washington.

On the collective approach itself, it seems that the Commonwealth Prime Ministers were more luke-warm than I had thought: and Leslie Rowan is quite gloomy because he thinks they won't support it in the end. Meanwhile R.A.B. has got less and less enthusiastic about either speed, or convertibility as a good thing. Today E.B. took a meeting of a small group (Rowan, Plowden, Brook, Lee, Liesching, Hall, Dixon) which has been set up after much prodding from everyone but Rowan to keep a watch over the negotiations. OF have prepared a paper to hand to the Americans to tell them what our ideas are, preparatory to discussions. It was almost an unexceptionable paper, in its stress on caution and risk, the need for the earning of dollars and the risks of a declining spiral if convertibility leads to the abandonment of discrimination too quickly.

I suppose one is hardly conscious of the changes in one's own mind so inclines to exaggerate the victory of one's own ideas. But I certainly feel that the final state is much more a vindication of all that I have been fighting for, than a demonstration of the rightness of the Bank and OF. At any rate we have gone a year without taking any rash step, our position is much improved in the meantime, and we have made our own action conditional on a number of things being done, none of which was included in the early Robot plan.

The next step is under discussion in a most confused situation. Probably R. Makins will hand the paper to the US about Jan. 30th. He has already sent several telegrams about the discussions. R.A.B. is most anxious to go himself, with one or two officials, to launch the talks, and he has suggested about Feb. 20th. He can't go between mid-March and early May, because of the Budget. The other possibility is that the talks will be between Makins and Rickett and the US on the official level and R.A.B. not go till June or July. No one will really know until after the Inauguration.

Meanwhile it is extremely awkward with the Europeans and OEEC generally. They know enough from leaks to have a fair idea of what is going on but we won't talk: they are extremely nervous of early convertibility, desperately afraid that we will break up EPU, and most jealous that we want to talk about their affairs to the US over their heads. All this had been foreseen but we were determined not to broach it to them until it has been opened with the US. Marjolin is coming to London tomorrow to try to find out some more.

Budget. I put in a preliminary paper to the BC [BC(52)27] before I went to Washington: the gist of it was that as we were now well below full output, and were limited in exports by markets and not by supply questions, there was room for a good deal of relaxation but that it was a matter of judgment how much we made, since we clearly were getting some benefits from the disinflation we had had. The whole situation is very interesting: OF and the Bank, and the Chancellor's policy, suggest that we ought not to let up at all. But politics, the Chancellor himself, E.B. and a good deal of pressure, are in favour of being as easy as I can be induced to say is safe.

I have been trying to bring out the conflict between Robot etc. and the Budget outlook but it is beginning to be a dead horse as there is no doubt that in this at least I can do what I like. I have been trying to conduct a campaign about the balance of payments target, arguing that we cannot possibly get the £300 or £350 mn surplus we say we must have, unless we lend people the money and find creditors who are willing to be repaid in goods. Maudling is helping as he has asked for an investigation into our power to lend abroad, and this will force my ideas to be ventilated.

All this sounds very egotistical but I feel rather bitter as well as fairly triumphant about what now seems to be the defeat completely of Robot and all that we have struggled for.

E.P. He is temporarily feeling very good as he has been completely taken back into favour by the Chancellor and OF are at least temporarily under a cloud. He now says he will stay till the Budget and then consider. His main fear seems to be that Oliver Franks will be offered his job. I saw O.F. when he got back from Washington and he said that he was going on six weeks' holiday before he even thought about the next step. But when he saw the Chancellor the same day he said 'What have you got to offer me?': and G. Crowther, who crossed on the same ship, reported to E.P. that he was desperate to get into Government service. I do not believe for a moment that he would give Crowther the slightest idea of what was in his mind. But it *is* a bit hard to know what he will do since he has turned down almost everything that seemed remotely or completely suitable. I would think that to be a 2nd Sec. in the Treasury was a bit *infra dig* after the Washington Embassy.

He will be back in a week or two now and then at last perhaps he will give me some idea – he has talked about it every time I have seen him for the last three years, but I am sure it is completely genuine that he didn't, probably doesn't, know what he wants. I am much the same but I don't talk about my uncertain state of mind to everyone all the time.

Tuesday, January 20th

The draft paper for the US on the Collective Approach [CP(53)22] was agreed yesterday and has been sent off for R. Makins' comments. When these have been received and digested, and Ministers finally approve, he will probably hand it in, towards the end of this month. Foster Dulles [incoming Secretary of State] is due in London about the same time, on a quick trip he and Stassen [Director, Mutual Security Agency] are making, no doubt to inspect the MSA Empire: and perhaps we can have a little talk with him in London.

Marjolin was here on Friday and saw officials, and then Butler and Eden, to ask what was in our plan and how we would handle it. I saw him at lunch at MacDougall's in Oxford on Sunday and he said that the trip was a waste of time. He had been refused any information and though he had protested that we clearly intended to break up EPU and damage OEEC, had been told that we simply had to speak to the US first. This is quite right and I think he takes it too hard. We had a talk about the present situation with production in Europe slowing up and a stagnant appearance – and agreed that the problem of our time was to maintain inflationary impetus while avoiding inflationary prices. The balance of payments aspect could be handled if we were more sensible in our arrangements.

My NEW [National Economy in War] Working Party met again yesterday, after six weeks' break, to begin on the Draft Report which Grieve-Smith has prepared. We have come to much the same conclusions as the Man-Power Committee, about the total that will be available for defence production *and* the Armed Forces, but hope to make our recommendations much more concrete. It is full of unverified and indeed arbitrary assumptions which can't be checked until we talk to the US. But in any case it is now quite out of date, as it works on the old strategic hypothesis, for which a much more drastic one is now being substituted.

Wednesday, January 21st

President Eisenhower was successfully inaugurated yesterday so we ought to know fairly soon some of the things his Administration will think. The stories in the papers are very contradictory and often unlike the impressions I got in New York.

There was an inner Budget Committee yesterday afternoon to consider a note I had written which said that the ordinary rules were not applicable this year since we were not assuming full output, nor could we assume any particular connection between deflation and exports. Leslie Rowan was there and though he agreed that no further deflation would help, he certainly didn't want anything the other way. I raised also the question of how we could earn the overseas surplus for which we were budgeting, and which the Programmes Committee now consider unattainable. I could not feel that Leslie understood at all the influence of monetary demand upon output, either from home or from abroad. William Armstrong made the most constructive suggestion as he said he thought it would be out of the question to have a deficit above the line at this time.

Thursday, January 29th

Oliver Franks came to see me on Wednesday, and stayed about 75 minutes: I was a little annoyed as I had told him I was busy and asked how long he wanted and he said an hour. He was just beginning a round of consultations about what he should do next, and set out all the considerations at great length. In brief they were:

(a) He didn't want to teach but would not mind an academic job such as Head of a House, or Vice-Chancellor. The most promising thing going now was the Chairmanship of the UGC.
(b) He wouldn't mind a business job if it were exactly right – not otherwise. He didn't want a nationalized industry.
(c) He *did* on the whole want something in Government service, either FO or Treasury. But neither William Strang [Permanent Under Secretary of State, FO] nor E.B. were capable of saying 'Here is a man with such and such qualities, what can we use him for?'! They just offered him whatever was next on the list. He wanted my views on the offer from the Chancellor of the (or a) Treasury job.
(d) Finally, if it were better to wait, he could get a reasonable competence for several years as a Research Fellow, without conditions, from the Rockefeller Foundation.

My own feeling was slightly for (d). But of course the Treasury job is the one that interested him most and concerned me most. I was a bit surprised to find he wanted it as I had not expected him to. I told him I thought the main difficulty was that neither the Chancellor nor E.B. were capable of making up their minds, R.A.B. by constitution and Edward by exhaustion. Therefore they couldn't solve the Treasury problem and wanted someone to do it for them. But was there any hope that they would support him? I didn't think so, and felt that in the complex situation with so many deep interests involved, including the jealousy of Permanent Civil Servants against Temporaries, he would not really be more successful than anyone else. I don't know if this was the best advice but E.P. will resign if O.S.F. comes and this would not be good for either. Nor on the whole do I think O.S.F. is quite the man to pull the Treasury together (in case I have not written it down yet, they want someone to be a real Deputy to the Perm. Sec. and over *all* the Economic work, i.e. a man between the Perm. Sec. and the present layer of 2nd Secs.).

Actually O.S.F. would do better as the Perm. Sec. but the job has been promised to N. Brook both by the PM and by E.B. and I think he would do it very well.

I took William Armstrong to lunch yesterday and found that it was *his* idea to get Oliver into this job. I am not sure that he is right, i.e. I still feel as in the last paragraph though I think William is a very sound and sensible young man. He is 37 and will clearly be very high in the Civil Service before long.

The Budget is going very nicely as far as I am concerned and I think the Armstrong formula of a small above the line surplus is about right.

Wednesday, February 11th

Nothing more about O.S.F. so far. Plowden is convinced that he is coming to the Treasury, and says he is determined to resign if he does. I feel very doubtful and think it more likely that he will do nothing for the present.

The main interests have been the Budget, preparations for Washington, and arguments about our capacity to invest abroad. On the Budget, E.B. is anxious that we should not take too optimistic a view and is trying to prevent me from saying that I think there is a margin in hand.

We all had a meeting with the Chancellor on Monday and E.B. and B.W.G. were very negative and depressing. Yesterday afternoon the Chancellor sent for me by myself and we had a long talk. He is most anxious to take a little bit off the Income Tax and I think feels that the pressure from his back-benchers will be irresistible. I don't see myself why he should not do this. It will be necessary to do a little on PT and we all want to do something for industry, which from the Nat. Inc. point of view is indifferent to the inflationary–deflationary aspect.

The Chancellor is seriously worried because the Treasury forecasts of [government] income and expenditure have turned out so badly and feels it is very shameful that his experts should have got it so wrong.[14] I tried to comfort him but not very successfully. Otherwise he is mainly worried about the speech – he says it will be very dull and must have 'light and shade'. He said he deliberately made last year's speech like a symphony – I am afraid I get a little lost in these aesthetic similes.

There have been great ups and downs about who would go to Washington, now settled for early March. I thought that the team should be small and unobtrusive. The Chancellor and the F. Sec. are going, also Dixon, Rowan, Plowden, Frank Lee and Otto Clarke. At first they wanted me too. As N. Brook said, who else *could* they take? However, it is now decided that I won't go, and I think Frank Lee may be made to fly. Meanwhile heat continues to be generated among the European countries against the whole plan, especially because EPU will not be able to keep on with convertibility. OF have promised us a plan to manage them together but it has not appeared yet.

The Investment Abroad controversy arose from OF really committing us to aim at a surplus of £300–£350 mn a year, which was stated in the reply to an OEEC questionnaire and which is now getting rather publicized. Maudling sent a minute to various people asking how much we *could* invest abroad and OF and the Economic Section have been arguing about it.[15]

Tuesday, February 24th

The Chancellor, E.N.P., Rowan, Otto Clarke and [Matthew] Stevenson of OF leave by sea on Thursday night and Frank Lee is going by air on Friday. The US side have asked a lot of questions which we shall have to try to answer: and a lot of briefs have been prepared here. The most critical one is about the future of EPU where our hands are quite empty, and indeed where I don't think even yet that we realize how incompatible a regional system is with true convertibility and non-discrimination. There is plenty of evidence that the US will be worried on this one. The Europeans of course are very worried indeed and have protested more on this score than on any others.

Partly connected with this in polemics at least have been the discussions about the Budget and about what we could afford to invest overseas. OF have been arguing either that there was no slack in the system, or that if there was it would weaken our competitiveness to do anything about it. They also felt very reluctant to admit that there was any connection between our foreign lending policy and the amount of our overseas surplus. Strath and I have had several long and heated discussions with Otto Clarke, which I enjoyed very much as Strath showed an unexpected degree of academic detachment and ability to chop logic, so that between us we more or less defeated Otto (who seems to me incidentally to be rather in retreat just now, perhaps because he senses that he has lost this battle). Although we have not really agreed on our doctrine, we have at least got it on record that one school of thought thinks there is a connection between what we are willing to lend, and the amount of our overseas surplus. Otto, and Leslie Rowan who is really nothing but his creature now, have been moving more and more to a very severe old-fashioned doctrine that 'competitiveness' is the only thing necessary to salvation.

Meanwhile the pre-Budget discussions have continued but here I think I am more or less having my way. At any rate the Chancellor has accepted and no one really rejected the conclusion of the Economic Section paper [BC(53)15] that there was a bit of slack in the system: and the particular uses to which we should put it are the ones I have wanted, at least I think they will be – the Chancellor has (wisely from a tactical point of view) refused to make any final decision, but he has made it pretty clear which of the alternatives he finds attractive. E.B. and B.G. and to some extent even E.N.P. were very much against doing anything for the final buyer (as A. H. Abbati used to call him – at least I think so – it is so long since he used to send me all that literature on Unclaimed Wealth – there are plenty of claimants for it now!). I felt that it was not very sensible to accept a figure for the amount of slack and plan to use it in ways which would either not materialize till next year, or which could only be transfers within the savings account. I hope also to have got into my hands the first drafting for the Speech.

There has been a curious trend this year. In the past the horrors of having to raise more taxes have led almost everyone except perhaps Rowan to accept the Economic Section calculations. This year there seems to be nearly as much horror at the idea of giving anything away, especially on the part of B. Gilbert who propounded the doctrine that we should either accept the Section target, or aim at a substantial surplus above the line, whichever was the bigger.

Wednesday, February 25th

Edwin told me yesterday that Oliver had refused to come to the Treasury – which I had all along said he would not do – and also turned down the UGC which I felt more doubtful about. So he still really does not know what to do – indeed more than ever for when he saw me both of these seemed real starters in his mind. I begin to feel sorry for him.

The Economic Survey, which used to cause me so much agitation and bitterness at this time, has almost ceased to be a pre-occupation at all. This is no doubt partly that familiarity has lessened its terrors: but it is also because it has gradually ceased to go in for forecasting and because, as this has happened, the CEPS have become more and more responsible for it. I think my real disillusion came from the realization that practically no Ministers cared about what was in it except from the point of view of its impact on the public: so that all our struggles to get the shades of doctrine or prediction right were completely wasted. Every Minister read it to see whether he or the Government were praised enough and to make sure that any note of criticism was removed. The device of having a Ministerial and 'true' version first, to be suitably debased in the draft for publication, was never operative because Ministers, and Permanent Secretaries before them, would regard the draft from the first as the one to be published.

However the coup de grâce was given by the present Government who had spoken so much against planning that they convinced themselves that if they did not make any forecasts except subconsciously, they were therefore not planners. In fact they are all inveterate planners in the 18th century or paternalist sense: whenever anything happens that they do not like, their first instinct is to use the power of the State to stop it. Eccles and Macmillan interfere at every turn in order to build 300,000 houses. Recently when various price changes have been suggested – transport, coal, steel, for example – there has been a strong party in favour of preventing the changes, if necessary by increased subsidies. It is not very surprising that Tories have no principles to speak of, it is historically right and probably inherent in Conservatism. But it is surprising that they are such cowards.

Leslie Rowan has not broken up yet but still seems very near it. There is now always *some* disgruntled Perm. Sec. in Whitehall who finds his manners intolerable and the air of bitter theological controversy almost too painful to be endured. I think even E.B. is aware of all this and at least considers moving him. Of course Frank Lee who wants his job is the most consistent but he is so naive on these occasions that he does not carry much weight.

Thursday, February 26th

A long telegram from Washington yesterday giving preliminary questions on the document we have handed in 'from Professor Bissell, [H.] Linder and [W. R.] Burgess'. They must have brought Dick Bissell back to MSA either for this occasion or in general – he had told me in December that he was right away from current affairs. It really was rather like an examination paper and I spent a good deal of the day writing answers to the questions about UK internal stability. Curiously, however, these were in absolute terms and not related to convertibility at all. An enormous mass of material is being prepared, as usual, for this visit and much of it is being printed. There will be no chance to use more than a fraction in the four or five days available, but I suppose it is necessary to be ready for anything. E.P. got cold feet at the last minute and decided to take D. A. V. Allen to help him deal with any questions that may come up. Leslie Rowan is taking Stevenson as well as Otto.

I had Hitchman for lunch yesterday to meet Colin Clark. The latter is now Director of the Oxford Inst. of Agricultural Economics where I used to know the staff so well long ago when C. S. Orwin was Director and Ruth Cohen and Keith Murray on the staff. He resigned from his job in Queensland late last year and is now living in Keble Road with his wife and I think 7 of their 8 sons – I have seen him several times there.

Hitchman is trying to get an Agricultural Economist or really an economist *tout court* to advise the M/Agriculture. They have never really replaced Enfield and the present adviser is a young man called Kirk who is more statistician than economist and who is not very strong or good. So Hitch wants to meet various people and pick their brains. He has already asked me if he could send his people to talk to one of mine regularly, but I have no one available. Yesterday we talked about agricultural efficiency and land tenure and why the Danes and the Dutch produce so much more than we do. Clark wants to introduce land taxation and at the same time more freedom of tenure which he thinks would drive out bad and small farmers. I am always inclined to think that until we get bigger holdings we will get nowhere. Hitch did not show his hand, and I imagine that he has decided nothing in so short a time. But he talked a good deal about systems of education and of providing expert advice and services from the centre.

Tuesday, March 3rd

The party got away in the end, on Thursday night. In the afternoon the Chancellor rang me up to say goodbye – it is one of his endearing traits that he does that sort of thing; so did Cripps. H.G. was too young and insecure to think about cosseting his staff. I expect he thought of them as being at least as grand and more self-assured than he was.

Yesterday the Planning Board took the Economic Survey, but as only Clegg and Tewson were there from the non-official members, it was not much of a run for it. It seemed to go through all right, although a man called Little, a Welsh economist borrowed by the Ministry of Supply for a year, made a lot of observations, including some which questioned the National Income tables. Both he and Bowyer [Deputy Sec., Ministry of Supply] appeared to think it was very wrong even to suggest that any relaxation of consumption was possible. The February unemployment figures, which I saw yesterday, show quite a big drop from January, but I think these are very seasonal: there is no evidence yet of a real return to anything like boom, nor do I expect there to be one.

Dow is doing quite well as my new Assistant Secretary, and is much more constructive than Butt was. On Friday he put forward quite firm ideas about the long-term prospects and organization of the Section. He thinks we should gradually increase in numbers to about 50: the junior people to be nearly all research assistants, getting up facts and figures: the senior ones who are to be let out to meetings, to be where possible on the A/Sec. level so that they would have some authority in Whitehall.

Wednesday, March 4th

The Steering Committee took the Survey yesterday so it is through all its official stages. There is still a good deal of confusion about the decline in production which we have consistently argued is a clear sign of deflation. Most people would like to advocate more deflation *and* measures to increase production at the same time. The instinct behind this is quite sound but they entirely overlook all the work of the past 20 years on the relation between demand and output.

We have at last almost finished the Report of the National Economy in War Working Party, about the size of the forces in war.[16] This argues that there is a strict limit to the size of the Forces we can arm ourselves – the upper limit is set by the needs of the civil population but before this is reached an earlier one is likely to be set by steel supplies, and perhaps by industrial capacity. However the whole report will be obsolete before it appears as the new 'strategic hypothesis' about bomb damage in the early stages is so much more drastic than the one we were told to take. My party may have to do the new report too which will be, as is now said, a 'Dennis Wheatley' report, painting the outlines very broadly.[17] I feel fairly clear about the picture which is essentially one where you have to make do with what is available in the smaller towns.

Monday, March 9th

At Norman Brook's briefing meeting this morning (the weekly meeting to discuss the briefs needed for the PM and other Chairmen of

Committees of Ministers), a telegram from Washington was brought in which said that the talks had achieved nothing but the establishment of friendly relations. The US thought that we were not yet strong enough to move to convertibility! Later on there was another telegram to say that we would not now be able to explain the details of our scheme to the Europeans. All this looks as if the plan is dead at any rate for the time. I had hoped for something like this and naturally feel very pleased about it, though it is perhaps counting chickens a bit in advance. At any rate it is nice that the Americans say the same as I have been saying for a year.

Meanwhile the Bank of England have discovered another £100 mn in last year's invisible income and consequently in our overall balance of payments surplus. It is said to be the result of about 20 different small errors all in the same direction. The chances of this happening are about 1 in 1048575 but I do not suppose they will admit to any systematic bias though it is obviously due to Otto Clarke's wanting to persuade us to more austerity this year, so I suppose it will be the higher truth. I am not sure what difference this will make to the forecasts. The surplus is now £170 mn odd without US aid and about £280 mn with it, and as we have not run down stocks of imported materials in the process we cannot be said to have been nearly as phoney as we were in 1950.

E.B. took the third draft of the Budget speech this afternoon. I had written a good deal of it and it is a relief to have got as far as this. The first draft is always repetitive and rather formless but all the subsequent ones are a great deal easier. I have now been told about four times by E.B. *not* to argue in documents for the public that the changes in employment and production are credible evidence of disinflation. I cannot get used to this especially as the Chancellor is so sensitive to the accusation of the Bank Chairmen that we are still in a state of inflation.

We seem well forward with the Speech but of course it will be re-written a great many times, and we are not at all clear about the proposals. I saw Maudling this afternoon – he wanted to talk about credit policy and the future of hire purchase. I gathered that he had it in mind to lower Bank Rate at the Budget but I think I persuaded him against this – as E.B. says, you can do it any Thursday at lunch time if you think it is needed. However I promised to let him see the Economic Section paper on credit policy and the effects of the past year's operations [EC(S)(53)2]. Our view is that Bank Rate played only a small part – but no one knows what caused the stock reduction, which was the biggest deflationary factor.

Wednesday, March 11th

Frank Lee came back from Washington yesterday and in the afternoon Bridges had a meeting, mainly to hear him but also to consider the statement from Rowan that we could not now make anything like a full disclosure to the Europeans on March 23rd. Frank said that the new Administration had no experience, distrusted their civil service intensely, and were unduly afraid of Congress. Consequently they had made no commitment whatever – on the whole had said they believed in the objectives but thought the approach premature. Also no money for anyone until they are more aware of where they are and what they can do. He said that Butler had made a very good impression both by his mastery of the facts (!) and by his ability to use words like 'moral' and 'right' which the Americans thought quite proper though British civil servants could not bring themselves to use in a business deal. He couldn't say much about the Europeans as there hadn't been time to think about it when he left.

We all felt in varying degrees how awkward the European problem was and how difficult it would be, especially after our telegram begging them to wait, if we said very little. On the other hand if we say too much it will reveal too clearly the rebuff from the US. My view is that they will find out all about what happened anyway.

I have to see Cherwell today and no doubt he will feel very pleased, as on the whole I do. But OF show no signs of error or of anything like a change of heart.

Friday, March 13th

Norman Robertson (High Commissioner for Canada) came to see me yesterday morning to ask how the talks had gone – he had heard nothing of course, and they were only going to Ottawa that day. I told him what I knew and he was as always extremely sensible and helpful. We agreed that the immediate problem was the OEEC meeting on the 23rd and he suggested bringing Wyn Plumptre [Head of Canadian Delegation] from Paris next week, in order to brief him about the line we would be taking. Norman said, when I told him that no one was so anxious to move forward as we were except perhaps the Canadians, that even they were very anxious not to press us to do more than we thought our strength could bear.

In the afternoon I saw Norman Brook, to whom I had sent an account of Bridges' meeting with Frank Lee. He is also worried about the line in Paris and his fears had been exacerbated by a call he had made on Cherwell who wanted to stir things up again. I had seen Cherwell on Tuesday and we had had a somewhat triumphant post-mortem followed by an alarmed consideration of what it was exactly that was dead. Norman felt that our best chance in Paris was to admit that we had not made much progress in Washington and that we were going now to do our best to have a strong EPU, for the next 12 months. He thought that if we did this we would have the best chance of not talking too much about the details of the plan. He is worried about a tendency on E.B.'s part, stimulated by O.F., to avoid having meetings of the small group set up to deal with the after-Commonwealth and pre-Washington talks. I found the discussion very helpful and encouraging.

MacDougall dined with me on Wednesday night and we exchanged ideas on the Budget, where we are quite close together, and on all this Robot business where I still find him a bit unrealistic. I went over most of last year's events to see where I had gone wrong and I felt he did not know enough about how to handle these affairs to appreciate the errors. He is still far too much inclined to want to fight and to let the truth speak for itself and to regard a defeat as almost as good as a victory – one ought not to be in practical life if one thinks that.

Wednesday, March 18th

They all came back on Sunday and I saw Plowden on Monday and also went to a BC taken by the Chancellor where L. Rowan was. E.P. says the trip was very successful in making the US think about the problems, and that R.A.B. had a great personal success as he convinced them that he was very well up in everything and also they liked and indeed admired him. He confirmed what Frank Lee said, that the US said *we* were not strong enough for convertibility and *they* could not at this stage get any action from Congress. Leslie and probably Rab want to keep up what they call the 'momentum' but I don't quite see how this can be done.

The Chancellor made a lot of remarks about looking again at the Budget objectives to see if they were deflationary enough and also in the light of the possibility of a US recession later on but no one seemed to want to do anything different. All the Tory Ministers are very keen on income tax changes and also they feel that p.t. changes are frittering away money and gaining nothing politically.

Thursday, March 19th

I saw the Chancellor alone for about an hour yesterday. He told me that he was devoting the day to 'the moral aspects of the Budget', by which he meant the needs, having regard to opinion at home and abroad, of the whole situation but especially the balance of payments. However both the Governor and B. Gilbert (and also Leslie Rowan) have said that they do not object to the main lines which I have been advocating. The Chancellor said he wanted me to participate in three studies being made:

(a)   What do we do if there is a US recession?
(b)   What should we ask the US to do to help our balance of payments?
(c)   What about a floating inconvertible rate?

On the 3rd he said the Bank were now saying that it was practicable.

Thursday, April 16th

For several reasons I have been too much occupied to write this diary, and consequently all the pre-Budget alarms and excursions are not recorded.

The main lines remained unchanged, i.e. 6d off Income Tax, initial allowances restored at 20%, and a cut of ¼ in the rates of Purchase Tax. The only new proposal of importance was the decision to announce the end of EPL [Excess Profits Levy] next year. This was done at Plowden's insistence and rather against my views, though I did not care much. But I don't like announcing changes too far ahead.

The weeks before the Budget were made almost unpleasant by the apparent hesitations and wavering of the Chancellor. No doubt he exaggerates them, partly to be sure that you really mean what you say, and partly to have an excuse if things go wrong. But it is a most unpleasant trait and shows a strong streak of moral cowardice. At the end I felt that my nerve was almost breaking as it might do under constant pressure from Secret Police in iron curtain countries! However Bridges and Gilbert who originally thought I was too bold, stuck to their guns very manfully, and E.P. who is himself given to such doubt, took a strong line whenever he saw R.A.B.

The Budget itself seems so far to have had a great success and the papers yesterday were almost all enthusiastic though the more serious pointed out that there were elements of risk.

However I doubt if this would have been so a month ago, when the same papers were much more gloomy about the prospects. The combined effect of the Economic Survey and of talks I had with Wilfred King of *The Economist* and Maurice Green of *The Times*, led to some articles which paved the way for all this. Wilfred especially wrote a long article in *The Banker* which had a very good effect including on the Chancellor, who underlined almost every sentence in red ink in his copy.[18] He said to me that I might have written it which was slightly embarrassing as I had inspired it, not because of the analysis but because his forecasts (which we had *not* discussed) came so near the mark. However I think everyone likes me to talk to financial journalists.

Wednesday, April 22nd

The Chancellor gave the Budget dinner at No. 11 last night. I used to think that this was an old institution but apparently my first was also *the* first as it was introduced by Stafford. The Chancellor goes to Paris today. We are told that the Americans will approach us and later NATO (it is the NATO meeting) to say that they are going to cut their defence spending, including Aid. This is because they don't think they can get their Budget through Congress but they want to put it on the 'new' strategic appreciation which they rejected last autumn.

E.P. and I got hold of the Chancellor after dinner to tell him we thought it was essential to plug the political effects of the economic effects a big cut in aid would have in Europe.

From April 22nd until the end of the year Hall made only six entries. Nineteen fifty-three, however, was a fairly uneventful year. The Chancellor continued to worry over the possibility that the budget might be heading for a deficit 'above the line', if not in 1953–4 then within a year or two. Fears continued also of an American depression and by the autumn it looked as if one were on the way but that it might be relatively mild (entry for October 4th). Little was heard of the 'collective approach' in the second half of the year.

Early in June Hall decided to resign from the Treasury, partly on financial grounds (he had two daughters at Oxford University to support), partly because of the continuing friction with OF. The Chancellor, who had only recently asked Bridges (without success) to create an Economic and Planning Division of the Treasury under Hall ('whom I intend to regard as my Chief Economic Adviser'), was very much taken aback. On his instructions, arrangements were made to move the Economic Section from the Cabinet Office to the Treasury. Hall's salary was increased and at the end of the year he was knighted. Otto Clarke, who had dominated OF thinking, was moved to the Social Services Division of the Treasury.

In two concluding entries Hall gives his impressions of Harold Macmillan after a dinner with him and Plowden on October 5th and looks back on the events of 1952–3 before setting out for a Conference of Commonwealth Finance Ministers in Sydney on January 2nd 1954.

Washington, Thursday, June 25th

This is the longest gap since I began to keep this diary and has occurred mainly for personal reasons – that is, because other things pressed on me rather than work, which has not really been more strenuous than usual.

The Budget is an old story now. Its main interest was in the gradual acceptance by almost everyone, of what at first they all would have regarded as very rash and wrong, that is the acceptance of a much reduced above-the-line surplus and the complete abandonment of the 'principle' which Stafford had so misguidedly erected, of an overall balance. Although we had always protested against this, he had felt that there was some curious rightness that the inflationary gap could be met by the Government saving enough to pay for its own investment outgoings.

However the fact that the fiscal year closed with a much smaller surplus than had been intended, although our balance of payments was quite healthy and unemployment much more than a year before, provided some help. The strongest force was undoubtedly that it was extremely convenient to the Chancellor to be able to reduce taxes a bit and especially the income tax where he had been so heavily pressed by Conservative back-benchers. He was indeed so pleased that I told him that he *could* do this, and that I was in favour of it, that my influence was much increased. However he had continual qualms about how rash he was being and once the decision was taken he kept on recurring to its propriety.

Fortunately Wilfred King had a very good article in *The Banker*, not uninspired, which put all my arguments over again and this proved a great comfort. The Budget itself was a success in the country as no one could bring themselves to attack it seriously lest they might be thought to be against the reduced taxes. And although a number of critics thought that the Chancellor was taking a gamble, they mostly said that it was the right thing to do. E.P. did not want income tax reduced except for the earned incomes between £2,000 and £5,000; he wanted initial allowances at 40%. I did not care much what happened to them but could not possibly have got the BC, let alone the Chancellor, to agree that they were almost neutral as fiscal weapons. They would not even feel strongly that since they would not operate for 12 months they were almost irrelevant to the current situation. Everyone wanted to repeal EPL, which won't operate for 2 years.

The Purchase Tax changes were made mostly because the officials all felt that some move would be necessary: the Ministers rather felt it was a waste of money. It is clear, however, that the tax in its present form cannot last indefinitely and it is at least something to be getting it gradually down. Frank Lee and I, and Customs, too, want to make it a lower tax with a wider spread but this is generally regarded as politically impracticable.

It is now 2½ months since the Budget and so far as one can tell so early, things are working out as we expected. Production is increasing but does not show much sign of rising very far above 1951. Employment is rising seasonally but I feel a bit doubtful about whether it won't fall fairly soon once the Coronation peak is over.[19] The foreign balance remains good and the reserves are still rising. Exports are often said to be difficult but even they keep up well and there is at least as much evidence that we are competitive as the other way. Small savings are better.

The Chancellor is very worried about next year's Budget and even more about the 1955 one because his revenue will be falling and his expenses rising unless he can really take a stand against defence which seems to go up steadily whatever one does. He told me that this is more a political than an economic worry as he feels that it would be bad for confidence and for his position if he has to Budget for an above-the-line deficit.

Things have changed quite a bit on Robot, the Collective Approach and all that. The US more or less turned down our proposals; they said that they were very interesting and that they would need to think about them, but privately we heard that they thought them ill-advised and mostly it is thought now that the plan is dead. The Europeans have been subjected to a series of meetings of indoctrination by Leslie Rowan and Otto Clarke but they have not reacted very favourably to the particular things that concern them most and especially the demise of EPU. The Commonwealth Prime Ministers at the finance talk they had after the Coronation were all very gloomy about whether the US could ever do the things we wanted, and they talked a good deal about the need for an alternative plan: though they did not seem to know what this meant. Macmillan is one of those who thinks the plan dead, and I am very doubtful whether any Ministers can see movement in the near future – some of them say that our objectives are the same but their realization is much further off.

All this means that the ideas we formulated last December and put to the US have very few friends, in fact in my view the main friends are OF and the Bank who have been pushing convertibility and the floating rate so violently, in every conceivable form, for the past 15 months. They wanted it when our reserves were apparently going to run out: just the same when we made it a condition that the US should be a good creditor: and recently have said that we should do it if there was a US recession, i.e. when the US was being a bad creditor. In fact it is the universal nostrum.

Meanwhile the Chancellor has been a changed man since the Washington visit. He came back believing that he had done well to go but that he had been misinformed about the probable US reaction. He also found an undercurrent among some of his colleagues that his policy had received a severe set-back and should be abandoned. Finally he became aware of some of the other matters mentioned above, i.e. that his plan had very few friends anywhere. So he has decided to beat a retreat and indeed he has several times said that there was very little between my ideas and his. But Leslie Rowan is being very un-cooperative in allowing him to change his mind, and to a large extent is frustrating by administrative action what I think the Chancellor wants. However things are not going too badly at present and I am not seriously worried about the economic situation or about the dangers of rash policy decisions.

A great deal of time has been taken up about the future of Treasury organization and of E.P. For nearly all the time R.A.B. has been here, he has not felt very much confidence in Edwin, and Edwin has been aware of this and of course like me has suffered very much from the split between OF and the rest of us. He has also wanted in some ways to have a good business job as there is no pension attached to his Civil Service one. Thus he has been more and more restive and slowly deciding to leave, though very reluctantly. If R.A.B. had really wanted to keep him he would I think have stayed, as Deputy Sec. of the Treasury. But with R.A.B. so lukewarm it was inevitable that he should go, and this was announced on Tuesday (June 23rd).

I do not know whether I am sorry or glad. We have always worked very closely together, and I think it is fair to say that he took my advice on questions of policy. But he was certainly much more influential than I, and in the short run more forceful. So that we have really been a team, and a powerful one – as William Armstrong said after the 2nd rejection of Robot – 'The Plowden–Hall team is the strongest force in Whitehall, since Ministers will not accept anything that they strongly disapprove'. Personally he could not be nicer to work with and he is a particularly loyal person, as I discovered when there was a whispering campaign against Oliver on the ground that he knew no one in Washington: Edwin took great pains to force the FO to say that they did not feel any criticism of Oliver.

But nevertheless I feel that Edwin is much less happy and has much less of a role, when R.A.B. does not really want him – a great deal of his influence before came from his special relationship both to Cripps and to Gaitskell. This feeling, that R.A.B. was at best a doubtful supporter, had a very bad effect on Edwin's efficiency, as it might well do on anyone else. In addition, he had made so many demonstrations about resignation that it was becoming a bad thing for him that he should go on saying it and not doing it. And it was probably necessary for him to become a permanent Civil Servant if he were going to stay much longer. Thus, although it will be a great loss to me, I think on the whole it was the right decision, certainly for Edwin and I am inclined to think for the organization.

I had been getting increasingly distressed about the relations between OF and the Economic Section and came more or less to the conclusion that I would also leave, if I could find a suitable job. To my surprise this produced quite strong reactions from the Chancellor and to a less extent from Bridges. The Chancellor I think has decided for the time being that my advice has been consistently better than anyone else's, so he doesn't want me to go. Bridges feels that it would be a bad thing politically if Edwin and I both resigned, as it would be argued that the Government were throwing overboard all the principles of planning, and especially full employment. At any rate great pressure was brought on me to stay, and in very flattering terms. The Chancellor indeed said that I was to have whatever assurances I might want 'to make me happy'.

E.B. saw me several times and I finally wrote him a letter saying that I did not think the head of the Economic Section should stay forever anyway, and that I would need to find a more remunerative job soon, but that my main objection to staying was that I could not get along with OF and that if it would help to ease the position at all, I would be glad to resign. This produced what was almost an emotional scene and I was assured that everything would be done to make people work more as a team in future. There were also hints that Otto might be moved.

The upshot of all this is that I am likely to go, with the Economic Section, to the Treasury in October, at a higher salary and with the title of Economic Adviser to the Government. No announcement has been made yet but it certainly looks as if this will be done.[20]

Wednesday, July 1st

The above was written in Washington and I am writing now on the way to New York, where I hope to bring the diary up-to-date. I left London on June 23rd and had the quickest trip I have ever had, being in Washington by 10 a.m. on the 24th. I have seen a great many people and on the whole feel pleased with the trip and reasonably pleased with the situation.

I met Folsom [Under Secretary, Treasury], Burgess, Rose, Willis and some lesser officials in the Treasury. Martin and Riefler in the FRB. Hauge at the White House. [Arthur] Burns the new Chairman of the

CEA. Bill Elliott of the National Security Council Planning Board. Bowie who succeeded Paul Nitze as Head of the State Dept Planning Staff. No one else in State and no one from Commerce. Also Joe Alsop, Paul Nitze, Lew Douglas, as well as Roger Makins, Denis Rickett, Hall-Patch and a number of UK officials including my Fred Atkinson who is doing very well.

The main general impression I got was that the new Administration is feeling its way rather carefully and is much less cock-sure than the old one. This is partly after a long period out of office, they do not know how much power they have nor are they very clear about the situation with which they are dealing. They are very like the Conservatives in many ways, having to abandon campaign promises that are out of touch with the facts. I was told also that it is politically essential that Eisenhower should be seen to be leading the Republicans and not going over their heads with the help of Democratic votes (as he has had to rely on Democratic votes to get through the more liberal aspects of his policy, it is all the more important that he should seem to be a Republican).

Wednesday, August 19th

The announcement about the transfer of the Economic Section to the Treasury was made while I was still in America. It is to take place when Plowden goes, at the end of October. There was a little criticism on the ground that the Section might be losing its independence, but in my view, this was quite misjudged unless independence is to be preferred at whatever cost in ineffectiveness.

Ian Little, who succeeded Crosland at Trinity after me, came to the Section as Deputy Director early in July. He is a very nice young man and very distinguished for one so young (35±) and I think that he is going to do well – his only fault so far seems to be extreme nervousness which leads him almost to wring his hands when he talks to one – not that he is a coward, anything but. He has already begun to bring some coherence into the Section views on external economic policy and written a very good first draft of a paper to draw together the voluminous work now nearing its end, on economic policy prior to and during a US recession. Plowden (now on leave) has been charged with doing this and Strath is making a start this week. Little is generalizing the proposition that one should extend enough credit to the debtors, to keep up more or less the pattern of trade.

Sunday, October 4th

It seems impossible to keep up-to-date, but now that the winter is beginning I will try.

Edwin Plowden is moving inevitably to his departure at the end of this month. He has been very uncertain about what he wants to do, but is now between Bowater's Paper Co. as Deputy Chairman, and Head of the new Atomic Energy Board which is to be set up soon to take over from M/Supply. Although the Bowater job is a very good one, interesting, half in Canada and US, £10,000 to start and the reversion of the Chair, I have been advising him to go to the other because it is more important and because he will still be in the stream of public events. I think he is almost certain to go but there is a difficulty about a pension, due to the penurious attitude of the Labour Government to salaries and pensions for nationalized boards. They felt morally that £5,000 or so was enough for anyone and have tended to understaff themselves since and to create a precedent, which (e.g. in this case) hampers them quite unduly. However they are paying for this and other similar sins; at the Margate Conference the trend was very much against nationalization.

Meanwhile E. has recovered his poise and his dignity, which he was in danger of losing in the bitterness of his resignation, and is really going in a blaze of glory. He has been in charge of a great exercise on what we should do in a US slump, and has got Departments and Working Parties to produce a great mass of very competent documents, and has got these through the Steering Committee and got them approved by the Planning Board, with only improvements in the process. These get, on doctrine, nearer to an agreed line among officials than there has been since Robot appeared in February 1952: the line is reasonably near the Economic Section one. Part of the credit for this must go to Ian Little who handled most of it for us during the critical stages – I was on leave, and then in Paris, for three weeks at the end of August and early September.[21]

The process was helped, however, by some pressures on OF from E.B. and also by some forthcoming changes. At last Otto Clarke is being moved, to do Social Services on the Supply side. Herbert Brittain is to take Gilbert's place as head of HF and Supply, when Bernard becomes Deputy Secretary. Eddie Playfair is to succeed him, William Armstrong is to take the place of Flett who is going to Washington to replace Allan Christelow. And Arnold France is going to OF to replace Otto. Thus the changes are:

Rowan	Rowan	*Second Secretary*
Brittain	Playfair	*Third Secretary*
Clarke	Copleston	
Flett	Armstrong	*Under Secretary*
Copleston	France	

Playfair is no doubt a bit of a Robot man but is quite different from either Brittain or Otto. William Armstrong is of course the ex-Private Sec. with whom I have worked so closely in the past. France has been Strath's deputy on MAC and ONC and a very sensible man. At any rate, any change would have been better than none, and I find these a great improvement in prospect: and the fact that they are taking place has been a solvent in the anticipatory period. It still seems to be true that the Chancellor puts a great deal of trust in me and this is fairly widely known and no doubt this helps also.

The economic situation has remained reasonably calm and not too bad. I cannot see any trend either way but if there is any it is deflationary. The price and wage levels have been stable and with the terms of trade continuing to get better, the balance of payments has been easier and easier. Stocks have been built up, the reserves have gone on rising, and though the sterling balances have risen too we have been improving our position. Indeed next year's Programme Committee forecast shows a surplus on overall account of about £325 mn though I don't think we shall get it unless we lend more money to our customers. I have been trying to stir up arguments about this but find it very difficult to make much progress. The doctrines of living within one's means, and not making 'unrequited exports' sank so deep that I can't get them out at a time when they are a barrier to reaching the objective of a £350 mn surplus year in year out on overseas account (see *Economic Survey for 1953*).

I feel fairly sure that the American recession has actually begun now and that when we look back on these months from a year ahead we will say that the turn took place about June. However the economy is holding up very well so far and the Government is so determined to avoid getting blackened by the 1929–32 labels, that I don't expect it to be at all a bad one.

I was in Paris from Sept. 7th to 11th, at a meeting of economists chosen by 7 of the OEEC countries to make a study of the situation for the 5th Report. [22] It was not particularly interesting except to feel the strong desire for integration, a common market etc. among all the others, and because Germany was represented – it was the first time I have sat with Germans as full members.

However Gabriel Hauge, Eisenhower's Special Assistant for Economics, was the US representative, which was a great catch and gave me a chance to consolidate the acquaintance I had begun last December in the [Hotel] Commodore and renewed in Washington at the end of June. He had impressed me then with the strength of his feeling against having a slump and he had already begun to have a study made (under Arthur Burns) of measures to counteract one. In Paris he was much more forthcoming and practically said that they would not allow there to be a slump – only mild recessions or 'adjustments'. He was also very liberal in his views about US tariffs, foreign aid, European integration etc. In fact about as enlightened a Republican as could be found, and I cannot but think that it is very lucky that such a man is so close to the President.

I met lately Philip Graham the publisher of the *Washington Post* who was in London and whom I liked very much. As the views of the *Post* are so well known there is no point in adding his. We talked a good deal about the problem of Europe, and especially the relative position of France and Germany, which are now so prominent. He can understand the US desire to back Germany which is reviving at the expense of France which is so demoralized. But I think nearly all Europeans except the Germans feel that a solution with France in a minor role and still weak, is not a solution at all.

Tuesday, October 6th

Last night Edwin Plowden had me and Harold Macmillan to dinner in his flat – it was arranged at my request as I have been coming round to the view that R.A.B. will have to work with H.M. The PM clearly cannot last much longer and all my distinguished doctor friends tell me that it is very doubtful whether Eden will again be the man he was. Apart from Butler, Macmillan is the man who has made most impression in this Government. And I suspect that he will be Foreign Secretary before too long, or perhaps Chancellor if *both* the PM and Eden go. Not that I hope for this as I do not think R.A.B. is by any means an ideal PM. I had not met Macmillan for a long time – I must have seen him during the war but I was in humble circumstances and made no impression on him and I simply cannot remember him at the M/Supply, or at later meetings when he was over from N. Africa. However we had a pleasant evening and he stayed till 12.15, having ordered his car for 9.45. So presumably he enjoyed himself.

He has a restless and not very orderly mind and it could hardly be called a reasoned conversation, in fact it was largely a monologue. We had wanted to say something about Europe, Schuman and EDC and so on and he was very responsive here and asked us if we thought he should have resigned when the Conservatives in office turned out to be so much less forthcoming than they had been in opposition. We said of course not but did make the point that we were losing ground and prestige in Europe and that in general we behaved as if there was much more time than there was. On this and other things, it was fairly clear that he shared R.A.B.'s view that the PM has been there far too long and is now inhibiting action. He talked quite a lot about the decontrol of rents or rather the first step in this direction which they will take this autumn – he will be in charge of the Bill. We agreed that the Opposition would try to make it a great case but that it would not be easy. He thought Nye Bevan would see this and concentrate on the hard cases, the old age pensioners. Most of them were getting their rents paid by Public Assistance already.

Wednesday, December 30th

This year has been a dead loss as far as the diary is concerned. The reason is nothing to do with the work but that I got over-strained by a combination of worrying about Robot and a private worry and early in the year came rather near to a break-down. I recovered almost at once but found that I had more to do than I could manage and remain unstressed, and in reducing my activities to a bearable compass I let the diary go. I have just been to Switzerland for 8 days' holiday and am going on January 2nd to the Commonwealth Finance Ministers' Conference in Sydney. The Chancellor and most of the party went today and there isn't much to do.

The main events of the year for me have been first the Budget, in which the Chancellor took entirely my advice (it suited him to do so but he took it): then Edwin Plowden going and my removal to the Treasury, again on the Chancellor's insistence: then my new title and my salary put up (to £3,750 p.a.): and on January 1st I shall be made a KCMG. So personally or from a career point of view, I have had a good year, it is a peculiar sort of result of a year (1952) in which I suffered so much from being opposed to the Chancellor in a matter he had set his heart on (Robot etc.) and I suppose that if I had not opposed him Edwin Plowden and Roger Makins would not have done so, and he would have been able to carry it through the Cabinet; though I believe it would have had a bad time in Parliament, the Conservatives would probably have had to follow the Whips and we would have made the move.

However, the Chancellor, I feel almost sure, came to realize that he had made a mistake politically, and as a matter of prediction all the disasters Otto Clarke and the Bank foretold did not happen, quite the contrary, so that they both argued at the end of 1952 that we had missed our chance in March because we were on the verge then of a period of extreme strength of the £ – I think they had quite forgotten that they had said in March that the reserves would be so low in April (later moved to July) that we would have no alternative but to float convertible. Anyway the Chancellor told me, practically in plain terms, that he had been wrong about this but that 'I would be generous if he acknowledged that he had been wrong'. I put all this down, not in any spirit of exultation, as I do not regard anyone as very secure because R.A.B. happens to trust him for the time being – but because my growth in prestige for the time being is such a curious outcome of the struggle.

Otto is gone and he and I have become fellow conspirators against the increase in Social Services, he being in charge of that bit of the Treasury now. The relations with OF are slowly improving under the combined influence of Playfair, Armstrong and France, though Leslie Rowan still regards all those who have been against him with a latent fanaticism which doesn't need much to flare out again. Edwin Plowden went to be the Chairman-designate of the Atomic Energy Corporation on November 1st and I have seen him quite a bit though not of course as we used to. I think he is quite enjoying it – he got all his financial stipulations met, or near enough, in the end and now he is working at trying to get the three scientists who head the three big establishments to work as something like a team. Apparently they hardly ever spoke to one another before E.P. came, as each thought he would have the best chance of being left alone if he did not try to interfere with the others.

In the Treasury, we now have B. Gilbert as Deputy to Bridges, with Rowan and Brittain under him on the 2nd Sec. level, and Strath and I also but Strath as 3rd Sec. and me as 2½ Sec. Bernard is trying hard, he has meetings of CEPS on Wednesday as Edwin did, and a new meeting called Friday Forum, of Rowan, Brittain, Compton, Crombie, Strath and me on Fridays at 10, to discuss general issues. It does not exactly duplicate the 2nd Secs. on Tuesday but gets somewhere near it. It has not worked very well so far as Leslie Rowan is too jumpy to be able to talk calmly about the fundamental questions. However he is calming down slowly.

We did the first BC paper early in December [BC(53)26] – it was designed to keep the way open and did so quite effectually – it said the system was pretty well in balance but with a tendency towards deflation which would become marked if the US recession went on. It has been rather a disappointing year from the national income point of view – production recovered almost exactly as we had predicted and the last few months showed a big rise in exports; but all this was done with much fuller employment than we had expected, i.e. we are now about 3% above 1951 production with about the same level of employment, though we had thought that in 2 years we ought to have been able to do this with a smaller labour force. Thus, although I don't think there is any real inflation in the system, there isn't as much deflation as we had thought. So all my young men are being forced to reconsider their views, and the deduction seems to be that one can only get the advance in production, of which the system is obviously capable, by driving it so hard that there is more inflation than is comfortable.

The year closes with the UK in very good shape, except for the industrial and wage situation. A railway strike was only stopped by the Cabinet in effect giving way over the head of the Railway Executive. This was, however, probably right as the railwaymen had a very good case and public opinion thought they had. There is a threat of trouble in the engineering industry though I still think it likely that it will be settled for some such increase as 5/– a week which is probably bearable.

The US recession is well under way and the statisticians have done a revised paper on the prospects, they expect it to go down quite a lot more by mid-1954 and then it will depend on what the Government has done in the meantime. I still feel moderately optimistic about the outcome and find that the down movement is very slow and well-controlled. Leslie Rowan and I will go back from Australia by Washington, and Denis Rickett has arranged for us to see Hauge and all the three members of the new Council for Economic Advisers. By then the various messages to Congress will be available and we shall be able to form a clearer idea of what the Administration intend.

It is too early to say how the move to the Treasury is affecting the Economic Section but I think it will be all right as soon as we have settled down and especially as the OF situation improves. My room is now the one E.P. had, to be close to the Chancellor. The Section are still where they were so it is rather a long way between us. Ian Little seems fairly happy and nearly all the others are good people – Keane who was least satisfactory has gone to the Iron and Steel Board as an economist to help Robert Shone.

Notes

I *From the convertibility crisis to devaluation, 1 September 1947 to 15 September 1949*

1   The sterling balances referred to were short-term liabilities, mainly incurred during the war in countries like India and Egypt and amounting at the end of 1947 to about £4,000 million compared with reserves of gold and foreign exchange of about £500 million. The Economic Section was critical of the Treasury's failure to block wartime accumulations more completely.

2   The papers referred to in this and the entries immediately following are in PRO T230/277 'Balance of payments general policy' and PRO T230/63 'Economic survey long-term 1948–51'. The work in progress related mainly to the prospects for the balance of payments and the level of imports that could be afforded either in 1948–9 (12 September) or over the longer term, taken to be 1948–51 (10 September).

3   The issue of diversion of exports to dollar markets was a pressing one because the United Kingdom normally earned relatively few dollars from such exports in comparison with outgoings on dollar imports. It made up the balance before the war from dollars earned in trade with other members of the sterling area, mainly Commonwealth countries. In the postwar years few of those countries were in surplus with the dollar area.

4   This refers to the period in July/August 1947 when the pound was briefly convertible. The total loss of dollars in the third quarter of 1947 was over $1,500 million.

5   The document which Hall had been preparing for Plowden was a 'Review of the present position', EPB (47)10, considered by the Planning Board on 18 September. An estimate of the balance of payments between mid-1947 and mid-1948 was prepared simultaneously and showed high capital exports continuing into 1949 (PRO T230/277).

6   Humphrey Mynors was a Director of the Bank of England from 1949 to 1954 and Deputy Governor from 1954 to 1964. His brother Roger was Corpus Christi Professor of Latin Language and Literature at Oxford from 1953 to 1970.

7   The Planning Staff was asked on 1 August 1947 to review the investment programme urgently with an eye to reducing inflationary pressure and proposed a reduction in the annual rate of fixed investment by £250 million (about a sixth) by the end of 1948. In spite of the cuts, however, fixed investment continued to increase almost as fast as before.

8   In 1947 all repairs to housing costing £10 or over required a licence.

9   Franks (then Provost of Queen's College, Oxford) had presided in Paris in the summer of 1947 over the Committee for European Economic Co-operation (CEEC) in the preparation of a report in response to General Marshall's offer of aid in European reconstruction. Franks was about to

lead a small group to Washington to present the report as a basis for an approach to Congress for a grant of aid (the European Recovery Programme or ERP).

10 This may have related to arrangements for an *Economic Survey for 1948*, on which work began later in the month, but the entry for October 7th suggests that what was in dispute was the revision for publication of the draft *Economic Survey for 1948–51*, presumably in place of an annual Survey.

11 A paper on 'Wages policy' (EPC(47)4) was circulated by Cripps and discussed by the Economic Policy Committee on 27 October. It was probably drafted by Hall after discussion with Plowden.

12 On 3 November the Economic Policy Committee took four papers on 'Dollar aid' and discussed whether an approach should be made to the USA for help in maintaining reserves (EPC(48)7–10). See also below, entry for November 4th.

13 In 1941 W. Averill Harriman was stationed in London as the Special Representative of the President in Great Britain. The use in British exports of materials being supplied under Lend-Lease was subject to stringent conditions set out in a White Paper (Cmd 6311 of 19 September 1941) on which see R. S. Sayers, (1956), pp. 398–405.

14 Anthony Crosland was Robert Hall's successor as Fellow in Economics at Trinity College, Oxford.

15 Cripps's Central Hall speech was made on 12 September 1947 to 2,000 delegates from all parts of the country. He announced ambitious export targets by groups of industry to be reached by the end of 1948. These added up to 188 per cent of the 1938 volume for manufactures and 164 per cent for total exports but did not distinguish between exports to dollar or hard currency areas and other exports. Cripps also suggested that it might be necessary to make cuts of £200 million in investment (entry for September 24th) in order to clear the way for exports.

16 The paper by Cripps and Dalton, 'Dollar programme in 1948', CP(47)283, was designed to reduce the prospective 'dollar drain' in 1948 by $700 million, mainly through cuts in imports. The Cabinet was still in doubt whether Congress would vote Marshall Aid and did not think it safe to bank on it. Nevertheless, as the *Economic Survey for 1948* stated in March 1948 (paras. 46–8), if no aid were forthcoming 'further heavy cuts' would have to be made in imports from the Western hemisphere.

17 'Unrequited' exports (EPB(47)24) were exports paid for in soft currency that could not be usefully spent on items in the import programme so that no counter-flow of imports resulted. 'Frustrated' exports were exports denied a market by quota restrictions.

18 The Cabinet approved the proposals, but the matter was reopened on 23 October by Bevan (Minister of Health), Wilson (President of the Board of Trade) and others. Eventually the original decision was reconfirmed. A month later, Dalton having resigned in the meantime, Cripps, now Chancellor, submitted a second paper (CP(47)311) dealing with the non-dollar balance of payments in 1948 and his proposals were approved (see entry for November 12th).

19 The Cabinet had agreed in the middle of the convertibility crisis in August to legislate for a reduction in the period over which the House of Lords could exercise a veto from two years to one (see entry for October 21st 1948).

20 Cripps's speech (on 23 October) was made during the Commons debate on the King's Speech. He announced measures designed to reduce the 'dollar

drain' from an estimated £475 million in 1947 – it was in fact £1,024 million – to £250 million a year at the end of 1948.

21 The figure that appeared in the *Economic Survey for 1948* (pp. 43–4) was 450,000.

22 The White Paper ultimately appeared as *Capital Investment in 1948* (Cmd 7268).

23 The Economic Section had insisted repeatedly since August on the danger of excessive repayments of sterling balances. The net outflow of capital in 1947 is now put at nearly £650 million (much higher than was thought at the time), and in 1948 at £430 million. Taken together, these figures add up to more than the US and Canadian loans of 1946. But only a limited part of the total represented a run-down of sterling balances, which fell by £300 million over the two years.

24 The 1947 budget had estimated that the surplus 'above the line' in 1947–8 would amount to £318 million and the November budget estimated that it would add £48 million to tax revenue (and so to that total) in the current financial year. The surplus proved to be much larger than expected – £635 million (compared with a *deficit* of £569 million in 1946–7).

25 Swan's thesis is developed in an Economic Section paper, 'The theory of suppressed inflation' (EC(S)(47)39, 22 December 1947). 'Our paper on inflation' may be the 'Note on inflation' circulated to the Budget Committee as BC(48)3.

26 The budget divided items 'above the line' (ordinary revenue and expenditure) from items 'below the line' (in respect of which borrowing was authorized). But the division was far from coinciding with a division between current and capital expenditure and provided a highly imperfect measure of the impact of the budget on economic activity. The CSO used a quite different classification to measure the 'revenue surplus' of the government in the White Papers on National Income and Expenditure. A third measure could be arrived at using 'the alternative classification' introduced in the postwar years but rarely used in debate. John Hicks was ultimately persuaded (see entry for May 20th) to undertake an analysis (published in 1950 as *The Reform of Budget Accounts*) but there always seemed to be good reasons for deferring reform.

27 Douglas Jay had written to Dalton in November 1947 suggesting that the prospective budget surplus should be used to effect a reduction in the money supply. For later developments see pages 37–8 *et seq.*

28 This may have been so in peacetime but the budget of 1941 is generally regarded as the first attempt to set the budget in the context of the economic situation as a whole.

29 The 'Special Levy' was Cripps's substitute for a capital levy. It was a once-for-all payment, based on the previous year's investment income.

30 The Committee on Wages and Prices Policy met under Bridges, starting in January 1948, shortly before the issue of a *Statement on Personal Incomes, Costs and Prices*. On 12 April it considered a draft report (ED(SP)(48)6) dealing with the implications of the *Statement* for price policy. The Chancellor had already circulated on 18 March a paper by Bridges on price policy (EPC(48)20). The (incomplete) papers of the committee are in PRO T233/57.

31 Hall had made this suggestion a month earlier in a minute to Plowden which was circulated to the Budget Committee on 12 April. He was concerned about the level of government expenditure and the impact of the tax structure on incentives. Plowden, in minuting Bridges, pointed out that the budget was now an integral part of economic planning and that there was a

dearth of economic knowledge on which to frame policy (PRO T171/397). It was agreed that the Budget Committee should meet over the summer about once a month.

32 At the meeting of the Budget Committee on 20 April (on the basis of minutes by Hall and Plowden in March) Hall was asked to do a paper on government expenditure over the next five years and the scope for reductions in taxation to improve incentives. He was also to report on the statistical basis of budget accounting (PRO T171/397).

33 After the convertibility crisis a statistical unit was created in the OF division of the Treasury under Sam Goldman.

34 This may have been a draft of a paper on 'Controls and efficiency' circulated by Bridges as WPP(48)5 for a meeting of the Wages and Prices Policy Committee on 4 June (PRO T233/57). A committee to report on the subject by the end of July was set up and its *interim* report was considered on 16 October 1948. For some reason the papers of the committee (PRO CAB 134/89) have not yet been released but some of the papers submitted to it by its secretaries, Christopher Dow of the Economic Section and Polly Hill of the Board of Trade, are in PRO T230/28.

35 The bilateral agreement on ERP was discussed by the Economic Policy Committee at no less than seven meetings from 3 June to 26 June before agreement was reached. Ministers objected to the tone and substance of the draft, which 'there could be no question of accepting'. It made 'excessive demands for statistics', stipulated that the budget must be balanced in all years in which aid was received, made it possible for the US to put pressure on the UK to alter exchange rates and envisaged the continuation of the UK's obligations under the agreement for 'too long a period' after aid ceased.

36 A Fortnightly Economic Report to the Cabinet was circulated to the Cabinet starting in November 1947 (CP(47)309).

37 The Economic Section had prepared a paper on 'Signs of deflation' early in May (EC(S)(48)15) and now arranged to do one monthly. The fears that the budget had been too deflationary arose largely from recollections of the slump in 1920–1 and the widespread expectation that something of the kind would happen again.

38 'Economic consequences of receiving no ERP aid', memorandum by the Chancellor of the Exchequer, 23 June 1948, CP(48)61.

39 Unfortunately the records of the Committee of Second Secretaries (which had a long life after reporting on Controls and Efficiency) do not appear to have survived.

40 The bilateral agreement did not commit the United Kingdom to granting most favoured nation treatment to Japan.

41 The *Draft Economic Survey for 1948–52,* EPB(48)25, prepared by Austin Robinson, was circulated to the Economic Planning Board on 29 July 1948.

42 In response to the Budget Committee's request for a paper on public expenditure over the next five years (above, note 32), Christopher Dow drafted a lengthy memorandum ('Budgetary prospects and policy 1948–1952') which was then redrafted by Hall, boiled down into a six-page draft for the Chancellor and discussed with him on 15 September. It envisaged a net fall in government current expenditure by £130 million by 1952 on current policies but the Budget Committee thought this too optimistic (PRO T171/397).

43 An airlift to supply Berlin, which was blockaded by the Russians, began on 28 June and continued until the blockade ended ten and a half months later.

44 Vertical committees in OEEC dealt with the problems of particular industries or groups of industry.

45 The gifts were labelled 'drawing rights' but could only be used if the country given drawing rights was in deficit with the country granting them to the extent assumed. The payments schemes devised in 1948–9 proved unsatisfactory and were superseded in 1950 by the formation of the European Payments Union (EPU).

46 *The Long-Term Programme* was submitted to OEEC on 1 October and published in December (Cmd 7572), but without detailed tables.

47 Published (without tables), the first in October as Cmd 7545, the second as part of Cmd 7572 in December.

48 Exports in the year July 1948 to July 1949 were put at 137 per cent of 1938 when they were already at 134 per cent before the year began and rising rapidly (see entries for November 18th and December 1st).

49 Industry complained that the Inland Revenue increased the cost of keeping capital intact by allowing depreciation for tax purposes only on the basis of historic cost when replacement cost might be twice as high or more (see entries for October 21st 1948 and January 13th 1949).

50 It has not been possible to trace this note.

51 'The balance of payments problem of Western Europe', EC(S)(48)37, 1 November 1948. This was followed by a paper by Marcus Fleming and Nita Watts, 'European viability in 1952/53', EC(S)(48)39, 16 November 1948 (revised 8 December 1948). For this see note 56.

52 The Defence Estimates for 1949–50 were up by £67 million on the previous year excluding supplementaries but were slightly lower if they are included and actual expenditure was also lower than in 1948–9. Expenditure on the National Health Service was expected to increase by £164 million.

53 This seems to refer to 'Budget prospects 1949' which Hall submitted to the Budget Committee on 6 December in advance of a larger paper that could not be completed for lack of the necessary statistics.

54 This was the beginning of a campaign for freer trade with other members of OEEC, coupled with an intra-European payments scheme, leading up to proposals in OEEC in 1949–50 for trade liberalization and the European Payments Union.

55 A dining club of which Keynes was one of the founders which discussed economic and political issues.

56 'The viability of Western Europe in 1952/53' by the Economic Section was circulated to various groups, including the London Committee (on 3 December) and the Planning Board (EPB(48)33). It showed that the members of the OEEC (other than the UK) would still be in heavy deficit with non-members in 1952 if their plans were fulfilled and that their hopes to be in overall balance were illusory because each of them counted on large surpluses in trade with the others.

57 The Lynskey Tribunal was appointed to investigate charges of corruption in the administration of government controls. Much of the evidence related to the Parliamentary Secretary to the Board of Trade, John Belcher, a former railway clerk; but there were hints that other ministers, including even Hugh Dalton, had had dealings with a Mr Stanley who took some pride in his ability to find ways round the controls.

58 The first of these relates to the Ministerial version of the *Survey*, not to the document published in March 1949 (see entry for January 13th).

59 From 1948 the Economic Section submitted an assessment of the prospective economic situation in the year ahead usually in January as a back-

ground to the formation of a budget judgement. The 1949 paper was entitled 'The problem of inflation in 1949' (BC(49)10 Revise, 20 January 1949). It suggested that 'to hold the position' the budget surplus would need to be at least £150 million higher than seemed likely on existing policies; and that there was 'an urgent need for re-examining the likely costs, and methods of paying for, the social and other services'.

60 The views of senior civil servants in January 1949 on links with Europe emerge from the note of a meeting of permanent secretaries in Clarke, 1982, p. 208.

61 The Economic Section and the Treasury had been pressing for cuts in the food subsidies for a long time. They already amounted to 20 per cent of personal expenditure on food and seriously distorted the price structure. The Budget Committee, however, accepted three days later that it was not possible to tackle the matter in 1949 on political grounds.

62 This probably refers to 'The UK long-term programme and European viability', EPB (49)6, 4 February 1949. The papers of the three groups are in PRO CAB 130/42.

63 Article 9 of the Washington Loan Agreement required the United Kingdom to refrain from discrimination (e.g. against imports costing dollars) in its use of quantitative restrictions on imports.

64 This was a meeting of a Working Group of the Steering Committee set up by Bridges in May, with Plowden in the chair. It had already taken papers on 'Possible import licensing relaxations' (ED(W)(49)3–5) and an Economic Section paper on 'Economic policy in a depression' (ED)(W)(49)6). On 12 July (see below) it took a Board of Trade paper on 'Import prices and the dollar shortage' (ED)(W)(49)7).

65 The 'two worlds' problem arose from the effort to limit purchases from the dollar area by buying elsewhere at higher prices. Since this raised costs, it tended to perpetuate the uncompetitiveness of British exports in dollar markets and split the dollar world off from the world of soft currencies. More generally there was danger that a bloc of countries might pursue protectionist policies designed to make the group largely self-sufficient on a long-term footing.

66 The main decision at the Commonwealth talks was that member countries should make a cut of 25 per cent over the next twelve months in their imports from the dollar area. A reduction of 25 per cent was in fact achieved.

67 The note was signed by Bridges, Plowden, Hall, Eady and Wilson Smith (Cairncross, 1985, pp. 181–2).

68 The $1,500 million asked for in Marshall Aid represented nearly half the total amount likely to be available to OEEC. The revised bid caused much indignation in Paris among other members of OEEC.

69 Douglas had accidentally hooked one of his eyelids while fishing.

70 Bevin and Cripps proposed that the price of bread, which was still at its prewar level, should be increased by 1½d and the extraction ratio raised so as to yield a whiter loaf. These proposals were rejected by the Cabinet which agreed, however, to an increase of 1d.

II From devaluation to the change of government, 26 September 1949 to 15 October 1951

1 'The internal financial situation', memorandum by the Chancellor of the Exchequer, EPC(49)102, circulated on 5 October 1949.

2 The OEEC Plan of Action 1949 set out a number of economic objectives including control of inflation, raising productivity, developing dollar exports and fixing realistic exchange rates.

3 It was ultimately decided to send Jukes. From 1949 onwards a member of the Economic Section was stationed in Washington, usually for a two-year spell of duty, both to supply economic advice in the Embassy and to provide up-to-date intelligence about the American economy to Whitehall.

4 Although many of Britain's trading partners devalued simultaneously, the terms of trade moved against the United Kingdom by about 10 per cent. This created a danger of inflation because wage-earners might seek compensation for higher prices by demanding higher money wages.

5 The Second Report of the OEEC was due to be completed early in 1950 for transmission to ECA as a statement of OEEC policies and prospects and as a background to an approach to Congress for Marshall Aid in 1950.

6 Fleming had written the first of a series of papers on an intra-European payments scheme at the beginning of November (EC)(S)(49)29) but did not carry the trade and payments committee examining such schemes (PRO CAB 134/720). Triffin played a part in devising the scheme put forward by ECA later in the month.

7 Cheap sterling was sterling dealt in abroad outside the Exchange Control regulations and at rates below the official rate. Foreign exporters using cheap sterling to purchase raw materials were at an advantage in competing with British exporters dealing at official rates.

8 The reserves, which had fallen to $1,340 million when the pound was devalued, rose to a peak of $3,867 million at 30 June 1951.

9 Lionel Robbins's article on 'The sterling problem' appeared in the October issue of *Lloyds Bank Review*.

10 'Economic planning and liberalization', memorandum by the Minister of Fuel and Power, 7 January 1950, EPC(50)9, in PRO CAB 134/225. Gaitskell defended the use of controls as the distinguishing feature of British socialist planning and regarded import restrictions and exchange control as indispensable *permanent* instruments of policy. Without them it would be necessary to rely exclusively on fiscal and monetary policy to prevent unemployment.

11 For these developments see Tomlinson, 1987, ch. 7. The British government had taken the initiative in 1949 that led to this report by an international group of experts including N. Kaldor. Its object was to induce other governments to commit themselves to policies of full employment and to set an employment target at which to aim.

12 'The sterling balance problem', by J. Jukes, EC(S)(50)7, 28 January 1950. Mrs Hemming's paper has not been traced.

13 Robert Hall's memorandum would appear to have dwindled to a 'Note on central planning' by R. L. Hall and D. A. V. Allen, in PRO 230/143.

14 'Full employment and cost inflation' by J. Downie, EC(S)(50)14, 8 March 1950.

15 This was the committee which had just been set up by Robert Hall to produce regular forecasts of national income and known subsequently as the National Income Forecasts Working Party.

16 The calculations are set out in NIF(50)12, 13 February 1950, in PRO CAB 134/521, and their implications are expounded in a note on 'The budget position', 1 March 1950, and a 'Note on increases in the national income', 2 March 1950, both in PRO T171/400.

17 Gaitskell had been appointed to the Treasury as Minister of Economic Affairs after the election in February.

18   Bevin and Cripps had approached the TUC for agreement to a standstill in wages provided the cost of living was held within 5 per cent above its pre-devaluation level and this received a narrow majority at a conference in January 1950. Ministers contemplated concessions in the budget to improve the chances of success in holding down wages but were advised by Tewson, the General Secretary of the TUC, against such concessions.

19   The paper finally circulated was CP(50)35, 15 March 1950, in PRO CAB 129/38. Addison was an early supply-sider, arguing that what was taken in taxation was either at the expense of personal savings or of a loss of output.

20   The talks with American officials followed an exchange of letters between Cripps and Snyder (Secretary of the US Treasury). Snyder had asked for a full statement of British trade and payments policies in the context of the Loan Agreement of 1945 and this set off a controversy on 'fundamentals' within the Treasury between Gaitskell and officials which was at its height in late April. Gaitskell had just persuaded Cripps to circulate a memorandum on 'fundamentals' on 27 April (EPC(50)44) expressing views similar to those in the entry for April 17th (see also entry for June 6th).

21   The view of the Economic Section (EC(S)(50)29) was that the manager of a buffer stock should sell at the top of the agreed price range and buy at the bottom, but not deal at his discretion at intermediate prices as the rest of the committee thought desirable.

22   The Gordon Gray Report was a report to the President of the United States on foreign economic policy.

23   Pierre Uri was a close associate of Monnet and had been one of the experts who produced the UN Report on *National and International Measures for Full Employment*.

24   Some foods (e.g. tinned foods) were grouped together for rationing purposes and the consumer was allowed to choose between them by using up a fixed total of 'points' per week, each item being priced both in cash and in points.

25   The Communists had come to power in China and the Russians had developed their own atom bomb.

26   The Committee of Four was a subcommittee of the Programmes Committee formed in September 1949 to save the time of the parent committee. It was composed of representatives of the Treasury, the Planning Staff, the Economic Section and the CSO and its work was largely statistical.

27   The National Executive Committee of the Labour Party (Chairman, Hugh Dalton) issued a statement entitled *European Unity* which appeared on the same day, 13 June, as one by Attlee in the House of Commons explaining why the United Kingdom would not join what became the European Coal and Steel Community. The Executive Committee insisted on the need for the United Kingdom to have regard to her worldwide responsibilities and to retain her freedom of action in the management of the British economy and argued against surrendering to a European body power over two key British industries. Its statement was widely regarded as more or less tying the government's hands in its attitude to the Schuman Plan.

28   The National Economy in War Committee was set up in March 1950 under Norman Brook to provide the Defence Committee with guidance on the broad financial and economic assumptions on which departments could base their plans.

29   The British government was anxious that other countries should adopt policies of full employment and wished to use the NIFE Report for this purpose at a meeting of the Economic and Social Council of the United Nations (see above, entry for January 31st). Gaitskell put forward a figure

of 3 per cent for the level of unemployment that would be an acceptable norm and called on other countries to announce similar full employment norms.

30 The Royal Commission on Taxation of Profits and Income. The Chairman was Lord Radcliffe and Professors Hicks and Kaldor were both members.

31 Planning had hitherto proceeded on the assumption of an increase in labour productivity of 2½ per cent per annum but alternative calculations had been made to show the consequences of a 4 per cent increase in 1950 and this alternative was now adopted as a basis for government plans.

32 For the three years 1951–2, 1952–3 and 1953–4 the programme agreed on 3 August had added up to £3,400 million while the maximum that could be achieved, relying on the country's own resources, was put at £950 million a year or £2,850 million in all. This left £550 million to be supplied in aid, and was half the difference between the pre-Korean estimate of £2,300 million and the post-Korean estimate of £3,400 million.

33 Gaitskell made it clear to the House of Commons on 14 September that no formal assurance of the aid requested had been received from the United States.

34 The US proposal became known as 'the Nitze exercise' or 'formula' after its originator, Paul Nitze. At this stage it was expected to yield the United Kingdom substantial dollar aid. Marshall Aid to the UK, it was coming to be accepted, would cease at the end of 1950, as in fact it did.

35 The Snoy–Marjolin formula for the division of aid dated back to the autumn of 1949 when, following the British bid for $1,500 million, the members of OEEC were all (except for Belgium) dissatisfied with the recommendations to Council made by the screening committees. Council invited Baron Snoy (the Belgian Chairman) and Robert Marjolin (the Secretary-General) to make fresh proposals and these were accepted 'with resentful acrimony' (Milward, 1984, p. 206). The national allocations for 1949–50 were then adopted at the suggestion of the British as the basis for division of aid in later years.

36 FEA was the wartime Foreign Economic Administration. OEC was the Office for Economic Co-operation.

37 'The finance of defence', memorandum by the Chancellor of the Exchequer and the Secretary of State for Foreign Affairs, DO(50)91 in PRO CAB 131/9, 23 October 1950.

38 For 'the White Paper that never was', see Tomlinson, 1987, pp. 130–7.

39 The ES Committee was the new Steering Committee (see entry for September 20th).

40 The defence programme for the three years 1951–2, 1952–3 and 1953–4 had increased from a pre-Korean total of about £2,300 mn to £3,600 mn in September and £4,700 mn in January (excluding stockpiling). Munitions production was to be increased fourfold by 1953.

41 In a general post, Isaacs, who was Minister of Labour, became Paymaster-General, Marquand moved to the Ministry of Health and Bevan took over from Isaacs at the Ministry of Labour.

42 'Prospero' was the code-name for a revaluation of the pound which had been considered by officials in January. Kaldor had argued for a floating rate (see Cairncross, 1985, pp. 235–8).

43 The figures changed a good deal over the following weeks but the Budget Committee stuck to its estimate of a worsening of the situation by about £150 mn.

44 The traditional budget accounts included such items as 'strategic stock-piling' (£150 million in 1951–2) which were not included in the 'alternative

classification' of current expenditure. On the *Economic Survey* basis there were further differences: for example, it counted in expected tax liabilities, not just actual tax receipts during the year.

45 Whereas in February it had been assumed that higher import prices could swell the import bill by £330 million in 1951, by the middle of March this had been revised upwards to £700 million.

46 Aneurin ('Nye') Bevan had just been moved to the Ministry of Labour and Herbert Morrison had replaced Ernest Bevin as Foreign Secretary.

47 The government issued a White Paper (Cmd 8274) announcing its intention to ban resale price maintenance but lost office before it could legislate.

48 In EPC(51)65 the Chancellor stated the case for and against revaluation of the pound and came down against.

49 Under Article 5 of the Loan Agreement of 1945 the United Kingdom could ask for a waiver of interest due in any year provided certain conditions were met. The waiver was never operated as originally devised.

50 Stocks in 1951 increased more than in any year between 1945 and 1960.

51 This may refer to 'Coal supplies' (GEN 380/4 in PRO CAB 130/71), 27 September 1951, drafted by Francis Hemming of the Ministry of Fuel and Power.

52 Clarke was, if anything, too cautious. The loss of reserves in the second half of 1951 and the first quarter of 1952 was £775 mn out of an initial total of £1,380 mn.

53 The Iranian government led by Moussadeq had taken over the large oil refinery at Abadan and cut off oil supplies to the United Kingdom.

III The first six months of Conservative government, 24 October 1951 to 11 April 1952

1 The Strath Working Party's papers are in CAB 130/71 (GEN 380). Their 'Report on economic prospects for 1952' was circulated to the Steering Committee as ES(51)57.

2 Salter was appointed Minister of State for Economic Affairs, Swinton Chancellor of the Duchy of Lancaster and Minister of Materials. Lord Cherwell (below, November 5th) joined the Cabinet as Paymaster-General.

3 Lord Cherwell (then Professor Lindemann) had been head of Churchill's 'statistical section' during the Second World War and for most of that time Donald MacDougall had been his chief economist.

4 The official description of the three 'wise men' was the Temporary Council Committee (TCC) of NATO and their staff (the TCS) was headed by General McNarney.

5 These proposals were endorsed by the subcommittee at its first meeting on 3 December 1951 (EA(E)(51)1 M in PRO CAB 134/856). The subcommittee's 'Report on the economic situation' (CP(51)48) was circulated a fortnight later.

6 Just as the Labour Government had contemplated a White Paper on Wages in 1951 against the background of full employment without ever issuing one so the Conservatives prepared to issue a White Paper on Wages and Inflation but never did (entries for January 3rd and February 5th).

7 The Alternative Classification, which was used in Budget Committee papers and had been included in the 1948 Budget statement, was a move in the direction of separating current and capital transactions more accurately

than in the traditional distinction between items above and below 'the line'
– a distinction based on whether or not parliamentary approval had been
given for borrowing. The proposed Economic Classification involved the
adoption of the principles that had governed the treatment of government
income and expenditure in the White Papers issued by the CSO since early
in the war. These were on a calendar year basis and had been used by the
Economic Section in budget discussions. The Treasury, however, preferred
to stick to the traditional form of accounts as an effective instrument of
control and resisted any alternative that would weaken that control
(Tomlinson, 1987, p. 149).

8 It may have been 'a bad week for dollars' but the exchange rate which had
been at the lower limit of $2.78 more or less continuously since January rose
after the budget and touched $2.81 three days later (MacDougall, 1987,
p. 101).

9 'The future of sterling', memorandum by R. L. Hall, 25 March 1952, in
PRO T 236/3242. The OF reply (entry for March 28th) is in the same file.
On 4 April, OF re-stated the case for their plan in a document running to 60
pages ('External sterling plan', report to the Chancellor of the Exchequer,
in PRO T 236/3243).

IV Convertibility after Robot, 24 April 1952 to 30 December 1953

1 The paper – 'Economic policy', memorandum by the Chancellor of the
Exchequer – was re-drafted several times and was not circulated to the
Cabinet until 17 May. It gave a general outline of policy under a series of
headings and continued to insist on the need for early convertibility but
recognized that it was necessary to postpone action until Menzies, the
Australian Prime Minister, had been consulted on his arrival in London in
June. Cherwell (in CP(52)171) said he agreed with almost all of the paper.

2 The Economic Policy Committee (*not* the Cabinet) agreed on 26 March to
set up a Committee on Commercial Policy but it was not formally
constituted until 19 May with the Lord Privy Seal (Crookshank) in the
chair. A number of papers were submitted to it by the Economic Section,
the Board of Trade and Donald MacDougall (they are in PRO CAB
134/787) but the committee met only twice before its work was absorbed by
preparations for a Commonwealth Economic Conference (entry for June
20th; see also Lee to Hall, 23 June, in PRO T 230/220).

3 'Defence and the balance of payments', EPB(52)4, 10 May 1952. By this
time it was being urged that exports should take priority over the defence
programme but the difficulty was to find export markets to absorb the
capacity released in the metal-using industries.

4 The papers on 'The balance of payments crisis' (CP(52)172) and 'The
balance of payments and the metal-using industries' (CP(52)173) were by
the Chancellor. He expected a loss of gold in the second half of 1952 at an
annual rate of £255 million, put the current account deficit of the sterling
area at £700 million a year (of which the rest of the sterling area accounted
for £150 million) and argued in favour of a steady annual UK surplus on
current account of at least £300 million, requiring an increase in the volume
of exports (mainly to difficult markets) by 20 per cent. Macmillan dimissed
these objectives as unattainable (CP(52)196) and called for 'a plan'. It soon
emerged that Butler was too pessimistic.

5   These were circulated to the Committee on Commercial Policy. One was on 'The basis of post-war international reconstruction', the other on 'The effect of world economic development on GATT'.

6   The intention had been to get agreement from the meeting of Ministers at 10.30 p.m. on Monday night and put the scheme to Cabinet next morning. The Chancellor's paper on 'External financial policy' (CP(52)217) was circulated on Saturday, Cherwell's (CP(52)221) on Monday and a further paper by the Chancellor (CP(52)223) – all with the same title – on Thursday 3 July. The Governor warned that if no change in financial policy arrangements were made over the summer, this 'would involve a grave risk to the currency and therefore to the economy' of the UK and the sterling area. The Chancellor expressed agreement with 'the very weighty and almost unanimous advice which I have received from the world of banking that a change in our system is necessary'. Hall's own memo is presumably in one of the two Robot files that has yet to be released.

7   W. King, 'Should sterling be freed?', *The Banker,* June 1952.

8   The papers (eight of them) are in PRO T 230/245.

9   H. Morrison, *Government and Parliament: A Survey from the Inside* (London, Oxford University Press, 1954).

10 Macmillan made his bid for a big housing programme in 'Housing – 1953' (CP(52)241), supported by Eccles in 'The investment . programme' (CP(52)239), while the Chancellor at first upheld the need to hold the ring through for some form of investment programme (CP(52)240). A few days later, on 22 July, the Defence Ministers put round their paper (CP(52)253), which showed a rise to £1,850 million in 1954–5 compared with a peak of £1,700 million in 1953–4 in the 1951 programme.

11 Figgures had been Director of the Trade and Payments Division of OEEC and only recently rejoined the Treasury as an assistant secretary in OF.

12 The preparatory meeting of Commonwealth officials drew up four reports for submission to Governments covering short-term balance of payments prospects, development policy, commodity policy and finance and trade. These were circulated to the Cabinet on 31 October as part of CP(52)373. The proposals which the Cabinet was asked to approve (for discussion at the Prime Minister's Conference) are annexed to CP(52)376. These envisaged action in agreement with a 'nuclear group' consisting of France, the Netherlands and Belgium (and, at a later stage, Germany) as well, of course, as the USA and Canada. The support fund for the operation, which at one time was to consist of $5 billion advanced by the United States, was now to be made up of a drawing of $1.3 billion from the IMF (i.e. up to the quota limit) and a further $1 billion from the USA (which would also have to supply the IMF with dollars for the drawing).

13 Cherwell circulated his paper to the Cabinet on 31 October ('The collective approach to convertibility', CP(52)377), attacking the scheme as likely to produce 'the worst financial crisis in history'. It 'might end in a serious setback in the cold war'.

14 The 'above-the-line' surplus in 1952–3 of 'ordinary' revenue over 'ordinary' expenditure, estimated in April 1952 at £510 mn, turned out to be only £88 mn. These estimates were not made by the Economic Section which was more interested in forecasts of *national* income and expenditure.

15 The Economic Section was arguing that a surplus on current account had to tally with a new outflow of capital of the same magnitude and that in the absence of foreign investment on the necessary scale the surplus on current account would tend to fall to the same level.

16 This committee, set up in March 1950, had been disbanded a year later. It was reconstituted as an inter-departmental committee in August 1952, with Sir Norman Brook in the Chair, 'to formulate broad planning assumptions regarding the economy in war and to co-ordinate the preparation of plans for the most effective use of resources in war'. The papers have not been released.

17 Dennis Wheatley was a best-selling novelist and inventor.

18 W. King, 'Budget hopes and fallacies', *The Banker*, April 1953.

19 Queen Elizabeth was crowned on 2 June 1953.

20 These events are discussed in Cairncross and Watts, 1989, ch. 10.

21 For these documents, see 'Studies of measures to guard a recession in the United States and to strengthen the economy', EPB(53)30, 18 September 1953, in PRO CAB 134/879.

22 This group continued to meet with Hall as Chairman and was in many respects the forerunner of Working Party No. 3 of the OECD.

Appendix 1: Committees

Budget Committee (BC)

A Treasury committee of officials, but sometimes attended by the Treasury ministers, which advised the Chancellor of the Exchequer on all budgetary matters. As well as senior Treasury officials, other members included representatives of the Boards of the Inland Revenue and Customs and Excise. Between 1952 and 1954–5 there was also a Budget Committee Working Party, of which Hall was the chairman (PRO T171).

Official Steering Committee on Economic Development/
Official Committee on Economic Development (ED)/
Economic Steering Committee (ES)

A committee of the permanent secretaries (or official heads) of the economic departments, appointed in 1945 and chaired by the Permanent Secretary of the Treasury. It was the main official body coordinating economic policy and reported after October 1947 to the Economic Policy Committee (see below) but met irregularly after the establishment of the Planning Staff until it was reconstituted as the Economic Steering Committee in October 1950. In May 1949, the Committee's Working Group (ED(W)) was set up to deal with any urgent problems and, in practice, it concentrated on overseas issues. There were also various other subcommittees of the Committee, amongst them the Economic Survey Working Party (see below) (CAB134/186–93, 263–6, 884–7 and 202–3 for the Working Group).

Economic Planning Board (EPB)

A committee of businessmen, trade unionists and senior officials appointed in July 1947 and chaired by the Chief Planning Officer, Sir Edwin Plowden, until he left the Treasury in 1953. There was no ministerial representative and the Board was thus advisory, with its members meant to act as individuals rather than representatives (T229/28–38, CAB134/210–14 and 877–9).

Economic Policy Committee (EPC, and from 1951 EA)

Appointed in October 1947 as the major ministerial committee below the Cabinet dealing with both external and internal economic policy. It was chaired by the Prime Minister (CAB134/215–30 and 841–9).

Economic Survey Working Party (ESWP)

An interdepartmental group which supervised the preparation of the annual review of economic prospects and problems (the *Economic Survey*) by the

Economic Section in conjunction with the Planning Staff and CSO for the Official Committee on Economic Development. The Survey was first published in 1947 but was originally also intended to act as a means of eliciting planning decisions from ministers, with the published version being prepared later. After 1951 only a published version was prepared (CAB134/267–8 and 892).

European Economic Cooperation (London) Committee (ER(L))

An interdepartmental committee appointed in July 1947 and chaired by Otto Clarke which drew up the reports to be submitted to various international bodies and served as the London base for negotiations on the Marshall Plan. In June 1948 with the establishment of the OEEC the Committee was turned into a standing committee and most of its work from then on related to the submission of reports to that body. It did not operate after 1951 but whilst in existence was served by a large number of subcommittees and working parties (CAB130/21–6 and CAB134/232–54).

Investment Programmes Committee (IPC)

A committee of officials appointed in August 1947 to draw up a plan to curtail capital investment programmes and reconstituted as a standing committee in December 1947 to maintain a continuous survey of investment, replacing the Investment Working Party. It had a Planning Staff chairman (Weeks, then Strath and then Turnbull) and for most of its existence had four other members drawn from the Economic Section, the Board of Trade and the Ministries of Supply and Works, although they acted in a personal capacity. Its papers were prepared by the Committee's Working Party and it was also served by three working parties. It was replaced by the Treasury Investment Committee at the end of 1953 (CAB134/437–42, 982, and 444–57 and 983–4 for its Working Party).

National Income Forecasts Working Party (NIF(WP))

An interdepartmental committee set up by Robert Hall in January 1950 as a subcommittee of the Economic Survey Working Party to prepare forecasts of the economic situation. Its first chairman was C. T. Saunders of the CSO (CAB134/520–2 and 1058–9).

Overseas Negotiations Committee (BP(ON) and ON)

An interdepartmental committee of officials appointed in September 1947 and chaired first by Leslie Rowan then Alan Hitchman, and which dealt with the various bilateral trade negotiations in progress (CAB134/46–8, 555–75 and 1087–96. For the working papers of the Committee see T238).

Production Committee (PC)

A ministerial committee appointed in October 1947 and chaired by the Chancellor of the Exchequer to supervise the formulation and implementation of various programmes and generally to deal with internal economic policy. It tended to concentrate more on day-to-day issues than the Economic Policy Committee. The committee was abolished with the change of government in October 1951 (CAB134/635–52).

Programmes Committee (P)

An interdepartmental committee appointed in June 1948 and chaired by Otto Clarke. It met frequently. Its main function was to collate and record the progress of all programmes to be submitted to OEEC (in particular, the import programme) but it also advised the Treasury on expenditure of foreign exchange and took over some of the functions of the Exchange Requirements Committee which kept track of payments to be made in dollars and other currencies in short supply. (CAB134/608–23 and 1123–8).

Second Secretaries Meetings (2S)

A committee of second secretaries or their equivalents appointed in 1948 by Edward Bridges and chaired by him. It met weekly to coordinate economic policy. It is not known what has happened to the records of these meetings.

Appendix 2: Main characters referred to

Armstrong, William (later Lord) 1915–80 Private Sec. to Sec. of War Cabinet 1943–6; PPS to successive Chancellors of the Exchequer 1949–53; Under Sec. OF Division, Treasury 1953–7; Third Sec. 1958–62; Jt Perm. Sec. 1962–8; Head of Home Civil Service 1968–74; Chairman, Midland Bank 1975–80.

Attlee, Clement R. (later Lord) 1883–1967 Deputy Leader (1931–5), and Leader (1935–40) of the Labour Party; Deputy Prime Minister 1942–5; Prime Minister 1945–51.

Bevan, Aneurin ('Nye') 1897–1960 Minister of Health 1945–51; Minister of Labour and National Service 1951.

Bevin, Ernest 1881–1951 Gen. Sec., Transport and General Workers' Union 1921–40; Member of War Cabinet 1940–5; Sec. of State for Foreign Affairs 1945–51.

Bissell, Richard 1909– Assoc. Prof., later Prof. of Economics, MIT 1942–52; Exec. Sec., Harriman Committee on Foreign Aid 1947–8; Asst. Administr. Program, ECA 1948–51; Acting Administr. Sept.–Dec. 1951; Spec. Assist to Director, CIA 1954–9, Dep. Director Plans 1959–62; business consultant 1974–.

Bolton, George (later Sir) 1900–82 UK Exec. Director (1945–52) and alternate Governor (1952–67), IMF; Director of Bank of England 1948–68; Chairman, Bank of London and South America 1957–70.

Bridges, Sir Edward (later Lord) 1892–1969 Secretary to the Cabinet 1938–46; Perm. Sec. UK Treasury 1945–56.

Brittain, Sir Herbert 1894–1961 Entered Treasury 1919; Treasury Officer of Accounts 1937; Under Sec. and Head of HF 1942–6; Third Sec. 1946–53; Second Sec. 1953–7.

Brook, Sir Norman (later Lord) 1902–67 Additional Sec. of Cabinet 1945–7; Secretary 1947–62; Jt Perm. Sec., Treasury and Head of Civil Service 1956–62.

Butler, R. A. (later Lord) 1902–82 Under Sec. of State for Foreign Affairs 1938–41; Minister of Education 1941–5; Minister of Labour June–July 1945; Chancellor of the Exchequer 1951–5; Lord Privy Seal 1955–9; Home Secretary 1957–62; Deputy Prime Minister July 1962–October 1963; Sec. of State for Foreign Affairs 1963–4; Master of Trinity College, Cambridge 1965–8.

Caine, Sydney (later Sir) 1902– Deputy Under Sec. Colonial Office 1947–8; Third Sec. HM Treasury 1948; Head of UK Treasury and Supply Delegation Washington 1949–51; Vice-Chancellor, University of Malaya 1952–6.

Campion, Harry (later Sir) 1905– Reader in Statistics, University of Manchester 1933–9; Director, Central Statistical Office 1941–67.

Cherwell, Lord ?–1957 Prof. of Experimental Philosophy, Oxford University 1919–56; Personal Assistant to Prime Minister 1940; Paymaster-General 1942–5 and 1951–3.

Christelow, Allan 1911–75 Ass. Sec., War Cabinet Secretariat 1944–5; Ass. Sec.

1945–8, Under Sec. 1948, UK Treasury Delegation to Washington; Acting Exec. Director, IBRD 1948, Director 1953.

Clarke, R. W. B. ('Otto') (later Sir Richard) 1910–75 Financial journalist in 1930s; war service with Ministry of Production; Ass. Sec., HM Treasury 1945; Under Sec. 1947; Third Sec. 1955; Second Sec. 1962; Perm. Sec., Ministry of Technology 1966–70.

Cobbold, Cameron F. ('Cob') (later Lord) 1904–87 Exec. Director, Bank of England 1938; Deputy Governor 1945; Governor 1949–61.

Compton, Edmund (later Sir) 1906– Entered Treasury 1931; Under Sec. 1947; Third Sec. 1949–58; Comptroller and Auditor-General, Exchequer and Audit Dept 1958–66.

Cripps, Sir Stafford 1889–1952 Minister of Aircraft Production 1942–5; Pres. of Board of Trade 1945–7; Minister of Economic Affairs 1947; Chancellor of the Exchequer 1947–50.

Crombie, Sir James 1902–69 Entered Civil Service 1926; served in Customs and Excise Dept, Treasury, Ministry of Food, Foreign Office; Chairman, Board of Customs and Excise 1955–62.

Crosland, Anthony 1918–77 Fellow of Trinity College, Oxford 1947–50; held various offices in Labour Government 1964–70; Sec. of State for Environment 1974–6.

Dalton, Hugh (later Lord) 1887–1962 Reader in Economics, LSE 1925–36; Minister in Coalition Government 1940–5; Chancellor of the Exchequer 1945–7; Chancellor of the Duchy of Lancaster 1948–50; Minister of Town and Country Planning 1950–1.

Dean, Maurice (later Sir) 1906–78 Entered Civil Service 1929; Deputy Under Sec. of State, Foreign Office 1947–8; Deputy Sec., Ministry of Defence 1948–52; Additional Second Sec., Treasury 1952; Second Sec., Board of Trade 1952–5; Treasury 1963–4; Perm. Sec., Ministry of Technology 1964–6.

Eady, Sir Wilfrid 1890–1962 Ministry of Labour 1917–38; Chairman, Board of Customs and Excise 1940–2; Jt Second Sec., HM Treasury 1942–52.

Edwards, L. John 1904–59 Staff Tutor, University of Leeds 1932–6; Gen. Sec., PO Engineering Union 1938–47; Labour MP 1945–59; Parl. Private Sec. to Cripps 1945–7; Parl. Sec., Ministry of Health 1947–9, Board of Trade 1949–50; Econ. Sec. to Treasury Oct. 1950–Oct. 1951; Chairman, Public Accounts Cttee 1951–2.

Figgures, Frank (later Sir) 1910– Entered Treasury 1946 after military service; Director of Trade and Finance, OEEC 1948–51; Under Sec., Treasury 1955–60; Sec.-Gen., EFTA 1960–5; Second Sec. 1968–71; Director-Gen., NEDO 1971–3.

Flett, Martin (later Sir) 1911– Entered Dominions Office 1933; Treasury 1934; Under Sec., Treasury 1949–56; Deputy Sec., Ministry of Fuel and Power 1956–61; Perm. Under Sec. of State, Air Ministry 1963–71.

France, Arnold (later Sir) 1911– Entered Treasury 1945 after military service; Assistant Sec. 1948; Under Sec. 1952; Third Sec. 1960; Chairman, Board of Inland Revenue 1968–73.

Franks, Sir Oliver (later Lord) 1905– Fellow of Queen's College, Oxford 1927–37 and Provost 1946–8; Ministry of Supply 1939–45 (Perm. Sec. 1945–6); UK Ambassador to USA 1948–52; Chairman, Lloyds Bank 1954–62; Provost of Worcester College, Oxford 1962–76.

Gaitskell, Hugh 1906–63 Reader in Political Economy, University of London 1938; Minister of Fuel and Power 1947–50; Chancellor of the Exchequer 1950–1; Leader of the Labour Party 1955–63.

Gilbert, Sir Bernard 1891–1957 Entered Treasury 1914; Jt Second Sec. 1944–56.

Hall, Robert (later Lord) 1901–1988 Fellow of Trinity College, Oxford 1927–50;

Ministry of Supply 1939–46; Director, Econ. Section of Cabinet Office 1947–53; Economic Adviser to HM Govt 1953–61.

Hall, Wm Glenvil 1887–1962 Barrister; Labour MP 1929–31, 1945–51; Financial Secretary to the Treasury 1945–50; Chairman, Parl. Labour Party 1950 and 1951.

Hall-Patch, Sir Edmund 1896–1975 Ass. Under Sec. of State, Foreign Office 1944; Deputy Under Sec. 1946–8; Chairman, Exec. Cttee of OEEC 1948; UK Exec. Director of IMF and IBRD 1952–4.

Harriman, W. Averill 1891–1986 Special Rep. of President Roosevelt in UK 1941; US Ambassador to USSR 1943–6; to UK 1946; US Sec. of Commerce 1946–8; US Special Rep. in Europe under ECA 1948–50; Director of Mutual Security Agency 1951–3; Governor of New York State 1954–7.

Helmore, Sir James 1906–72 Board of Trade 1929–52; Second Sec. 1946–52; Perm. Sec., Ministry of Materials 1952; of Ministry of Supply 1953–6.

Hitchman, E. A. (later Sir Alan) 1903–80 Under Sec., HM Treasury 1947; Deputy to Chief Planning Officer 1948–9; Third Sec. 1949–51; Perm. Sec., Ministry of Materials 1951–2.

Hoffman, Paul 1891–1974 President, Studebaker Corporation 1935–48; ECA Administrator 1948–50; President, Ford Foundation 1951–3.

Jay, Douglas (later Lord) 1907– Fellow of All Soul's College, Oxford 1930–7 and 1968– ; staff of *The Times* 1929–33, *The Economist* 1933–7 and *Daily Herald* (City Editor) 1937–41; Ministry of Supply, then Board of Trade 1941–5; Pers. Assist to PM 1945–6; Labour MP 1946–86; Econ. Sec. to Treasury 1947–50; Financial Sec. 1950–1; President, Board of Trade 1964–7.

Katz, Milton 1907– Professor of Law, Harvard University 1940–50 and 1954–78; Deputy US Special Rep. in Europe (under Harriman) 1949–50; Special Rep. 1950–1; President, American Academy of Arts and Sciences 1979–82.

Knollys, Viscount 1895–1966 Governor of Bermuda 1942–3; Chairman BOAC 1943–7; Chairman Vickers Ltd 1956–62; UK Rep. at International Materials Conference 1951–2.

Lee, F. G. (later Sir Frank) 1903–71 Colonial Office 1926–40; HM Treasury 1940–4; Treasury Delegate to Washington 1944–6; Ministry of Supply 1946–8 (Dep. Sec. 1947–8); Minister at Washington 1948; Perm. Sec., Board of Trade 1951–9; Ministry of Food 1959–61; HM Treasury 1960–2; Master of Corpus Christi College, Cambridge 1962–71.

Leslie, S. C. (Clem) 1898–1980 Rhodes Scholar; Senior Lecturer in Philosophy, Melbourne University 1924–5; Publicity Manager, Gas, Light & Coke Co. 1936–40; Director, Council of Industrial Design 1945–7; Head of Treasury Information Division 1947–59.

Liesching, Sir Percivale 1895–1973 Entered Colonial Office 1920; Ass. Under Sec. of State, Dominions Office 1939–42; Second Sec., Board of Trade, 1942–6; Perm. Sec., Ministry of Food 1946–8; Perm. Under Sec. of State, Commonwealth Relations Office 1949–55; High Commissioner for UK in S. Africa 1955–8.

MacDougall, G. D. A. (later Sir Donald) 1912– Prime Minister's Statistical Branch 1940–5; Fellow of Wadham College, Oxford 1945–50; Director, Economics Division OEEC 1948–9; Paymaster-General's Office 1951–3; Fellow of Nuffield College, Oxford 1950–62; Director-Gen., Dept of Economic Affairs 1964–8; Head of Govt Economic Service 1969–73.

Makins, Roger (later Lord Sherfield) 1904– Entered Foreign Office 1928; Minister at Washington Embassy 1945–7; Ass. Under Sec. of State 1947–8; Dep. Under Sec. of State 1948–52; Ambassador to USA 1953–6; Jt Perm. Sec. of the Treasury 1956–9; Chairman, Atomic Energy Authority 1960–4.

Marjolin, Robert 1911–86 Head of French Supply Mission in USA 1944; Director, Foreign Economic Relations, Ministry of National Economy, Paris 1945; Joint Commissioner-General, Monnet Plan 1946–8; Sec.-Gen. OEEC 1948–55; Prof. of Economics, Nancy, 1955–8; Vice-Pres., EEC Commission 1958–67.

Marquand, Hilary 1901–72 Prof. of Industrial Relations, University of Wales, Cardiff 1930–45; Labour MP 1945–61; Sec. for Overseas Trade 1945–7; Paymaster-General 1947–8; Ministry of Pensions 1948–51; Ministry of Health Jan.–Oct. 1951.

Martin, William McChesney 1906– Chairman and President, Export-Import Bank 1946–9; Ass. Sec., US Treasury 1949–51; Chairman, Board of Governors, Federal Reserve Board 1951–70.

Maudling, Reginald 1917–79 Called to the Bar 1940; Conservative MP 1950–74; Ec. Sec. to the Treasury, Nov. 1952–April 1955; Ministry of Supply 1955–7; Paymaster-General 1957–9; President of Board of Trade 1959–61; Chancellor of the Exchequer 1962–64; Home Secretary 1970–2.

Meade, James 1907– Economic Section of (War) Cabinet Offices 1940–7; Director 1946–7; Prof. of Economics at LSE 1947–57; at University of Cambridge 1957–68; Nobel Laureate 1977.

Monnet, Jean 1888–1979 Deputy Sec.-Gen., League of Nations 1981; Member of British Supply Council, Washington 1940–3; author of Monnet Plan 1946; President European Coal and Steel Community 1952–5; Action Committee for the United States of Europe 1956–75.

Morrison, Herbert (later Lord) 1888–1965 Home Secretary 1940–5; Deputy Prime Minister and Lord President of the Council 1945–51; Foreign Secretary March-Oct. 1951.

Muir, Edward (later Sir) 1905–79 Under Sec. Ministry of Works 1946–51; Dep. Sec., Ministry of Materials 1951–4.

Nicholson, E. M. (Max) 1904– Perm. Sec., Office of Lord President of Council 1945–52; Director-Gen. Nature Conservancy 1952–66.

Nitze, Paul 1907– Vice-Pres., Dillon Read & Co. 1939–41; Vice-Chairman, US Strategic Bombing Survey 1944–6; Deputy to Ass. Sec. of State for Economic Affairs, 1948–9; Director, Policy Planning Staff, Dept of State 1950–3; Sec. of Navy 1963–7; Dep. Sec. of Defense 1967–9; Head of US Negotiating Team, Arms Control Talks, Geneva 1981–.

Playfair, E. W. (later Sir Edward) 1909– HM Treasury 1934–46, 1947–56; Perm. Under Sec. for War 1956–9; Perm. Sec., Ministry of Defence 1960–1; Chairman, ICI 1961–5.

Plowden, Sir Edwin (later Lord) 1907– Ministry of Aircraft Production 1940–6 (Chief Exec. 1945–6); Chief Planning Officer and Chairman, Econ. Planning Board 1947–53; Chairman, Atomic Energy Authority 1954–9; Chairman, Tube Investments 1963–76.

Robbins, Lionel (later Lord) 1898–1984 Prof. of Economics, LSE 1929–61; Director, Economic Section of War Cabinet Offices 1941–5; Chairman, *Financial Times* 1961–70.

Robinson, E. A. G. (later Sir Austin) 1897– Jt Editor, *Economic Journal* 1944–70, Economic Section, War Cabinet Offices 1939–42; Ministry of Production 1942–5; Econ. Adviser, Board of Trade 1945–6; Member of Economic Planning Staff 1947–8; Prof. of Economics, University of Cambridge 1950–65.

Rowan, Sir Leslie 1908–72 Ass. Sec., later PPS, to Prime Minister 1941–7; Perm. Sec., Ministry of Economic Affairs 1947; Second Sec. HM Treasury 1947–9, 1957–8; Economic Minister to Washington 1949–51; Managing Director, then

Chairman, Vickers Ltd 1962–71; captained England at hockey 1937, 1938 and 1947.

Salter, Sir Arthur (later Lord) 1881–1975 Civil servant 1904–22; Director, Economics and Finance Section of League of Nations 1919–20, 1922–31; Prof. of Political Theory and Institutions, Oxford University 1934–44; MP 1937–53; Chancellor of Duchy of Lancaster 1945; Minister of State for Economic Affairs 1951–Nov. 1952; Minister of Materials Nov. 1952–3.

Snyder, John Wesley 1895–1985 Director, Office of War Mobilization and Reconversion 1945–6; Secretary of US Treasury 1946–53.

Strath, William (later Sir) 1906–75 Ministry of Aircraft Production 1940–5; Ministry of Supply 1945–7; Central Economic Planning Staff 1947–55; Member, Atomic Energy Authority 1955–9; Perm. Sec. Ministry of Supply 1959, of Aviation 1959–60.

Thorold, Guy (later Sir) 1898–1970 Ministry of Economic Warfare 1939–45; attached to UK Delegation to OEEC 1948; Head of UKTSD and Economic Minister, Washington 1957–9.

Trend, Burke St J. (later Lord) 1914–87 Entered Treasury 1937; PPS to Chancellor of the Exchequer 1945–9; Under Sec., HM Treasury 1949–55; Dep. Sec. of Cabinet 1955–9; Secretary 1963–73; Rector, Lincoln College, Oxford 1973–83.

Weeks, Hugh (later Sir) 1904– Director of Statistics, Ministry of Supply 1939–42; Ministry of Production 1943–5; Deputy to Chief Planning Officer 1947–8; Director, Finance Corporation for Industry 1956–74.

Wilson, J. Harold (later Lord) 1916– Secretary for Overseas Trade March-Oct. 1947; President of Board of Trade 1947–51; Leader of Labour Party 1963–76; Prime Minister 1964–70 and 1974–6.

Wilson Smith, Sir Henry 1904–78 HM Treasury 1930–46; Perm. Sec., Ministry of Defence 1947–8; Additional Second Sec. HM Treasury 1948–51.

Woods, Sir John Henry 1895–1962 HM Treasury 1920–43; Perm. Sec. Board of Trade 1945–51.

Appendix 3: Members of the Economic Section 1947–53

Note: This appendix omits members of the Section who left in 1947 (A. J. Brown, P. Chantler, J. E. Meade, R. S. Sayers, R. C. Tress).

Abramson, S.	1948–50	(later Under Sec., Department of Trade)
Atkinson, F. J.	1949–69	(later Sir Fred; Head of Government
	1977–9	Economic Service 1977–9)
Bensusan-Butt, D. M.	1946–54	(Professorial Research Fellow, ANU, Canberra 1962–76)
Bretherton, R. F.	1949–51	(Jt Deputy Director, 1949–51; Under Sec., Board of Trade 1954–61, Treasury 1961–8)
Day, A. C. L.	1954–6	(Prof. of Economics, LSE, 1964–)
Dow, J. C. R.	1945–54	(Ass. Sec.-Gen., OECD 1963–73; Exec.
	1962–3	Director, Bank of England 1973–81; Adviser to Governor 1981–4)
Downie, J.	1948–61	(Ass. Sec.-Gen., OECD 1961–3; died 1963)
Fearn, J. M.	1947–8	(Sec., Scottish Education Dept 1973–6)
Fleming, J. Marcus	1942–51	(Deputy Director 1946–51; Deputy Director Research Dept, IMF 1964–76; died 1976)
Fleming, J. Miles	1952–4	(Prof. of Economics, University of Bristol 1970–8)
Forsyth, Miss J. M.	1947–9	(Under Sec., HM Treasury/Dept of Transport 1975–84)
Franklin, M. D. M.	1952–5	(later Sir Michael; Perm. Sec., Ministry of Agriculture, Food and Fisheries 1983–7)
Grieve-Smith, J.	1949–57	(Senior Bursar, Robinson College, Cambridge 1982–)
Hall, R. L.	1947–61	(later Lord Roberthall; Director 1947–61)
Hopkin, W. A. B.	1948–50	(later Sir Bryan; Head of Government
	1958–72	Economic Service 1974–7; Professor of
	1974–7	Economics, University of Wales, Cardiff 1972–82)
Howell, Miss K. (Mrs Jones)	1945–60	(Sec., National Institute of Economic and Social Research 1968–)
Jefferies, G. P.	1946–9	(later Ass. Sec., Dept of Trade and Industry)
Jones, D. J. C.	1950–3	(Minister for Hong Kong relations with EEC 1982–)
Joseph, Miss M. W. B. (Mrs Hemming)	1940–3 1947–55	(Senior Research Officer, NIESR 1956–70)
Jukes, J. A.	1948–54	(Dep. Dir.-Gen., Dept. of Economic Affairs 1964–7; Member, Central Electricity Generating Board 1977–80)

Keane, J. W. P.	1947–53	(Director, International Affairs, British Steel Corporation 1973–87)
Kelley, Miss J.	1949–54	(Under Sec. HM Treasury 1979–87)
Lawler, P.	1952–3	(later Sir Peter; Australian Ambassador to Eire and the Holy See 1983–7)
Le Cheminant, P.	1950–2	(Second Perm. Sec., Cabinet Office 1983–4)
Licence, J. M. V.	1948–52	(Managing Director, Economic Planning, British Gas 1972–82)
Little, I. M. D.	1953–5	(Deputy Director; Prof. of Economics, University of Oxford 1971–6)
Neild, R. R.	1951–6	(Prof. of Economics, University of Cambridge 1971–84)
Ross, C. R.	1952–5	(Dep. Sec., CPRS 1971–8; Vice-Pres., European Investment Bank 1978–)
Scott, M. F.	1953–4	(Fellow in Economics, Nuffield College, Oxford 1968–)
Shackle, G. L. S.	1945–9	(Prof. of Economic Science, University of Liverpool 1951–69)
Swan, T.	1947–9	(later Prof. of Economics, Australian National University, Canberra)
Watts, N. G. M.	1941–55	(Vice-Principal, St Hilda's College, Oxford 1967–81)

Appendix 4: Initials and abbreviations

2nd Secs.   meeting of Second Secretaries
A   Clement Attlee
AO Committee   Atlantic (Official) Committee
APU   Atlantic Payments Union
A/S   Assistant Secretary
AUTE   Association of University Teachers of Economics
B   Budget/R. A. Butler
BC   Budget Committee
B/E   Bank of England
BEA   British Electricity Authority
BEC   British Employers' Confederation
BG/BWG   Sir Bernard Gilbert
BIS   Bank for International Settlements
BISF   British Iron and Steel Federation
BoT   Board of Trade
BRMM   British Raw Materials Mission in Washington
C   Chancellor/Cherwell/Churchill/Convertibility)
Conv.   Convertibility
CEA   US Council of Economic Advisors
CEGB   Central Electricity Generating Board
CEPS   Central Economic Planning Staff
CGT   Confédération Générale de Travail (French TUC)
CIGS   Chief of the Imperial General Staff
CO   Colonial Office
CoS   Chiefs of Staff
CPRB   Combined Production Resources Board
CRMB   Combined Raw Materials Board
CRO   Commonwealth Relations Office
CSO   Central Statistical Office
DEA   Department of Economic Affairs
DJ   Douglas Jay
DSIR   Department of Scientific and Industrial Research
D(T) Committee   Defence (Transition) Committee
EB   Sir Edward Bridges
ECA   Economic Cooperation Administration
Ec. and Emp. Commission   Economic and Employment Commission of the UN
ECE   (UN) Economic Commission for Europe
ECOSOC   Economic and Social Council of the UN
ED   Official Steering Committee on Economic Development
ED(W)   Official Committee on Economic Development Working Group
EDC   European Defence Community
EIU   Economic Information Unit
E/EP/ENP   Sir Edwin Plowden

EPB   Economic Planning Board
EPC   Economic Policy Committee
EPL   Excess Profits Levy
EPU   European Payments Union
ERC   Exchange Requirements Committee
ERP   European Recovery Programme
ES Committee   Economic Steering Committee
ESP   External Sterling Plan
ESWP   Economic Survey Working Party
FAO   Food and Agriculture Organization
FBI   Federation of British Industries
FEA   Foreign Economic Administration
FEB   Finance and Economic Board of NATO
FO   Foreign Office
FRB   Federal Reserve Board
FS   Foreign Secretary
FSSU   Federated Superannuation Scheme for Universities
FST   Financial Secretary, Treasury
GATT   General Agreement on Tariffs and Trade
GNP   Gross National Product
HC   House of Commons
HE   His Excellency, the UK Ambassador
HF   Home Finance, Treasury
HG/G   Hugh Gaitskell
HP   Sir Edmund Hall-Patch
HWS   Sir Henry Wilson Smith
IBRD   International Bank for Reconstruction and Development
IDT   Information Division, Treasury
IEPS   Intra-European Payments Scheme
IMC   International Materials Conference
IMF   International Monetary Fund
IPC   Investment Programmes Committee
ITO   International Trade Organization
J   Eric Johnston
JHW   Sir John Henry Woods
JIB   Joint Intelligence Branch
JWPC   Joint War Production Committee
LP   Lord President
LR   Sir Leslie Rowan
M   Robert Marjolin/Sir Roger Makins
MAC   Mutual Aid Committee
MCA   Mutual Cooperation Administration
MD   Minister of Defence
MFN   Most favoured nation
MFP   Ministry of Fuel and Power
MoF   Ministry of Food
MPA   Motion Picture Association
MSA   Mutual Security Agency
NATO   North Atlantic Treaty Organization
NB   Sir Norman Brook
NCB   National Coal Board
NEW   National Economy in War
NFM   Non-ferrous metals
NI   National income

NIESR National Institute for Economic and Social Research
NIFE National and International Measures for Full Employment
NIFWP National Income Forecasts Working Party
NJAC National Joint Advisory Council
NPACI National Production Advisory Council for Industry
NUM National Union of Mineworkers
NUR National Union of Railwaymen
Nye B Aneurin Bevan
O/OF/OSF Sir Oliver Franks
OEC Office for Economic Cooperation
OECD Organisation for Economic Cooperation and Development
OEEC Organization for European Economic Co-operation
OF Overseas Finance, Treasury
OGL Open General Licence
ONC Overseas Negotiations Committee
P Sir Edwin Plowden
PC Production Committee
PEC Preparations for (Commonwealth) Economic Conference
PEP Political and Economic Planning
PM Prime Minister
PPS Principal Private Secretary
PRO Public Record Office
PT/p.t. Purchase Tax
q.r. Quantitative import restrictions
RAB R. A. Butler
RFC Reconstruction Finance Corporation
RLH Sir Robert Hall
RM Sir Roger Makins
RMC Raw Materials Conference
RMD Raw Materials Department of Ministry of Supply
RMIA and RM (PW) Branches of RMD
RSA Rest of the sterling area
RV Revaluation
SBAC Society of British Aircraft Constructors
SC Sir Stafford Cripps
TCC Temporary Council Committee of NATO
TCS Temporary Council Staff
TLR Sir Leslie Rowan
TUC Trades Union Congress
UGC University Grants Committee
UKCC UK Commercial Corporation
UKTD UK Treasury Delegation in Washington
UKTSD UK Treasury and Supply Delegation in Washington
USG US Government
W Winston Churchill
WE Sir Wilfrid Eady
WS Sir Henry Wilson Smith

Bibliography

Boyle, Lord 'The economist in government' in J. K. Bowers (ed.) *Inflation, Development and Integration* (Leeds, University Press, 1979).

Brittan, Sam *The Treasury under the Tories* (Harmondsworth, Penguin Books, 1964).

Butler, Lord (R. A. Butler) *The Art of the Possible* (London, Hamish Hamilton, 1971).

Cairncross, Sir Alec *Years of Recovery* (London, Methuen, 1985).

Cairncross, Sir Alec 'Prelude to Radcliffe' (*Rivista di Storia Economiche*, December 1987).

Cairncross, Sir Alec (with Nita Watts) *The Economic Section: A study in economic advising* (London, Routledge, 1989).

Clarke, R. W. B. (ed. Cairncross) *Anglo-American Co-operation in War and Peace* (Oxford, Oxford University Press, 1982).

Dow, J. C. R. *The Management of the British Economy 1945–60* (Cambridge, Cambridge University Press, 1964).

Fforde, J. S. *The Bank of England 1945–58* (in preparation).

Hicks, J. R. *The Problem of Budgetary Reform* (Oxford, Oxford University Press, 1950).

Hogan, M. J. *The Marshall Plan* (Cambridge, Cambridge University Press, 1987).

Jay, D. P. T. *Change and Fortune* (London, Hutchinson, 1980).

Jones, Russell *Wages and Employment Policy 1936–85* (London, Allen & Unwin, 1987).

Kaplan, J. J. and Schleiminger, G. *The European Payments Union* (Oxford, Oxford University Press, forthcoming).

King, W. 'Should sterling be freed?' *The Banker,* June 1952.

King, W. 'Budget hopes and fallacies' *The Banker,* April 1953.

MacDougall, Sir Donald *Don and Mandarin* (London, John Murray, 1987).

Milward, A. S. *The Reconstruction of Western Europe 1945–51* (London, Methuen, 1984).

Morgan, K. O. *Labour in Power 1945–51* (Oxford, Oxford University Press, 1984).

Morrison, H. *Government and Parliament: a Survey from the Inside* (Oxford, Oxford University Press, 1954).

Plowden, Lord Edwin *An Industrialist in the Treasury 1947–53* (London, André Deutsch, 1989).

Rees, G. L. *Britain and the Post-War European Payments System* (Cardiff, University of Wales Press, 1963).

Robbins, Lord 'The Sterling Problem' (*Lloyds Bank Review,* October 1949).

Sayers, R. S. *Financial Policy 1939–45* (London, HMSO, 1956).

Seldon, A. *Churchill's Indian Summer: the Conservative Government 1951–55* (London, Hodder and Stoughton, 1981).

Shonfield, Sir Andrew *British Economic Policy since the War* (Harmondsworth, Penguin Books, 1959).

Tomlinson, J. *Employment Policy: the Crucial Years 1939–55* (Oxford, Oxford University Press, 1987).

Worswick, G. D. N. and Ady, Peter *The British Economy 1945–50* (Oxford, Oxford University Press, 1952).

Worswick, G. D. N. and Ady, Peter *The British Economy in the 1950s* (Oxford, Oxford University Press, 1962).

For official documents see the references in the text and in Appendix I (Committees). The papers of the Economic Section are in PRO T 230 and those of OF Division in PRO T 236. For a fuller bibliography, see *Years of Recovery* and *The Economic Section*.

Index